EUGENE A. FORSEY

EUGENE A. FORSEY

AN INTELLECTUAL BIOGRAPHY

BY FRANK MILLIGAN

UNIVERSITY OF
CALGARY
PRESS

University of Calgary Press
2500 University Drive NW
Calgary, Alberta
Canada T2N 1N4
www.uofcpress.com

National Library of Canada Cataloguing in Publication Data

Milligan, Frank, 1952-
    Eugene A. Forsey : an intellectual biography / Frank Milligan.

Includes bibliographical references and index.
ISBN 1-55238-118-8

1. Forsey, Eugene A. (Eugene Alfred), 1904-1991.
2. Social reformers—Canada—Biography.
3. Legislators—Canada—Biography.
4. Canada. Parliament. Senate—Biography.
5. Canada—Politics and government—20th century. I. Title.
FC601.F67M54 2003   971.06'092   C2003-905789-5

 **Canada** We acknowledge the financial support of the Government of Canada
through the Book Publishing Industry Development Program (BPIDP)
for our publishing activities.

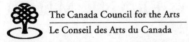 The Canada Council for the Arts
Le Conseil des Arts du Canada

This book has been published with the help of a grant from the Canadian Federation
for the Humanities and Social Sciences, through the Aid to Scholarly Publications
Programme, using funds provided by the Social Sciences and Humanities Research
Council of Canada.

Printed and bound in Canada by Transcontinental Printing Inc.
∞ This book is printed on acid-free paper.

Cover design by Mieka West.
Page design and typesetting by Kristina Schuring.
Frontpiece photo by Jean-Marc Carisse / www.carisse.org

To Nancy

TABLE OF CONTENTS

FOREWORD

Eugene Forsey's life as a politician, academic, constitutional expert, and Christian activist places him in the midst of many reform movements during the past half-century. By analyzing the factors that influenced Forsey's thought processes, one gains a deeper understanding of the principles that many of these reform associations advocated. But more importantly, by studying Forsey's personal intellectual thought, one gains a deeper understanding of the intellectual forces from within Canada and from abroad that shaped his thinking, and which were expressed through his spoken and written words and through the doctrines of the organizations with which Forsey chose to associate.

Through his participation in the Conservative and CCF parties; the Fellowship for a Christian Social Order; the Canadian Civil Liberties Union; the Canadian Congress of Labour and Canadian Labour Congress; the League for Social Reconstruction; and a number of additional organizations in which he participated to a slightly lesser degree, Forsey contributed a great number of ideas and a substantial amount of work that in turn helped shape the manner in which those organizations responded to the social, economic, and political problems facing Canadian society from the early 1920s through the 1980s.

Forsey's intellectual thought represents a cross-current of many forces. From his middle-class conservative boyhood home, Forsey went on to study at McGill University and at Oxford before returning to academic and political life in Canada. During these early years Forsey adopted the political philosophy of nineteenth century British Tory democracy and a belief in Christian activism. Faced with the economic upheavals of the 1920s and 1930s in Canada and Britain,

Forsey adopted a strain of socialism that blended with his conservatism and religious beliefs. His resulting philosophy represented a strain of Canadian conservative reformism and constitutional traditionalism that placed Forsey in many different intellectual homes and makes him an interesting subject for an intellectual biography.

PREFACE

This book is a study of Eugene Forsey's intellectual thought from his youthful days in Ottawa and Montreal's McGill University, through to his days as a senator in the early 1970s.

The examination of Forsey's intellectual thought is an effort to reveal the intellectual underpinnings and external forces that shaped the way Forsey thought in the earlier phases of his life. In addition, this study of his intellectual thought seeks to describe Forsey's role within and contributions to those associations which Edmund Burke called the "small platoons" of society and with which Forsey chose to become involved. In this sense this intellectual biography indirectly illustrates some of the intellectual links that kept those associations functioning as cohesive units. As such, this book may provide some much-needed insight into Canada's various social, economic and political reform movements dating from the post-World War I era.

The term "intellectual thought," as used in this work, takes in many of Forsey's personal views on myriad issues and concerns that were also, at least in part, the *raison d'être* of such reform movements as the reform elements within the United Church; the Student Christian Movement (SCM); the League for Social Reconstruction (LSR) and the Co-Operative Commonwealth Federation (CCF); the Fellowship for a Christian Social Order (FCSO); the Canadian Civil Liberties Union (CCLU); the Canadian Congress of Labour (CCL); and the Canadian Labour Congress (CLC). Forsey was an active participant in each of these movements, though the degree of his commitment and actual influence upon the direction that each organization took, or the issues it chose to advocate, varied from organization to organization and from time to time.

This book also suggests that Forsey's thought reflects some concepts that became important intellectual principles for these particular movements. By examining Forsey's personal beliefs, therefore, one gains a greater understanding of one of Canada's great thinkers, as well as a deeper insight into the philosophical underpinnings of many of Canada's early twentieth century political, economic, religious and social reform movements.

This work traces the ever-changing, though consistent, beliefs that underlay Forsey's early middle-class, Protestant, conservative upbringing in Ottawa, through his radical period of the Depression era and into his later efforts as one of Canada's leading constitutional authorities. Eugene Forsey was, to a tremendous extent, influenced by various people and events throughout his life, and quite naturally those people and events helped to shape Forsey's views on the issues of the day. This biography documents those forces, and assesses their relative influence on Forsey by monitoring Forsey's private reflections and public utterances on related issues.

This work is a study in ideas. It is not a study of the various movements listed above. For the most part that work has been done in published works and in theses and unpublished papers. Although revisions to those works will undoubtedly occur, the primary purpose of this work is to examine Forsey as an intellectual participant in those movements. This work, therefore, seeks to provide insight into Eugene Forsey as an individual Canadian groping to contribute solutions to Canada's twentieth century problems. In some cases, as in the CCF and church-related organizations, Eugene Forsey's views reflected the beliefs of a substantial percentage of Canadians. In other cases, Forsey's truculent, rebellious, and somewhat independent "crusades" represent little more than the solitary pleas of a man who defies political labelling. This in itself is valuable, for it illustrates the somewhat contradictory and confusing ramifications inherent in labelling individuals. Such is the value of the intellectual biography, for it provides the crucial perspective that permits the historian to identify the individual strands of thought that provide the collective intellectual "glue" that unites society's "small platoons."

The relations between Forsey and the individual reform movements examined in this study are discussed in roughly chronological order. The first third of the book (Chapters 1 to 4), examines Forsey's conservative, middle-class Ottawa upbringing and the British "Tory democratic" principles that he adopted while a student at McGill between 1922 and 1926. A second theme in this section is the central importance Christian moralism had for Forsey in his early years. Thirdly, this section traces Forsey's gradual acceptance of the need to implement his form of "Tory democratic Christian reform" through the planned efforts of the socialist state. The last segment of this section (Chapter 4), examines Forsey's experiences between 1926 and 1929 as a Rhodes scholar at Oxford and European traveller. These years reinforced all three of the themes mentioned above.

The second section of this biography (Chapters 5–7) examines Forsey's intellectual thought as it evolved through the era of the Great Depression. These chapters record the effects that disastrous period had upon Forsey's intellectual foundations as developed to that point. Here one sees the gradual radicalization of Forsey's conservative form of Christian-oriented social reform. The last section (Chapters 8 and 9) focuses on Forsey's ideas for reconstructing Canada's post-World War II social and political policies within the context of the planned society. The reforms Forsey advocated during this period reflected his belief in the need for gradual, yet fundamental changes in Canada's economic and social structures. These changes, however, could for the most part be accomplished through the existing constitutional framework inherited through British traditions.

This "British connection" is an important theme that permeates this work, for a fundamental argument made in this work is that Forsey shares many similarities with early British conservatives and later nineteenth century Tory democrats. His brand of political pluralism, moral reformism, and constitutional democracy derives directly from his family upbringing in Ottawa, his reading of British history and politics, and the influence of his childhood hero and later best friend, Arthur Meighen. In this regard Eugene Forsey's intellectual beliefs represent a particular strain of Canadian conservatism with which much historical work remains to be done.

THE EARLY YEARS

Eugene Forsey's family roots ran deep into Canadian soil. A fifth-generation Canadian himself, Forsey's ancestors came to the Maritimes over two hundred years ago and to Quebec over a century ago. Delighted to describe himself as an "English ethnic," Forsey's Anglo-Celtic family antecedents were of English, Scottish, Irish, and Welsh extraction.[1] His great, great maternal grandparents, the Thornes, were New York Loyalists who came to Nova Scotia in 1783,[2] while his maternal grandfather's family, the Shaws, were pre-Loyalists who came from Massachusetts "in or before 1760."[3]

Forsey's paternal family emigrated to Newfoundland from Devon late in the eighteenth century. His paternal grandfather, George Robert Forsey, was born in Grand Bank, Newfoundland in 1843 and was listed as a magistrate and merchant in the Family Records. In 1868 he married Jane Forsey, and the couple named the first of their eight children Eugene.[4] Eugene Forsey senior lived a multi-faceted life: a onetime able-bodied seaman,[5] he also exhibited a keen interest in his father's lobster-fishing activities,[6] and taught school for a time in Newfoundland. Eugene Forsey senior attended a Methodist College in St. John's and Mount Allison University in Sackville, New Brunswick. He later became a teacher and "Methodist probationer," having resigned from the Methodist Church ministry after fulfilling all but the disciplinary requirements necessary for ordination.[7] In 1896, while studying at Mount Allison, Forsey met Florence Elivia Bowles. Born in Ottawa in 1876, Florence had attended various Ottawa schools before enrolling at Mount Allison.[8] Eugene senior and Florence were married in Ottawa in 1902, after which they worked as missionaries for a time in Mexico City.[9]

Eugene Forsey senior died in Mexico City of heart complications in 1904. Attending his funeral in that city's Methodist Episcopal Church South was his former friend C.H. Cahan, who afterward assisted a very pregnant Mrs. Forsey with the funeral arrangements and advanced her "a good-sized sum" of money for her trip north to Newfoundland.[10] The Forseys' only son, Eugene A. Forsey, never forgot the help that Cahan had given his mother following his father's death: "Cahan is a very old friend," Forsey later wrote, "to whom I am greatly indebted."[11]

Politics seems to have been an accepted career in Eugene Forsey's maternal families, with the Thornes and the Shaws each contributing a member to the Nova Scotia legislature before Confederation, and the Thornes an added senator. Of particular interest to Forsey's intellectual development was the political influence of his maternal grandfather, William Cochrane Bowles. Forsey grew to know grandfather Bowles very well, for immediately after Forsey's birth in Grand Bank, Newfoundland on May 29, 1904,[12] Eugene and his mother moved into the Bowles' Ottawa home, where Forsey was raised by his mother and grandfather, both of whom had a tremendous influence upon him.

Bowles, whom Forsey later described as "a bilingual Quebec City Anglo-Scots Irishman of the first generation born in Canada,"[13] was born in Quebec City on September 23, 1841,[14] and entered the service of the Assembly of the Province of Canada in 1855.[15] Bowles entered the government service permanently in 1866 as the Chief Clerk of Votes and Proceedings, a post from which he was forced to retire in 1915 due to ill health.[16] Upon his retirement both Robert Borden and Wilfrid Laurier paid tribute to his efforts in the House of Commons, where for some years he served as secretary to Sir John Bourinot, from whom he acquired a mastery of parliamentary procedure.[17]

Bourinot was a former Conservative newspaperman who had risen through the ranks of the civil service to become Clerk of the House in 1880, an appointment he held until his death in 1902.[18] The scholarly Bourinot possessed one of the finest library collections of historical, constitutional and literary books in the country. During his tenure as President and later Secretary of the Royal Society of Canada, Bourinot supervised the publication of the Society's nineteen-volume *Proceedings and Transactions* series. Bourinot later published at least six major works on parliamentary procedure and politics and helped to develop many of Canada's own parliamentary traditions.[19]

Forsey's grandfather was tremendously influenced by his association with Bourinot and his constitutional ideas. One very important constitutional principle that Bowles advocated was the importance of "tradition" in the British constitutional system. In a statement that Bowles and Forsey would paraphrase many times throughout their lives, Bourinot called on Canadian intellectuals to contribute to the development of "a new country at a time when its institutions have to be moulded, [by collecting] precedents and principles from the storehouse of the past for the assistance of the present."[20] Bourinot was convinced that the Canadian political and constitutional system, as descended from Canada's British imperial connection, was the matrix in which Canadian liberty was born and nourished.[21]

It was from Bourinot that William Bowles acquired not only a mastery of parliamentary procedure, but a conviction, later attacked by environmental historians, that Canadians should look to Britain, and not to the rivers and forests of Canada or to the United States, to find its constitutional and cultural roots. Forsey later placed himself firmly in this Bourinot-Bowles tradition through his own vehement denunciation of the environmentalist-nationalist historians, and in his support for the philosophy and politics of the "highly conservative British" household in which he was raised.[22] "There was a sort of family tradition of British institutions and British ideas which I grew up with," Forsey later recalled, "and we just took it for granted for the way things were done and not done."[23] Forsey also stated that whatever he received from his father's family was rooted in a similar British constitutional tradition.[24]

It was in the bilingual Bowles household that Forsey learned from his mother and grandfather the basic traditions of Canadian government. Here they discussed politics and literature on a regular basis. As a result, Forsey later wrote, "I frequented the Canadian Parliament Buildings almost from the time I was able to walk. Where other boys played, watched and talked baseball or hockey, I listened to parliamentary debates."[25]

Forsey and his grandfather seemed to have established a strong personal, as well as political, bond. The Forsey Papers contain a number of notes and letters to Forsey from his "affectionate Grandpa," and many proud references about Eugene in letters from Bowles to other family members. In 1911, for example, Bowles circulated to family members a poem written by his seven-year-old grandson: "He is quite pleased with it," wrote the proud grandfather, "and thinks now he will be a poet when he grows up."[26]

Though fatherless, Forsey did not lack for fatherly direction or a stable home life. Forsey fondly recalls his childhood household years as a "genteel, comfortable lifestyle" in which family members shared what could be termed as standard middle-class values: "I recall them as pretty good days," Forsey later said, with summer holidays to the Maritimes and American and other Canadian resorts every summer. In addition to these extensive vacations with his mother and grandfather, Forsey would help tend gardens at the Ottawa home and care for their household pets.[27]

Learning was the most popular pastime in the Bowles' home. The close-knit family shared a love for reading: "You and Eugene must not read much but spend all your time in the open air," directed William Bowles, but one suspects that the books received at least as much time as did Ontario's sparkling waters and fresh air, for Forsey was a voracious reader who had developed a remarkable vocabulary at a very young age.[28]

Scholastically, Forsey received many honours certificates and scholastic prizes during his years at the Ottawa Normal Model School and Ottawa Collegiate Institute. Forsey capped off these awards with a First Class Honours standing in all of his Upper School Matriculation Examinations, a record achievement for any student at that time. It was an accomplishment that ensured his admittance to McGill University later that year.[29]

Forsey grew especially close to his mother during his boyhood years. Florence Forsey shared with her son her special talents for painting and writing and worked for many years as the Librarian of the Geological Survey and Museum in Ottawa.[30] Forsey, a single child, and his widowed mother enjoyed a close relationship, and the two kept in almost constant communication with each other following Eugene's departure from his Ottawa home for McGill in the autumn of 1922.

Eugene Forsey was eighteen years old when he rode the train from Ottawa to McGill University in Montreal in October 1922. In three years he would graduate with a First Class Honours Bachelor of Arts in Economics, Political Science, and English. In 1926 Forsey received a Master of Arts in Economics, *summa cum laude*. These McGill years were tremendously influential for they provided him with an opportunity to expand his intellectual horizons and pursue personal interests free of family direction.

Like most arts students entering McGill in the early 1920s, Forsey's first year courses included his Honours subjects and extra courses, which included History, English, and French. Forsey's first interest, however, was Economics and Political Science, and during his first registration procedures Forsey met two professors in that faculty who would become very important figures in his life.

By 1922, Stephen Leacock had been a permanent member of the McGill Department of Economics and Political Science for almost twenty years. The latter half of this period he had spent as department chairman, during which time he had been successfully engaged in expanding his department as part of an overall upgrading of the faculty of arts.[31] His appointment proved to be critical to the development of the social sciences at that university, and more particularly to the development of political economy as an academic discipline in Canada.[32]

It was from Leacock that Forsey gained first-hand exposure to social criticism, for Leacock had developed a reputation for satirizing the mannerisms and morals of early twentieth century Canadian society and expressing his disillusionment and concern over the destructive effects of material progress on the labouring classes of society. He had, like many other academics in post-war Canada, welcomed the rise of political economy, which was defined variously in the post-war era as economics, political science, sociology or a combination of all three. Leacock also mixed in with this new discipline his general educational and religious idealism. By the 1920s Leacock was firmly opposed to what he perceived as a general slide in Canadian society toward socialism. As one of the leaders of the fragmenting, yet still present, post-World War I "progressive element" in Canadian society, Leacock could not, and would not, acquiesce to such a slide.[33]

While at McGill, Leacock taught Forsey Economics and Political Economy.[34] Later Leacock taught him courses on British and Canadian government that seemed to be a natural extension of information he had been raised with. Leacock was, said Forsey, "a masterful teacher who built on the foundations my home had laid."[35] Leacock later helped Forsey in the young student's decision to pursue Economics in graduate school, and assisted him in obtaining a lecturer's position at

McGill in 1929.[36] Though the two men's politics grew to be substantially different, they continued to share a respect for the British tradition and the importance of empirical research in political economy.[37] Leacock also helped broaden Forsey's perspective on economics and helped Forsey to appreciate its many facets, which to Leacock included "the literary ... and philosophical side of economics, or the purely commercial side, or monetary or perhaps the National (Canadian) or the economic aspect of the Empire."[38]

Professor J.C. Hemmeon was an academic with a less visible public profile than Leacock, but was equally influential in Forsey's career development. Hemmeon taught one of Forsey's first-year Economics courses,[39] and later was instrumental in encouraging Forsey to pursue his M.A. at McGill.[40] Following Forsey's return to McGill in 1929 to pursue a teaching career and a Ph.D., Hemmeon joined Forsey in the League For Social Reconstruction. The two men worked closely with Frank Scott, writing public pamphlets and making speeches on social and economic issues.[41] Hemmeon and Forsey also shared an interest in furthering the cause of civil rights during the 1930s, and the two worked together for some time on the Executive of the Montreal Branch of the Canadian Civil Liberties Union.[42] Their friendship grew stronger after Hemmeon played an instrumental role in arranging for Forsey's sessional lecturer's position at McGill in 1929. "You are among my few good friends," Hemmeon wrote Forsey in 1943, and their friendship continued well into the 1950s.[43]

Despite Leacock and Hemmeon's encouragement, Forsey had difficulty in deciding upon his major area of study. He had always been fascinated with reading English Literature, a passion which caused him to be on the receiving end of friendly verbal abuse from his Economics professor on more than one occasion.[44] But in the end he chose to study economics and political economy: "All knowledge has the strongest fascination for me," wrote the exuberant Forsey to his mother,[45] and that desire to learn was increasingly applied to the workings of Canada's economic and political machinery.

Typical of the books Forsey studied extensively in McGill's Economics and Political Science Department during the mid-1920s was a book written by two Americans, J.W. Jenks and Walter Clark, entitled *The Trust Problem: Economic Power in a Free Society*. First published in 1900, *The Trust Problem* is a prime example of turn of the century American progressive economic reform impulses. The book was written from data collected by Jenks, an economist and federal Immigration Commission employee. Most of his information emanated from his work on the United States Industrial Commission investigating trusts in 1899–1901 and during later trust investigations between 1913 and 1915. Clark, the other author, was employed as a Professor of Economics at the College of the City of New York.[46]

Generally speaking, *The Trust Problem* reflected American progressivism's "broader impulse towards criticism and change that was everywhere so conspicuous" in the United States in the late nineteenth and early twentieth centuries. Richard Hofstadter, an American historian of the progressive era in the United States, has stated that these progressives were "often of two minds on many issues." The progressives, he argued, felt that the new great corporations and big business in general, though perhaps a menace to society and all too often manipulated by unscrupulous men, were nevertheless aware that the newer organization of industry and finance was the product of a social revolution. The new industrial giants, Hofstadter wrote, had their beneficent sides and were undoubtedly here to stay.[47]

The Trust Problem, which Forsey studied at length, presented a similarly balanced view of the evolution of trusts in the United States in the post-Civil War era. The book documented the negative effects of diminishing competition and government policies that were enacted in response to increasing consumer prices and unemployment for union workers. "Apparently," wrote the authors, "the trust has not been operated to secure to the public or its labour the savings of monopoly which it might have divided between them." This type of progressive literature presented a conflict of interests that often required a judgement on the student's part.[48] For their part, Jenkins and Clark made their judgement very clearly understood: "The majority which has been injured is also the social group which, in terms of economic welfare, needs most to gain and can least afford to lose." The conditions, the writers concluded, called for a "sound treatment" of trusts and monopolies because the monopolist must not be allowed to frighten great, maturing democracy. The authors did add, however, that the honest cost-cheapening trust should be welcomed if it was operating in "the fair field."[49]

This rather typical progressive assessment of current economic ills favoured a form of federal government regulation but not outright government ownership. These progressive economists did not seek solutions in fear-inspired, anti-monopoly legislation that sought to thwart or defeat the natural evolution of monopoly. The task at hand, rather, was to initiate national legislation that would set officials "free to do the stimulating, progressive work of guiding and directing the nation's great energies to their utmost achievements."[50] Such studies of modern economic problems that were inherent to both the American and the Canadian state in the 1920s challenged Forsey to critically examine the nature of economic power in Canadian society, and the best methods for rectifying its associated problems.

By his third year, having made his choice to pursue economics and political economy, Forsey quickly set out to master the subjects and establish both his capabilities and his credentials as a social scientist and economist. His McGill transcripts reveal that he was at the very top of his class. In his second year he was awarded first class distinction in his economics, which included Economics I (Elements of Political Economy); Economics II (Elements of Political Science); History 2 (British and European History); English 4 (English Prose From Bacon to Stevenson); and French 2 (French Language). Forsey also won a First Class Honours Award and the First Mackenzie Scholarship Award in Economics and Political Science.[51] In the following two years of his undergraduate work Forsey received first class standings in all of his eleven Political Economy subjects and his five minor courses and received the Charles William Snyder Memorial Scholarship and the Allan Oliver Gold Medal.[52]

In recognition of Forsey's outstanding academic accomplishments, Leacock took the opportunity at Forsey's graduation to recognize Forsey as "one of the most brilliant students [he] had known in twenty-five years of university teaching.... He has a wonderful record in the Department," said Leacock, "and has gained the gold medal and the highest honors."[53]

Forsey's success in studying Political Economy while continuing with English as a minor area to a large degree shaped the nature of his dissent and commentary. He developed the ability to assess economic and political developments and then express his opinions and recommendations in print effectively. It was significant in this regard that in his Fourth Year Honour Certificate Forsey was the only graduating student to carry three disciplines: Economics, Political Science, and English.[54]

Forsey was also active outside the classroom as a member of the McGill Debating Club, President of the Council of the McGill Mock Parliament, Vice President of the McGill Conservative Club, President of the Political Economy Club, and a member and Vice President of the McGill Literary and Debating Society. These experiences greatly improved his public speaking to the point where he won the Talbot-Papineau Memorial Cup for oratory over eighteen competitors by taking the negative on a resolution that Canada should adopt a more liberal policy toward immigration.[55]

For Eugene Forsey, therefore, McGill provided an academic environment ideally suited to fostering the intellectual development of a bright and intellectually eager student intent on mastering the subtleties of political economy. Forsey's enthusiastic involvement in this subject area, both in the classroom and in extramural endeavours, reflected the enthusiasm and organizational momentum that political economy was enjoying in many Canadian universities during this time.

In the early 1920s social scientists, and particularly those social scientists in the expanding political economy subject areas, were successfully making a "special claim to special recognition" for their accumulating expertise. D.R. Owram, for example, has recently illustrated the post-World War I social scientific drive "for organization, distinctiveness and recognition" which was revealed through the proliferation of associated professional associations and journals. This, in turn, was made possible because of the increasingly important role the social scientists held within Canada's universities.[56] Owram specifically documents the emergence during the 1920s of political economy as a "mature discipline" led by social scientists who increasingly "thought of themselves as specialists in their disciplines rather than as deviant historians, philosophers or theologians."[57] At Queen's University in Kingston, for example, the Political Economy Department was energetically expanding its scope with new appointments and curricula to offer interested students.[58] At McGill Leacock, Hemmeon, and others such as John Farthing and John Day provided a similar atmosphere of growth, energy, and relevance to Canadian society.[59]

An excellent indicator of the nature and quality of Forsey's own work in this field was an especially lengthy and detailed paper he wrote in 1925 on Adam Smith's *The Wealth of Nations*. This paper provides some revealing insights into Forsey's personal economic views during these early years at McGill. Forsey delved into Smith's classic, chapter by chapter, and his comments suggest that Forsey possessed an exceptional breadth of understanding of world events and economics as well as some well-developed personal opinions on many of the leading economic issues of the post-war period.

In the opinions he expressed in his review of *The Wealth of Nations*,[60] it was obvious that Forsey was very much a part of the growing empirical and realistic form of critical inquiry defined by A.B. McKillop.[61] But Forsey rejected Smith's adherence to a "true philosophical spirit of inquiry." He also critically viewed the fact that:

> Smith never divorced Economics from Politics and Jurisprudence, nor from the parent study of philosophy.... The work is loose in structure, full of inconsistencies and contradictions; and the style is often ponderous and tiresome.[62]

Though Forsey appreciated the unique, "eminently practical" and reformist aspect of Smith's work,[63] he held it suspect because it was:

> in style, but still more in method,... the child of the eighteenth century [and] inevitably fashioned by the ideas and circumstances of the time. This was the golden age of universal, a priori reasoning and Natural Law. Sentimentalism and optimistic Deism were in the air, and the greatest names of literature and philosophy united in believing in a beneficial and harmonious Natural Order which appears (spontaneously) wherever Nature is left to itself. Rousseau, the prophet of the new gospel, had already applied it to politics. Smith would have denied any sympathy with Rousseau's theory; but he had absorbed from Hume its really fundamental ideas.[64]

Forsey agreed that Smith's philosophy was pervaded by the theory of nature "in a form given to it by theology, and by political history, and by the cast of his own mind." In this sense Smith had accepted the classical conception of nature's "harmonious code" as it blended with theology, producing the Law of Nature as an article of religious belief.

This philosophy seemed overly optimistic to Forsey. He questioned any theory in which the principles of human nature were accepted "as being necessarily beneficial to society and man's fellow man." Though he acknowledged that Smith avoided extremes in this regard, Smith did share in the optimism of the age, as was evidenced by his description of the merchant's being led by an invisible hand to promote the interest of society while simultaneously intending only his own gain. In this regard, Forsey rejected Smith's "sentimental theory of Political Economy as revealed in every page of his book."

To support his point, Forsey referred to Smith's statement regarding the "establishment of natural liberty" as a result of diminished economic control.[65] In this sense Smith's inductive approach reasoned from "the ills of government regulation to the necessity of economic liberty." Forsey had little use for the eighteenth century belief in the positive role played by "natural liberty" and the need to maintain "economic liberty" at all costs.[66]

Forsey differed, for example, with Smith's basic interpretation of the nature of human abilities as related to the growth in the division of labour. This is an important argument because it reveals Forsey's own conservative view of man as a being pre-eminently varied in abilities. Forsey rejected Smith's expressed skepticism as to the existence of any great differences in natural talents among men and women and his argument that any visible differences were "rather the effects of environment – habit, custom, education." Though Forsey acknowledged many good arguments in Smith's account of the origin of the division of labour,[67] the work was nevertheless a "glaring example of the vicious results of pure deduction [a system in which] Truth and error get hopelessly tangled." Smith's "error" was his failure to recognize the extreme variety in men's talents and abilities, and his stressing of environmental factors in its place.[68]

Forsey acknowledged that at times Smith had a low opinion of human nature and believed that "economic man" was somewhat vain and governed by the economic motive most of the time.[69] But Forsey found Smith's assertion that "greater zeal makes for better morals among the lower orders" ridiculously simplistic and wrong: "God help us, what a morality!" Forsey exclaimed. "The constant emphasis on the economic motive shows an unlovely mind."[70] Whereas Smith's eighteenth century view of man suggested that "economic zeal" would rectify any minor differences in basic abilities between makers of society, Forsey always believed that mankind was "rather stupid, reasonably well-meaning, and often very ignorant and unimaginative."[71]

Similarly, Forsey disagreed with some of Smith's key economic arguments, such as the value of monopolies and concentration. Forsey felt that Smith's treatment of them and their effects on society showed the limitations of Smith's time. For example, Forsey agreed with Smith's definition of the monopoly price as "the highest that can be squeezed out of the buyer," but he disagreed that this was necessarily due to "keeping the market constantly under-stocked."[72] Smith had argued that the "natural price," that is, the price resulting from competition in the marketplace, was the lowest that "the sellers" could commonly afford to take and at the same time continue with their business. Enlarged monopolies, in Smith's view, kept the market price of particular commodities above the natural price.[73]

This seemed rather too simple for Forsey, who countered that "Smith had no conception of the wastes of competition, the diminishing costs per unit, or a constant revenue curve." This statement, though admittedly minimal in descriptive value, suggests that Forsey accepted, at least in part, the arguments of American progressives who saw in "efficiency" a major positive force in society. In *The Trust Problem*, for example, the authors concluded that "in many industrial lines cost-cheapening is an outcome of combination" and it was therefore incumbent upon society to "let the honest cost-cheapening Trust be welcomed."[74] Similarly, Forsey recognized the benefits of monopolization, though he realized that the possible negative effects on society had to be assiduously scrutinized. In this regard Forsey's views on the trust issue seem in line with the interpretations of American progressives as persons seeking a harmony through technological order and a moderate degree of control along with the utilization of new industrial forces. This view pictures man not as an isolated individual in nature but rather in a communal perspective and part of nature and "a group."[75]

Forsey was, therefore, critical of Smith's "inveighing against corporation privileges, and the evils of meetings of people in the same trade, which [always] end in a conspiracy against the public or some contrivance to raise prices."[76] Forsey did not fail to mention that Smith was well aware of "the immense power of the monopolists and their unscrupulous tactics."[77]

The "Protective System" was a second major issue that was discussed at length in *The Wealth of Nations*. Smith's book represented, in effect, an outright frontal attack on the merchants and manufacturers who supported mercantilism, as well as an attack on the value of economic protectionism as a beneficial governmental policy. Such a system, Smith argued, could only harm the nation by destroying public revenue and "diverting capital and labour into what are admittedly less productive channels." In words that Forsey would soon echo himself, Smith concluded a chapter on the mercantilist system by unequivocally stating his belief that:

> In the mercantilist system, the interest of the consumer is almost constantly sacrificed to that of the producer; and it seems to consider production, and not consumption, as the ultimate end and object of all industry and commerce.

Smith viewed the mercantilist system as being continued by the producing class, namely the merchants and manufacturers, to the sacrifice of not only the interests of the consumer but also "some other sets of producers."[78]

Forsey viewed Smith's discussion of the protective system rather favourably. He found Smith's argument regarding the consumers' interests vis-à-vis the producers' interests "profoundly suggestive" and he concluded that at least one contemporary economist's harsh review of Smith's arguments on the protection issue had been less than fair. "Smith's original contributions," Forsey wrote, "are really very great."[79]

Closely associated with the protection and mercantilist systems was Smith's contention that the state was "by its nature unfit for economic functions," thus leaving the Sovereign "responsible only for natural defences, the administration of justice, and erecting certain public works."[80] Forsey acknowledged that Smith's well-known arguments on this issue had been "an anti-socialist arsenal ever since," but Forsey pointed out that Smith "lived in a world in which State interference had been nearly all bad, in which State industry had rarely succeeded, and in which the extravagant British government was 'unfit to manage more than the Post Office.'" Forsey also argued that since Smith's time, governments had gained knowledge of economic conditions and could now give industry the minute attention it needed, while the civil service was more careful and efficient. "The change which has taken place," Forsey explained, "shows the danger of applying Smith's principles to totally different conditions."[81]

In Forsey's detailed review of *The Wealth of Nations* one can identify the beginnings of Forsey's overall economic philosophy that would emerge as a Canadian form of British "Tory democracy" within two years. Forsey's favourable review of Smith's sympathetic treatment of the value and positive role of labour in society, for example, would emerge as a humanitarian concern for the role of the working man in industrial society. Similarly, Forsey's view of man as part of a communal, social and interdependent system,[82] and his support for a moderate, consumer-oriented protective system, would soon form two additional philosophical pillars in Forsey's Tory democratic thought.

EUGENE FORSEY
AND TORY DEMOCRACY

The early to mid-1920s were an especially important period for Eugene Forsey's personal and intellectual development. They were also extremely unstable years economically in Canada as economic fluctuations and recessions adversely affected many groups in Canadian society. Some of this instability was due to the fact that during this period the Canadian economy underwent a transformation from one based on primary production to one in which the secondary sector of manufacturing and construction emerged as the largest contributor to national income.[1] One result of this economic transition was a deteriorating business climate early in the decade. The Gross National Product, for example, declined 20 per cent in 1921 and continued its decline in 1922.[2]

Public realization of the extent of economic collapse in Canada steadily increased during the early 1920s as the length of the unemployment lines increased across the country. By the winter of 1924–25 over 200,000 Canadians were without work as the financially beleaguered municipalities found themselves unable to provide jobs and forced to restrict relief to married men with families. Conditions in the early 1920s in some ways closely resembled the conditions of the Depression era as thousands of unemployed single men joined in "an endless trek of jobless transients across the country searching for work or a meal and a place to sleep."[3]

As a result of this increasing distress in the 1920s, both Arthur Meighen's and Mackenzie King's governments were besieged with demands for new initiatives in the fields of social and economic policy. The Ontario government, financially pressed in the 1920s, led the attack on Ottawa's seemingly dormant social and financial policy makers.[4] In Quebec the dismal years of the early 1920s drew very little political response to the needs and demands of the growing number of unemployed, though a few gestures toward the most vulnerable workers, women, and children were necessary. Industrial accidents, deteriorating working conditions, and mounting unemployment continued to be the major problems facing working people in Montreal, where Forsey was studying, and in Quebec as a whole.[5]

Along with the economic situation, health conditions were also deteriorating in Quebec. Despite efforts by municipal institutions in this period to improve Montreal's poor sanitation facilities, the network of health institutions remained insufficient to meet the needs of the population, especially that part of the population who were in no position to pay the cost of treatment.[6] In the 1920s, for example, Montreal's tuberculosis rate was three times that of Toronto, and its basic social service level was estimated at 66 per cent of that of other major cities.[7] In Montreal Forsey was exposed to the contrasting lifestyles of Mont Royal and St. James Street on the one hand, and the charitable refuge homes and the slums on the other.

Conditions in other regions of Canada were no better. In the Maritimes, where much of Forsey's family lived, civic leaders were "spurred to near desperation by the virtual collapse of their economy, as the early 1920s saw a widespread recession turn into a lingering depression."[8] On the Prairies, the emergence of the Progressive Party was an expression of the farmers' revolt against the old economic system based on protection and against post-war inflation, indebtedness caused by wartime expansion, and the return to the free market in wheat caused by the termination of the Wheat Board in 1920.[9]

An observer of the Canadian scene during the early 1920s could not but agree with the statement: "The Canada that emerged from the election of 1921 seemed ungovernable."[10] For his part Mackenzie King responded to the emerging social crisis by referring issues to newly created boards and agencies that neither developed nor advanced any new economic theories.[11] In many cases patterns emerged in the 1920s that resembled the patterns in the late nineteenth and early twentieth century period that Forsey was studying in his political economy classes. In the 1920s, for example, the increasingly powerful manufacturing class continued to lobby Ottawa to establish institutional protection against the impact of rapid socio-economic change, such as the effects of competition in an increasingly protective world economic climate, control of labour unrest, and protection against the implementation of radical prairie political policies. Despite evidence of massive price-fixing schemes, "informal arrangements," and King's 1923 Combines Investigation Act, scant protection existed for consumers. In the ten years following World War I the number and size of Canada's mergers continued to increase.[12]

A decade earlier a heated debate had emerged in the United States over the progressives' efforts to raise tariffs "as the sovereign remedy for the huge business combinations that were arising in the face of business lobbying."[13] So too did the tariff issue play a large role in political debates in the 1920s.[14] The tariff remained the prime focus of much of the decade's political debate largely because of Mackenzie King's efforts to placate demands for lower tariffs to keep consumer costs low. In King's view the formulation of a tariff policy constituted an essential part of the "daily compromise" needed to maintain the stability of the established social order.[15]

King's answer was to defer as much of the debate as possible to the newly created Board on Tariffs and Taxation. According to historian Tom Traves, this Board "prepared safe ground for the Cabinet" by functioning as the organization in which the competing class interests "spent their force in tedious and lengthy hearings."[16] Despite some minor adjustments, however, no dramatic changes in the basic three-tiered tariff structure that had been in place since 1907 occurred, and the debate over the advantages and disadvantages of a protection continued to exacerbate Canada's interregional and class tensions throughout the 1920s.[17] Given the period's economic transformation, the economic effects that the tariff policy had on Canada's regions and classes, and King's policy of deferment, it was natural that the tariff issue remained the focus of much public and political debate.

The importance of this debate was augmented politically by the fact that the two traditional political parties, the Liberals and the Conservatives, were themselves seriously split into rival factions on the issue. The tariff debate illustrated the fact that during the 1920s one could not "identify conservatism with the Conservative party or liberalism with the Liberal party."[18] The debate, in fact, illustrated the ways in which varied opinions were contained within the Canadian brokerage system of parties, as the two major parties gave expression to a multiplicity of views on the question of protection for home industry.[19]

In the early and mid-1920s Eugene Forsey was a leftist member of the Conservative Party and an admirer of its leader Arthur Meighen,[20] who during this period exercised a tenuous hold on the leadership reins following his 1921 defeat by Mackenzie King. One of the most glaring policy debates within the Conservative Party after that defeat was over its policy on the tariff. Following the 1921 defeat Meighen had set out to crystallize the Conservative Party's position on the tariff, quite aware that his personal preference for maintaining the tariff might succeed in uniting protectionist Liberals with like-minded Conservatives.[21] Meighen was undoubtedly aware that his tariff theme would please relatively few people in western Canada, including members of his own party, but he held firm to his conviction nonetheless, believing it was a risk he had to take in order to gain strength in central and eastern Canada; and because the national interest, as he conceived it, required the maintenance of the protective system.[22]

Meighen's moderate tariff plan was similar to the policy he put forward during his own administration,[23] and despite the potentially divisive nature of the issue and an undisciplined, somewhat raucous caucus, Meighen held to his policy throughout the 1922 and 1923 House of Commons sessions, when the tariff dominated the political agenda.[24] When in the 1924 session the Liberal government's budget reduced tariff duties, manufacturers were alarmed, for they saw the Liberals' promised tariff stability disappear and uncertainty and conjecture take its place.[25] As dissension broke out in the Liberal ranks, Meighen spotted just the opportunity he had been waiting for, and he attacked the new tariff proposals and reaffirmed his faith in a protectionist tariff.[26]

Given the above scenario, Meighen seemed to have "the clear, clear fight" he had long sought, but unfortunately for him the "definite verdict" he sought in the 1925 campaign left his 116-member caucus on the outside watching King's Liberals cling to power with Progressive support.[27]

From his Montreal location Forsey witnessed first-hand one of the major factors in the Conservative Party's continuing problems, that being the Montreal business community's opposition to Meighen's leadership. Meighen, the man who nationalized the Grand Trunk Railway, would never be a friend of the St. James Street power brokers, a powerful, united group of railway, manufacturing, and press tycoons.[28]

Observers of the Montreal political scene like Eugene Forsey had anticipated the Conservative's 1925 defeat a full year earlier in the autumn of 1924, when the Montreal business group had interfered with Meighen's campaign strategy in a by-election in Montreal's St. Antoine riding. The election was the result of a protectionist Liberal's resignation over the 1924 budget vote, and two Conservative candidates, a Meighen man and a St. James Street candidate, campaigned against each other until a few days before the vote. Confusion in the Conservative ranks ensured a Liberal victory in St. Antoine, and the Montreal *Star* was quick to lead the condemnation of Meighen's leadership abilities after the result was announced.[29] In many ways, then, St. Antoine was a foretaste of the 1925 election results.

Forsey closely followed the political debates of the early 1920s from both his Montreal home and from a country home on the cool shores of Lake Ontario, where he was employed for a time at Vincent Massey's Batterwood home as a tutor for the Massey children. The setting could not have been more aesthetically or intellectually pleasing for the young McGill student. Located a few miles north of Port Hope, Ontario, Batterwood was a modest country home until converted into the Masseys' principal residence in 1927. The Masseys had purchased the old farm house and property in 1918, and it was a splendid site, located on rising ground above a river with surrounding rolling hills to the north and Lake Ontario to the south.[30]

The setting made an obvious and immediate impression on Forsey, who described the scene as he approached Batterwood for the first time in the Massey's chauffeured automobile: "The place is beautiful – rolling country, lightly wooded here and there with a stream ending in a mill pond almost below the hill window." This rural and rustic setting was a pleasant change for Forsey, who had lived his whole life in either Ottawa or Montreal. He especially appreciated the surrounding farmland and the fact that the house was "quite in the pioneer stage."[31]

Forsey was hired to teach the two Massey boys reading, poetry, and history, and to lead a daily nature study session. His letters to his mother over the course of his tenure show that he thoroughly enjoyed the experience with his two young pupils. In addition to providing him with much-needed income, the job gave him an opportunity to experience activities such as archery, arrow making, fishing, wildflower gathering, and sailing as well as the "harder work" with the books. Overall he found the work delightfully interesting and challenging, and his various antics over the course of his three-week stay seem to have brought out the boy in him.[32]

More stimulating perhaps was the intellectual flavour surrounding Batterwood, for the Massey home was filled with good books and a seemingly constant flow of politically, culturally, and academically oriented visitors. Vincent Massey had been acquiring books since his early boyhood, and he eventually collected a library of over six thousand volumes, consisting largely of British, Commonwealth, and Canadian history, but with a substantial amount of English literature as well.[33] With his work day with the boys finished by 5:00 p.m., Forsey was free to spend evenings reading and writing. When he was not engaged in either of these two activities, Forsey socialized with the Masseys and their many visitors, who in the course of his stay at Batterwood included: a Professor Smith of the University of Toronto's History Department, a great friend of the Massey's and a frequent visitor to Batterwood[34] whom Forsey found "most interesting and witty"; Principal Maurice Mutton, a University of Toronto classicist; and George Wrong, Professor of Modern History at the University of Toronto. Wrong was Massey's long-time mentor and friend who had "assumed his ecclesiastical robes" nine years earlier to assist in Massey's marriage to Alice Parkin, daughter of Sir George Parkin, whom Massey had met while at Oxford.[35] Wrong had also been instrumental in bringing Massey to the University of Toronto as a special lecturer in history following Massey's return from Balliol College in 1913. Massey, in fact, had first seen the Batterwood property in 1917 while visiting the Wrongs, who owned property adjacent to the Massey home.[36] Additional visitors to the Massey home included another University of Toronto academic, Charles Cochrane, a contemporary of Massey at Oxford and later Associate Professor of Classics at Toronto and a major international scholar;[37] the son of British Prime Minister Ramsay Macdonald, whom Forsey described as having "a clear head and plenty of information and ideas without being at all self-conscious or forward"; and a young Austrian, Fritz Thalman, "a most interesting chap with an excellent mind."[38]

Although Forsey quite enjoyed participating in the political, theological, and academic discussions with the Masseys and their guests, he took even more delight in the Massey library and in his private discussions with Massey himself. It is through these two venues that one discovers the first thorough expression of Forsey's political and economic positions on issues such as the tariff and the nature of Canadian conservatism.

In the early 1920s Vincent Massey was a man on the verge of public life who saw himself playing a public role in helping to set the course of the nation. He had a special interest in education, world trade, and industrial peace, and by 1924 his passion for these issues had fostered both a theoretical and practical interest in politics.[39] But politics was a secondary interest to Massey's concern for the welfare of the family's agricultural implements business. By 1924 the Massey firm, like most enterprises during the early 1920s, had witnessed a collapse of its Canadian market which forced the firm into the overseas market.[40] As the chief executive of a business involved with national and international trade, Massey favoured the maintenance of a moderate to high tariff. Politically he had been accused of being a "renegade Conservative," but Massey saw himself as holding "stock liberal ideas" on the major issues of protection and the future of the empire.

It is difficult, however, to define what exactly was a "stock liberal idea" on the tariff issue during the mid-1920s. Massey had met privately with Prime Minister King following the Liberals' reduction in a number of manufacturing and agricultural items in the March 1924 budget.[41] King later recorded in his diary that during that meeting Massey made a "last plea on behalf of the mffr's [sic] of implements against a reduction especially on binders. He claims it will work havoc with the industry.... I gave Massey little encouragement."[42]

Like so many Canadians in the early 1920s, Massey yearned for a clarification of political, social, and economic policies by both the Conservatives and the Liberals. He believed that if the Liberal Party "swings to the left, Liberalism in Canada [stood] some chance of meaning something again." On the other hand, Massey believed that:

A low tariff radical Liberal party would throw the type of Liberal, who is an ultra-Conservative under another name, into the Conservative camp where he belongs, and we may have some chance of having two great parties sincerely divided on the ancient lines. If this happens, and a revived Conservative party, with protection and the greater emphasis on the Imperial tie, emerges on the

21

one hand, confronted on the other by a new Liberal party adhering to the low tariff or free trade, and with its emphasis on Canadian nationalism, then I think the political air will be very much clearer, and the utterances of politicians inevitably more sincere.[43]

Massey later ran, and lost, as a moderate, tariff-supporting Mackenzie King Liberal in the 1925 general election, but he later joined King's 1925 Cabinet as a Minister without Portfolio.[44]

Massey had much in common with the young Meighen-supporting tutor he employed in 1924. "Mr. Massey said he and John Buchan[45] had agreed they were the only two Tories in the world," Forsey wrote his mother, adding: "I think I am the third."[46] Politically Forsey shared Massey's frustration with the government's lack of clearly defined economic policies: "The Government," wrote Forsey, "still plays the old double game – Stewart[47] declaring (for Western consumption) that the Budget is 'the death knell of Protection,' and Cardin[48] (for the East) that the Tariff has been scarcely touched."[49]

As a political economist Forsey was being trained to develop the facts clearly and to assess their implications. He therefore had nothing but contempt for Mackenzie King's style of political decision making. Forsey believed that on the tariff issue the Liberals were in a "dam-tight [sic] place" but they had been in similar positions in the past and had "wiggled out of it more successfully than any similar collection of mediocrities ever did before." They had managed to do so primarily because they were conditioned to act from motives of expediency. "If there is a principle behind their tariff policy," Forsey wrote, "no one is likely to drag it from the labyrinthine depths of Mr. King's speeches." "He is," added Forsey, "the perfect mystifier."[50] Politically, Forsey respected clearly defined policy and intellect and found "Tory personnel ... far more imposing than Whig. Meighen has brains, King is a pleasant fool in a good many regards."[51]

As far as his own Conservative Party was concerned, Forsey found the results of the St. Antoine by-election extremely disheartening, though he believed that it had offered the Party the opportunity to make a choice between the two disparate factions that sought its leadership.[52] "St. Antoine was a hard blow for the Conservative Party," Forsey wrote his mother, "but it is a far harder one for Philosophical Industrialism."[53] This was a reference to the "sky-high" tariff tycoons who so wished to replace Meighen with their own man. The failure of this faction to win St. Antoine with their own candidate, therefore, hardly displeased Forsey, who wrote that "THE GREAT BUSINESS MAN is evidently without due honour in the city supposedly dedicated to him."[54]

Forsey supported Meighen because he believed in Meighen's form of moderate conservative philosophy, though he was concerned that Meighen had "lately deferred rather too much to the 'orthodox' Tory-private enterprise view."[55] For Forsey, opportunity to cleanse the Conservative Party of right wing elements and set it on a more progressive direction provided solace for political defeat:

> I see the Montreal gang are out for Meighen's head, and are going to form a new party under Sir Arthur Currie! I wish them luck. Good riddance to bad rubbish as far as the Tories are concerned. It means that Meighen (whom Montreal *never* could control and therefore hated) will be positively driven into the direction of Tory Democracy. Montreal capitalism would be a poor cornerstone for Quebec Toryism anyway. It has too much contempt for the French. Toryism dominated by Montreal interests is a nightmare; the possibility of which we are now happily freed.[56]

The concept of Tory democracy referred to in the above quotation was a political doctrine that Forsey had been increasingly favouring for some time. He had been writing draft copies of an article on the philosophy of Tory democracy when he had been back visiting in Ottawa following the end of the previous academic year. He had also spent most of his free evenings at Batterwood reading additional books on the subject of Tory democracy as espoused by its two chief spokespersons, Benjamin Disraeli and Randolph Churchill.

The term "Tory democracy" emerged in the latter quarter of the nineteenth century and was first identified as "Disraelian" Conservatism, a central feature of which was a commitment to social reform. In this sense Tory democracy addressed the material needs of the masses and served as a philosophical rallying cry by which the Conservative Party would encourage class harmony, guarantee social stability, and gain increased popular support.[57]

Disraeli's emphasis on "the elevation of the condition of the people" is commonly regarded as one of his most important contributions to the development of his party because it enabled the Conservatives to come to terms with the rising social and political power of the working classes in the late nineteenth century.[58] Disraeli's efforts to adapt the British Conservative Party to the realities of the new industrial age in Britain rested on his belief in the traditional British institutions of the Crown and the Constitution. This duality of progressive reform and constitutional traditionalism was unique to its day. The philosophy was well described in a 1914 book entitled *The Tory Tradition*:

> [The Tory Party's claim] to represent the non-agrarian masses of the people ... is his [Disraeli's] contribution to the Tory party. It is his contribution to English political philosophy. Mob-rule Disraeli feared as much as any man, and even applied to it the name of Democracy, which he contrasts more than once with what he termed "popular government." In this he saw the People, united with the Crown, buttressed by their institutions, able only by this method to resist a dominant clique that would enslave them. Toryism [therefore could] never tire of protesting against the control of the nation and its destinies by any single class.[59]

In addition to the political arena, Disraeli was also able to express his ideas through his theatrical plays and novels, for he was an accomplished writer as well as politician. In his most popular novel, Sybil, Disraeli used the effects of the industrial revolution on English society as his principal theme. Believing that British life had been fundamentally transformed by economic change, Disraeli hoped to develop a policy that would take account of that change and provide leadership in a country split into two classes. The Tories' role was to heal wounds and reconcile Britain's deep split between its two social groups, its "two nations" – the rich and the poor.[60]

Though he has been criticized for failing to transform his zeal for social reform into concrete measures,[61] Disraeli did sponsor legislation to protect the working man (Disraeli's real "Tory democrat"), restrict hours of work, and revise poor laws. He also maintained and strengthened the monarchy and the empire and the ideas they represented, such as law and order, religion, and the clarification of political party platforms that would provide the electorate with clear-cut choices.[62]

Disraeli believed that the people were represented not solely by their elected members in the House of Commons, but by "the popular throne," their peers, and the Commons, three entities which taken together represented the trusteeship of the nation. This interpretation of the balanced elements in the constitution made possible the extension of suffrage. The dominant will of the Disraeli nation was to be vested in these three "estates," and his emphasis on the balanced nature of the British constitution represented an essential component in Tory democratic ideology, though Disraeli left it to Lord Randolph Churchill to popularize that ideology later in the nineteenth century.[63]

Like Disraeli, Churchill worked to create a central role in the Conservative Party for the working man.[64] Though Churchill was somewhat caught "between the progressive and reactionary, between Tory Democracy and the older Toryism,"[65] he steadfastly pursued his reformist goals,[66] many of which were achieved after his resignation from the Party.[67] Most historians agree, therefore, that the Tory democratic movement successfully achieved the enactment of various Tory legislative measures, which a contemporary writer of the Tory democratic movement described as "social, economic, and political reforms which look to the betterment of the people, without endangering the nation's institutions."[68]

Taken as a whole, Disraelian-Churchillian Tory democracy introduced into the personality of Conservatism an element that assisted it in coming to terms with the new industrial order and the rise of labour.[69] While maintaining the traditional Conservative principle regarding centrality of religion and a belief in the existence of a transcendent moral order, Tory democrats advocated the need for greater democracy by rooting the new industrial masses in traditional conservative traditions and introducing Tory neo-imperialism and the "second British empire."[70] Constitutionally, Tory democracy sought to safeguard a balanced constitution by preventing the domination of any one class, especially the "alleged plutocrats of big business." Tory democrats sought to achieve this goal by demonstrating to the working men the value of rooting themselves in traditional institutions by passing legislation that would satisfy their needs within that framework, rather than a Marxist class war framework.[71]

Disraeli's Tory democracy, sometimes referred to as "Tory social democracy," or "Tory socialism," represented, therefore, a strain of conservative social consciousness that addressed social problems through the social action of the state. For nineteenth century conservative spokesmen such as Lord Hugh Cecil, such a philosophy represented a unique form of conservatism which maintained that conservative social reform need not proceed on purely individualistic lines. With Tory democracy there was, according to Cecil, "no antithesis between Conservatism and Socialism [because] Conservatives now had no difficulty in welcoming the social activity of the State."[72]

Eugene Forsey's interest in the type of conservatism advocated by Benjamin Disraeli and Churchill increased during the summer of 1924. He had spent much of the summer in Ottawa researching and writing an article he planned to call "Tory democracy," and he had brought some of his notes with him to the Massey home where he continued to work on the paper.[73] Upon his arrival at Batterwood, Forsey soon realized that his host shared his own interest in the subject, and the two men discussed the possibilities of adapting and applying Disraelian and Churchillian policies to twentieth century Canada. "Mr. M. [Massey] thinks, as I have more than once thought," wrote Forsey shortly after his arrival, "that the future of the world lies with a Disraeli-Churchill Toryism."[74]

Forsey was pleased to find that the Massey library contained valuable books on the subject of Tory democracy, including a biography of Churchill entitled *Lord Randolph Churchill* that Forsey required to continue his work at Batterwood but had left at his home in Ottawa. Reading the biography rekindled his interest in completing his "Tory democracy" paper: "I am surprised and delighted to find how closely I agree with that great man [Churchill] in my general idea of Toryism and what it stands for or *should* stand for," Forsey wrote his mother. He added that he had found in his most recent reading on the subject a renewed inspiration to get on with the writing of the "Tory democracy" article, and he immediately set to work on that task.[75]

Forsey was soon applying his knowledge regarding the nature and importance of Tory democratic principles to the Canadian political scene. He concluded, for example, that the Montreal business tycoons who were cheerfully advocating "blatant Protectionism" had so linked their "philosophical industrialism" with the Conservative Party in the public's mind that they had ended "all hope of a change of Government." "If Quebec and the West held firm," Forsey predicted,

"Ontario, British Columbia and the Maritime Provinces may go to the dickens" as far as the Liberals were concerned. But Forsey was not dismayed at such a prospect. He assessed the relative merits of each party on the basis of policy as opposed to any strong partisan loyalty. The prospect of a Montreal-dominated Conservative Party, however, held little interest for him. Forsey predicted if that were to occur and Meighen was ousted from the Party's leadership:

> The Grits – both wings – may breathe freely: we shall have another fifteen years of Liberal rule. I cannot say I am pleased at the prospect, though the Tories have only glimpses of the real Toryism; and I have sincere respect for the Liberal railway policy as well as the Superannuation Act.[76]

Like many British Tory Democrats and Canadians, Forsey actively participated in the tariff debate. Basically his was a practical and moderate view since he did not see the tariff as a great unyielding principle. Forsey's main criticism of the Liberals' policy of gradually lowering the tariff barriers centred on the resultant loss of revenue that accompanied such a move. Forsey was therefore undecided as to the specific level of protection that should be offered to the manufacturers, but he was adamantly opposed to seeing "Toryism as the hand-servant of Protection," and its plutocratic adherents.[77] "I cannot share the anti-Budget fever of Philosophical Industrialism," wrote Forsey, "at least not fully, or for the same reasons; but *how* anyone can think the Government Protectionist I cannot see."[78]

Forsey's main concern with King's 1924 budget lay with its tax reduction measures. In terms of revenue, for example, the lowering of the sales tax was the most significant change and involved the probable loss of twenty-three million dollars in government revenue.[79] Despite the fact that the government was working with its first surplus since 1913,[80] such a drastic measure bothered Forsey. His chief concern lay with the Liberal's apparent disinterest in maintaining a consistent, traditional financial policy and the associated threat this posed to the country's financial stability. This too was a concern quite in keeping with the fiscal principles of Tory democracy. Forsey explained his position on this issue by arguing that:

27

> My real objection to their (Liberals') fiscal policy lies in two things:
> it is likely to be financially ruinous at a time when we need every
> cent we can get; and being based on absolutely no principle, but
> veering round according to the political wind, it contains no prom-
> ise of permanence or stability, just when stability is most needed.[81]

What was needed, he believed, was cautionary reform leading to progressive change. This called for "a scientifically revised tariff, coming
gradually into force under favourable conditions." Such a policy, Forsey
believed, "would improve the efficiency of our industries and the general condition of the country [and] quiet most of the talk of Free Trade,
or anything approaching it."[82]

Forsey personally favoured the implementation of a consistent fiscal
policy, one that would vigorously enact "generous and progressive
measures, and real economy." Such a policy combined Tory democracy's adherence to fiscal economy with its call for socially progressive
measures. As far as the tariff was concerned, this involved the immediate enactment of "differential Protection," which Forsey described
as "a duty sufficient to equalize our costs of production with those of
our competitors – and so maintain the standard of living" of Canada's
increasing numbers of working men. These were words that might well
have been drawn from the Churchill biography he had just read, for
like Churchill and Disraeli before him, Forsey steadfastly supported
the need to create and maintain a strong economic base that would
support necessary social reforms: "A tariff for the masses – Fair and
Imperial Trade with due considerations for the revenue and the interests of trade," concluded Forsey, "that must be the policy of Tory
Democracy" in post-World War I Canada.[83]

But Forsey's "Tory democracy" also recognized the needs of Canada's
farmers, who at this very time were expressing their frustrations
through their political support for the Progressive Party. The Tory
democracy of Disraeli and Churchill had sought to utilize education
and social reform to alleviate Britain's rural economic distress in its age
of rapid industrialization, thereby linking the farmer with the urban
factory worker.[84] So too did Forsey look beyond what he felt were the
short-term Liberal solutions to rural Canada's plight:

> By the time we come to power the farmer will probably have got
> nice economic concessions, so we need not worry about them on this
> (the tariff) score. The problem of agricultural distress will survive, in
> a less acute form, and will have to be met by various means, social
> *and* educational as well as, and I think rather more than, political.[85]

It is apparent that Forsey was assimilating his growing academic knowledge with his ubiquitous interest in history and politics. In terms of
his knowledge of political economy, Forsey consistently defined his
personal philosophy in a progressive conservative mould along British
Tory democratic lines.

Environmental factors must play a significant role in any discussion
of the growth and development of Forsey's political and economic philosophy during the tumultuous post-World War I decade. This was
especially true in the autumn of 1924 when Forsey departed Batterwood
and returned to McGill. There he was faced with Montreal's many visible economic and social problems, which his ongoing education and
practical experience was training him to critically assess. At McGill,
Forsey enrolled in a joint Political Economy-English programme that
at least three professors warned him included too many courses.[86]
Forsey not only refused to drop any of his courses, he began to publish public articles on political issues. One such project was Forsey's
lengthy, three-part article entitled "My Discovery of Montreal" which
was published in the McGill Daily *Literary Supplement*. The articles are
an important yardstick in Forsey's intellectual development, for they
mark his first major effort at political commentary for public consumption. After repeated urging by the paper's editor and a number of "small
subtractions" by the author, the articles were finally published in the
late autumn of 1924.[87] Forsey believed the articles were "too savage for
the paper's purpose," and refused to sign his full name, but following
consultations with Professors Hemmeon and Files, the latter being an
English professor who had urged Forsey on throughout the autumn,
Forsey agreed to sign his initials to the articles.[88]

In the "My Discovery" series, Forsey satirized Montreal's business
community "for opening a new era in human knowledge and differing radically from all previous systems in having outgrown the silly

superstition of thinking." "Philosophical Industrialists," Forsey added, do not need to think for "they already know, and so with characteristic energy, decision, and finality they have waged war on the evil source of all our troubles – theories and ideals." For older ideas, however, such as "Laissez-faire it keeps a sentimental kindness, even condescending to use them." In the words of one of its critics, Montreal "looks upon new ideas as positively immoral."[89] In this regard, Forsey wrote, socialism and government ownership were dismissed "as one and indivisible with Marxian Communism and other kindred manias [and] very roughly handled." Forsey mentioned the "radicals" who implemented the "Canadian National Railway policy" as an excellent example of radical Lenin fanaticism at work in Canada.[90]

In the third instalment of the series, Forsey drew on his increasing sensitivity to the working class and wrote of the capitalists' pleasure with the docile and respectful French-Canadian worker: "They are, in fact, the indispensable hewers of wood and drawers of water in Philosophical Industrialism's Utopia to which that employers' Paradise, Montreal is the nearest approach."[91] Forsey also added the industrialists' support for widespread immigration, but certainly "not because an immigration flood lowers wages, but because therein lies the road to greatness." Yet another "article of religion" for the capitalist was "a good stiff tariff," for the capitalist would be more than happy to explain that "Free Traders, 'Bolsheviks,' Prohibitionists, and criminal lunatics are much the same class of people."[92]

Nor did Forsey forget the spiritual dimension that Philosophical Industrialism lent to Canadian society:

> So much for the temporal concerns. But Philosophical Industrialism does not neglect the spirit. It has discovered the cause of religious decay. Christianity has lost its hold on account of ecclesiastical weakness and stupidity. Priests and ministers have become entangled in theories and 'isms', forgetting the Church exists for the business man. He remains firm; it is the Church which has drifted away. But by purging itself of the taint of Trade Unionism sympathies; by humble submission to business control and a whole-hearted devotion to business interests, it may yet transform itself into a spiritual department store able to regain the confidence of the market.[93]

Forsey had clearly adopted much of the satirical style of his instructor Stephen Leacock. But all was not satire in his writing, for he did directly denounce the Montreal business community for blindly opposing government ownership without first examining the management skills of its own people who administered its railways and hotels. This group, Forsey maintained, was totally ignorant of the facts to the point of inviting derision. How else, asked Forsey, does one respond to Montrealers being so fearful of the Labour Party's rise in England, where it had increased its popular vote by over one million from the 1923 election total, winning one hundred and fifty seats in Parliament?[94] Forsey ended his series by satirizing certain Montrealers' fear of "flaming red shirts brandishing banks in both hands." Surely, he wrote, Labour's recent political success was the precursor of the political arrival of a "mob of rough, ignorant and fanatical working men with no knowledge of business – backed by an overwhelming Parliamentary majority thirsting for blood." "And surely," Forsey cried out in mock alarm, this was "Russia over again!"[95]

Forsey also felt it was important to lend direct support to the incorporation of the working class and the Canadian trade union movement into the mainstream of Canadian politics. To do this he once again took direct aim at the St. James Street business community:

> Montreal has a deep seated distrust of the economic group in politics, whatever its platform. It feels perfect confidence in the good old system of two parties safely controlled from St. James Street. But when a group takes on a 'Bolshevik' hue it becomes anathema; and their metropolitan friends have long since endowed Messrs Wood and Irvine with horns, hoofs and tails.[96]

And then, with his pen planted firmly in cheek, Forsey praised "the Philosophical Industrialist" for insisting "that people stand on their own feet [and for] his efforts to save the 'duped' working man from the clutches of the professional foreign agitator, who lives by concocting strikes and taking employed bribes to call them off." It was, added Forsey, undoubtedly an oversight on the Industrialist's part that "in his anxiety to preserve his little flock of wolves ... he occasionally forgets such trifling details as wages and living conditions."[97]

Despite his flippancy in writing the "My Discovery" articles, their publication made Forsey extremely nervous. His academic work was extremely important to him, and he fully expected the "college people" and university officials to recognize the "E.F" initials on the articles.[98] Forsey's discomfort was intensified by the thought that Sir Arthur Currie, a close associate of many Montreal businessmen and President of McGill, would soon know the authorship of the articles. There was, however, no official response to the articles.

Despite this apprehension, Forsey continued his political commentary, publishing major articles defending Meighen's leadership amid the rising tide of opposition from within and outside the Party to Meighen's imperialist position.[99] He also published reports that the Montreal tycoons had established a slush fund to defeat Meighen in his Manitoba riding.[100] Not surprisingly, Forsey recalls that he and the four editors of the McGill *Fortnightly Review*, one of whom was Frank Scott, were "called up on the mat by Currie who accused us of attacking the St. James Street gang."[101]

The action by Currie was almost to be expected, for as Forsey would later recall, the atmosphere in Montreal in the early 1920s was "very odd indeed for one was considered to be wrong in the head ... a lunatic for writing to newspapers." This was especially true for those who chose to lash out at the City's power brokers.[102]

For Forsey, however, these early McGill years represented his 'coming out' into the world of public commentary on the nature of Canada's political and economic scene. The McGill authorities would have to wait another six years before they could repay Forsey for his unwelcome actions.

During his undergraduate years at McGill from 1922 to 1925, Forsey combined his expanding knowledge of political economy with an interest in the principles of Tory democracy to arrive at a conviction that the principles embodied in that late nineteenth century form of conservatism were suited to meet the challenges of Canada's twentieth century industrialized society. Progressive social reform recognizing the needs of the working class and the farming community was desperately required, he believed, as was a moderate tariff that guaranteed an adequate level of protection for the employer. This was a practical and moderate programme of economic and social reform that had, by 1929, provided the foundation upon which a significant portion of his future economic and political commentary would rest.

CHAPTER 3

THE ROOTS OF CHRISTIAN ACTIVISM

While Eugene Forsey's "Tory democracy" represented a distinct form of British and Canadian conservatism in the areas of political and social reform, and economic moderation based on "scientific principles," it also retained one important founding principle of British conservatism, and that was the importance of Christianity and Christian morals in establishing standards of right and wrong in society. In this regard, conservatives apply to politics the Christian doctrine of man's innate Original Sin,[1] which assumes that men are not born naturally free or good but "naturally prone to anarchy, evil and mutual destruction."[2] Thus Conservatives tend to fit man into a "stable, durable framework, without which ethical behaviour and responsible use of liberty are impossible."

This conservative concept dates back at least to Edmund Burke, who argued that the essence of social conservatism was preservation of the ancient moral traditions of humanity. Recently, historians of conservatism such as Russell Kirk have reaffirmed the centrality of religion as one of six canons of conservative thought: "Belief in a divine intent rules society as well as conscience," wrote Kirk, "forging an eternal chain of right and duty which links great and obscure, living and dead." Kirk concluded his argument with the statement that for the conservative, "Political problems, at bottom, are religious and moral problems."[3]

Kirk has cited Burke's argument favouring a world governed by a strong and subtle purpose, with revelation, reason, and an assurance beyond the senses telling man that "the Author of our being exists, and that He is omniscient; and man and the state are creations of God's beneficence." Kirk believed that this sense of Christian orthodoxy was the kernel of Burke's philosophy, and since Burke is generally considered to be the founder of modern conservatism, the Christian element has embedded itself as a basic tenet of conservative thought.[4]

Burke, and most conservatives since his time, have pointed to the religious foundation of society as reason for approaching reform with caution, for if the world was indeed ordered in accordance with a Divine idea, man ought then to be cautious in his tinkering with the structure of that order. Burke's idea had some similarities to the philosophy espoused by Social Gospel advocates in early twentieth century Canada, for Burke strongly believed that the church must be interwoven into the fabric of society so as to create the kingdom of God on earth.[5] "The principle of true politics," said Burke, "are those of morality enlarged [and these principles are] moulded into the nature and essence of things."[6]

Later Conservatives, including Disraeli and Churchill "Tory democrats," affirmed Burke's religious principle as one of the major principles in conservative philosophy. Lord Hugh Cecil, in a small but enlightening book entitled *Conservatism*, wrote a chapter called "Religion and Politics" in which he linked the Christian moralist with active social reform: "The burning uneasiness which Christian teaching has planted in his mind," Cecil wrote, "forces him to embrace the opportunity and take the field as a politician and social reformer. The spiritual life to which he is called, purely individual as was his entrance upon it ... involves him in social activity." In this regard, Christianity rested on social reform, and conservatism itself necessarily insisted on the national acceptance of Christianity. "The championship of religion is therefore the most important of the functions of Conservatism," wrote Cecil. "It is the keystone of the arch upon which the whole fabric rests."[7]

By 1924, Eugene Forsey had come to accept religion as the standard by which the plans of politicians had to be judged. He had been brought up in the Methodist Church in Ottawa, and the missionary flame that took his father to Mexico flickered within the young McGill student. This interest led Forsey to aggressively explore Christianity during his early academic years in Montreal.

The period between 1922 and 1926, when Forsey was first at McGill, was a turbulent period for many Canadian Protestant churches. Richard Allen's penetrating study of the Social Gospel movement clearly illustrates that the early 1920s witnessed a gradual moderation of the post-war Social Gospel emphasis on transforming the social order.

This movement, which had emerged in the late nineteenth century, reached its zenith during the early 1920s and went into eclipse by 1925. Allen defined the Social Gospel "as a religious expression, striving to imbed ultimate human goals in the social, economic and political order" by transforming the social order. It was, Allen wrote, "a call for men to find the meaning of their lives in seeking to realize the Kingdom of God in the very fabric of society."[8]

In Allen's immediate post-war "radical" phase, the Methodist Church had called for complete social reconstruction by a transfer of the basis of society from competition to co-operation. Much of the impetus for this radicalism came from the progressive and radical social gospellers who by war's end, had reached positions of considerable power and consequence within movements for social and industrial reform.[9] By 1921, however, the social gospellers had for the most part splintered apart in the face of rising secular reform agencies, new political reform movements like the Progressives, and a growing internal controversy within the Social Gospel movement itself between its receding progressive and radical wings and its emerging conservative advocates.[10]

These conservatives placed greater emphasis on the inclusiveness of the church, and this in turn prompted them to minimize the conflicts of interest and ideology that divided workers from management and social activists within the church.[11] This group stressed the transcendence of God and the central role of the church in "mediating the knowledge of His will,"[12] but their acceptance of the existing social order and orthodox beliefs could not make up for their inaction in the face of the injustices suffered by workers and unemployed persons. "In their rightfulness," concluded Allen, "they had nothing to say."[13]

It was within this atmosphere of ongoing debate within the Protestant church in Canada that Forsey, in the autumn of 1922, attended his first service in the Douglas Street Methodist Church in Montreal. As he continued to attend this Church regularly during the mid-1920s, Forsey became particularly interested in the Church's Minister, the Reverend Allsworth Eardley, who had made a powerful first impression on Forsey by delivering what Forsey described to his mother as a magnificent sermon on "The Real Presence and Real Life Preparatory to Holy Communion."[14]

Eardley was born in 1873 and he, like Forsey, had arrived in Montreal and the Douglas Street Church in 1922. Eardley remained there until 1926, when he was transferred to the Dominion United Church in Ottawa. In 1931 he was posted to Fort Rouge Church in Winnipeg and resigned from the Manitoba Conference of the United Church in 1937. Forsey's written references about his new Minister suggest that Eardley adhered to the social gospel philosophy that sought moral improvement in Canada's post-war society. Specifically, Eardley preached a message that combined references to modern society with a certain sense of idealism. This combination of worldly empirical references and a strong idealistic vision had been "the first strength" of pre-World War I social gospellers such as J.S. Woodsworth, and in essence reflected the same types of concerns that stirred the Reverend Eardley and Eugene Forsey during the 1920s.[16]

In rousing sermons with titles such as "The Challenge of Jesus," "The Christian Use of Money," and "The Things That Remain," Eardley focused on the Christian's responsibility to sacrifice and to actively work to improve the conditions of modern society that interfere with the realization of God's Kingdom on earth. Therein lay the individual Christian's route to freedom and salvation, and society's pathway to "liberty."

Typical of this approach was an Eardley sermon called "Spiritual Freedom," which Forsey described as "one of the finest sermons I have ever heard in my life."[17] In this sermon Eardley spoke of an idealistic vision of "Christian liberty" which could be achieved through the power of the "living Christ." Eardley pronounced to his congregation that:

> Human progress has, from the very earliest times been a struggle for liberty. The great deeds of human life have been enacted on the battlefields of liberty and the noblest sacrifices of history have been the price paid for freedom.

It was, preached Eardley, the power of the "living Christ" that set men free from "the phantom hosts of haunting memories, and the temptations and oppression of modern society." This power, he said, "enable[d] us to triumph over the force of circumstance [and] to be more than conquerors through him that hath loved us."[18]

Forsey found Eardley's focus on the nature of "Christian liberty" especially compelling. In his advocacy of "Tory democracy," Forsey had acknowledged that personal freedom and liberty included a responsibility to the common welfare of the community, and Forsey linked liberty in personal moral and ethical issues relating to the spiritual welfare of the community. For example, Forsey wholeheartedly concurred with Eardley's definition of Christian liberty as being "the freedom of thought, and mind, and conscience, and will." In Christ's terms, Forsey agreed that this was best described as man's right to do right. Forsey explained to his mother that Eardley had, "with marvelous power and eloquence," described this form of liberty as man's decision to break free of secular controls, for any man who was a slave to habit of any kind could be "no true servant of the Lord Jesus Christ. Such a man was condemned to misery, for Christ called upon the Christian 'to grapple with [habit] as your dangerous enemy!'"[19]

Forsey particularly praised Eardley's belief in the omnipresent power of Christ to set men free from "the shackles of particular prejudices." This was illustrated, Forsey wrote, by Christ's struggle with the Pharisees, who were "bound by prejudice and tradition [while] Our Lord was not. Consequently they attacked him and disputed Him every time he opened His mouth."[20]

Forsey's belief in the need for social and economic reform reflected his belief that the world could be improved, and it was within this context that Forsey equated "personal liberty" with Eardley's "Christian liberty." This was not, however, an "individualistic" form of liberty that served the needs and interests of lobby groups in society, because they did not represent the community's interests at large. Referring to the pro-liquor lobby, for example, Forsey wrote that:

> Last night I attended a St. Francis of Assisi lecture which we all very much enjoyed; except I profoundly disliked particularly uncalled for taunts at prohibition! To my mind one of the worst things that afflict this day and generation is the semi-cynical, insidious, unthinking ridicule that meets every attempt to better the world. Surely it is enough that we should have to face the envenomed assaults of the army of the devil, without the would-be humour of every empty-pated fool in Christendom without sufficient mental capacity for real wit.... And by the way has it ever struck that every-thing which "'Personal Liberty' people urge against prohibition is equally, and sometimes more than equally, applicable to the laws against narcotic drugs? Yet we hear no plaintive wails of 'Let the

37

addict have his drugs. Do not interfere with his glorious personal liberty!' Oh! No! *Hypocrites!* Personal Liberty is but a cloak for self-ishness and greed.[21]

Freedom, in Forsey's view, more closely followed Eardley's description of "Freedom of Conscience," that is, an individual's freedom to *act* his or her everyday life according to Christ's will. Forsey, therefore, responded favourably to Eardley's message to his listeners that if they had come to his church just to hear him tell them what they ought to think, and believe, and say, and do, they might "Just as well sell their soul to a Roman priest as to a Methodist Minister, and [they] might just as well sell it to the devil as either."

Individual freedom of conscience and action was especially important in Eardley's view of religion, for he saw the Christian's challenge as acting on the decision "to make the presence of the living Christ a reality in his daily life." This decision could not be made by a person's Minister: "I don't covet the power to tell a man what he must think, and believe, and say and do," said Eardley. "In the last analysis the thought and the decision must be his own."[22]

Clearly Eardley was challenging his congregation to resist modern society's secular temptations and to follow Christ's call to live his Kingdom on earth. This was a message that drew Forsey ever closer to the Methodist Minister and his family between 1922 and 1926. During that period Forsey was a regular visitor to Eardley's home, where he enjoyed good food, entertainment, and many stimulating discussions on theological and social topics. Eardley enjoyed reading passages to his family members and house guests in order to stimulate such discussion.

One particular book he chose for one such evening's discussion was entitled *This Freedom*. This was a new novel written by A.S.M. Hutchinson, whom the ecumenically-minded Eardley had first heard about at a sermon he had attended at a Jewish synagogue. Forsey was impressed with Hutchinson's insights and he continued to read the author long after his reading of *This Freedom*, the central theme of which was the individual's freedom to choose Christ's message over the temptations of modern secular society.[23]

Hutchinson's book in many ways illustrates the nature of many of the social and moral issues with which Forsey and his post-war generation were most concerned. The novel traces the life of a girl named Rosalie, who grows up determined to avoid living her mother's lifestyle, which was one of continued household work and constant good deeds for others.[24] To this end Rosalie pursues a successful banking career and marries a rich lawyer, all while "raising" three children. Rosalie and her husband are the toast of the social pages in the local newspaper, which describes Rosalie as being "unique among professional women" because of her ability to combine rare business acumen with the raising of three beautiful children and maintaining a marriage to a "brilliant husband."[25] Their "thoroughly modern" lifestyle involves their employing a professional childcare worker to raise their children in "the right and scientific way, thought out and administered" with the goal of developing their children's reasoning powers. The parents accept this professional's belief that it is never necessary to punish a child, but "only to reason with it." This is the "modern scientific maxim" practised by the nanny in her "private domain in the nursery." There is no such thing as a naughty child in the modern post-war world; only a sick child or an unreasoning child. There is, therefore, no need for crude appeals to the emotions, but only reason. The entire process is "kind, wise, effective, easy."

What follows for this family, which holds every advantage except love, is disaster upon disaster, including rebellious children; family crime; premature death; the family's unanimous rejection of God; and a total indifference to each other by all the family members and especially toward Rosalie by her children. The author's message is clearly summarized by Rosalie's confession that she alone has been responsible for her family's destruction: "Life is sacrifice," lamented Rosalie in the book's closing pages, "[and] I never sacrificed. Sacrifice is atonement. It is now not possible for me to atone."[26]

Eardley's interest in *This Freedom* partially reflected a general concern in Canada during the interwar years over the pragmatic tone of "advice literature" that was "rooted in the relativism of the social sciences." Doctors, social workers, psychologists, and teachers became the "new experts" who eroded traditional family roles.[27] Eardley's message was a clarion call for Christians to reject the materialism and impersonal lifestyles of the "new society," and to escape the security of the "safe harbours" of indifference, in order to achieve true liberty. Eardley delivered a direct challenge to those who resisted such a call:

These people that are always talking about "safe harbours" make me *tired*. Get out of your "safe harbours" you lazy folk; sail out into the deep in search of truth. Never mind where it is leading you. When you're searching for truth, God is leading you and not the devil....The highest Christian liberty was the liberty to serve: he frees himself who bears another's charms.[28]

This message struck close to Forsey's belief in the central role of the Christian in society, and he excitedly wrote his mother about Eardley's "wonderful and rousing sermon" from which the above quotation was taken: "The rafters rang and it is badly needed nowadays," he wrote, adding that he was anxiously awaiting Eardley's upcoming sermons entitled "Free, Yet the Slaves of Christ,"[29] and "The Romance of Missions." In this latter sermon Eardley expanded on the importance of Christ's missionary message to Peter that any man who left family, friends, and material possessions to follow Him would be repaid "a hundredfold."[30]

Eardley's advocacy of Christian duty in action was quite similar to the idea of Christian responsibility espoused by Canadian philosophers such as John Watson twenty years earlier. The core of Watson's social philosophy focused on the individual's desire to identify himself with the "social good." Only by doing this could the individual realize "that the moral life [was] the gradual realization of ideal life." Watson insisted that it was not true that the ideal of humanity was a mere ideal; rather, he argued, the ideal of humanity was something that was "continually in process of realization." This in turn became for Watson a call to action, similar in nature to Eardley's message of individual freedom and liberty through active service: "The individual man can find himself, can become moral," wrote Watson, "only by contributing his share to its realization. He must learn that, to set aside his individual inclinations and make himself the organ of the community is to be moral, and the only way to be moral."[31]

A.B. McKillop has linked this sense of man's "moral imperative" to twentieth century figures such as Stephen Leacock, George Grant, and Donald Creighton. It was based, argues McKillop, on an idealistic vision of human life as an organized whole that set out a conception of the social good in an industrializing civilization. The "moral imperative" rejected individualism, and advanced a truly moral society by virtue of one's performing "moral acts of real flesh and blood persons, not the acts of hypothetical distance and abstract selves." This necessarily involved the making of concrete choices in the world and a denial of abstract laws of nature.[32]

Advocates of this "moral imperative" believed in the necessity of an ordered society; that things could not be understood without that order.[33] Despite some differences, Watson's arguments were basically similar to the arguments of post-war social reformers like Eardley and Eugene Forsey who believed that morality consisted ultimately in acting.[34]

Eardley's call to this form of Christian moral activism must be placed within the context of the post-war rise of secular materialism and empirical relativism in Canada. His challenge was to resist modern society's temptations and the empirical "relativism of the social sciences." He also implored his listeners to reject the "cold detachment towards questions of social justice" that typified the decade of the 1920s.[35] As S.E.D. Shortt explained, "the fundamental battle of the period had been decided: the idealists were defeated and the empiricists, secure as victors, slipped into relative complacency."[36]

For Forsey, Eardley's form of idealistic thought, which stressed a central role for moral Christian duty, was a stark countervailing force to his empirical academic training. Whereas Eardley's message stemmed from the idealism of the Victorian period and viewed society's leaders as moral tutors, Forsey's social science instructors stressed the importance of the academic as secular instructor in a specific academic subject.[37] Just as Eardley's philosophy places him in the tradition of the "moral imperative," so too does Forsey's enthusiastic response to his preaching indicate Forsey's personal belief that society's leaders, and in fact every Christian, had a moral responsibility to assist in ameliorating social ills through active social and moral leadership.

By the time of his undergraduate convocation in the autumn of 1925, Forsey had fully accepted this need for Christian action to regenerate Canada's secular industrializing society. By 1925 his belief in Christian activism had blended with his Tory democratic social beliefs. Forsey expressed his developing philosophy to his fellow Arts graduates in his 1925 Arts Valedictory Address. To great applause Forsey drew on the religious theme "Who chooseth me must give and hazard all he hath," and he challenged his fellow graduates to attempt the "impossible" and sacrifice for their country:

That is the thrill of Canadian citizenship. We cannot afford to be practical, selfish and money-grubbing. Canada is such a geographical absurdity that her only chance of survival lies in idealism. On that basis she was founded: that is the sole justification for the policy she has followed: and only on the hard road of self-sacrifice can she arrive at national prosperity.[38]

Forsey appealed to his classmates not to join in "the trek south [to the United States] in quest of the dollar pure and simple [but to] let it be known unto all such that there are some who will not serve their gods, nor worship the golden image which they have set up."[39] The "future builders of Canada," Forsey predicted, had "a great part to play in the development of our Empire." Canada's greatest hope, he predicted, lay in the diversity of the graduates themselves:

We are a perfect museum of conflicting view points. This year's graduating class in Arts, for example has Protectionists and Free Traders, socialists and individualists, Western radicals and Maritime Rights enthusiasts, prohibitionists from Ontario like myself and others to whom the Quebec Liquor Commission stores are wayside shrines (waves of laughter and applause). Where would you find broadmindedness if not here?[40]

Turning to the twentieth century intellectual debate between the rise of the natural sciences and the traditionally powerful "arts," Forsey encouraged his Arts classmates to think positively about their role as "the hub of the universe." This was especially true now that the war had shown them not to be the "outcasts and useless luxuries" they had been viewed as in the pre-war era:

Twelve years ago, everyone looked to the natural sciences for the regeneration of the race. But the War taught us that science without the soul is a hideous monster and arch-fiend seeking whom it may devour. We are realizing that humanity must be the master, not the servant, and that regeneration can only come from the spirit. That is the message that Arts men should never tire of proclaiming to Canada.[41]

Forsey's conviction regarding the importance of mankind working to overcome moral indifference is especially important for it represents a view that salvation lies in a "regeneration" of the individual's spirit. This belief was illustrated in one particular valedictory address comment: "Canada's troubles are fundamentally due not to her Government," said Forsey, "but to her people: to their gross indifference, their lack of real patriotism, their failure in moral earnestness ... their apathy and laziness." Sounding very much the Christian activist in the John Watson and Allsworth Eardley tradition, Forsey called on his audience to turn their backs on the "cowardice which prefers to shut its eyes to our problems rather than grapple with them." To great applause the young economist announced that "natural salvation does not lie in Bolshevism or business government or in the abolition of the Senate, but in a change of heart in the Canadian people."[42]

Forsey concluded his address by challenging his listeners to become the active leaders of society that modern Canadians so desperately needed. He emphasized that they, the graduates seated before him, were the natural leaders of society who possessed the necessary education, experience and talents to lead Canadian society out of its post-war materialism and moral apathy. This form of belief in the superior abilities of some men to become the natural leaders of society has been shared by most conservatives from Edmund Burke's era through to twentieth century Canadian conservatives such as W.L. Morton. These conservatives have called upon society's "natural leaders" to guide the "weak, imperfect and limited" members of society and in fact *all* mankind flawed by the presence of original sin.[43]

In Forsey's mind, the reality of the flawed human spirit and the resultant need for both natural leaders and a continued individual effort to overcome personal limitations brought into focus the need for continued, active efforts by mankind toward the necessary regeneration of the spirit. He addressed this need in the closing section of his valedictory speech:

> Some of us look forward to teaching, some to journalism. Some will be occupied with the great work of social readjustment or the development of a new philosophy of life. Others ... the gifted few ... are going out to preach Christ to a world which never needed

> Him more. We can all touch public opinion at many points. Our
> common ground is the necessity of idealism, and our work the cre-
> ation of a broad and noble patriotism. If we fail, fifteen years will see
> the end of Canada. "Where there is no vision the people perish."[44]

Forsey's emphasis on "Christian reform" was, therefore, a natural
response to the rising secularization of the age.[45] With his personal
conservative belief in a need for guidance, order, and moral duty firmly
established since childhood, Forsey lamented the emergence of "a
new variety of liberalism" oriented toward individualism, pragmatism,
and secularism.

Forsey's sense of Christian duty and responsibility to lead, reform,
and regenerate society was reinforced during the 1920s by his acceptance of the need for social and economic reform along "Tory democratic" lines. His developing philosophy was in turn reinforced even
further during the research and writing of his M.A. thesis.

It is significant that it was Forsey's former instructor, J.C. Hemmeon,
who recommended to Forsey that he write a Masters thesis on the economic aspects of the Nova Scotia coal industry. Hemmeon, a Nova
Scotian, had little trouble in convincing Forsey, who always considered
himself "partially Nova Scotian," to pursue this topic. More important,
however, was the fact that by 1926 Forsey had developed "a keen interest in labour matters,"[46] and was concerned with the possibility that the
negative aspects of Mackenzie King's "Colorado" labour plan would be
implemented in Canada.[47]

Another reason that Forsey readily accepted the topic was that the
situation surrounding labour relations in the Nova Scotia coal industry in the mid-1920s was "very bad for both the workers and the
Province."[48] A few years earlier the British Empire Steel Corporation, a
post-World War I coal syndicate that was economically unstable in the
early 1920s,[49] demanded wage reductions of 30 to 50 per cent.[50] Violent
strikes ensued throughout the early and mid-1920s. In August 1925,
just as Forsey ended his undergraduate programme, Nova Scotia's new
Conservative government arranged for the miners to accede to the
British Empire Steel and Coal Company's (BESCO) wage cuts in order
to save their union shop.[51]

Forsey began his research by using some of his Maritime connec-
tions to acquire an unreleased copy of the Duncan Commission Report

from the BESCO office in Montreal.[52] This Report, which was not publicly released until the politically turbulent summer of 1926, produced a catalogue of far-reaching recommendations as to how Ottawa could assist in the recovery of the slumping resource economy.[53] Forsey concluded that the Commission had made "several very definite and constructive recommendations and had laid bare what had gone on [in the coal industry] over a long period of years."[54]

Forsey supplemented his research with interviews and background reading in British labour writings by Fabian-leftist authors such as Sidney and Beatrice Webb's *History of Trade Unions* (1920) and *Industrial Democracy* (1920). Forsey was encouraged by Hemmeon to read as much British labour material as possible. Hemmeon, Forsey recalls, was a "declared socialist" at this time and did not lack for suggested reading material.[55] Hemmeon specifically recommended that Forsey read Harold Laski as well as the Webbs, who were at that time advocating a socialistic alternative to the capitalist system.[56] For his part, Laski was putting forward concrete proposals for the introduction of a pluralist state in Britain.[57] Through his extensive reading of this material Forsey became more and more sympathetic to the plight of English labour and was "moving more and more towards Labour and Socialism."[58]

Forsey's M.A. research was, therefore, a major factor in his continuing intellectual development during the 1920s. His explorations took him physically as well as intellectually into the "abysmal working and living conditions" of the Nova Scotia miners and their families.[59] He also became interested in the history of the Canadian labour movement as he documented the formation of the Provincial Workingmen's Association in the Nova Scotia coalfields, "the first wholly Canadian craft and miners' union in North America."[60] Forsey also quoted extensively from the Webb's *Industrial Democracy* in stating the grounds of the coal workers' "stubborn dislike of compulsory arbitration and establishment of fair and consistent salary levels."[61]

Though he was shocked by the dehumanization of the "very nasty example of capitalism" that he saw at work in the Nova Scotian coalfields, Forsey did not abandon his Tory democratic principles in formulating his responses. In fact, he felt at the time that his research and work was specifically linked with the "working man principle" of Tory democracy and very much in the true conservative tradition. The Duncan Commission, Forsey explained, was originally appointed by a Nova Scotia Tory government, and specifically by its "Red Tory" Minister of Mines, Gardiner Harrington, a "real progressive conservative" in Forsey's view and a man who later became Premier of Nova Scotia.[62] Harrington was liked and trusted by the unions because he displayed a genuine concern for the welfare of the worker in the true "Tory democracy" tradition.[63] This fact was not lost on Forsey, who later explained that he felt he "could proceed with the Thesis with a double-clear conscience because it was a Tory Government that delved into this and a Company that had done wrong with the workers."[64]

Forsey later acknowledged that it was BESCO's corporate manipulation, combined with Hemmeon's very close supervision, that helped push him to the left during 1926.[65] Hemmeon, Forsey recalled, "planted seeds of doubt and raised questions in my mind. It all became part of my continuing evolution towards socialism."[66]

Not surprisingly, Forsey's completed thesis was judged by his examiners to be "an excellent piece of work." But quite apart from the technical merit of the work was the fact that Forsey's M.A. thesis work consolidated in his mind the need to rectify the economic ills of a society that permitted the exploitation of man by man. His efforts also reinforced his decision to study economics and political economy in even more depth.[67]

Encouraged by his academic success and the support of his McGill advisors, who assured Forsey of a teaching post back at McGill,[68] and buoyed by the financial support of a Rhodes Scholarship, Forsey decided in 1926 to pursue further graduate work at Oxford. His decision to study History, Economics, and Political Science placed him in the "Final School of Philosophy, Politics and Economics."[69] The arrival of Oxford's acceptance letter ended all thoughts of summer employment with the CPR or permanent work with the Dominion Bureau of Statistics, and Forsey prepared for what promised to be an unforgettable overseas experience.

CHAPTER 4

THE OXFORD TRADITION

For many Canadians who preceded Eugene Forsey to Oxford, the first days at that venerable academic institution elicited an almost awestruck response: "It all seems like a dreamland," wrote J.S. Woodsworth on his first day at Oxford," and I wonder sometimes just where I am or how I got there and how it will all end." David Lewis recalled his first days in a similar tone: "I gazed at everything with the same feeling of reverence that a religious man must when he enters a house of God." Lewis had a feeling of unworthiness of his new surroundings, "which spoke eloquently of knowledge, of wisdom and of culture."[1]

Such respect seemed appropriate, however, especially because those men were entering Oxford's Balliol College, renowned as an institution of advanced learning and character. In the 1920s Balliol was generally regarded as "the undisputed intellectual focus of the university."[2] Special also was the atmosphere at Oxford during the interwar period. One resident of the college during those years recalled that "it was a brief, blessed interval when the lives of the young were neither overshadowed by the consequences of the last war nor dominated by the fear of a future one."[3]

The 1920s were also experimental and changing years for Oxford University, and particularly Balliol. "There can be no doubt," wrote one historian of the famed College, "that England and the world had changed with the First World War and that in 1925 Balliol was ... well up with those changes."[4] One particular academic change involved the accelerated expansion of the science and mathematics faculty, which represented a continuing trend since the turn of the century. A second academic change was the introduction of the "Modern Greats" school by the new Master of Balliol, A.D. Lindsay.

Lindsay's philosophy has been described as 'bearing the stamp' of T.H. Green,[5] whose multifaceted philosophy attempted to grapple with the social disruptions that accompanied the industrialism of nineteenth century Britain. Green's search for a "new cement for a society coming apart at the seams," led him to a theory built upon religious and "possessive individualist" foundations. This idealistic system, though it rejected the individualistic empirical tradition advocated by J.S. Mill, sought to retain the desirable values of individualism while discarding its excesses.[6] Green's attempt to reconstruct liberal principles after those principles had been rejected by laissez-faire economics, Benthamite Utilitarianism, and Mill's "atomic" individualism, resulted in his developing a positive theory of the state under which intervention in the life of the individual for reasons of public welfare was acceptable.[7]

Lindsay accepted Green's argument for the need to limit an individual's freedom to act for himself in society, but the new Balliol Master found his answers within the collectivist spirit of the Fabian Society and its political action group, Britain's Independent Labour Party. For this reason Lindsay's election as Master of Balliol was viewed as a radical step. Though the choice was not approved by many of the "encrusted Oxfords, it put Balliol in the lead again – or kept it in the lead in a period of startling change in England."[8]

Lindsay, therefore, like Green, who had also taught at Oxford, continued a Balliol tradition that stressed the need for social and labour reform, permeated with the dual themes of physical and moral improvement.[9] As a newcomer to Balliol, Forsey's exposure to this philosophy soon reinforced his own religious activism and interest in labour issues that had been fostered during his years at McGill. Forsey soon had occasion to meet informally with Lindsay, who was then Secretary-Treasurer of the Oxford Labour Club, which Forsey began attending shortly after his arrival.[10]

Lindsay's sense of Christianity was especially attractive to Forsey, who was still a very impressionable twenty-three years old when he arrived at Oxford in the autumn of 1927. A few short months earlier Forsey had been impressed with the Reverend Allsworth Eardley's "balanced view of spirituality and action" as well as his orthodox Methodist delivery. Eardley spoke with "great fervour," recalled Forsey, "and he read the Bible aloud magnificently with extraordinary power.... His very fine delivery appealed to me."[11] Now Forsey was similarly attracted to Lindsay's sermons, which he preached in the College Chapel in his capacity as Master. It was from listening to these sermons, Forsey recalls, "that I learned of Christian Socialism."[12]

A second important influence upon Forsey's intellectual thought came from his interaction with the faculty members who assisted Lindsay in his efforts to implement his new "Modern Greats" school. This school had been introduced largely because Lindsay felt that the twentieth century demanded a program that exposed students to ancient civilizations as a means of better preparing themselves for the modern challenges of industrial society. The additional Balliol instructors who played a considerable role in the development of the Greats' school were G.D.H. Cole, W.D. Ross, B.H. Sumner, and John Macmurray. These men taught the Modern Greats classes with enthusiasm inside their College, lectured for it in the University as a whole, and taught pupils from outside Balliol College.[13]

Taken as a group, these academics followed in the tradition of Green and the Scottish philosopher Edward Caird, Master of Balliol from 1893 to 1907.[14] Caird had been a close friend of Green's and he developed, but did not substantially change, many of Green's theories when he assumed responsibility at Balliol.[15] Drawing heavily on Hegel's theological philosophy, Caird argued that religion and science were not opposed but in fact formed part of a higher unity. He tried to show, therefore, that the conflict between conventional religion and materialistic science could be overcome by arguing that the doctrine of scientific law was itself spiritual. "No longer was it possible," wrote Caird, "as it once was, to intercalate the ideal, the divine, as it were surreptitiously, as one existence in a world otherwise secular and natural."

Caird's Scottish idealism was a philosophical theology that, unlike traditional theology, did not differentiate between Man, God, and Nature. Rather, Caird saw in all three the workings of a single spiritual principle that found worldly values in the realm of empirical facts.[16] Caird also firmly believed that religion, which was always his special interest, had to be studied historically, and this was a tradition that Forsey's three leading instructors firmly acknowledged in their own work. It had been in all probability also part of Forsey's own education in Canada.

B.H. Sumner, a fastidious and exacting scholar,[17] taught Forsey British Constitutional History,[18] a subject in which Forsey had been interested since his early exposure to the House of Commons as a young boy in Ottawa. W.D. Ross taught Forsey First Principles of Ethics,[19] for which Ross was eminently qualified, having published two books that followed the Modern Greats philosophy of tracing religion, science, and politics backward through eras to ancient civilizations. Ross argued within a pluralistic framework,[20] described politics as "the supreme practical science, or social science, [which necessitated] our fuller consciousness of man's membership of communities other than the state, yet 'individual' man is essentially a member of society." Ross viewed this relationship between man and his society as the essence of ethics and politics, which together constituted "the complete science of politics."[21] Ross focused his historical research primarily on Plato and Aristotle, and he identified Aristotle's conception of virtuous action as illustrating the fact that all action must have a virtuous end. Virtue, therefore, was the "springboard from which good activity" flowed. Ross also emphasized the importance of free will in virtuous action, a message that was similar in content to that preached by Reverend Eardley.[22]

Ross's emphasis on the importance of virtuous action was an example of Balliol's new approach to teaching ancient history. The planners of the Modern Greats School sought every way possible to emphasize to their students the contributions that history could make toward understanding modern society.[23] This approach was especially apparent in the teaching style and philosophy of Balliol's Philosophy Professor, John Macmurray, a man of "outstanding ability" who had been a fellow at Balliol since the early 1920s.[24] Macmurray was also the most important intellectual influence on Eugene Forsey during his years at Oxford, and is arguably the most important intellectual influence in Forsey's entire life.

Macmurray's arrival at Balliol from Glasgow University continued the traditional link between Scotland and the College. Founded by the parents of the King of Scotland, Balliol had, since the seventeenth century, been attended by Scottish students in inordinate numbers. Many were supported by "Snell contributions," scholarships established in the seventeenth century by one John Snell to enable students from Glasgow University to go to Oxford. It was later legally decided that Scottish students must go to Oxford to be eligible for the scholarship.[25] This academic connection between Scotland and Oxford continued into the twentieth century as Scottish-trained academics continued to teach Balliol students. Most of Forsey's instructors had been taught in Scotland at some time during their lives, and Forsey wrote to his mother shortly after his arrival that he had attended and thoroughly enjoyed an evening presentation describing "The Scottish Traditions at Oxford."[26]

Macmurray's career fits into this pattern, but it also reflects the conflicting forces at work at Oxford and many other British universities in the late nineteenth and early twentieth centuries. In the nineteenth century, natural science came of age as a social institution, invading schools and universities "and demanding that laboratories should stand side by side with libraries." The scientists proclaimed that science, and not classics or philosophy, was the true educator.[27] The emergence of natural science as a force to be reckoned with in academic circles followed the rise of the "realist" and "critical realist" nineteenth century Scottish schools of philosophy. Realist philosophy was adopted at English universities, most notably Oxford, as a challenge to the idealists who had achieved dominance in the nineteenth century.[28] Drawing on Immanuel Kant's philosophy, which combined a strong bias toward piety with a keen scientific interest based on "experience" and a sense of moral conviction,[29] the "critical realists" sought to combine the central role of the Deity with the emerging natural science schools.[30]

Macmurray's career epitomizes the challenges that faced these "philosopher-scientists." He had a long-time fascination with sciences, but the classicists had held sway throughout his academic career and he had studied arts. "My director of studies at Glasgow University," Macmurray later recalled, "convinced of the superiority of a classical education and the crudity of science as an educational instrument, insisted that I should not sacrifice what I had already gained at school [by studying sciences]."[31]

Macmurray pursued his "passionate belief in science and its application [and] fought a successful rear-guard action" by winning permission to study sciences at his Grammar School, Robert Gordon College in Aberdeen; Glasgow University, where he received his M.A. and LL.D. in 1909; and Balliol College, where he received an M.A. Macmurray took science as an extra course in his classical field, studying chemistry and geology. He was the only arts student in a large class of pure and applied scientists and mining engineers: "It was the only university class in which I carried off the medal," Macmurray later wrote.[32]

Macmurray repeatedly acknowledged that his solid grounding in science and scientific method had been of the greatest possible use to him as a philosopher in a country where few philosophers had any direct experience in science, and also in his second field of study, the religious field. "The question of the relation between science and religion," he wrote, "has been dominant during my lifetime."[33] This interplay between God and science represented one of the major areas of philosophical debate for many natural scientific philosophers in early twentieth century England,[34] and also continued a debate that had arisen after the arrival of Hegelianism at Oxford and the Scottish universities in the last third of the nineteenth century. This philosophy sought to explain history and reconcile religion and science while giving a sense of direction to political reform.[35] The Modern Greats course at Balliol was instituted in part to address this very debate.

Macmurray was Forsey's Professor of Political and Moral Philosophy, which Forsey found exciting yet somewhat intimidating: "Macmurray I like," Forsey wrote his mother, "but I expect to find philosophy heavy going."[36] Forsey seems to have met the academic challenge of this essentially new discipline,[37] for he graduated as one of nine "Firsts" in the Modern Greats School of Philosophy, Politics and Economics.[38] His "B" in Philosophy (and "D" in German, which was a mandatory subject due to his German-oriented philosophic studies), did not, however, match his five "A's" in his Economic and Economic History classes.[39]

Macmurray's influence upon Forsey went beyond the general classroom, however, for Macmurray was appointed Forsey's "Model Tutor," which meant that Macmurray not only taught Forsey formally in class, but in the true Oxford tradition, became Forsey's special tutor. During their twice-weekly tutorial sessions Macmurray's aim was to make Forsey think. Simply put, the tutor had overall responsibility for the student's intellectual advancement.[40]

Forsey came to share many of Macmurray's ideas. Macmurray, for example, had become active in the Student Christian Movement in 1909 during the height of its influence in British universities,[41] and Forsey became active in the SCM at Oxford during his second year at that University.[42] John Macmurray had converted to the Quaker religion as a means of escaping traditional and rigid church doctrines.[43] Some years later Forsey quoted Macmurray's concept of a "personal, infinite, super-personal" God in explaining his own conversion to the less rigid Quaker religious philosophy of "the Inner Light and the nature of worship."[44]

Forsey maintained an interest in Macmurray's philosophy following his return to Canada. He would write a lengthy review of Macmurray's views on the subject of Christianity and Communism,[45] and with his wife, would assume the rather substantial task of transcribing, editing, and publishing a series of lectures Macmurray delivered to a Belleville, Ontario Student Christian Movement Conference in 1936.[46] Later in that same year Forsey quoted Macmurray in a *Canadian Forum* article,[47] and drew extensively on his former tutor's SCM lectures and philosophy in writing two chapters of the book *Towards The Christian Revolution* which was a collective effort by a number of key participants in Canada's interwar Christian activist movement.[48] One Sunday afternoon in 1940 Forsey relaxed by reading Macmurray's most recently published book: "I rested Sunday, reading John Macmurray's *Clue To History*, most of the time [a fine book]," Forsey wrote his mother."[49] Forsey was still quoting Macmurray in his own published material as late as the 1950s.[50]

John Macmurray's teaching thus had a tremendous influence on Forsey's thinking, and it is important to note that during the period when Forsey was under his instruction, Macmurray's philosophical interests were focused on an effort to redefine religion based on a natural theology that was profoundly communal and social in character. Macmurray's "philosophy of religion" challenged the post-war world to redefine a theology that was "nurtured in the faith of the Christian community and productive of a philosophical inquiry."[51]

Macmurray's beliefs were shaped largely by his experiences in World War I, which had shattered his faith in idealism and led him to his central philosophical premise, that the heart of Christianity lay not in the truth of a particular doctrine or development of a specific idea, but in the continuity of an action.[52] Action necessarily involved the individual being in an active relationship with other persons, and this concept became the philosophical religious foundation for Forsey, guiding most of his own actions throughout his own life.

Macmurray's conception of a religion that was adequate for the post-idealistic, modern scientific world was similar to Kant's views on the subject. Like Kant, Macmurray rejected theoretical reasoning, advocating in its place a practical form of reasoning based on the premise and conviction that empirical evidence was more adequately explained through "man-in-activity."[53] Macmurray consistently claimed throughout his work that activity gave rise to genuine knowledge and that knowledge was always in the service of activity.[54]

Macmurray, like so many others of his era, was largely influenced by personal experiences during World War I. He had fought as a Lieutenant in the Cameron Highlanders at the Battle of the Somme, during which he was injured and returned home. He was later awarded a Military Cross.[55] This experience greatly influenced Macmurray's view of reality and idealism: "We went into war in a blaze of idealism, to save little Belgium and put an end to war," he later recalled, "[but] we discovered stage by stage what childish nonsense all this idealism was [and that we] had been played upon by men whose real interest was in their own wealth and power and prestige. Our eyes were opened."[56]

Macmurray rejected the Hegelian idealist principle that reality was an idea that asserted the primacy of thought over action and things. In place of this notion Macmurray argued that "realism makes the thing and not the idea the measure of validity, the centre of significance." Macmurray believed that any other view "[was] absurd and nonsensical,"[57] and that to accept Hegel's dialectical process and his adherence to idealism was "to live in make-believe" and to divorce the idealist's belief in progress from his modes of social activity.[58] In the idealist's world, Macmurray argued, progress remained an idea, "a dream, not something to be accomplished by deliberate, planned social and political action."[59]

For John Macmurray, the man of action had superseded the man of ideas in terms of his overall worth to society. He applied this formula to himself and his fellow academics by defining a new and proactive social role which had to be practical and real in order to be relevant. "A philosopher who is unconscious of the reference of his thought to the development of society," wrote Macmurray, "will find the meaning of his crucial idea in a world of ideas which has no reference beyond knowledge."[60] Macmurray believed that philosophy and science, in fact all the academic disciplines, had to have more practical value in society so that the student could then "have some practical value in society; some action upon oneself and society." This, Macmurray bluntly stated, necessarily "involved the reinterpretation of all, or nearly all of our important ideas and norms."[61]

During the 1920s Macmurray consolidated this belief that the foundation of realism in the modern world could lie only in a truly harmonious society which would reject idealistic thinking and the advancing dualism that the world had witnessed since the Medieval Age with the growth of materialism. In 1928 Macmurray contributed two articles to a book edited by an Oxford associate, B.H. Streeter, a man who shared many of Macmurray's beliefs. Streeter, for example, had published a book in which he challenged modern man to be committed to living out actively his Christian ideas. This, Streeter argued, was essential in order to test "whether prayer is really prayer, or merely pious auto-suggestion." The litmus test in this case would be "the extent to which prayer inspires to bold and constructive action and to moral initiative."[62] In his 1928 articles Macmurray continued Streeter's line of argument and concluded that it was essential for man to go beyond knowledge in his search for truth. What lay beyond knowledge, Macmurray argued, was action.[63]

Many British and American writers during this period concurred with Macmurray's rejection of the "dualism" that they believed dominated modern post-war society.[64] This dualism, which Macmurray referred to as the "New Materialism," represented the increasing gulf between religious and materialistic values; a gulf which could only be rectified through man's active participation in society through Christian fellowship in relation to his fellow man. This was the message that Macmurray delivered to his young Canadian student,[65] and to his Student Christian Movement audience in Belleville in 1936: "Reality is material," said Macmurray, "and was only to be found in action, in the meeting of bodies. Thinking and feeling can occur only in reference to action."[66]

The concept of dualism was central to Macmurray's thought because it represented the dichotomy between idealism and realism, and between intention and action. To illustrate this he drew analogies from his experience during World War I, which had resulted in the shattering of his faith in idealism:

> The idealist thinks that in the realm of action intentions are causes, that if you don't intend a thing it won't happen; if you do (with enough others) it will. This is not true. "The road to Hell is paved with good intentions." Causes are actions. Note the attempts to mobilize opinion against the war: all the good will had no effect,

> it probably makes war more certain. Usually the talk about good
> will is an escape from action. We very much want to change things,
> but we very much more want not to. So we do it in imagination,
> instead of working on the actual facts. Pacifism, I often feel is the
> last refuge of the idealist. Open conflict is the result of hidden con-
> flict. Intentions don't matter. Only action matters.[67]

Macmurray's "New Materialism" concept rested on his firm belief in
the need for an integral modern world, a world in which thought and
action were inseparable because action included thought and was not
something that could be distinguished from thought.[68] This necessitated a reversal of what Macmurray viewed as the continuing dualistic
nature of the historical process and human progress in general.

This growth of dualism could be seen in the increasing power of
individualism and materialism, in the growth of upper-class power, and
in the exploitation of man by man. These were all realities that Forsey
was aware of from his life and studies in Montreal. Real progress was
impossible in such a world, Macmurray explained, because "dualistic
consciousness is debarred by its very nature from conceiving progress
as a general idea applicable to history as a whole."[69] Macmurray was
certain that man's progress was doomed if limited to such a materialistic, dualistic environment, which made the "immediate and material
things of primary importance, glorifying the gratification of immediate
material desires and lusts." When Macmurray denounced a man as a
materialist, he meant "that he had no concerns for the higher things in
life, that he is selfish and self-seeking, and that he grasps at immediate
satisfaction of a materialist kind."[70]

The result of this dualism in society was the growth of unbridled
capitalism, which in turn was *only* possible in an idealistic society that
permitted, but did not acknowledge or accept, exploitation of one class
of man by another. Ignorance of such exploitation only fostered its
growth: "Capitalism can only exist," wrote Macmurray, "when people
think they are doing one thing when they are actually doing another."[71]
Concomitantly, Macmurray viewed the advance of industrial democracy as primarily the establishment of a particular class ideology that
rationalized and justified the rise of the middle and upper classes to
a position of dominance over the rest of society. Once the dominant
classes were ensconced in this position of power, it was extremely

difficult to dislodge them for two basic reasons. First, there developed an acceptance of a dualistic relationship in which equality and justice were addressed only in the religious sphere. Oftentimes this discussion became solely idealistic and no action developed, and so the reality of exploitation was allowed to continue. Secondly, the dominant class structure defined the welfare and goals of society in its own self-interest so that a change of class position necessitated nothing less than a new ideology. "We are thus brought back to our starting point," Macmurray explained, in that "the Dualism of thought and action makes the class struggle inevitable in the process of social development, because it leaves society unconscious of what is happening to it."[72]

The final point on the subject of Dualism relates to the difficulty of effecting change in society once the ideologies and classes are in place. In this challenge lies the core of both Macmurray's philosophy of action and Forsey's later adherence to this same philosophy as demonstrated through his participation in a number of religious and secular activist organizations after his return to Canada. Effecting change in a society controlled by the upper classes became, in Macmurray's view, a Herculean task:

> [To effect such social change] would mean, in social action, a complete break with the past. It would mean a radical reorganization of society, a redistribution of power, a trans-valuation of social values, something indeed, in society analogous to a religious conversion in the individual. Only under the pressure of dire necessity, when the mass of society has been convinced that such a radical change is imperative and unavoidable, can such an effort of social reformation come within the bounds of possibility.[73]

Eugene Forsey's socialist philosophy, which had been evolving from his Tory democratic beliefs and academic studies at McGill, fit very comfortably on the foundation of John Macmurray's philosophy of social and religious activism. Forsey's Christian socialism was based on the presumption that genuine and real reform was necessary to effect any worthwhile change leading to a more moral society. And Forsey's view was that change was a practical, concrete process. In his chapters written for *Towards the Christian Revolution*, Forsey emphasized that it was necessary to change economic society through such a realistic process:

> The first step towards changing society, is to understand the exist-
> ing society. We cannot start from a mental picture of the world we
> should like to live in then try to mould the real world into the like-
> ness of that idea. The real world is refractory material. We cannot
> push history in the direction we should like it to take in sublime dis-
> regard of the forces actually at work. We must start from the world
> as it really is ... then work in and with and through them to a new
> world which is possible. If we try to cross the purposes of reality we
> can end only by producing a result exactly opposite from that which
> we desire.[74]

Forsey accepted Macmurray's belief in an integrated society, and his
holistic approach argued against the prevailing concept of dualism as
epitomized by the growing separation of church and state and the
growth of secular power in general.

Opposed to this prevailing paradigm was one which the ancient
Hebrews had accepted that was based on the unity of religion and economics. Macmurray accepted this perspective and argued that "religion
[was] concerned with the reality of life and not with ideas, except insofar
as they embody themselves in life."[75] Similarly, Forsey began his chapter
on "The Economic Problem," in *Towards The Christian Revolution*, by
justifying a chapter on economics in a religious book: "The insertion
of a chapter on economics in a religious book ought not to need either
explanation or defence," wrote Forsey, "because the field of religion
is the whole of life. That should be explanation and defence enough."
Forsey argued that the Christian character did not develop in a vacuum
but rather was "forged in the struggles of daily life and most of the daily
life of most people is spent in the effort to satisfy economic wants."[76]

The integrated world that both Macmurray and Forsey envisioned
included a shared vision of the role of religion in the modern world.
World War I had shaken Macmurray's confidence in churches but had
reinforced his belief that Christianity not only had to "be rediscovered
and recreated," but that the religious issue was not "the most central and
most important issue" of his day.[77] Macmurray sought to reshape the
role of religion into the ancient Hebrew model, which integrated out-
ward religious practice with inner thought and reflection. In so doing,
Macmurray wrote, the Hebrews presented the modern world with the
only true example in history of a specifically religious civilization in

which "the elements of culture (science, morality, law and politics) have no autonomy. They are contained in religion and remain aspects of it." Such an approach presented religion as the synthesis of all human activity and not as "a particular sphere of human activity."[78]

Forsey accepted this holistic philosophy of religion: "The church is concerned with the whole of life, individual and social," he wrote, and "it cannot sign a treaty of partition leaving politics and economics to the devil." Unless Christianity was concerned with life in day-to-day existence it was unreal because it could not address the "here and now." As such, it was not real Christianity: "Jesus taught us to pray 'Thy will be done on earth,'" Forsey emphatically wrote, and so "the great religious ideas and emotions ought to be motives to action in this world. Too often we have cut the nerve between ideas and action."[79]

In another article Forsey emphasized that the Church could not be neutral on issues of the day and that it had "both a right and a duty to pronounce on political, social and economic questions in accordance with Christian principles." Forsey believed that to give up this responsibility "would be in effect to give a partition with the devil, handing over to him vast provinces of human life."[80] He wholeheartedly accepted Macmurray's argument that "The Real Business of Religion" was rooted in the integration of ideas and action. Forsey explained this integrated process by quoting his Oxford Tutor:

> The church must be concerned with the economic because it is concerned with the spiritual. As Professor Macmurray puts it: Our bodies are not ends in themselves. We live for knowledge and friendship ... when society goes bad, the economic organization of society is not the supremely important thing, but it is like the health of the body. If. economic organization falls sick, then nothing else is important for the time. No real human social life is possible till [sic] the economic organization is restored to health. We must recognize that the economic system is making personal life impossible, dehumanizing people. That imposes on Christianity the unmistakable duty of reconstructing the economic system [with a view] to ... abundant life.[81]

Many of Forsey's arguments in the 1930s rested on concepts expounded by John Macmurray. A section of Forsey's contributions in *Towards the Christian Revolution*, for example, drew heavily on passages from Macmurray's book, *The Creative Society*, which was published just two years before *Towards the Christian Revolution*. Forsey wrote of the need for "real religion" to challenge what Macmurray called "pseudo-religion," that is, "conventional ecclesiastical institutions [that reduce man's] vital concern for existing injustice." This was done whenever the church obscured man's social vision by its sanctions and its promises of heavenly kingdoms in another world. Quoting extensively from Macmurray's *The Creative Society*, Forsey stated that one's immediate task as a Christian was to:

> ... attack pseudo-Christianity openly and resolutely in all its forms, in the name of real Christianity. The religious revolution is the immediate and special responsibility of the Christians.... There must be war to the death between real and unreal religion, even if it should cleave organized Christianity in two and destroy all its existing forms. That is the primary task, it has to be achieved concretely in terms of the Christian denunciation and criticism of the existing structure of society, in its effects upon the lives of men and women.[82]

Forsey logically concluded that Christian values contributed to the betterment of all of society, but how was the active Christian supposed to effect the revolution? Forsey found his answer once again in Macmurray's denial of individuality, and his emphasis on mutual experience being the essence of religion. Both Macmurray and Forsey believed that this concept of mutuality denied any role to the individual, for there could be no individual except in terms of other human beings to whom he was essentially related. "Personality exists between people, not in individuals," Macmurray wrote. "A person's personality is born out of his relations with others." Science had no role to play in this process because the scientific approach was to observe, and one could not observe experience.[83]

In this approach religion's primary role lay in "raising and dealing with the intention of communion, community; the means by which fellowship can be restored." In effect the purpose of all religion, therefore, was to live in mutual brotherhood with fellow man.[84] "Without religion," Forsey believed, there could be no basis for either equality or democracy.[85] Like Macmurray, Forsey saw the Church as the institution for arbitrating class differences in society between farmers, organized labour, and the middle class.[86]

Forsey's vision of Christian action focused on action through the institution of the Church itself, to promote both an awareness of class differences and an understanding between classes in society. Here Forsey was advocating a very clear yet narrowly defined role for the individual within the context of a modern communal society. Such a limited role illustrated Macmurray's belief that tension was the inevitable outcome whenever the individual asserted himself in society: "Individualism involved a tension between two things," argued Macmurray, "on an individual acting consciously in his own way on his own initiative, and a tradition which demands that he should act in another way."[87]

Macmurray cited Luther's assertion of individualism against the established church as a visible example of this type of rebellion against the established authority of tradition. Luther had established the central thesis of the modern spirit, "the right of the individual to worship God in his own way." This right had led to two social movements, individualism and socialism, both of which were "concerned primarily with economic conditions." The former movement was concerned primarily with the economic freedom of the individual *only*, while the second, socialism, was concerned with the equal economic freedom of *all* individuals. While individualism produces capitalism, the second destroys capitalism, Macmurray wrote, in order to produce the economic equality of socialism. "Capitalism and socialism represent, therefore, two successive phases in the progress of civilization, corresponding to the two successive stages in the development of the modern spirit."[88] The result was the growth of two forces in opposition, the Church and the State, where once there had only been the Church. The associated rise of the democratic movement along with the birth of individualism led to the conviction "by the masses of the people that they were right in claiming to live better than before."[89] Forsey's previous exposure to the negative social impact of unbridled capitalism in Montreal and Nova Scotia meant that he had some practical knowledge with which to interpret some of Macmurray's more abstract philosophical points. Forsey agreed with Macmurray's limited view of individualism[90] and with his rejection of Benthamism because of the importance the Benthamites accorded to the individual and laissez-faire attitudes.[91]

What was needed was a balanced form of social co-operation to prevent the development of individualism that destroys freedom and equality. Macmurray was convinced that in order to create the form of community life which was compatible with the individuality of all its members, the economic class structure of capitalist society had to be replaced. [92]

Forsey also agreed with Macmurray's view of freedom and equality as religious ends.[93] Forsey believed that democracy in effect meant equality and that the democratic principle derived in the last analysis from Christianity.[94] Forging a sense of unity between the secular and the religious worlds would become a lifelong task for Forsey: the two were, in his view, mutually supportive. But it was to religion that Forsey, like Macmurray, turned for clarification regarding the concept of equality among fellow human beings and for his definition of democracy.

Religion for Forsey provided the force that functioned as a counterweight to the "natural forces" in society. Religion was for him, in fact, the only source that could ensure basic human equality and freedom. Here Forsey returned to his conservative view of human nature and its basic inequalities and weaknesses:

> Logically and historically, democracy is a religious conception and a religious creation. Democracy implies a belief in essential human equality. But the physical, biological, psychological facts are all against such a belief. Manifestly, human beings are not equal in physical strength, in beauty, in intellect; equality is nonsense. The only possible source of the idea of human equality is a conviction that, in spite of all the obvious inequalities, all men are equal in importance. That conviction is a religious conviction. Religiously speaking, equality is not nonsense but truth.[95]

Forsey's concept of equality and freedom, as expressed in his many public pronouncements, was rooted in Macmurray's philosophy of Christianity as a real creative force in society. The Christian's task was to help bring about a free society which would assist each person to realize his or her intentions.

For Macmurray, recognition of the existence of restraint in society was crucial to eventual freedom, for only through an awareness of restraint could real change occur. Real change, as cited in the example of Luther given above, occurred when traditions were challenged, and

Forsey, like his tutor, was well prepared to challenge social and economic traditions in the decades after his return to Canada. "The basis of any church pronouncements on social questions must be that human beings are persons free, responsible children of God," Forsey wrote. Their equality was an equality "in the sight of God," and ensuring their freedom was a fundamental Christian doctrine:

> This does not, of course, imply absence of social restraint or equal pay all round. But it does mean recognizing that "the poorest he that is in Canada hath a life to live as the richest he; that the baby in the slum is as important as the baby in the prosperous residential suburb; that discrimination on account of sex, race or creed is utterly contrary to the Christian Gospel.... It means also that these affirmations must not be left as mere affirmations, but must be translated into social reality ... based on the best information and expert advice obtainable.[96]

Forsey practised his belief in economic and social equality by assuming the responsibility for increasing social awareness of existing inequalities. By exposing inequalities and oppression, Forsey believed he was enacting the necessary first step to effecting real change and a real transformation of society.

This dedication to creating an awareness of social problems evolved from Macmurray, who advocated the necessity of changing accepted traditions in order to effect real democracy. The vehicles Forsey chose for this work were those "small platoons" referred to by Edmund Burke and other committed pluralists. For Forsey they included socio-religious associations such as the Student Christian Movement, the Fellowship for a Christian Social Order, and the United Church's Committee on Social and Economic Research. These associations were mechanisms for action in society; mechanisms for fostering a sense of class-consciousness in the minds of Canadians.

Macmurray had argued for the need to become class-conscious as the first step in bringing the class struggle to an end: "To become class conscious of the class situation and of our bondage to it is also to become conscious of the general interest of society," Macmurray reminded his audience in Belleville in 1936. "The Christian's business is to arouse people to the facts, not to prevent something from happening but to show people that war is being waged now." This, Macmurray believed, was the necessary first step to establishing a harmonious, co-operative society: "Nothing can be achieved towards real democracy," he wrote, "until people discover they don't have one."[97]

Forsey dedicated himself to this task and in so doing rejected once and for all any constructive role for idealism in modern Canadian society. "Class is a fact," he wrote. "If we deny it, that is sheer idealism, ignoring facts to escape doing something about them. If we want to get rid of class divisions and class conflict, the first essential is class-consciousness." Only when people realized that classes in fact existed would society become class-conscious and only then would class divisions begin to disappear. This awareness would then lead the proletariat into a share in the political and economic decision making process.[98]

Though Macmurray was the main source of these ideas during Forsey's time at Oxford, he was not the sole source. In addition to Macmurray's religious activism, Forsey became familiar with the writings of the socialist G.D.H. Cole, who had returned to Oxford in 1925.[99] Cole had turned his back on Fabian socialism, and had become very much a "rebel with a cause" in support of his concept of Guild Socialism. Cole, who had a stronger dislike for liberalism than he did for conservatism, advocated a resistance to utilitarianism; a respect for Tory traditionalism; a passionate hatred of social injustice; and a belief in the value of adult education and socialist-labour research.[100]

Forsey was immediately impressed with Cole when Forsey first encountered Cole in the Oxford Labour Club. "We had a brilliant speech by the famous G.D.H. Cole on 'The Case for Socialism,'" wrote Forsey to his mother.[101] Much later in his life Forsey would recall that Cole had been the only really excellent lecturer he had heard at Oxford and that Cole had been a "great influence" upon him.[102]

Forsey immediately joined in some of the political campaigns then raging in England. For example, during Cole's campaign as a Labour candidate in Oxford's University riding, and during the 1926 General Strike, Forsey performed in an operetta that Cole had written on that bitter labour strike.[103] He also regularly attended Cole's popular informal lectures and discussion groups that were held in the Cole home.[104]

Cole's socialism reinforced many of Macmurray's messages, including the need for a classless society based on human fellowship, with intellectuals serving along with workers as the movement's core.[105]

Cole preached that his form of guild socialism was "of its essence a missionary gospel with a message for all mankind" and he spoke of the need for a new form of society that would make democracy economic as well as political.[106]

Cole, like Macmurray, emphasized the importance of community and communal relations in achieving real progress. This was especially true for businesses and industries, which would be encouraged to maintain the willing co-operation of their workers by ensuring that their operations were conducted "in a spirit of real democracy and communal service."[107] The foundation for this form of "Industrial Democracy" rested on Cole's opposition to overpowering collectivism. Rather, Cole asserted the vital importance of individual and group liberty. Like Macmurray, Cole believed in the need to diffuse social responsibility among all the people by making them as far as possible masters of their own lives and of the conditions under which their daily work was done. An important word in this process was freedom, which to Cole had a twofold purpose – freedom from the fear of unemployment and freedom at work.[108]

If it was Cole's vision of real democratic socialism based on freedom and equality that provided the spark in Forsey's mind, it was Macmurray who continued to fuel the flame, if only because Macmurray and Forsey shared a belief in the important role that the Church should play in fostering the ideal Christian society. But Cole's influence was important, and many of his ideas were incorporated into Forsey's writings and works while he was employed by the Canadian Congress of Labour later in his life.

Forsey's Oxford experience was, therefore, tremendously important in the continuing development of his intellectual thought. He had come to Balliol at an important time in its academic development, for the College was alive with new professors and new courses, all of which aimed to rectify the past wrongs of a world that had led itself into a disastrous world war. The goal now seemed to be to prepare students to take an active role in social leadership and to utilize academic instruction to the betterment of society.

If Oxford meant exposure to new ideas and new political movements, the Rhodes Scholarship also provided Forsey with a remarkable opportunity to absorb new ideas and new cultures outside of the Oxford milieu. Forsey toured France and Switzerland following his first academic year, and during this trip he stayed three weeks in a Quaker hotel in Geneva.[109] By the summer of 1928 Forsey had completed a very successful Bachelor of Arts and was considering pursuing further graduate degrees. He was particularly interested in a Bachelor of Letters and had begun research with that degree in mind. Forsey was also especially pleased that he was the only Canadian who received a 'First' in his final examinations.[110]

At this time Forsey was seeking advice regarding his future. Leacock wanted him to do a Ph.D. at McGill, but Forsey was considering very seriously enrolling in a doctoral programme at Harvard.[111] But first there was time for another European excursion, and Forsey broke free of his growing interest in Labour Party politics[112] to spend the summer touring the continent, visiting Italy, Switzerland, Austria, and France.[113]

One particularly interesting stop on this trip was Geneva, where Forsey once again visited his Quaker friend with whom he had spent three weeks on his previous trip. Forsey also had the opportunity to view first-hand the diplomatic excitement surrounding the Ninth Assembly of the League of Nations.[114] This particular League Session offered Forsey a first-hand view of Mackenzie King and an assortment of Department of External Affairs staffers in action, for the Prime Minister had decided to lead a delegation to Geneva to represent Canada at the Assembly and personally sign the Kellogg Pact. This was seen at the time as an important step toward enhancing Canada's status in the world, representing as it had, a separate and individual international diplomatic act by the Dominion.[115]

Forsey personally denounced the general diplomatic trends then occurring in Geneva, particularly France and Britain's continuing "reactionary" and oppressive policies toward Germany despite her fulfillment of her reparation obligations "to the letter." Forsey did, however, enjoy watching the Canadian delegation, which he said was "cutting a great dash here," despite a very ordinary performance by the Prime Minister. Forsey was particularly impressed with King's Under-Secretary for External Affairs, O.D. Skelton, who "made an excellent speech ... wise, witty, shrewd and admirable in temper." "Everyone was vastly impressed," added Forsey. Despite some low points, such as a rough encounter with "Fascist border-guards" in Austria, the trip went very well.[116]

The autumn of 1928 brought further study, and in the new year Forsey received a greatly appreciated assurance from Hemmeon that McGill would do its best to receive him as a Ph.D. candidate with some lecturing responsibilities in either the 1929 or 1930 academic year.[117] Forsey completed his overseas experience with a two-month European tour with his mother, visiting seven countries before sailing from Southampton for home on August 24, 1929.[118]

CHAPTER

DEPRESSION-ERA CHRISTIANITY

That Eugene Forsey returned to Canada in 1929 with a strengthened personal commitment to socialism[1] should not be at all surprising. His previously established belief in the importance of "Tory democratic" social and economic reform principles had been shifting to the left during his last year in Canada in 1926, and this shift had been reinforced and radicalized during his Oxford years. This had occurred academically through his close connection to John Macmurray, by his exposure to the general philosophical position of individuals like W.D. Ross and G.D.H. Cole, through his observations of Britain's chaotic industrial society, and through his outside reading of British economic historians, especially R.H. Tawney.[2]

In many ways Tawney's writing style was similar to that which Forsey would develop during the 1930s. Both men believed in writing "in and of their times," not strictly for academic purposes but for the general public, in the belief that real social and economic reform depended on an educated adult population.[3] Tawney was also very much in the same intellectual tradition as many of Forsey's Oxford instructors. He too had taught at Glasgow University and Oxford, and he possessed a spirit of radical social criticism that had, by the 1920s, established his reputation as one of the most influential spokesmen of Anglican socialism. Tawney did not attempt to turn Christians into socialists, but to turn socialists into Christians by historically documenting the emergence of the capitalistic power and thus encouraging a spiritual resistance to capitalist modes of thought and behaviour.[4]

Tawney's form of spiritual reformism reinforced the formal economic training Forsey received at Oxford. The latter was in turn reinforced by the nature of Forsey's personal spiritual journey. Despite his Methodist background Forsey maintained strong "semi-Anglican" principles in his earlier years, but since the mid-1920s these principles had been repeatedly challenged by messages of spiritual activism. While at Oxford Forsey attended a local Presbyterian Church as well as a campus non-denominational church and had listened to a "mixed bag of preachers."[5]

Forsey quite enjoyed this spiritual variety, for he never strictly adhered to one denominational church; rather, he always found the message more important than the particular label which was affixed to it. It was during his time at Oxford, for example, that Forsey decided to become a Quaker, a religion he was not totally unfamiliar with, since he had grandparents who were Friends and had met Quaker Friends at Oxford, including John Macmurray and A.D. Lindsay's wife.[6] Forsey remained a Quaker until the Spanish Civil War, at which time his feelings presented too great a challenge to his Quaker pacifist principles.[7]

The Quaker movement was in many ways ideally suited for Forsey, especially during the 1920s, because its sense of freedom appealed to his freethinking Oxford mind. Forsey was specifically attracted to the Friends' belief in the "Inner Light" experience as the means of achieving individual grace directly from God.[8] One can also presume that the Society's "activist" ethical and faith foundations were an added attractive feature for Forsey, especially the Quakers' assertion that "Truth" was something that a person could be simply by living the life of Christ on earth. This concept closely resembled John Macmurray's philosophical and theological teachings.[9] The Friends' leadership in church-sponsored poor relief, public health advocacy, and additional social reform issues such as prison reform, for example, was a tangible sign of its belief in concrete social activism.[10] It was, in short, a living embodiment of much of what Forsey was being taught and had come to believe in during the ten years following his departure from Ottawa.

Forsey acted on his belief in the importance of religiously based social activism following his entrance to McGill as a Ph.D. candidate and sessional lecturer in Economics and Political Science in the fall of 1929.[11] Specifically, Forsey associated with three religiously oriented social activist associations: the Student Christian Movement (SCM); the United Church's Committee on Social and Economic Research; and the Fellowship for Christian Social Order (FCSO). Each of these organizations embodied the type of independent social unit which represented pluralism in action. Each association fit Burke's definition of a "small platoon" at work in society.

The Student Christian Movement in Canada was part of an international association called the World's Student Christian Federation, with headquarters in Geneva.[12] The SCM in Canada originated with the Young Men's Christian Association and the Young Women's Christian Association, but the major impetus to its growth came from students who had returned from fighting in World War I. Many of these men and women were "profoundly dissatisfied with the world as it was, and full of eagerness to make something more significant out of their own lives and out of society."[13]

The SCM's "call to battle" was dual in nature: it represented a call for the reordering of society through Christ and a call to individual improvement of Christian lifestyles. This combination of social and individual reform was based on the belief that "the foundations of society were wrong because the relations between man and man are wrong. We have failed to be Christians." The Movement aimed to improve an economic system "which robs so many of their birthright and joy and freedom."[14]

In choosing McGill, Forsey had joined a campus where Student Christian work had begun as early as 1882 through the initiatives of Sir William Dawson and D.A. Budge. Dawson was then the principal of McGill and one of Canada's most eminent scientists, not to mention a Presbyterian of "unshakable conviction."[15] Budge, who was at that time the General Secretary of the Montreal YMCA, had arranged in 1905 through the generosity of Lord Strathcona to open Strathcona Hall in Montreal in 1905 as the institutional centre of student Christian work in Canada.[16]

In 1920 the McGill YMCA reorganized and became part of the Student Christian Movement of Canada. With the voluntary assistance of SCM students and with the backing of the McGill faculty, the McGill SCM provided a needed spiritual service on that non-sectarian campus, for few provisions had been taken to meet the spiritual needs of the student body.[17]

The SCM acknowledged that it was difficult for churches to deal directly with problems of university life and thought, so it functioned on an interdenominational basis to help "students to face their common problems together." Communal study groups, chapel services, and "fireside meetings" were all held at McGill in the hope of providing students with an informal social learning atmosphere in which they could talk and listen to speakers on topics of "current importance." The SCM also operated annual spring camps after the conclusion of spring examinations. These were intended to help students "co-ordinate classroom knowledge in terms of Christian purpose."[18] The SCM was, therefore, actively engaged in real world issues and debates.

Forsey had been a member of the SCM as a McGill undergraduate,[19] and he continued his activity in the Movement following his return to McGill in 1929.[20] Forsey's interest in the SCM as an active spiritual force for reform had been intensified through his association with John Macmurray, who had joined the Movement in 1909. The years between 1909 and 1924 were formative ones for the SCM as it increased dramatically in importance because of its unique message regarding the important social role of Christian fellowship: "The SCM," Macmurray wrote, "taught me that religious fellowship could be fun."[21]

Forsey's return to Canada and the SCM came at an important time in the Movement's history, for the SCM was "rethinking its place and purpose in the life of the universities"[22] and entering its "radical Christianity" phase, which coincided with the years of the Great Depression. This change came about as a response to the growing conviction, within the Movement and within Canadian society as a whole, that real social change was necessary. Many individual SCM members were, therefore, joining associations that were committed to concrete programmes of action.[23]

This new approach was very much in line with Forsey's own belief in the need for Christians to take concrete action to rectify social ills, and he remained active in the SCM Movement at McGill until 1940.[24] In fact Forsey and R.B.Y. Scott, a Professor of Old Testament at United Theological College in Montreal, were instrumental in expanding the McGill SCM chapter to include students who had graduated yet wished to retain fellowship in the Movement. This newly formed section of the McGill SCM promoted ongoing fellowship among former SCM students after their graduation and provided a new source of ongoing financial support for the Movement. It also sponsored study groups, sent out materials to its members, and organized an annual week-long summer conference.[25]

This new section, established in 1932 and called the Graduating Co-Operating Committee, also re-established the neglected relationship between the SCM and its former members. Led by a small number of former SCM members, in particular Eugene Forsey, the Committee had as its guiding principle "the vision that the Kingdom of God could not be realized without the concerted efforts of all who ardently desire its coming."[26] The Graduate Committee was designed, therefore, to provide SCM graduates living in the Montreal region with "a continuous renewal of the inspiration they [had] received" during their school years, but who were now expected to "take their place in community life and ... identify themselves with the Church and the various institutions working for the betterment of society."[27] This provided an associative link between an individual and an organization in society dedicated to "the fashioning of a new and better order." Graduating members of the SCM would henceforth have their names transferred to the graduate list, thus retaining their connection with the Movement.[28]

The Graduate Christian Movement maintained an organized, working executive to co-ordinate a programme of conferences, lectures, and study groups that encouraged its members to:

> engage in critical and scientific study of religion, particularly in the life of Jesus, to gain a realistic understanding of social, economic and political forces; and to work together for increased religious consciousness and for the reconstruction of society on the basis of their religious convictions and in conformity with the life and teachings of Jesus.[29]

The Graduate Movement also exposed current SCM members to the knowledge and experience of former members employed on campus and in the community.[30] Forsey soon became integrally involved in the Graduate Christian Movement's efforts at McGill, serving on the Executive of the Graduate Co-Operating Committee and speaking at numerous conferences and study group meetings. [31]

The Movement's inclination toward active reconstructive work in society was based on its principle that Christianity had to express itself in "relations within a society." King Gordon later recalled that this principle followed in the tradition of religious fellowship espoused by many Oxford academics who believed that an expressed relationship between neighbours ensured the realization of a "society of neighbours [to protect] the rights of individuals within that neighbourhood." Such a Christian society had to ensure its individuals the means of fulfilling themselves as human beings.[32]

Gordon had also been an SCM member while he was at Oxford, where he met Frank Scott, a fellow Oxford student whom Forsey had also met there. According to Gordon, both he and Forsey had their "comfortable social philosophies shaken up by the likes of Shaw,[33] Tawney, Hobson, Cole, and the Webbs, either in person or bursting out very much alive from the cover of books or declaring from the Oxford stage."[34] Gordon went on to do graduate work at Union Theological Seminary in New York, where he studied under Harry F. Ward and Reinhold Niebuhr, "for whom Christian profession called for a radical analysis of the social situation and appropriate personal and collective action."[35]

Gordon performed his "field work" in Christian ethics in a strike-ridden steel mill in North Carolina, where striking textile workers had been shot by police.[36] Ordained a United Church Minister, Gordon had been invited to Montreal by the YMCA in 1930 to deliver a speech on unemployment at one of the YMCA's regular meetings on social issues. Gordon had obviously impressed his hosts, for he was hired a year later as professor of Christian Ethics at United Theological College.[37]

Forsey and Gordon shared an interest in social and ethical issues and a respect for individual rights, and they had both experienced first-hand the abuses that the trade union movements were encountering in Great Britain, the United States, and Canada. In Montreal, inadequate health services and a lack of built-in support for the unemployed provided the necessary incentives for Forsey and Gordon to implement the "call to action" that was encouraged through their affiliation with the SCM. This philosophy of action had been impressed upon them by their Oxford and American teachers. The messages of men such as Macmurray and Niebuhr continued to reach Forsey, Gordon, and others through the Graduate Christian Movement's organized study groups, where Macmurray's current works were studied[38] and special lectures given by Niebuhr.[39]

The SCM, in fact, referred specifically to Niebuhr and Macmurray as the two men most important in influencing the official positions taken by the Movement on Depression-related issues and World War II.[40] Gordon has confirmed that Niebuhr had an immense and fundamental influence on his own personal thought as well as the collective thought of the members of the SCM.[41] John Macmurray's influence on Forsey was equally prevalent. Both Macmurray and Niebuhr shared a commitment to the fundamental importance of action and realism, though Niebuhr tended to emphasize political action and Macmurray social and economic issues.[42]

And it was the deteriorating social and economic conditions associated with the advent of the Depression in 1929 that helped spur Forsey into this type of Christian social action. The dreadful impact of the Depression upon thousands of families worsened in the opening years of the 1930s, and there seemed little prospect of improvement for the unemployed and homeless. As Blair Neatby has written: "In retrospect the depression appears as an unmitigated disaster, a decade of impotent despair in which people could only wait helplessly for the return of better days."[43] And in the slums of Montreal the Depression only worsened the poverty and hopelessness of families who had known little else during the 1920s.[44]

These deteriorating conditions compelled Forsey and Gordon to action and strengthened their convictions. By 1932 both men had become actively involved in the Committee on Social and Economic Research, a committee of the Montreal Presbytery of the United Church. The Committee's members were Gordon, Forsey, and J.A. Coote, an Assistant Professor of Mechanical Engineering at McGill.[45] The Committee stated in its first *Information Bulletin*, published in 1932, that its objective was "to draw attention to aspects of the economic and social life of Canada which seem to call for careful consideration from the Church."[46] Recognizing the "need for a fresh interpretation of Christianity," the Committee put forth an open and radical challenge to "established religion" to respond to what the Committee called the growing conviction "among all classes of Canadians ... that our present economic system has broken down and that our most urgent task is to build a new and better one." The Committee asked why it was that as the economic and industrial situation grows "more and more urgent, established religion tends always to rationalize and sanctify the social situation in which it finds itself."[47]

Forsey, Gordon, and Coote openly challenged the Church to respond to the needs of its people and provide the active leadership that "all classes" of Canadians were seeking. "Will the conscience and vision of the Church awake soon enough," asked the editors of the *Bulletin*, "to exercise in the crisis a socialising and Christianizing influence soon enough to be potent in offering any direction or control to the forces of social revolution?"[48]

The Committee's work went beyond rhetoric, for over the course of three years the Committee sought to bring to the attention of the public and the federal government important facts and socio-economic trends.[49]

"We are acting as a Committee of our Church to make available social and economic information for our people and statistics for our use," Committee Chairman Gordon wrote to a member of Quebec's Womens' Minimum Wage Board.[50] The Committee publicized both facts and opinions on a number of socio-economic issues through its *Information Bulletin*. Funded by the Church, the *Bulletin* followed a format previously established by the Social Service Federation of the Methodist Episcopal Church in its *Social Service Bulletin*.[51] The Committee also drew on socio-economic research compiled by individuals such as Frank Scott, Harry Cassidy, and Leonard Marsh, who was then in the midst of his "formidable task" of leading a McGill University-sponsored and Rockefeller-funded project called "The McGill Social Science Research Project."[52]

The Committee also drew on statistics compiled by government agencies such as the Dominion Bureau of Statistics and the Department of Labour, as well as municipal agencies such as the City of Montreal's Family Welfare Association.[53] The Committee selected issues that it considered most in need of reforming, including corporate waste in the production of foods such as bread at a time when thousands were going hungry, and the trend to increasing "combination" by the large firms such as Quebec's milling companies.[54]

Forsey was especially active in the economic analysis of wages and dividends in the Quebec textile industry. He published a series of articles in the *Bulletin* entitled "Dividends and Unemployment," which highlighted the contrast between the actions of firms such as the Dominion Textile Company and Canada Cottons in holding down wages and laying off workers while paying out, in the first three years of the Depression, "the highest dividends in their history, $1,485,000.00."[55] Forsey's unpublished research notes on this subject indicate that he exerted a great deal of time and effort in the preparation of this series of articles.[56] His efforts were matched by Coote and Gordon, both of whom wrote detailed articles on subjects ranging from child mortality in Montreal to inadequate wages in other industries to unemployment, the major social issue of the era.[57]

The problem of urban unemployment was especially acute in Montreal, which grew faster than any city in Canada between 1931 and 1941. The city had expanded its population by almost 50 per cent in the twenty years between Forsey's arrival in the early 1920s and his departure in 1941.[58] The problem was aggravated by the lack of work for the growing urban population and the rapid decrease in per capita income for those who were fortunate enough to find work. In Quebec as a whole, per capita income fell by 44 per cent between 1928 and 1933, the years in which the *Bulletin* was published.[59] The situation was especially disastrous for destitute families, whose plight, as Blair Neatby has explained, illustrated the precarious nature of an industrial society in which willing, able-bodied men realized that through no fault of their own, they could not support their families.[60]

The Committee responded to the growing unemployment by taking an active lead opposing the Montreal Unemployment Commission's decision to close the City's Day Shelter for unemployed men. The Committee's tactic was to publicize a head count of Shelter users to illustrate the disastrous effect that the decision to close the Shelter would have on the 34,000 to 125,000 men who utilized the facility each week.[61] "The Committee on Social and Economic Research is strongly and unanimously of the opinion," stated an article in the November 1933 issue of the *Bulletin*, "that ways should be found whereby the Day Shelter could be immediately opened."[62]

The Committee illustrated for its *Bulletin* readers that the closing of services was linked to the transition "between the new system and the old [in which] the City Unemployment Commission, took over from the private agencies the distribution of Unemployment Relied to married men and families." The results of the change had been anything but beneficial to the unemployed; not only were the amounts paid out by the new Commission for fuel and clothing felt to be inadequate, but its new office arrangements were too small and crowded for the long lines

of unemployed.[63] The Committee also denounced the Quebec government for not keeping any official unemployment statistics and permit-
ting firms to fire young girls and replace them with boys whose wages
the Quebec Minimum Wages Commission had no control over.[64]

One particular issue that received heightened awareness during these
desperate years was the perceived infringement of the civil rights of
many of the Depression's victims and protestors. J.H. Thompson has
documented a widespread "movement of popular resistance that had
been evident in a number of important industrial centres as early as
the winter of 1929–30." Violent street confrontations occurred in many
of Canada's largest cities wherever "Communist or red trade union-
ists" could mobilize Canadians with the party slogan "Fight or Starve."
Among the Communist party's most dedicated supporters, Thompson
adds, were unemployed victims of Canada's collapsing railway network,
most of whom were European immigrants.[65]

The Conservative government's response to this increasing civil strife
was in part to initiate the massive deportation of immigrants who were
perceived to be engaged in the violent actions.[66] Then, in 1931, the
government invoked Section 98 of the Criminal Code against many
protesting groups.[67] These arrests of Communists and labour leftists
led men such as Frank Scott to take the unpopular step of objecting to
police behaviour that they believed infringed on the freedoms of speech
and association of Canadians during these crisis years. Scott also publicly criticized the absence of judicial and executive control over such
infringements. Through speeches and articles, Scott and other civil libertarians raised public awareness of personal oppression and infringements upon basic civil rights that were occurring in Canadian society.[68]

The Committee on Social and Economic Research, and particularly Eugene Forsey, took a specific interest in these cases involving
perceived infringements of civil liberties, especially in those episodes
involving "defenders of civil liberties, not its suppressors, who in a free
country are truly desirous of maintaining law and order."[69]

This article on abuses of civil liberties illustrates Forsey's tendency to view the need for economic reform and the threat to civil
liberties through the prism of social law and order. Forsey believed
that the preservation of law and order was inextricably connected
with the maintenance of basic freedoms guaranteed by the British
Constitution, and that this stability and freedom could only be pre-

served by society enacting those reforms in society that would prevent radical social revolution.

One illustration of this principle was the Committee's response to the "Zynchuk Case," in which a Montreal man, Nick Zynchuk, was shot and killed by a Montreal constable in March 1933. The shooting received widespread publicity in the Montreal press, largely because it took place during the victim's eviction over his failure to pay his rent, and because of the strong testimony from many eyewitnesses that disputed police evidence that the life of the constable who fired the gun was in danger at the time of the shooting.[70]

The *Bulletin* raised a number of civil rights violations surrounding the event, including charges of brutality and violence on the part of plainclothes policemen against onlookers of the shooting. While Forsey acknowledged that it was "not the function of the Committee ... to express its opinion on the attitude of official bodies in the Zynchuk case, it does feel that certain issues have been raised that are of vital concern to Canadian citizens and especially to Christian ministers and laymen."[71]

Forsey called on authorities to recognize the fact that, as the Zynchuk shooting had illustrated, the economic situation dictated that in such a general community of distress, a high percentage of unemployment evictions were bound to occur and "accentuate community unrest." Forsey called upon authorities to recognize and plan for the fact that inability to pay rent would continue to affect the unemployed, and to reform the relief system to ensure that an adequate and humane system of relief was in place. The *Bulletin* article also recommended that, since uniformed men had managed to maintain social order to date, the use of plainclothes men dealing with crowds be limited since they seemed to provoke violence and were inefficient in maintaining order.[72] This was an argument that Forsey would return to after the introduction of the Padlock Act.

Forsey also condemned the Immigration Act, which gave the power to the authorities to state that "foreigners" such as Zynchuk were communists, thus placing them outside the pale of justice where they were no longer entitled to full protection under the law. In the case of many immigrants, Forsey wrote, deportations could be enacted on the grounds of seeking relief, which he condemned as being ridiculous, given existing levels of unemployment and distress.[73]

Forsey's article also struck out at Section 98 in much the same way as Scott had done. Forsey specifically attacked the Code's clause stating that convictions for "unlawful association" could lead to prison terms of up to twenty years, as had been the case in 1931 when eight Torontonians were jailed for being communists.[74] The Committee urged the Montreal and Ottawa Conference and the General Council of the Church to encourage "its own Presbyteries to make earnest efforts through their relevant Boards and Committees to take steps to safeguard basic freedoms" and to lobby authorities to ensure police authorities did "not yield to panic, and the violence that panic produces." Rather, police should recognize that "firmness, with patience and understanding, [were] the qualities required in our distressed and critical days."[75]

Had the United Church officials on the Commission of Evangelism and Social Service, which had appointed the members of the Social and Economic Research Committee, given more thought to Forsey's and Gordon's background they might well have anticipated that the Committee would have stretched its mandate to "secure reliable information concerning the existing ... state of our social and industrial life."

Both men were conditioned to the need for social action based on religious principles. It was natural, therefore, that given the deteriorating socio-economic conditions of the early 1930s in Montreal, they would transform their original mandate into a "clarion call to thought and action." This message was clearly signalled in the December 1932 issue of the *Bulletin*:

> Your Committee recognizes:
>
> 1) That the efforts of the working masses to improve their lot, and even to effect a different social order, are inevitable in the present situation.
> 2) That the necessity for serious change in the social structure is widely recognized in intelligent and professional circles everywhere, and in the commercial community itself.
> 3) The Christian Church would be untrue to herself, a traitor to humanity, and an ally of reaction, if she were indifferent to the present tragic situation of the labouring masses, and their efforts after self-betterment.[76]

The Committee's three members relentlessly pushed the established Church toward a more active "offensive of militant Christianity [in the face of] the waste, the suffering, the human frustration resulting from the present constitution of our social order." "There is great hope," announced the editors of the *Bulletin*, "that the Church may yet call forth that ethical leadership so lacking in our economic and political affairs."[77]

The Committee members had also anticipated the revelations of the 1935 Royal Commission on Price Spreads, and had submitted a report to the Ninth Conference of the Montreal-Ottawa Conference of the United Church of Canada. This report stated that "the work of providing society with the primary necessities of life ought not to be made the occasion of exploiting the mass of the population for the benefit of a privileged minority." The Committee called for "thorough-going legislative control [to ensure] to the consumer the benefits of the economics of concentration of control over the provision of the basic necessities such as bread, milk and coal."[78]

The Committee went too far, however, in its approaches to the CCF in Ottawa,[79] and its strident "clarion calls to action." Such activity awakened powerful forces that did not share the Committee's passionate concern for reforming the social order. "I have been receiving printed *Bulletins*," wrote J.A. Ewing of the Sun Life Assurance Company to the Committee, "[and] I do not approve of them. On the contrary I consider them most unseemly and as constitutes a reflection upon the intelligence and good taste of the Church, in whose name they purport to speak."[80] In March 1934 the powerful Montreal *Gazette* blasted the churchmen for passing resolutions demanding the repeal of the infamous Section 98 of the Criminal Code. In an editorial entitled "Friends of Sedition," the *Gazette* berated the Committee for offering advice on an issue "utterly foreign to the mission of Christian teaching."[81]

Forsey personally received a strongly worded anonymous letter from an irate churchman who suggested that he "exercise ordinary courtesy and refrain from misusing the prestige of Divinity Hall for which you have no authority, and that you address your discriminatory propaganda – if you must continue it – from some other address."[82] The Committee also received a mild rebuke from Ernest Thomas, the Field Secretary of the Board of Evangelism and Social Service of the United Church of Canada. Thomas took issue with the *Bulletin's* interpretation of the General Council's statement on marriage.[83]

Though the Committee members attempted to be somewhat conciliatory in congratulating the General Council for taking "significant forward steps in the social ethical position of Western Liberal Protestantism,"[84] the Council took steps to control the Committee's statements and activities. In June 1933, a motion was introduced at a special meeting of the Council to appoint two new members to the Committee. These men, F.W. Kerr and J.M Graham, were two conservative-minded churchmen whose duty it was to balance the Committee's views.[85] A second motion that would have seen four conservative churchmen appointed to the Committee and required every article in the *Bulletin* be approved by the Presbytery's Executive Committee was defeated.[86] But the Council did pass one amendment that required the *Bulletin* to add a byline to its masthead stating: "The *Bulletin* is for information, its material has not been endorsed by the Presbytery."[87]

The fact that the noose was tightening around the Committee's neck was illustrated by the United Theological College decision not to rehire King Gordon. The College publicly cited budgetary reasons for its decision, but the move was widely interpreted as punishment for Gordon's "radical" views.[88] The Committee's work did challenge many established institutions, some of which were in positions of influence within the Church. The Chairman of the Board of Governors of the United Theological College, for example, was also the President of Canada Cottons, one of Quebec's largest textile companies and a firm that had come under direct attack in the *Bulletin*'s pages.[89]

The pressure exerted on this Church Committee coincided with similar pressures against the SCM. Murray Brookes, the General Secretary of the SCM during the early 1930s, wrote that although "Political reformers such as Gregory Vlastos, King Gordon, Eugene Forsey ... were in demand everywhere.... The SCM was soon in hot water for placing too much emphasis on social questions." The SCM was attacked for focusing on the economic and for being "a bunch of 'pink' socialists, that had no right to the name Christian, that had all turned 'red.'"[90]

Forsey participated in both the SCM and the Committee on Social and Economic Research because he believed in the goals of both organizations. In most cases his personal opinions on the various issues were identical to the SCM's and the Committee's policies, and in some cases Forsey's opinions helped shape those policies. Forsey's pacifist

Quaker beliefs, for example, were directly in line with the SCM's 1931 petition to Prime Minister Bennett and later statements by the SCM that related the problem of war to fundamental faults in the social and economic system.[91] As well, the SCM was continually supporting the condition of the working class within a general critical view of industrial society. Specifically, SCM publications questioned the belief that property was sacred and argued for social action to establish "the principle that a worker is at no time to be without income adequate to sustain efficient life." In a SCM document entitled "Society and Industrial Discord," the SCM addressed the question of the condition of the industrialized worker in the machine age: "How then can the elements of human nature, suppressed by machine productions, be liberated?" asked the SCM. "Is good will of the employer an adequate alternative to guaranteed freedom of expression through some form of unionism?"[92]

These words could well have been written by Forsey, for he was at that time publishing some of his first material concerning the need for socio-economic reform.

One such pamphlet, entitled "Unemployment in the Machine Age: Its Causes," was published by the Social Services Council of Canada, an organization which was on record in the 1920s as supporting "both scientific and Christian forms of social service."[93] Forsey's pamphlet linked Canada's serious unemployment and relief problems to the advent of the machine age and industrialism.[94] He rejected traditional theories designed to rationalize rising unemployment such as the "technological theory of unemployment," which connected rising unemployment to high labour costs, and the "underconsumption-over-saving theory," which focused on the industrialists' over-investing in new factories as a means of absorbing excess capital. Both theories, wrote Forsey, only partially answered the questions raised by the economic disasters of the 1930s.[95]

Forsey believed that the problems raised by the Depression's form of capitalism were "curable only by substituting an economy of abundance for the present economy of scarcity."[96] In his personal writings and in the organizations he chose to support, Forsey consistently emphasized the fact that Christian man had the power and the duty to rectify any economic dislocations and shape a more humane society. He summarized this concept in his conclusion to the "Machine Age" pamphlet:

> Unemployment is not the fault of the machine, but of the uses to which we have put the machine. It is not an inescapable price of economic progress. It is only part of the price we pay for sacrificing humanity to the economic institutions of a bygone age. Only when we are ready to reverse that process can we conquer unemployment and achieve the economy of plenty which is within our grasp.[97]

Forsey's thinking in this regard was directly in line with the direction many religiously oriented organizations were taking in the early years of the Depression. This direction could be termed an ideology of group action oriented toward living out Christian fellowship in community with one's fellow man.[98] For King Gordon this meant a belief shared by many that the attainment of "real democracy" involved discovering resources within society capable of changing its very nature so as to allow the Christian ideology of neighbourly relations to express itself. This, said Gordon, was something more than the individual feeling goodwill toward others. Rather it was a question of what could be done "by the Christian community – the Church, if you like," to effect real change in society's thinking and sense of priorities.[99]

This approach necessarily involved one's following in "the prophetic tradition" of the Church as a prophet, as opposed to "the institutional tradition" of the Church as a priest.[100] For John Macmurray, whose literature influenced many SCM members, the prophetic tradition referred to the call of the Christian to rekindle the flame of the first Christian Church "in the fulfillment of the Christian community; the Christian mission." This, Macmurray wrote, went beyond "institutional churches" with their differing theologies, "because the original community was founded before there were theologies or creeds, as a way of life on earth, as an instrument for the salvation of the world."[101]

This philosophy represented a unique paradigm within which Forsey's writing in the 1930s took place. This paradigm is defined succinctly by Forsey's comment that "We are in the world; not apart from it. The Christian must be involved in almost any public question. How could it be otherwise? To save the world, God loved the world."[102] Forsey called on his fellow Christians to reject the "treaty of partition with the devil," and, true to his Quaker beliefs, he challenged his readers to follow the "Light":

> We are Christians, followers of Christ. A people who believe he is
> the Light of the World, and calls us to be lights in the world ... *un
> faible reflect, O Maitre, de ton eclat radieux*, shedding light on the
> whole of life.

This mission called forth to action all those who believed "in freedom, and brotherhood, and not merely the hereafter; the early Church
revolutionary; militant. People who believe in God's grace; his power.
Storehouse is powerhouse."[103]

Forsey took on this commitment with a missionary zeal, for accepting such a challenge meant not only "keeping the faith," but keeping
it to pass on to others to spread and to use. This was a force to be
applied to the betterment of society, argued Forsey, like "Light, heat
and power, not to be hidden but to give light in darkness visible."
Forsey believed that there could be no middle ground for a person
committed to this course of action, for it called one forth to share
Christ's poor, "to make, or keep people mentally and spiritually healthy,
but not just that: healthy to love, to act therefore to love one another
as God has loved you."[104] This was a "staggering command," one that
Forsey and a small group of SCM associates increasingly believed
called for a new structure that could express more fully their shared
sense of the Christian fellowship necessary to actually bring about a
new social order.

The type of polarization that occurred between conservatives
opposed to the type of social action typified by the United Church's
Committee on Social and Economic Research, and others sometimes
referred to as "radicals," had been occurring simultaneously on a
larger scale within the United Church since 1933. In that year "radical" groups in both the Montreal-Ottawa Conference, led by Forsey
and Gordon, and in the Toronto Conference, had begun to openly
challenge "the established order" of the United Church. Forsey and
Gordon's conservative opponents were led by A.J. Ewing, who vehe-
mently disagreed with the Committee's radical views,[105] A.S. Piper,
a Montreal businessman, and Principal James Smythe of the United
Theological College.[106]

The Forsey-Gordon Report submitted to the 1933 Montreal-
Ottawa Conference condemned the capitalist system as unchristian

and called for the creation of a new Christian society in which there would be a socialization of banks, natural resources and transportation as well as a system of social insurance, old age pensions, unemployment insurance, and a minimum wage.[107] The Church officials, though not entirely prepared for the tone of this Report, had been aware that this sentiment existed. In 1932 they had created the Board of Evangelism and Social Service to contend with the increasing dissent within its Church.[108] The establishment of the Board was a recognition of, and an attempt to merge, the twin concerns of evangelism, with its emphasis on personal salvation, and social services, with their more communal implications.[109]

The General Council of the United Church responded to this growing debate by paying tribute to what evangelical Christianity had accomplished in the past, but declared it an inadequate method of solving collective problems or of reforming society. The Council established a commission of enquiry chaired by Sir Robert Falconer, the President of the University of Toronto, to ascertain what Christian principles should govern the social order; the extent to which they were already accepted in society; methods of further applying such principles to existing conditions; and to "define those particular measures which must form the first steps towards a social order in keeping with the mind of Christ."[110]

The General Council urged the Falconer Commission to submit its report within a year "in the hope of unifying the Church," and to facilitate this request the Commission organized itself into sixteen small geographical groups to study the various issues. The Montreal Study Group was led by Professor R.B.Y. Scott and the Reverend J.L. Smith.[111] Specific issues open for discussion included Finance, Manufacturing, Labour, the Church, Economics, and Ethics. The various Study Groups were led by persons as intellectually disparate as the Reverend John Line and William Amos of the United Farmers, to Arthur Meighen and W.E. Rundle of National Trust.[112]

It was within the mandate of the Falconer Commission Enquiry on Christianizing the Social Order that Forsey and Gordon presented their views at the 1933 Montreal-Ottawa Conference. The Falconer Commission was, in effect, a political response by the United Church's authorities to the movement within its Church, led by Forsey and the other "radicals," to review the merits of capitalism within the scope of

Christian society.[113] Their submissions were considered radical when compared to the submissions of people like Irene Biss, who sought a more "co-operative reconciliation with capitalism. "[114] Biss's arguments were typical of the "middle position" on social welfare that the Church, in the end, supported over the "extremist" views put forward by people such as Forsey, Gordon, and John Line, on the one side, and the "status quo" conservative forces within the Church on the other.[115]

In addition to dramatizing the polarization within the Church over this controversy, the Church's "moderate response" to the debate reinforced the perception held by the "radicals" that the Church primarily served the vested interests. In response to this perception, the Montreal group in 1934 joined forces with the Toronto faction to form the Fellowship for a Christian Social Order, commonly referred to at the time as the FCSO.

In his extensive and detailed introduction to the FCSO's major publication, *Towards the Christian Revolution*, the Reverend John Line set forth the Fellowship's determination to avoid the narrowness of evangelicalism while maintaining a fervent concern for the conversion of individuals, the utopian optimism of liberal modernism, and dualism.[116] For FCSO activists such as Queen's Philosophy Professor Gregory Vlastos, the essence of the task at hand for the new organization was to effectively address "the tension between a lingering divisive society of economic classes and new possibilities of co-operative community in a classless society."[117]

Roger Hutchinson, in his detailed theological analysis of the FCSO, concluded that *Towards the Christian Revolution* "was a systematic statement of objectives of the FCSO, as well as the philosophical, theological and scientific foundations upon which it was based."[118] Hutchinson concluded that the three key elements of the FCSO's pre-war position were: the demand for concreteness in thought and action; a belief in the unity of life and in the importance of viewing man "as a social being who is characterized by individuality and relatedness"; and an awareness of the comprehensiveness of the task of transforming society.[119]

Hutchinson also concluded that the FCSO's central belief "about God, church, world and self" was rooted in the Fellowship's rejection of individualism and its determination that the content and focus of the Christian faith were disclosed in the struggle for justice and right relations in man's actual daily life and historical existence. This concept, Hutchinson found, evolved primarily from the works of John Macmurray, whose writings were well known to *Towards the Christian Revolution* contributors Vlastos, Martyn Estall, and Forsey.[120]

John Macmurray's "natural theology" represented a philosophy of religion that looked beyond the individual and became the manifestation of genuine community among persons. Macmurray emphasized that it was only in personal relationships that selfhood evolved, and it was only as the individual came to maturity as a self that he was enabled to know his world. But this selfhood was not to be proven by abstract reflection; rather, it was the very condition of life itself, and therefore the precondition of reflection. Macmurray's emphasis on the radical inter-involvement of personal life pointed to the importance of man's social environment as an important factor in the context of human creation and development.[121]

Given the schism in the United Church between the conservative proponents of evangelical, individual Christianity and the radical group's rejection of such evangelicalism and support for a more socially based communal religion, it is understandable that the latter group would see Macmurray's theological philosophy as expressing their goals and beliefs. And Macmurray was present at a crucial time to reinforce his message in person.

It was in June 1936, just as Forsey was agonizing over his chapter for the *Towards the Christian Revolution*, that Macmurray visited Canada to deliver his series of lectures to the conference of SCM graduates in Belleville, Ontario.[122] Forsey had taken time away from his chapter for the upcoming FCSO book to attend the conference, and after Macmurray consented to having the lectures reproduced "for a limited public," the FCSO arranged for Forsey and Harriet, his wife of about one year,[123] to transcribe the week's lectures, including question and answer sessions.

The task was tailor-made for the Forseys, who shared a very strong interest in Macmurray's subject matter. Forsey had met Harriet at a SCM conference in the Laurentians in 1935. Like her husband, Harriet came from a middle-class British household and was well educated. Her father was of New Brunswick Loyalist stock, and her mother was from a northern Irish family. Harriet's family owned and operated a shipping and lumbering firm in New Brunswick.[124] Harriet later attended Dalhousie University on a languages scholarship and eventually received a Masters of Arts in modern languages before taking post-graduate work at the University of Lausanne in France. She later taught French for many years, including one year at Carleton College in Ottawa.[125]

Forsey considered his wife his intellectual superior who possessed a mind that sought constantly to analyze and probe.[126] Harriet was particularly interested in reading religious material by the psychologist Carl Jung and the American philosopher and psychologist William James, who applied empirical methods of inquiry to questions of religion and philosophy.[127] James, like Macmurray, was a pragmatist in the sense that he believed the truth of an idea depended on its concrete results when it was put into practice.[128]

It appears that Harriet at least partially accepted James's pragmatic philosophy, for although she maintained an interest in religion, Forsey did not think that his wife ever had a strong religious faith. "I don't think she believes in anything," he explained, though "she comes from a strong Anglican family." At one point Harriet joined the Quakers with her husband, but she soon became disgruntled with them. "The Quakers didn't cotton much to Jung," her husband explained. Though both he and his wife were well read and were involved in many causes and issues throughout their lives together, Forsey himself maintained that neither influenced the other to any great extent when it came to the area of ideas and philosophies.[129]

But the two did share a keen interest in learning and expanding their intellectual horizons, and they worked diligently to transcribe Macmurray's week-long series of lectures into a published manuscript. This lengthy transcription provided the *Towards the Christian Revolution* writers with a clear and vivid summary of Macmurray's overall philosophy concerning the "violent end of the individualist phase" of world history and the transition to the socialist phase. The individual, said Macmurray, was increasingly forced into community because only in community could the individual find the solution to the actual problems facing him. Macmurray also condemned materialism as being "profoundly immoral because behind it was an immoral right to solve our problems regardless of consequences upon others." "Like all real immoralities," said Macmurray, "this is profoundly impractical: we are interdependent in fact."[130]

In words that would soon be repeated in the pages of *Towards the Christian Revolution*, Macmurray called for "the transformation from economic anarchy to economic order ... an entirely new order, and entirely new kind of structure of human society, with new working ideals." Such a transformation was entirely contingent upon world leaders consenting to exercise conscious leadership based on Christian ideals: "This involves a complete revolution in the conception of the meaning of Christianity," said Macmurray. Christians, he added, "have lost the reference of religion to reality (not ideas and visions)." Macmurray forcefully emphasized that the task could only be done by "people who would find out the facts and act in terms of them."[131]

Macmurray's writings influenced many writers contributing to the FCSO's *Towards the Christian Revolution*. Forsey's particular chapter in the book was called "The Economic Problem," but like Macmurray, Forsey viewed religion as universal in its application to human activity and central to all human experience. To include a chapter on economics in a religious book, therefore, needed neither explanation nor defence, Forsey wrote, because "the field of religion is the whole of life. That should be explanation and defence enough."[132]

Forsey denounced those who continued to insist that the "business of religion is the development of Christian character in the individual and that if only we [could] produce enough sanctified individuals economic problems would solve themselves." Christian character did not develop in a vacuum, argued Forsey, but rather was "forged in the struggles of daily life ... to sanctify economic wants." He concluded this section by stating that man's first task was to master his economic environment because the economic factor conditioned everything else.[133] In this respect Forsey was responding to Macmurray's challenge for Christians to pursue knowledge as a means of restoring an ailing economy. In Belleville, Macmurray had said:

> If the economic organization of society falls sick, then nothing else is important for the time. No real human social life is possible till the economic organization is restored to health. We must recognize that the economic system is making the personal life impossible.[134]

Here Macmurray was returning to the need to achieve class-consciousness in society as the first necessary step to achieving real democracy: "As long as people are not class conscious, classes will persist,"

Macmurray told his SCM audience in Belleville, "[but] if they can be made class conscious class divisions will cease to exist."[135]

Macmurray had always favoured the working class as the class most likely to do the most good for the whole of society, and he had referred to Jesus as being "intensely class conscious."[136] This sense of class-consciousness underlay Forsey's economic arguments in *Towards the Christian Revolution*. He wrote that the first necessary step toward changing economic society was to understand that existing society first, and then to go forward in a realistic fashion. Forsey's methodology for transforming society was, therefore, a very controlled and realistic one in that he did not advocate, nor would he ever advocate, an idealistic vision of what might be. His was a reasonable approach which connected reformist measures with what was actually possible: "We must start from the world as it really is, try to find out what basic forces are in operation, then work with and through them to a new world which is possible."

Forsey's chapter in *Towards the Christian Revolution* followed this practical approach: he first sought to "understand the nature of the economic problem, and second the way in which capitalism works."[137] In pursuing this task, Forsey explained that he was applying the techniques of political economy, which he defined as "the science of the management of the public household, the community." Forsey used this approach in discussing the economic problems associated with a system that created unlimited wants, but retained only limited means of supplying those wants. Forsey pointed out that despite modern science's ability to make many more things available for the consumer, Canada's supply of natural resources and of machinery remained necessarily limited. "There is not now, and as far as we can see there never will be," wrote Forsey, "enough of everything to satisfy all of everybody's wants." In addition to that, he pointed out that in the capitalist system "our limited means have alternative uses," so the community had to decide what goods and services are to be produced and in what proportion: "how much of its limited means shall go to which uses."[138]

The bulk of Forsey's discussions in the *Towards the Christian Revolution* chapter addressed the means by which such decisions should be made. In a capitalistic society such decisions were made on the basis of the pricing mechanism and consumer demand, which in the end meant the money demand. This, Forsey believed, did not reflect need but rather the distribution of income, which in a capitalist system was "inevitably, grossly unequal." "Wants," he said, "made themselves felt not in proportion to their urgency but in proportion to the incomes of those who feel them." So, for example, while the rich could "afford" to gratify their slightest whims, "the poor could not afford even the ordinary decencies of civilized experience." The capitalist system, Forsey said, naturally responded to the former over the latter.[139]

Forsey's arguments in *Towards the Christian Revolution* provide the context within which the bulk of his Depression-era economic and political writings must be viewed. His form of Christian reformism rejected a dual view of society, that is, the separation of man's Christian life from the society in which he lived. Forsey preferred not to speak of the goodness or sinfulness of the capitalist or the worker, but rather to assess the system's "economic life" or the means by which life is lived. He applied this concept to Canadian capitalism and concluded that capitalist industry in Canada did not exist to supply needs but rather to make profits. The supply of needs, sometimes referred to by capitalists as "service to the public," was thus purely incidental. "If it pays we get it, if it doesn't we don't," Forsey wrote, and he cited census statistics on the unavailability of basic household services to rural Canadians to support his point.[140]

Forsey made it clear to his readers that he was not attempting any ethical judgement about capitalism but was establishing a fact which was valid irrespective of the moral or intellectual qualities of individual capitalists. "It is the qualities or defects of a system, not of individuals which are in question," he wrote.[141] Any capitalist who wished to remain a capitalist and pay dividends while meeting his long-term costs such as interest and rents, would be forced to look to wage cuts and layoffs as his first means of economizing. This decision had nothing to do with the capitalist's individual qualities or preferences, for "a flock of archangels administering capitalism would be under the same compulsion, and their actions could not be appreciably different."[142]

Forsey believed that man was largely shaped by the nature of the environment within which he lived and worked. "Capitalists are pretty much what capitalism makes them," he wrote, "[but] so are the rest of us. It is not a matter of blaming but of understanding." Forsey's reasoned and realistic approach to change was based on what was generally considered to be possible within an existing framework. He realized that any effective transformation in Canadian society, that is, any change that would rectify existing scarcities and inequities in the basic economic structure, would necessarily involve replacing that structure. He explained this important point in *Towards the Christian Revolution*:

> To see the problem in terms of good people and bad people is to rule out the possibility of solutions. That is a pathetic fallacy of some capitalist "reformers." No intelligent socialist has ever imagined that putting socialists in charge of capitalism – putting 'us' in place of 'them' and leaving the system still in operation – would produce any important result. The thistles would still go on producing thistles, and the thorns, thorns. We must therefore emphasize that this point is fundamental, and that unless it is clearly understood and borne constantly in mind, the whole socialist case will seem just a jumble of organized nonsense.[143]

Forsey established this argument in the first four pages of his chapter in *Towards the Christian Revolution* and used the balance of his fifty-page chapter to cite supporting statistics and further assess the Canadian capitalist system and the value of a number of capitalist reformist variables that emerged during the Depression. Forsey condemned the ongoing trend toward monopoly capitalism and its declining and wasteful variety of competition between large units. "The economics of combination are correspondingly large," he argued, "and the relatively small number of competitors makes the thing easy." Forsey cited agreements among producers, price-fixing, and other forms of industrial co-operation that had been published in the Price Spreads Commission,[144] to prove that modern capitalism was in effect monopoly capitalism.[145]

This form of capitalism, Forsey explained, resulted in a pattern of diffused and minority ownerships in which control of one or a "few companies means control of a whole industry ... and many different industries falling into the same few hands." This development was a natural by-product of the system and its associated accumulation of power by private individuals. Sounding much like a twentieth century Lord Acton, Forsey concluded that "power is poisonous to those who wield it."[146] The objection of Christians to this phase of modern capitalism should be not to the inevitable concentration but to the irresponsibility of "rulers" who, unchecked by responsibility to the welfare of the community as a whole, unconsciously identified the public interest with their own.[147]

Forsey particularly condemned monopoly capitalism's rigid price policy, which helped maintain the profits of shareholders while increasing unemployment for industrial workers and decreasing income for farmers, small businessmen and their employees in the competitive industries. Forsey also drew attention to the "transfer price" problem of monopoly capitalism that was created by "inter-industrial concentration" in which several industries and concerns were controlled by the same group of people with information on goods and services passing between them. He cited examples to prove this point, such as the "artificial pricing in the transactions of certain Canadian flour mills, bakers and Canadian branch plants with their parent concerns."[148] Forsey also repeated the Price Spreads Commission's information regarding the mass-buying practices of the massive chain stores, and the resultant decline of "consumer choice" under monopoly capitalism, in which the consumer has little choice but to accept the goods and services the monopolist had to offer. The resulting loss of "conscious freedom" was augmented by the monopolist's advertising power, which made many of the consumer choices for the public.[149]

The alternative choice for Canadians was what Forsey called "socialist planning, by responsible public servants, for the common good, planning for abundance." Forsey rejected the alternatives of either restoring competitive capitalism or enacting the form of "controlled capitalism" represented by the "New Deals" that dominated both American and Canadian political agendas in the mid-1930s.[150] He found that both of these "cheerful conclusions" suffered from the one fatal defect of disassociating ideas from the material realities to which they were supposed to refer. "This is the characteristic vice of Idealism, which Professor Macmurray describes as a pathological condition of the human mind." Forsey, for example, condemned the New Dealers' use of the phrase "state control" without any inquiry into the "material nature of the control of the material ends which it actually serves."[151] He was personally certain that in any form of capitalism, whether fascist or democratic, the strongest interests would always be the capitalist interests. "In any case," he wrote, "*government is business*," and to support his argument he quoted a 1934 Chamber of Commerce speech by CPR President Sir Edward Beatty, in which Beatty said that business "had long ago passed the stage ... where we feared the oppression of the state – for we long ago learned that we were the state."[152]

Forsey also reiterated Macmurray's belief in the need to create class-consciousness. He argued that under capitalism, "public interest" would get served only as far as it happened to coincide with the interest of the dominant class. This included the growth of public ownership, which capitalists "had excellent material reasons for establishing." He added that Canadians could be sure that if the existing degrees and type of public ownership did not serve the purpose of "business" tolerably well, it would not last long. Business, Forsey argued, "graciously permitted" the state to undertake essential but unprofitable services such as transportation and those services in which the chance of making big profits were lessened. This twentieth century form of "controlled capitalism" Forsey called "state-capitalist public ownership," that is, ownership by the state for the benefit of capitalists. This economic system, he added, inevitably produced a scarcity economy that could not solve the economic problems that Canada was facing.[153]

Forsey built a convincing argument for the need for a new economic system, but he rejected alternatives such as the Scandinavian form of consumer co-operative movement as viable even though he had been favourably impressed with that system during a 1932 visit to Scandinavia and Russia with King Gordon.[154] Forsey felt that the non-competitive nature of Canadian monopolistic capitalism was too large, powerful, and close-knit for co-operatives to get a firm foothold. The second limitation to co-operatives was that the movement did not solve "one of the main causes of war [which was] the struggle of rival national capitalisms to secure preferred access to raw materials, markets and fields of investment, especially for the heavy industries."[155] Planning without control of the producers' goods, industries, power, and transportation was, Forsey felt, impossible; and the co-operatives could not get that control, "hence its utter inadequacy to the central task of bringing in a new order."[156]

The new economic system that Canada required, and that Forsey was promoting, also required working-class control of the means of production. This was an essential component of the "new order" because it was crucial to end the capitalist class's control of the means of production in the form of plant, machinery, materials, and natural resources. Forsey felt that such control left the working class with the control of nothing but its own labour power without the means of production. Forsey believed that there existed an irreconcilable conflict between these two classes and that the working class "could never be secure or free (for there is no freedom without economic security) until it controls the means of production, and the two classes cannot control the same thing at the same time."[157]

Forsey quoted Macmurray's Belleville lectures at length in arguing that the separate communities of rich and poor were different in their whole emotional and moral attitudes. "To deny the fact of class struggle was to indulge in sheer idealism," wrote Forsey, and he explained how real substantial democracy "in which men and women are really, substantially [free] in their concrete life," could not occur as long as people in both classes went on thinking and feeling as if classes did not exist. Forsey once again explained his point by quoting his old Balliol tutor:

> As long as people are not class conscious classes will persist. When we become class-conscious it will be possible to bring classes to an end and establish real community, mutuality, genuinely personal relationships on a universal scale in a classless society.[158]

Forsey's personal vision of "Christian commonwealth" first and foremost called for an end to the "exploitation of the working class by the capitalist class for anti-Christian ends." He called on Christians "to learn to understand and apply the lessons of Marxism," especially Marx's principle that only the capture of political power and "the transfer to the state of at least the main industries and services now in capitalist hands" could bring in the new economic order. "The new society," wrote Forsey, "must be socialist through and through."[159]

Forsey's work in the Fellowship for a Christian Social Order, and most importantly his chapter in *Towards the Christian Revolution*, represented the synthesis of his multi-faceted search for a statement of Christian socialism. Forsey's work in the three religious associations mentioned in this chapter, the Student Christian Movement, the Committee on Social and Economic Research, and the Fellowship for a Christian Social Order, was the mechanism through which he formulated and expressed his personal statement on the need for a

Christian-oriented "revolution" in Canada's economic structure. The "new economic order" that Forsey advocated during the Depression years must be viewed through this prism of Christian principles if the messages he was disseminating are to be understood correctly. Forsey's Christian socialism was the expression of a philosophy that he had been slowly developing during his early years at McGill and his later Oxford experience. It was a message that Forsey soon expounded through secular as well as religious organizations.

"REAL DEMOCRACY": 1930–1935

The five years between 1930 and 1935 were important ones as far as Eugene Forsey's progressive intellectual movement toward socialism was concerned. During this period two major factors confirmed in Forsey's mind the fact that for him, as for many other Canadians, socialism represented Canada's only hope for long-term economic prosperity and individual freedom for its citizens. The first factor was the continued social and economic havoc of the Depression and the failure of either major political party to address the associated problems. The second factor was Forsey's 1932 tour through Russia with King Gordon.

By 1930 the debilitating affects of the Depression were being felt in every region of the nation. On the Prairies it marked the beginning of the "Dirty Thirties," a decade full of defeat and despair, "whirling plagues of dust and grasshoppers," cruel winters, hunger, and boredom. As westerners faced these conditions together, there evolved a "collective experience that was as important in the development of the West's regional society as the era of the pioneer." As a result, prairie farmers opposed both Liberal and Conservative high tariff policies and restricted markets, and small businessmen demanded to be compensated at the national expense just as the manufacturers were protected at the farmers' expense.[2]

In central Canada, Ontario's usually steady economy was caught up in the country's continuing economic decline,[3] and Forsey's home province of Quebec faced mass unemployment, falling incomes, breadlines, and deprivations affecting all sections of the people.[4] On the east coast, the numbers of Maritimers placed on the dole increased, as did their fear and uncertainty as their economy collapsed around them.[5]

Facing deteriorating conditions and increased provincial hostility to its narrow definition of its own responsibilities for the needy, the King government's past rigidity on unemployment turned into a disastrous political liability. In February 1930, with 323,000 homeless and unemployment standing at 12.5 per cent, King still refused to take the crisis seriously. It was, he maintained, only a "temporary seasonal slackness."[6]

Not all Canadians shared Mackenzie King's perfunctory attitude. At a small resort on the shores of Lake Wonish, north of Montreal, five men, Graham Spry, Brooke Claxton, Terry McDermott, Frank Scott, and Eugene Forsey, sandwiched between a good deal of swimming and "play of several kinds" three lengthy meetings regarding the production of a book dealing with the political, economic, constitutional, and social problems of the country.[7] Blair Neatby contends that the 1930s represented a turning point and the beginning of a new era marked by "the emergence of modern Canada, in which new institutions and new policies were initiated to cope with the problems created by the slumping national economy."[8]

Though such a breakthrough had not yet occurred in the 1930s, the search for new ideas had most certainly begun on the shores of Lake Wonish.

The "group," as they called themselves, had been working for over six months on the book project "in the belief that a sincere attempt to develop a consistent political theory for Canada would meet with widespread interest" by the general public for whom the book was being specially prepared.[9] Just six days prior to the Wonish sessions, Canadians had given R.B. Bennett's Conservatives 137 of 245 seats in the House of Commons, the most decisive singular Conservative victory since the nineteenth century.[10] Though all five of the men who gathered at Wonish had voted Conservative, their general feeling was that the election had "showed more than ever the useful purposes of such a book."[11]

This proposed book was to be the first of many projects generally referred to as "the scheme," whose goal was to present a fresh and consistent system of political thought encompassing politics; the constitution; fiscal and monetary policy; external affairs and in particular Canada's relationship with the Empire; transportation, industry, and commerce; labour; immigration and assimilation; French and English relations; and the accumulation of Canadian art and culture through the promotion of the arts.[12]

The specific purposes of the book were outlined in the introduction to the manuscript. They included the necessity of filling "the widespread need for a general description of the distinctive Canadian Character" and putting forward a consistent political theory that would not be specifically Canadian, but also neither anti-British nor anti-American. It was rather, to be "Liberal, Conservative and progressive," while maintaining and developing the Canadian character "without closing the cultural door."[13]

This theme was pursued in detail in a proposed chapter entitled "Co-Operation" that outlined the unique potential Canada possessed for co-operative citizen participation in the workings of the state. This was already occurring, the authors pointed out, through the active involvement of Canadians in co-operatives such as the wheat pools, provincial hydro and telephone companies, "the proposed radio control and others such as the Bankers Associations, Chambers of Commerce, and Canadian Clubs." But despite this involvement, Canadians showed "qualities and defects of intense individualism." The book, therefore, addressed the significance of the "two manifestations" of pluralistic co-operation and rampant individualism existing in the same country and offered suggestions on how the two could work more harmoniously.[14]

The fact that the book was never published is not as important as the interest and concern that its planning reflected. Forsey's participation in "the scheme" reveals how deeply he felt the need for new solutions to Canada's economic and social ills. But for Forsey the project was only a beginning, and he remained very active throughout that decade in expressing his views on the inherent weaknesses in Canada's political and economic system and his solutions for rectifying those problems.

Forsey was employed throughout the 1930s as a Lecturer in Economics at McGill, but he never enjoyed the luxury of more than a one-year appointment at any time. Though he was very much involved in expressing his beliefs through the religiously oriented associations discussed previously, Forsey's position at McGill allowed him to express his views as an individual "professional social scientist" through secular organizations such as the League for Social Reconstruction (LSR). But because of many personal frustrations and preferences, Forsey also wrote for public consumption as an individual, free from the auspices of the League. Through his involvement in secular organizations such as "the Group" and the LSR, and in his personal work, Forsey practised his motto that an academic economist had a dual responsibility to work as scientist and as citizen.

To Forsey, the economist as scientist was a "technical expert," whose business was not "to denounce Communism or praise capitalism, or vice versa; nor to say what kind of economic system was ethically most desirable." The expert's role, rather, was to explain how different economic systems worked and how efficiently these systems succeeded in doing what the particular country or society intended them to do. "Whether a particular social objective is admirable or detestable," said Forsey in a radio address on McGill's Graduate Society Radiologue, "is to the economist in his purely professional capacity – in the classroom for example – a matter of complete indifference."[15] If discussing the tariff, for example, the "expert economist" would impartially present the facts, agreeable or otherwise, to all parties and explain its economic effects. This would provide material for "intelligent ethical judgments." A second, more urgent and socially conscious duty of the economist as technical expert was to help spread economic enlightenment by "demolishing the flood of well-meaning economic nonsense; facts, quackeries and plausible fallacies of every conceivable kind, based on ancient economic errors which were particularly prevalent during periods of industrial depression."[16] Forsey's performance in the former of these two roles seemed to be limited to his classroom work at McGill. Almost all of his writings and extracurricular work during the 1930s fell into the economist's second, more socially active role.

"The economist is not merely an economist," Forsey said in 1934, "he is also a citizen, with a citizen's ordinary rights and duties, and a peculiar obligation to use his special knowledge in performing a citizen's function." This role differed dramatically from that of the "pure" economist, who was "not concerned with the justice or injustice of the social order." Forsey further explained the economist's role as citizen:

> As a citizen, he has the same rights as anyone to state his views and act on them. He is entitled, for example, to join a political party, to work for it as actively as conscientious performance of his professional work will allow, and especially, to do what he can to ensure that the economic policies it adopts are effective means of reaching the goal the party has set itself. In so doing he serves not only the party, but the community in general, for a party which "goes it

blind" without sound economic advice, is likely to do a good deal of mischief even with the best intentions.[17]

Forsey bolstered his argument by citing a list of British dons, including Laski and Cole, who in recent years had taken an active role in political parties as energetic campaigners and pamphleteers.

Forsey added that in this respect McGill "followed the British tradition." Frank Scott, J.C. Hemmeon, and Leacock, were, for example, three McGill academics who served on Royal Commissions and Labour Conciliation Boards, stood for Parliament, "took the stump" for different political parties, and lectured and wrote books on various political and economic subjects. Forsey praised McGill's Principal Sir Arthur Currie for understanding and defending academic freedom, "especially for the several members of the McGill staff who were members of the League for Social Reconstruction." Forsey included himself in the ranks of McGill academics who were active in society in a citizen's role. "My own work in the past year," he said, "has included over forty public lectures and speeches, ... a political convention, a church conference, two non-partisan summer schools, a pamphlet now at the press, and a chapter or so contributed to a forthcoming book on Canadian economics."[18]

Spurred on by the deteriorating social and economic conditions of the early 1930s, Forsey plunged deeply into the more public "citizen" economist's role and in actual fact he published very little technical economic material. He preferred to write material in which he could argue for the type of social and economic changes he felt were necessary in Canadian society. Following the demise of the Wonish book project, Forsey wasted little time in stating how he would personally rectify the serious inequalities of the Canadian capitalism and democracy. Both, he argued, were controlled by the "pure economic individualism [of society's] vested interests." Forsey's major goal throughout the Depression was to define those inequalities, identify the mechanisms by which the "vested interests" shaped the policies that produced those inequalities, and recommend how the system could be improved to eradicate, or at least minimize, those inequalities.

By 1932, then, Forsey felt that he had discovered the essential ingredients for change. In a speech to the Canadian Political Science Association in that year, Forsey addressed the failure of "pure economic individualism, mitigated by factory acts, social services, minimum wage laws and trade union action." The only practical policy, Forsey thought, was one that reflected "some attempt at conscious intelligent direction and social control of our economy," based on a national planning effort. But how much planning was Forsey, the "Tory democrat" of the 1920s, prepared to accept in the depression-ridden 1930s? Simply stated, Forsey believed that four basic ingredients were essential to any national plan: central banking, export marketing, control of investment, and control over labour supply.

First, Forsey argued that it was essential to ensure a stable level of general prices because it was impossible for any planning agency to make calculations "for years ahead in terms of a unit of measurement which varies from month to month." Control of the price level through central banking machinery would ensure the monetary stability that was required for long-term national planning.[19]

The second essential element required in any national planning exercise involved control of foreign trade. This meant that Canada would have to continue to protect herself from sudden international economic action such as "temporary or sporadic dumping" of goods into her home market. Forsey argued that this control need not mean "protection," but rather the unified selling of exports by export boards and the bulk purchase of imports by import boards. This would ensure that the Canadian economy would be thoroughly integrated and allow Canadians to more easily realize "how silly it was to make expensively at home what we can buy cheaply elsewhere." This could only serve to stabilize prices and assist the consumer. For Forsey the key to the success of this planning mechanism was the action of the planning authority, whose aim was to sell Canadian exports for as high a price as possible and use its foreign credits to supply the import needs of the community at as low a price as possible. The export boards, Forsey explained, would then "sell their foreign bills to the planning authority or some subdivision of it, which would re-sell them to the import boards." Export and import boards taken together would have a monopoly of foreign trade.[20]

Thirdly, the planning authority must be able to control investment. One of the worst features of the economic anarchy of the early 1930s, Forsey said, was the waste of capital and natural resources which occurred through the overdevelopment of certain industries such as Canadian railways and the coal industry in Alberta: "To put an end to this sort of thing involved negatively, the power to veto the establish-ment of new enterprises or the extension of old ones; positively, the direction of investment into socially necessary channels." The planning authority would ensure that banks, insurance companies, and other financial institutions would be required to hold certain proportions of their funds in specified investments.[21]

A fourth feature of Forsey's planned economy was control over the labour supply. This involved controlling levels of immigration and "the industrial transference" of hours and wages. Forsey explained that:

> This effective planning would clearly involve either bringing new
> people into the country at one time or keeping them out at another,
> shifting workers from place to place and industry to industry, and
> seeing that they get enough wages and enough leisure at least to
> keep them fit for their jobs.

Inseparably bound up with these four controls, he added, was the power to force reorganization of any industry which did not reach a prescribed level of efficiency. A planned economy could not tolerate incompetence.[22]

These four essential controls defined the parameters of Forsey's socialism throughout the 1930s and into the post-World War II recon-struction era. Whereas the principles of Christian brotherhood pro-vided the reasons why change was essential, these four economic controls identified the guidelines for the planned system that would ensure that change occurred. Without at least these powers, Forsey could not "see how any kind of planning authority, socialist or capital-ist, could function at all." This speech, and his subsequent work, illus-trate Forsey's desire to create a sense of Canadian class-consciousness. This was a goal that Forsey, since his exposure to John Macmurray at Oxford, had been convinced was an absolute prerequisite before Canadians would accept the need for any comprehensive national plan-ning process. Forsey had been taught, and had come to accept, that only by convincing Canadians that class differences really existed in their society could "real democracy" occur.

Central planning, Forsey argued, could never work within a capi-talist system because "any attempt at capitalist planning [was] bound at once to run up against stiff opposition from vested interests." He believed that a stable pricing level, while good for the community as a whole, might not by any means be advantageous for everyone in the community. Central banking, he suggested, would be subject to heavy pressure from "interested groups to deflect it from its proper work." Even the miniscule amount of central banking that had been attempted in Canada, he said, was resisted to the "last gasp" by the commercial bankers.[23] Forsey cited evidence given by Canadian bankers before the House of Commons banking committee in 1923 and 1928 to support his argument.[24] "Any real efforts to control imports for the public good," he believed, "would meet similar opposition, and control by industry itself would be nothing more than a new and obnoxious form of exploitation."[25]

Forsey rejected the argument that in a capitalist system "enlightened self-interest would induce competing firms to unify their sales organizations," and he cited "depressing" examples from British, American, and Canadian experience to prove his point. The life of the few central selling agencies which had been formed voluntarily had, he added, been as a rule "poor, nasty, solitary, brutish and short." Voluntary reorganization "from within," whether in the banking or industrial sectors, he felt, was at best a "slow and painful process," and capitalist governments were even slower to force the pace:

> To suggest that capitalist business or its political instruments will ever undertake to control investment seems, to me the pinnacle of futility. Indeed the only part of the whole planning notion to which capitalism is likely to take to at all kindly is a "suitable" form of control of the labour supply. That, no doubt, it would accept with enthusiasm. But even this country which seems easily to bear away the palm for docility, would hardly, one hopes, be prepared to hand over its entire working class to the arbitrary discretion of a group of employers.[26]

Forsey believed that the powers that were indispensable to any planning authority were far too great to be entrusted to private persons or to a capitalist-controlled government. "The prospect of import boards made up of, or under the control of, persons interested in domestic industries which might suffer from foreign competition," Forsey concluded, was one which "no man could face with equanimity." Here

Forsey drew on his knowledge of Adam Smith in arguing that the acts of such vested interests would be those of a class whose interest was often to deceive and oppress the public "and who have accordingly on many occasions both deceived and oppressed it."[27]

Forsey rejected a system which permitted "irresponsible authorities to bring into the country whom it chose, send people where it chose, pay them what it chose, work them as long as it chose or establish whatever industries it chose." Such a freely organized power "would be a tyrant without parallel in history." Powers of this kind, said Forsey:

> ... were simply intolerable except in the hands of disinterested persons responsible to the community, and limited by a hundred percent rock-ribbed trade union organization with a recognized right to strike, in every industry in the country.[28]

A natural plan was required, but in early 1932 Forsey was still advocating a very tempered social message that shied away from any suggestion of radical class antagonisms. He told his Political Science Association audience, for example, that only a socialist government could produce a plan which would be effective and "safe for democracy, [but that the] object of the whole thing [was] not a fundamental social change but merely the ironing out of fluctuations; the steadying, regulating, stabilizing of our present social order; more security for all classes, but security in their present relative positions." This objective was, in Forsey's view a limited one; but it was unattainable except under socialist government "bent not only on the public good, but socialist in that it fostered economic democracy based on something like equality of income" to balance each class's political power and influence.[29]

Forsey's call for a redistribution of wealth was in his view the only effective policy that would eradicate "the vast gulf which still divided the 'two nations' of rich and poor." It was also the only permanent policy which would "get the sources of wealth into public ownership and under public control ... to use not a fraction but the whole of the proceeds for public purposes." This was Forsey's political rallying cry for the 1930s. He had by 1932 abandoned any hope of effecting the necessary degree of change through Canada's two major political parties. A new political movement was required:

> Unless we are prepared to turn the world upside down, prepared
> to work a social revolution – not necessarily by violent means – we
> cannot build up a political movement strong enough to apply any
> kind of plan. The task is immense. The driving force must come
> from the mass of the people, from the uncomfortable classes. To
> think that we can rouse them to the necessary pitch by offering them
> security in their discomfort is to my mind perfectly fantastic. Just try
> to run an election on a slogan to that sort and see what happens.[30]

The degree of social transformation required by the planned economy, he now believed, could not be accomplished by traditional reform
measures such as taxation and social services, but was now dependent
upon the acceptance of a "communist philosophy." Forsey was not,
in this instance, referring to "hopelessly stuffy Marxian economic
theory," but rather to the type of democracy discussed by "the Master
of Balliol," A.D. Lindsay, in his little book called *The Essentials of
Democracy* when he wrote, "the poorest he that hath a life to live as the
richest he."[31]

In his book, which was a collection of speeches that had been published in 1929, Lindsay discussed the essential social role of voluntary
associations. Not only did they help to make and form public opinion,
but they could also fight the "abuse of political power by powerful
interests against the individual [who was] singularly helpless on his or
her own individual accord."[32] There was, therefore, a great need for
church, university, and reform-oriented associations that could create
"real public opinion" and alter the public's complacent optimism about
democracy. Forsey saw in Lindsay's work another expression of the
need to raise class-consciousness.

In his speech to the Canadian Political Science Association, Forsey
had identified the principles and philosophy he was prepared to fight
for. He intended simply to perform his citizen economist role by convincing the Canadian public that the planned economy was needed,
and that necessitated a frontal attack on the vested interests. Only after
clearly identifying the activities of those interests could Forsey's driving
force for change emerge from the mass of the people. Forsey's socialism at this point seems, therefore, to have been connected to raising
public awareness of the basic inequalities of the capitalist system, with
the expectation that the proletariat would then be awarded more power

through the political process and through reasoned class and group negotiations associated with the pluralistic society.[33]

Forsey had for some time prior to his spring 1932 speech to the Canadian Political Science Association been working with a small group of Montreal academics and professionals to plan a society that might play a similar role in Canada as that played by the Fabian Society in Britain.[34] The Montreal sessions were hosted by Marion and Frank Scott and followed discussions that Frank Scott had undertaken the previous summer with Toronto historian Frank Underhill.[35] Attending the 1931 autumn meetings along with Scott and Forsey were King Gordon, David Lewis, then a young McGill law student, and Joseph Mergler, a Montreal labour lawyer.[36] By November of that year the Montreal group had forwarded to Underhill and his fellow Torontonians a programme for the proposed society.[37]

Over the following winter the two urban-based groups discussed the many details of the proposed society, including its name. Perhaps because the American theologian Harry Ward had just given a speech in Montreal called "The Need for Economic Democracy," the Montrealers favoured the name "The League for Economic Democracy." The Toronto group preferred "The League for Social Reconstruction."[38]

Forsey's notations on the amended draft programme which circulated between Montreal and Toronto over those months indicate that he preferred a more concise statement of principles but he fully supported the as yet unnamed society's main contention, which was capitalism's "failure to evolve a planned economy [and the] inherent evils in an economic system based on private profit." The League recommended "a new social order which [would] substitute a planned economy for the present chaotic competitive individualism and which [would] aim at that equality of opportunity for all citizens without which real freedom is non-existent."[39]

Forsey continued to participate actively in the newly formed League for Social Reconstruction, though his contributions were very much in a supporting research capacity during the League's earlier years. In January 1932, he travelled by train to Toronto with Scott, Gordon, Lewis, and Mergler to work out the details of the proposed organization.[40] By February the LSR's Reconstruction Manifesto, which was largely the work of the Montreal group, according the League's historian Michiel Horn, was completed.[41] It called for the establishment of a social order in which "the basic principle regulating production, distribution and service will be the common good rather than private profit." The Manifesto's proposed methods of achieving the planned and socialized economy almost completely mirror the mechanisms which Forsey presented that same winter to the Canadian Political Science Association. These included socialized banking and investment "to direct investment into socially desirable channels"; public owner-ship of transport and major utilities; the establishment of import and export boards for the regulation of foreign trade; extensive social legis-lation; augmented Dominion powers ("to deal effectively with urgent economic problems which are essentially national,"); and a foreign policy designed to obtain international economic co-operation and to promote disarmament and world peace. These were policies that Forsey had urged in his Canadian Political Science Association speech, and also in an earlier article in the Supplement to the McGill *News* in which he publicly recommended "moral considerations" in the eco-nomic policy formulation process. This, Forsey argued, was important so that we could "make reasonably sure that our morality is valid, and that we [could] realize the economic consequences of our action."[42]

At the inaugural meeting of the Montreal Branch of the LSR, Forsey declined election to the Branch Executive but accepted a position on the Branch's Research Committee along with Leonard Marsh and a Dr. Frank Pedley.[43] In keeping with the League's commitment to public education, the purpose of the research committees was to organize the preparation of pamphlets that would be written by members of the League. Two such pamphlets, one dealing with tariffs and the other with "constitutional problems," were soon underway. In addition, two subcommittees were activated; one to investigate the power situation in Montreal and the other to conduct a survey of the condition of employment in certain Montreal department stores.[44] The findings of these two subcommittees were then to be reviewed by the Research Committee before they were made public. Membership on both the subcommittees was to remain anonymous in order to give opportuni-ties for useful work to members "whose position or employment made it difficult to associate themselves publicly with the particular inquiry." Apparently the members of the Research Committee were attempting to protect the League and themselves from any negative responses from establishment figures.[45]

In keeping with the League's stated aim to educate Canadian public opinion in the principles and proposals outlined in its Manifesto, the League's Constitution encouraged local branches to hold public meetings and forums "to which members of the general public [were] invited to hear speakers who expressed in general, the point of view of the League." Branch members were also encouraged to provide speeches "to clubs, church groups, trade unions, farmers' organizations, and other bodies which are receptive to the League's ideals."[46]

Such a publicly oriented propaganda programme was ideally suited to Forsey, and he was nominated to speak in an upcoming debate entitled "Canada's Way Out."[47] To accommodate the public this debate was held in the Strathcona Hall, a location that Forsey was familiar with because of the many SCM functions he had attended there. On April 23, 1932, he faced his opponent, Mr. Francis Hankin, who was not a LSR member.[48] Hankin argued as an "advanced liberal" on the need for Canadians to make use of their "existing economic and political order" in working toward a more wisely planned economy. He contended that in its established entities such as its Railway Boards and the Public Service Commission, Canada had "much of the necessary machinery" to implement that planned economy but reiterated his belief in the need for a new political and economic system to replace Canada's existing capitalist system. He argued that "the attempt to humanize the capitalist order by appointing guardians to watch over it had always failed and would always fail," basically because those "guardians" would always represent "the moneyed classes whom they are supposed to control." What was needed, he emphasized, was "no less than the eradication of opportunities for the private exploitation of the sources of wealth."[49]

Forsey's commitment to socialism strengthened during the summer following his Canadian Political Science Association speech and LSR debate, when he and Gordon toured through Russia, Scandinavia, and Germany. The trip offered Forsey the opportunity to personally compare two vastly different political ideologies at work. On the one hand Forsey was shocked at the "advanced stage" of fascism in Germany,[50] but he was tremendously impressed with the socialistic state that had evolved in Russia from the ashes of World War I. Both he and Gordon returned to Canada with a deepened commitment toward practicality and humanity associated with the planned socialist state.

Russians in the summer of 1932 exuded confidence that their first experiment with the national economic planning had worked. The success of the socialist experiment seemed to be affirmed for many Russians when Stalin declared the first Five-Year Plan fulfilled and launched the second.[51] In many ways the Russian system centred around its "Gosplan" planning agency, which determined how much of every article the country should produce, how much of the national effort should go into the formation of capital and how much into producing articles for daily consumption. It also, they discovered, determined workers' wage levels. The Plan, according to R.R. Palmer, "undertook to control ... the flow of resources and manpower which under free capitalism was regulated by shifts in demand and supply, through changes in prices, wage levels, profits, interest rates and rent."[52]

Forsey's diary of his Russia trip, as well as his and King Gordon's personal recollections of the experience, suggest that much of what Forsey saw, heard, and read during the entire trip had a major impact on his personal socialistic beliefs. For example, Forsey read three books "on the organization and workings of Soviet industry, trade and finance" during the boat trip to Europe. He wrote in his diary at that time that he was a socialist and was committed to socialism because it involved the "speeding up of the enrichment" of the working class and it opposed the capitalist urge to increase production merely to enrich employers.[53] And with the infringements of civil liberties in Canada fresh in his mind,[54] Forsey wrote that while Canadians must avoid the Russian Revolution's "horror and hysteria," they must also learn from the Russian experience. "The more stupid repression our government goes in for," Forsey wrote, "the more drastic a retribution it's preparing for itself."[55]

The first impression of Russia that Forsey wrote about to his mother was his observation that "one couldn't but be impressed by the air of competence, quiet efficiency and good discipleship, yet *comradeship* in the place."[56] He was also particularly impressed with the "unmistakable spirit of hope and confidence everywhere here." An American journalist, a reporter from the *Cleveland Plain Dealer*,[57] and one of only two others who travelled with Forsey and Gordon in their very small entourage, explained to Forsey what an enormous change for the better had occurred in Russian society since he had been in the country three years previously. This improvement, the American explained, was not only material but psychological as well: "Three years ago they hoped the show would succeed," wrote Forsey, "[but] now they feel sure it will, and all of us feel sure it will. The young people are especially amazing."[58]

Forsey, being well grounded in John Macmurray's philosophy of concerted thought and action, was particularly impressed with the evidence that the Russians had successfully followed the "fundamental principle of uniting theory and practice." It was also not surprising that the evidence of economic and social progress impressed Forsey, given the deplorable and deteriorating circumstances he had left behind in Canada. The Russians' socialist planning task, Forsey recorded in his Diary, was "the biggest job, far and away, that any government undertook [after the War] and it's being done staggeringly fast, faster than anything like it has ever been done."[59]

Forsey was also particularly impressed with Russia's excellent health and education systems. He observed that children's health standards seemed to be very high. Russian children for the most part seemed to be healthy and happy, an observation that was supported by a discussion he had with a doctor who had worked in England and who was convinced that the Russian public health system was better than England's system. Forsey also spoke with an "Oxford man who professes to have seen great achievement in training peasants to be good nurses in one year." He concluded:

> There's no question that in this regard they're doing admirable work and on large scale. There are big, clean and modern clinics, for example, wherever one goes. They are very well equipped and thoroughly good ... complete with most ingenious special sections for children.[60]

Forsey was also impressed with the Russians' overall perspective toward health as involving both psychological and physical care. This was illustrated for him during a visit to a creative cultural centre for children. Forsey was certain that "no one knew we were coming," and he was most fascinated with the philosophy of exposing children to a variety of musical, dramatic, and recreational experiences at a young age. If Forsey suspected any propagandistic aspects to these "creative cultural centres," he did not indicate so in his diary.[61]

113

Forsey was similarly impressed with the competence of the staff of an Economic Institute he visited. He agreed with his hosts' conclusion that "the prime necessity was to establish a basis of heavy industries, the foundations from which alone a civilized Socialist society could arise."[62] Forsey was particularly struck with the broad and positive perspective of Russian students. He wrote, for example, that

> one of the most striking things about Russia is the enthusiasm, the spontaneity of the students and young people generally; their feeling of entering into a larger life and being part of a vast and splendid work for humanity; as contrasted with the apathy and drift of our students, their feeling of hopelessness or doubt or fear about their future. Their complete lack of relation to any social work. [sic][63]

Forsey also visited the Gosplan State Planning Commission, where he took "copious notes regarding the details of the technical aspects of planning." While there, he had lengthy discussions with Gosplan officials regarding his Quaker religion and about the fact the he was "not actually a member of any political party." Regarding that discussion, Forsey later recorded in his diary that: "I am in opinion an advanced Socialist, and very sympathetic with much that the USSR is doing, and trying to do. I am not now actually in any Party."[64]

Forsey and Gordon toured Russia for a month and both read a great deal during that time. Forsey was particularly impressed with two economists, Julian Huxley and Gustav Cassel. The latter economist, Forsey wrote, "was the post-war economist," and his writings definitely increased Forsey's sense of urgency with respect to socialistic change for Canada.[65] As Forsey was preparing to leave in late July, he wrote to his mother that he was very impressed with the Russians' "hard thinking of the large questions (freedom, economics etc.)." He added that his experience had focused his concern about the future of Canadian socialism and the prospect that the failure of peaceful change would result in the polarization of politics in Canada as had occurred in Germany:

> Unless Socialists who believe in peaceful change show at least as much capacity for hard thinking, hard work and self-sacrifice as the Communists have shown in Russia, and unless they show it quickly, I'm convinced that we shall have to choose not between what we

have and what we should like to have, not between the actual and the ideal, but between what we have and the best of several not very pleasant alternatives. Events everywhere are moving at a terrible pace. It may not be long before other countries reach the place where Germany now is – where the only alternatives are Communism and some form of Fascism. The worst of it is that our governments are so stupid, and the dice are so heavily loaded against any peaceful revolution.[66]

For Forsey the Russian trip was "quite the biggest thing that ever happened to me.... Russia's given me a better sense of proportion." Forsey was now anxious to return to McGill to share his observations, though he realized that "this winter I may find that I'm not as free academically as I should be."[67] The trip had reinforced his commitment to help preserve civil liberties as a necessary part of the advancement of peaceful socialistic change. He was, therefore, convinced that he had a responsibility to become active in leading the "peaceful revolution that would be associated with the necessary transformation from capitalism to socialism."[68] The alternatives, he wrote, were less attractive:

I'm convinced also that the revolutionary changes which are needed can be brought about by peaceful means. But I'm sure at the same time that the sands are running out. If we don't very soon do the job peacefully, it will be done otherwise, but done it will and must be. Those of us who believe in peaceful methods have a job quite as big as the other one here.... It calls for quite as much heroism, self-sacrifice, and hard realistic thinking [and] higher leadership than Lenin's.[68]

Given this sense of urgency, and the missionary zeal with which Forsey returned to McGill in the fall of 1932, it is not surprising that he plunged into LSR work with renewed energy.

Despite his extremely hectic workload at McGill, and his church-related commitments as outlined previously, Forsey readily accepted the task of forming an LSR Study Group dedicated to examining the details and benefits of national planning.[69] Later in 1933 Forsey accepted an opportunity to become integrally involved in the cause of Canadian socialist planning. In January of that year the Provisional National Council of the newly formed Canadian Commonwealth Federation

(CCF) requested the assistance of the LSR Research Committee in drawing up a tentative draft of a political programme based on the CCF principles established at its Calgary conference held the previous August. The timing of the CCF request was interesting, for the Montreal Branch had just opposed Underhill's recommendation that the LSR affiliate with the CCF.[70] The Montreal Branch's opposition was naturally on record as supporting the CCF, but it also passed a motion that the LSR not become affiliated as a "constituent member" of the new party.[71]

Though he cites no references, Michiel Horn has written that the Montrealers feared that too close an association with the CCF socialists would interfere with the LSR's attempts to reach the intelligentsia.[72] Though it is true that the Montrealers wished to remove any reference to the word "socialist" in LSR matters, there are additional reasons for its opposition to political affiliation. At the September 1933 Montreal Executive meeting the point was made that the main reason for opposing affiliation with the CCF was that there were "no steps" which could be taken by the LSR to assist the CCF in Montreal "owing to the absence of any real political labour organization in this city."[73] At the LSR's second annual convention in late January 1933, the debate raged on, and those opposed to affiliation advanced five reasons for their position: participation in political action would divert the League's research and education duties; the League might have to modify and compromise its opinions to keep pace with the CCF; affiliation would necessarily alienate certain individuals, notably civil servants and those in official positions who would be of inestimable value to the League; and lastly, association with the word "socialist" would alienate the Roman Catholic Church.[74]

Such points did not necessarily preclude assisting the CCF in the drafting of its Manifesto and various organizational details, but Forsey and his fellow Montrealers viewed their LSR duties very much in a public educational role. This role included assisting the CCF, but at this point there was little support for any steps that might lead to a more highly visible political role for the League. More important was the research and background writing required to implement the planned state.

Forsey, Gordon, and Joseph Parkinson did, however, agree to assist the CCF in drafting its own Manifesto at its Regina Convention in the summer of 1933. The three men set out by car for the west, with a copy of Underhill's draft CCF manifesto, to lend whatever assistance they could. Forsey and Parkinson had had time to discuss the draft while the two men attended a YMCA Institute on Politics and Economics at Geneva Park, Ontario earlier in the summer. On their way to Regina the three travellers attended a second YMCA Institute at Lake of the Woods where they were received as guest speakers and reviewed Underhill's draft once again.[75]

Their reception in Regina was somewhat less enthusiastic than they anticipated, although they were invited to participate in two days of closed discussions with CCF organizers. These discussions were followed by two more days of discussion in the Convention itself, and by all accounts they "took a prominent part in all the proceedings of the convention." Yet Forsey recalls that they were not totally welcomed by the westerners. Their inquiry into the specifics of the western-sponsored agricultural policy, for example, was met with a rude suggestion that their watered-down eastern brand of socialism was not welcomed in the west. They were rather abruptly advised to keep their opinions to themselves.[76]

Forsey's major contribution to the socialist cause of the LSR, and indirectly the CCF, lay not with his participation at the Regina Conference, but his continuing efforts at defining the planned economy and the policies that best articulated that goal. Joseph Parkinson, an economist at the University of Toronto during the 1930s, later recalled that neither he nor Forsey were as interested in socialism in the doctrinaire Marxist sense during the 1930s as they were with their own version of social democracy. As Parkinson explains:

> We addressed ... the problems of organization and management of production and distribution. We were most concerned with the allocation of resources for the general good of society – that is using all our human and material resources in the most effective manner.

Parkinson and Forsey assumed that the planned society could be implemented without their thinking about the consequences of the loss of market forces or political corruption in the allocation of resources such as occurred later in Soviet Russia. "There was," said Parkinson, "a feeling that we couldn't lose under socialism."[77] Parkinson recalled that the social views that he and Forsey shared addressed the general moral

principles of a social and economic system "that left many on the outside with little chance to contribute."[78] In this regard Parkinson specifically recalled Forsey's concentration on exposing the monopolistic
tendencies of Canadian capitalism and its threat to the welfare of certain Canadian classes.

This was a reality that Forsey addressed in his first major article in
the *Canadian Forum* entitled "Concentration in Canadian Industry."
This article is an important expression of Forsey's commitment to creating class-consciousness in Canadian society, and his decision to publish in the *Forum* was a natural one because the *Forum* had been since
the 1920s, "the voice of left-wing political attitudes" and in the fore-
front of intellectual radicalism in Canada.[79]

In his article Forsey chronicled the fact that "financial and industrial power in this country was concentrated in the hands of a very
small group."[80] He analyzed the financial system of banks, trust and
loan companies, and life insurance companies, and found in all cases
"the development of combination ... particularly striking." So too with
power companies, the pulp and paper industry, the iron and steel and
nickel industries, the cement industry, oil companies, textile, milling
and tobacco companies, and the breweries and distilleries. In just a few
pages Forsey provided a detailed analysis of interrelated directorships
and the extremely small numbers of powerful men who controlled virtually all of Canada's industrial apparatus. "A handful of titans," Forsey
wrote, "perhaps a hundred persons, here and abroad, decide what
we shall eat, what we shall drink, wherewithal we shall be clothed, and
most other of our activities." Forsey also dismissed the argument that it
was a dispersed group of shareholders, not the directors, who controlled
these industries. Few Canadians, he argued, made enough money to
invest in shares, since "only about 144,000 people in Canada receive
income enough to be taxable, about 82,000 of these get $4,000.00 a
year or less, and that three percent of the population gets 20 percent
of the income." Forsey concluded by illustrating the inadequacy of
Canada's existing economic system and its methods of self-regulation:

> Whatever one's opinion of the tendency towards concentration of
> control in Canadian finance and industry, the fact itself is inescap-
> able and sheds a somewhat lurid light on proposals for "controlling"
> capitalism in this country. Quis custodiet custodes ipsos?[81]

Forsey's role as "citizen economist" was to reveal for Canadians the facts that underlay the reality of class divisions in Canadian society. Only by doing this would the Canadian public accept the need for socialist planning and initiate a "peaceful revolution" associated with the redistribution of income and power in Canada. To this end it was necessary to illustrate for wage-earning Canadians the effect that extreme corporate concentration had on their lives. This Forsey attempted to do in two subsequent publications. In a *Canadian Forum* article published in November 1933, entitled "Equality of Sacrifice," Forsey examined the interrelationship between dividends, salaries, and wages, and concluded that in the first phase of deflation, such as the Depression Canada was then encountering, firms were inclined to economize by first reducing their wage bills by layoffs and a reduction of wage rates. In contrast, dividends and salaries were less "susceptible to easy adjustment" because it was more essential to the corporate image and administrative framework to do so. Economizing was essential due to combined falling prices and reduced sales. But with steady fixed charges, such as bond interest, the firms would necessarily turn to forms of wage control. The salary staff contracts were usually for a longer period of time and often went to the members of the owning class, who might even be important shareholders in the firm that employed them.[82]

This pattern of keeping dividend and salary payments "up to their prosperity level while wage-bills go down," Forsey argued, "was especially the case with monopolies and semi-monopolies, especially if they sell in a protected market." In a style that was now becoming his trademark, Forsey supported his argument with detailed dividend, salary, and wage statistics from dozens of Canadian industries between 1930 and 1933. He contrasted "sheltered" and "unsheltered" industries; the latter being those most dependent upon export markets. From his myriad of statistics, Forsey concluded that in 1930 it was clear that "the real income of shareholders increased while the real income of wage-earners fell."[83] Forsey repeated his analysis for 1931 and 1932 and concluded that:

> In short, Canadian industry in 1930 not only economized on wage-
> bills to the extent necessary to keep dividends up to the 1929
> level, but actually used the depression as a pretext for increasing

dividends at the expense of wage-earners. In 1931 and 1932 the sheltered industries continued to tread the same path as far as they could, keeping up dividends and cutting wage-bills, or at least cutting wage bills by much greater percentages than dividends. That the unsheltered industries in 1931 and 1932 behaved differently seems due rather to the lack of means to do ill deeds imposed by dependence of shrunken export markets than to anything else.

In his pamphlet *Dividends and the Depression*, Forsey reinforced these arguments and stressed the emerging contrast between the wage-earning Canadians and salaried and dividend-holding Canadians. He pointed out numerous cases of industries which simultaneously increased dividends and reduced wage bills. "Such is the tale of wages and dividends," wrote Forsey, "an amazing record, lurid of melodrama."[84]

In this work Forsey sought to illustrate the basic inadequacies of the capitalist system and to urge Canadians to realize that "to any humane person this sort of thing is normally hideous and intolerable." He urged his readers and listeners to reject the capitalist class propaganda arguments that they were "sacrificing their profits to the welfare of their employees." Such propaganda, wrote Forsey, was "positively indecent" when contrasted with the ugly background of the facts.[85] Forsey re-emphasized for his audience that it was no use blaming individuals or "shouting for human sacrifices or thinking that everything would be all right if only all businessmen would be honest and unselfish." The situation was not the work of "a set of crooks who have turned to evil uses a system in itself beneficent," but was "the normal result of the working of capitalism in one of its inherent periods of deflation." It was the system, not the nature of the men working that system, that required "regeneration." "I see no reason to believe that businessmen are less honest or unselfish than their critics, the preachers and professors," wrote Forsey, "nor that those virtuous persons placed in the same situation would do differently." He hoped that all Canadians would soon come to realize that:

It is not easy to be unselfish in an economic system whose beatitude is "Blessed are the greedy, for they shall inherit the earth"; whose biological function has been described as "the survival of the cunning and the vulgar and the crafty and the cruel." A flock of archangels *administering our present economic system* for the last four years would probably have produced very much the same state of affairs as we see around us. Is there any remedy short of a complete change of system?[86]

One can see very clearly the dramatic effect that the Depression was having on Forsey as he urged the public to reject the myth that Depression-era Canadians were "all poor together." His statistics proved that "the brunt of the depression has fallen and fallen heavily on the wage earners and no humane person [could] think this an agreeable story." Forsey challenged each and every Canadian who disliked the result to "help devise economic arrangements which [would] produce different results."[87]

Forsey had always believed that it was the role of society's educated natural leaders to define an overall workable system for such "fiscal arrangements" as were required for the new system, and he began that task with a small group of eight to ten men in the winter of 1933. Forsey joined with Frank Scott, King Gordon, and Leonard Marsh, who in turn began collaborating with Graham Spry, owner and editor of the newspaper *The Farmer Sun*, and University of Toronto economists Parkinson and Harry Cassidy, in another scheme to publish a book for the general public that would describe the planned economy in detail.[88]

In April 1933, this group met in Burlington, Ontario with two dozen additional persons who were interested in the project. Over the course of four days these men and women, most of whom were from the ranks of the LSR and CCF, made solid progress in the organization of the book's various chapters and the editing of semi-prepared drafts. Subsequent work proceeded more slowly as academic duties, speaking engagements, and increasing demands for political assistance by the CCF left few uninterrupted stretches for sustained writing.[89] It appears that a speech to the LSR's 1934 Annual Conference by a Mr. E.A. Radice, former director of England's New Fabian Research Bureau, provided a much-needed impetus for the writers and production subsequently increased.[90] Later in the winter of 1934 Cassidy could report that 90 percent of the manuscripts were complete, though editorial work progressed slowly over the summer. In addition, editing work was shifted to Montreal and taken over by Forsey, Marsh, and Scott.[91] But time was always so short. In November Forsey told Underhill that he hoped to have the remaining work on the book done before the end of the year, but "all sorts of things keep creeping into my telephone and I have weakly promised five speeches between now and Christmas."[92]

Four months later Forsey had written or rewritten almost all of the book's second section and had co-ordinated the writing of another section with King Gordon. Marsh and Scott were also hard at work editing,[93] but it was becoming a tedious affair, especially given the increasing pessimism of former collaborators like Underhill, whom Frank Scott described as having been "in his best pessimistic mood." The Montreal group, Scott added, had only one contribution left to the floundering LSR and that was "the completion of this book."[94]

After taking some time off for his wedding, Forsey returned to work on the book and applied himself diligently to that task over the spring of 1935.[95] The book, called *Social Planning for Canada*, was finally published in the autumn of 1935, and to Forsey's pleasure it received a great deal of publicity.[96]

Frank Underhill later recalled that *Social Planning* was important because it represented "a systematic exposition of what we thought a Socialist regime would amount to in Canada."[97] For Forsey, the central element in such an exposition was central planning, and this theme permeated the section of the book that he wrote, as well as the larger section that he rewrote. Just as Forsey's work in *Towards the Christian Revolution* summarized Forsey's belief in the need to retain Christian moral principles in the reconstructed society, so did his work in *Social Planning* summarize the necessity for, and nature of, the planning process that would actually implement that transformation from capitalism to the Christian social democratic state.

Many of the arguments are familiar: "half-hearted capitalist planning" and negative regulation had shown that "a hybrid system of laissez-faire and state control [was] too defective to remove the major inequalities of the present economic society." Capitalist planning was necessarily planning for the capitalist. True moral planning, on the other hand, would put the interests of the mass of the population first. That could "be done by grafting the organs of expert direction onto our present democratic machinery." What was essential, therefore, "was not so much a fixed plan, as continuous planning" by technical experts on a National Planning Commission who would be in "organized relation

with the organs and aims of government." This mechanism could organize industry to "serve the interests of the many, as both consumers and
producers, rather than the interests of the few."[98]

Forsey went on to argue that this type of planning was unavoidable
with the evolution of machine production and specialization which "has
made it essential to co-ordinate ... the work of multifarious human and
mechanical specialists." To support his case, Forsey cited the efforts of
scientific planners such as the American, F.W. Taylor, and the Russians'
successes in providing the necessary economic co-ordination, "not only
within each industry but between the different industries and aspects of
the whole economy."[99]

The Depression had convinced Forsey that international capitalist
planning could not prevent such disastrous dislocation in the future:

> A national planning authority is essential therefore, if the task of
> deliberately effecting the necessary re-adjustments is to be taken up
> as efficiently as possible, in order to reduce the severity and length
> of the depressions unavoidably thrust upon us by conditions beyond
> our borders.[100]

Flexibility of organization was necessary "in the face of economic
change," and this could be "secured only through the deliberate action
of a competent national authority, with power and discretion to revise
the terms of contracts in which economic relationships are embodied." Forsey argued that without such authority in place the burden
of adjustment was unequally shared. Integral, cohesive planning was
essential for "the rationalization not merely of one firm, or one trade,
but of the whole economic life demands that all the units in the economy should work together." He emphasized that the "sectionalism"
which was the "curse of the Canadian economy must be overcome."[101]

To Forsey, the only alternative to this form of planning was "the
mass of inflexible contractual relationships and price systems which
today intensify depression and throttle recovery."[102] This capacity for
change is an important element in Forsey's overall intellectual development. Previous chapters have indicated Forsey believed that individuals
could change themselves through spiritual regeneration resulting from
their Christian social action. It was inflexible economic systems such as
the Canadian system, however, that prevented men and women from

realizing such regeneration. The answer was to introduce a new system that was flexible and changeable. Closely tied to this was Forsey's belief in the need to maintain a flexible constitutional system that could adapt to a changing economic system.[103]

But how could Forsey, the Christian 'Tory democrat' who prized the preservation of individual freedoms through a pluralistic society of independent, influential associations, each representing legitimate citizen concerns and views, argue for a monolithic central planning authority? Forsey recognized that there would "always and inevitably [exist] a conflict between the demands of personal liberty and the necessities of order and organization." He argued, however, that the conflict was superficial. "Order is itself a necessary condition for the full realization of personal freedom," he explained, "and willing co-operation in concerted social action is a prerequisite of the enlargement of individual liberty in the fullest sense."[104] In the current economic system, he argued, each Canadian's liberty was already restrained by virtue of being "individually dependent for an income" either by having to sell a crop or secure a particular form of employment. Canadians, Forsey believed, were "unavoidably subject to the control of outside forces over which we have no personal power." Forsey concluded his argument with a key paragraph:

> An unemployed man, a wheat farmer whose crop has failed, or a store-keeper who has lost his business through the unemployment of his customers, may be legally "free," but not in any real sense. True freedom – opportunities for unfettered personal development – can only be enjoyed by people whose work and incomes are secure against arbitrary disaster and afford them a reasonable chance of a decent living and leisure. In the age of machinery and minute specialization this basic economic welfare depends entirely on the healthy operation of the economic organization as a whole. This can only be realized through such deliberate centralized organization as we have termed national economic planning. The control which is needed to secure economic efficiency is therefore the essential prelude to a truer personal liberty than we have as yet achieved.[105]

Forsey acknowledged that the price paid for this organization was "notably the surrender of some measure of independence of action," but he believed the sacrifice was not only unavoidable but that the resultant gain made it "well worth while." It was unavoidable, he explained, because Canadian society had passed the age of nineteenth century capitalism which brought "incalculable improvements in industrial technique," but which now required consolidation and effective organization in order to apply these industrial advances effectively for the benefit of all members of society.[106]

Forsey admitted that the individual initiative was invaluable "in the frontier stages of economic development, whether pioneering new techniques or in exploring virgin resources." But he warned that it was highly dangerous when it was exercised without restraint or direction in an economy that had passed the frontier stage, and when "effective co-ordination [had become] urgently necessary." This was especially required during the depression periods:

> The problem of securing order without imposing a deadening tyranny, of maintaining freedom without suffering chaos, is indeed difficult of solution. But of late chaos seems to have predominated. Control is primarily needed to redress the balance.[107]

Freedom of action and personal initiative were, Forsey emphasized, already disappearing with the advance of mergers, the financial integration of private businesses, and the rapid assumption of the giant corporation.

The type of planning authority Forsey visualized "would be alert to maintain flexibility and freedom of the individual and local action to the fullest possible extent." As he had explained earlier in the 1930s, one method of ensuring this flexibility and freedom was to secure "economic democracy." This could be achieved by replacing the existing political process, which was "at the mercy of the special interests and fed by a press dependent for its existence upon advertisement-revenue from capitalist private industries."[108] Under central planning, the House of Commons would continue its role as the legislative body responsible for enacting policy and proposals, but the formulation of those policies and proposals would be the responsibility of the "thinking body," the Planning Commission, with input from the different parts of Canada rather than to specific interests. Its role was neither to legislate nor administer, for those functions would remain with the House of Commons and the departments respectively; rather the Commission's role was specifically to investigate, study, and propose a continuous plan of economic development.[109] This plan, in turn, would be the result of a pluralistic process dependent upon the consultation with its "auxiliary organs" throughout society.[110] In those manufacturing and industrial areas that required decentralization, or were best left to operate on a small scale, "a large part of the secondary co-ordination could be secured through the formation or reconstitution of Trade Associations."[111] These associations, along with business organizations and councils, would all offer an opportunity for representation of the various interests involved.[112] The addition of a strong trade union movement and its machinery was also required to settle disputes and provide the "industrial democracy" necessary for co-operative economic planning by all elements of society.[113]

These central messages of Forsey's contributions to *Social Planning for Canada* were repeated in a revised form of the book called *Canada Needs Socialism*, which was published in 1938. This latter book reiterated Forsey's personal view that individual freedom was best achieved by removing the poverty and insecurity inherent in the capitalist economy. Forsey's work on wages and dividends, and his contributions within the Fellowship of Christian Social Order were best expressed in *Democracy Needs Socialism*. That book clearly repudiated "the Capitalist's travesty of Christianity which preaches that the rich shall be saved through their charity and the poor through the patient endurance of their poverty." The alternative system provided by the pluralistically planned state broke the "material shackles" which held Canadians back from their highest fulfillments. The socialist saw "in man an infinite possibility for spiritual development and creative activity."[114] Therein lay true individual liberty.

CIVIL LIBERTARIAN

AND THE FORCES OF REACTION

Perhaps nothing better illustrates Forsey's sincere commitment to preserving individual liberty within the socialized state than does his personal dedication to the cause of civil liberties during the latter half of the 1930s. As noted earlier, Forsey had been active in civil liberties work through the United Church Committee on Social and Economic Research in 1931. The League for Social Reconstruction, to which Forsey dedicated himself for a short time after his return from Russia, was similarly committed to the cause of civil liberties. The LSR's Official Programme, for example, stated that "[because] work of this nature involves a great expenditure of time and effort, the defence of civil liberties can probably be carried on most effectively by organizations which are not committed to fairly definite political views." But there was a definite limit to the LSR's level of commitment in this area. The LSR's official policy, for example, stated "that it does not seem appropriate for League branches to put too much emphasis upon civil liberties work."[1] Accordingly, the LSR's sixteen-page "What To Read" pamphlet, which listed hundreds of books and articles in nineteen different categories, included a rather limited list of references to civil liberties.

Though not directly related to the LSR's attitude toward civil liberties, Forsey's interest in the League did decrease as the 1930s progressed. Coincidentally his concern with, and interest in, the cause of civil liberties in Canadian society increased during this same period to the point that he became deeply involved in the formation and advancement of a new organization whose sole goal was the advancement of that cause. It was through the new Canadian Civil Liberties Union that Forsey pursued most actively his goal of heightening class-consciousness among Canadians for the ultimate purpose of encouraging working-class and middle-class Canadian support for his planned society.

Frank Scott, the most prominently recognized civil libertarian of this era,[2] had been corresponding with various individuals regarding the need for an independent Canadian civil liberties association since 1932. Much of the interest in such a society had come from Edmonton, where the Canadian Civil Liberties Protective Association had been organized in January 1933.[3] In the spring of 1934, Scott indicated to the Albertans and representatives from the American Civil Liberties Union that a Civil Liberties Union was in the process of being formed in Montreal.[4] By the following spring a draft constitution had been worked out, although Scott was apprehensive because there was a move by left-wing elements to control the new organization.[5] In Toronto, Graham Spry had indicated his interest in initiating support for the new organization.[6]

In Quebec, increasing apprehension over infringements upon free speech forced the Montreal LSR Branch, in June 1935, to support Scott's move to appoint a Civil Liberties Committee within the League Branch. This Committee was empowered to devise a strategy for organizing public opinion for the preservation of civil liberties and to establish contact with "progressive and fraternal associations with liberal-minded individuals regarding the provincial threat to civil liberties."[7]

By 1937, as Forsey observed Canada slowly recovering from the throes of the Depression,[8] he had come more and more to link the nature of Canada's recovery with what he perceived as the increasing frequency of civil rights abuses. In that year Forsey published an article in *Canadian Forum* in which he cited dividend and wage levels between 1935 and 1937 as proof that the unemployed were continuing to suffer while "recovery" proceeded, "at least for some people."[9] "What emerges from the mass of the statistics," Forsey wrote, "was that the capitalist class is getting the lion's share of the new prosperity."[10] Forsey perceived that the Depression had had little of the "chastening effect" one might have expected from Canadian capitalists who were opposing trade unionism and frequently rejecting workers' requests for increased wages and benefits.

The violent 1937 General Motors strike at Oshawa, Ontario, accelerated the growing conflict, as did Ontario Premier Hepburn's failed attempt to crush the American-organized Committee for Industrial

Organization (CIO). Irving Abella has written that Hepburn's actions did little more than turn the nascent labour movement "into a violent crusade," a landmark in Canadian labour history.[11] Unfortunately for the labourers, their enthusiasm was met with a combined offensive from both government and business against the CIO's efforts to organize and improve workers' conditions.[12] In Quebec, however, workers remained determined to gain their fair share of recovery through improved conditions and higher wages,[13] a goal that Forsey had personally worked toward with King Gordon in the United Church's Committee on Social and Economic Research since 1931.[14]

J.H. Thompson has described 1937 as the year that witnessed "the most widespread class conflict since the end of the Great War."[15] Though much of this increasingly bitter class conflict still lay ahead, Forsey believed that both the Depression and recovery had destroyed the capitalists' "old feeling of corporative security [and stiffened] their opposition to any suggestion of important social change." Forsey enveloped the various strains of his perceived capitalist reaction into five separate categories:

> It is now clear that the chief social-political consequence of recovery is an intense and bitter campaign of reaction. This takes five forms, by no means unrelated to one another – first increased armaments expenditures and postponement of further social services; second, more immigration; third, drastic relief cuts; fourth, stiff resistance to trade unionism; fifth, ruthless disregard or, if necessary, suppression of civil liberties.[16]

Apart from the continuing work on his Ph.D. thesis and his McGill lecturing, most of Forsey's energies between 1937 and 1940 went into exposing these five elements in the "campaign of reaction."

Early in 1937 Forsey attacked the "drive for more armaments," which he believed was related to the cancellation of the National Employment Commission's low-cost housing scheme. That scheme had been introduced in 1936 to strike at the root of unemployment by putting construction and general workers back to work. The policy was also intended to remedy the appalling lack of low-cost rental accommodation in slum areas, which contained the greatest number of the unemployed. According to the NEC's Economist, W.A. Mackintosh, those conditions "had a direct relationship not only to unemployment but to public health."[17] Forsey was convinced that given the increasingly chaotic nature of social service funding, "almost any further adequate social legislation must be by the Dominion; [but] the Dominion perhaps cannot, and almost certainly will not move until the BNA Act has been amended."[18]

But such was not to be the case, for Mackenzie King was determined to reduce the federal government's unemployment obligations. J.S. Struthers has written that throughout 1937 King "cut into the dole with a tenacity and determination that even Bennett would have admired." In that year alone the total federal spending on grants-in-aid to the provinces, for example, was cut by 34 percent. This move necessarily increased provincial responsibility, yet the provincial revenues were not equal to the task. Not surprisingly, King had soon added Quebec's Premier Duplessis and Ontario's Hepburn to the growing list of provincial premiers antagonistic to his relief strategy.[19]

Ottawa's action, or inaction if you will, in the relief field, spurred Forsey to action. In two *Canadian Forum* articles published in the spring of 1937, he lashed out at the federal government's "drive to cut down relief and wages of unskilled and semi-skilled workers,"[20] while simultaneously increasing expenditures on armaments.[21] Forsey denounced public calls for a "downward revision of relief payments, at least to a point which would render employment more attractive to the 'practically minded workers.'" These denunciations of the relief scales and relief programmes in general were initiated, Forsey argued, by capitalists and a capitalist-controlled press, who denounced the migrations of the total unemployed to urban areas where they could more effectively voice their concerns. "In other words," Forsey wrote, "the unemployed refuse to starve quietly in the country."[22]

Between October 1937 and March 1938, the number of unemployed Canadians had increased dramatically by almost 25 percent, but Ottawa's freeze on provincial grants-in-aid to their 1937 levels threw "the brunt of the depression ... on the backs of the provincial municipalities who in turn passed it on to the unemployed."[23] Forsey cited Dominion Bureau of Statistics unemployment figures as a "a damning indictment of [the government's] whole policy, or lack of policy, on the subject." Though recovery resumed its pace after the 1938 recession,[24] Forsey's statistics showed an increase in unemployment among previously employed wage earners: "Taken in conjunction with the figures of dividend and interest payments," wrote Forsey, "the statistics were a perfect illustration of the class character of our society."[25] Forsey renewed his call for the Dominion to assure "the whole burden of relief, the raising of relief rates above their present slow starvation level ... and the abolition of the local residence requirement." This would ensure that people in need would be looked after regardless of whether they happened to have moved from one municipality to another.[26]

Forsey also encouraged the Liberal government to reverse its "present policy of total paralysis" and introduce its promised Unemployment Insurance Act. The Act, which had been drafted in 1938, was awaiting both King's endorsement and unanimous provincial consent, since it required a constitutional amendment. Such action had not been forthcoming to date, and Forsey questioned the validity of the entire approach:

> How much longer will the country put up with the preposterous excuse about the necessity of getting unanimous provincial consent for any change in the British North America Act? Everyone who knows anything at all about the history of the Canadian constitution knows that the "compact theory" is unadulterated nonsense. If the Government again pleads the compact theory as the reason for its failure to go ahead with the insurance scheme, it should be told in plain terms that it is talking humbug.[27]

Forsey urged the government to implement its own National Employment Commission recommendations, which King had been resisting for years.[28]

Forsey continued to preach his now familiar message that "a complete solution to the unemployment problem was impossible within the framework of capitalism." He urged his readers not to allow the government to "skulk" out of its responsibilities on the plea of lack of funds. "The money is there," Forsey wrote, and he cited record-high dividend and interest payments to prove his point. He also assured Canadians that "capitalists did extremely well for themselves in this country last year [1938] and are confidently predicting even greater things in 1939." Though he doubted action would be taken, Forsey challenged the government to implement a "good stiff Dominion succession duty, a tax on undistributed profits, and a levy on wealth to reduce debt charges."[29]

131

Throughout 1939 and 1940, Forsey repeated his call for increased Dominion powers and revenues through such means. He also continued to increase public awareness of low corporate taxes and relief for the rich, despite increases in dividend and bond interest figures. To Forsey these patterns reflected adherence to the philosophy of "To him that hath shall be given." He did, however, praise the Liberals' 1940 budget, which gave "the rich, for the first time in Canadian history, a taste of real taxation on something approaching the British scale."[30]

Forsey also opposed the "vested interests'" immigration propaganda mills, which were going "full blast" in 1936 and 1937. He rejected calls by these "men of wealth and substance" from industry, the church, and politics who were utilizing their "immense political and economic power" to convince Ottawa to "fill up Canada's great open spaces while millions of people were still on relief, and farmers [were] unable to make a decent living." He argued that less than 30 percent of Canada's land was useful agriculturally, and concluded that the largest number of people Canada could ever be able to support was 35 or 36 million.[31] In addition, less that a third of the country's forested land carried accessible merchantable timber. Taken together, only 25 to 28 percent of Canadian land was potential agricultural land and accessible for lumbering. "For economic purposes," Forsey wrote, "Canada is not an empty empire or a thinly peopled half-continent, but a rather narrow ribbon of territory along the United States border."[32]

Forsey also refuted the vested interests' call for more skilled immigrant workers, arguing that "there were plenty of unemployed unskilled labour available for training." He demonstrated that since Confederation "we have brought to Canada at great expense four times as many people as we could absorb." New immigrants had to become producers and to find markets for their products, otherwise they, and native Canadians, would emigrate or go on relief. He warned that the immigrant level would be used by the capitalists "to break down our standard living and to mask what feeble trade union defenses the working class has been able to build up." "The price of human suffering," warned Forsey, "will be appalling."[33] Forsey reiterated his immigration arguments in an LSR pamphlet entitled *Does Canada Need Immigrants?* which was published in the autumn of 1937.[34]

Increased armaments and decreased social services, stiff resistance to trade unionism, relief cuts, and more immigration were, therefore, four elements that Forsey perceived in the capitalists' reactionary campaign, and Forsey's arguments on these issues indicate that he considered them to be very serious. But he considered the fifth element in the "campaign of reaction," the threat to civil liberties, as perhaps the most serious of this group, and he dedicated himself to that cause, though one wonders how he ever found the energy or the time for doing this, as he was severely overextended in his commitments during this period of his life.

In addition to his heavy lecturing schedule at McGill, which included frequent filling in for regular professors,[35] and his work on his doctoral thesis, Forsey remained active in the SCM and the FCSO throughout the 1930s. The steady demand for his LSR pamphlet and the success of *Social Planning for Canada*, evident in the increasing requests from the public for copies of the book,[36] reinforced Forsey's commitment to writing public educational materials. Added to this list was Forsey's participation in various LSR-sponsored lecture series during the mid-1930s.[37] By 1937 Forsey was singled out as the lone member of the Montreal group who was still committed to LSR-sponsored publications.[38] Forsey also accepted added administrative duties for the League when he was elected to the LSR's Executive Committee in 1937 and again in 1938.[39] His status as a major LSR spokesman was recognized when he was introduced by Underhill as the principal speaker at the LSR's 1937 Convention.[40] Both Eugene and Harriet, who was also an active member and contributor to the LSR, participated in joint LSR ventures. Harriet, for example, prepared a pictorial pamphlet for LSR publication and was a member of the Montreal Branch's Executive in the late 1930s.

But Forsey's prime focus remained civil liberties and the need for an association dedicated to that cause. Forsey at first believed that the most effective vehicle for pursuing the civil liberties issue was the CCF and, generally speaking, he devoted a great deal of his time to that party during the 1930s despite its dismal electoral showing in the 1935 federal election, when it elected only 7 of its 118 candidates.[41]

Following that election Forsey expressed to Frank Underhill his disappointment over the personal defeats of King Gordon, George Mooney, and Ted Garland, but did his best to keep a positive attitude. "If we work hard, play our cards right and have the luck to see the Social Credit turn itself out before the next election, we may

achieve something in four or five years. But meanwhile that majority!"[42] Forsey was realistic enough, however, to admit that the immediate future was not promising: "It looks as if the CCF policies will
hardly be practical politics in our time," he wrote to Harry Cassidy.
"Or am I too pessimistic? I mean to keep pegging away in one form or
another of work, but with fewer illusions!"[43] And peg away he did. In
the spring of 1936 Forsey participated in two closed LSR-CCF meetings, one in Montreal and a second in Ottawa. In these sessions Forsey
and other LSR National Executive members recommended policy and
generally presented their views on the direction they felt the CCF
should take.[44]

That same year Forsey also accepted the position of President of the
Provincial Council of the CCF in Quebec, which involved frequent
meetings, speeches, and organizational duties.[45] This position, however, gave Forsey direct input into the CCF's National Council, and
he began immediately to aggressively encourage the Party to advance
certain causes that he felt important. The relationship between Forsey
and the CCF, however, would be a stormy one.

Forsey assumed his position on the CCF's Quebec Council in 1936,
just as David Lewis became active in the national organization of the
party as its volunteer National Secretary. Working out of an Ottawa
"lean-to" complete with mud floor, Lewis later admitted that his first
steps in the CCF were not always astute ones. He specifically mentioned that his failure to recognize regional and cultural differences
within the federated party "no doubt irritated some people."[46] Lewis
later singled out King Gordon and Frank Scott as two LSR members in
Montreal who were especially helpful to him during these early years.
This was mainly because both men agreed with Lewis's policy that it
was essential to give more guidance from the national office to the provincial councils.[47]

The absence of Forsey's name on Lewis's list is to be expected given
Forsey's continued prodding of the national CCF office on a number of
issues, including the need for more active leadership. In March 1937,
Forsey discussed the inefficiency of the national office in providing
necessary election literature with Ted Garland, an Ontario CCF organizer in Ontario. Garland was at that time fighting a losing battle to
help the lone provincial CCF MPP in that province hold on to his
legislative seat in the provincial election.[48]

Garland was convinced that the national office was ignoring his written pleas for election material:

> Where the hell is it? What the devil is the use of staging a full dress
> campaign if we cannot get the ammunition? When are we going to
> get it? Where is the material? Hells bells-Spanish bells-Blue bells.

In desperation Garland turned to Forsey for material even though he felt Forsey worked "too blasted hard anyhow."[49] Forsey wasted little time in relaying his own displeasure to David Lewis, who quite obviously did not appreciate his efforts: "Thank you for your letter ... as well as the indignant advice contained in it," Lewis responded, "I must, however, say that both your indignation and advice is at this particular time unnecessary." Lewis explained to Forsey that he, Lewis, was "a little peeved with the tone" of Forsey's letter, though he admitted that he "may have fallen down in a number of important things." Lewis concluded his letter by extending the olive branch for he could hardly afford to alienate his chief CCF organizer in Canada's second largest province:

> Having got that off my chest I am sure I do not have to add that in
> reality I did not mind your letter in the least. A comradely attempt
> to spur each other on in this work should always be welcome and
> quite seriously I assure you that although I felt it my duty to defend
> myself as I did above, the resentment which I express was less than
> skin deep.[50]

Forsey's commitment to battling the "reactionary forces'" frontal attack on civil liberties was, however, more than skin deep, and the CCF's continued reluctance to respond to his suggestions to activate itself on the issue strained their already acrimonious relationship even further. Forsey continued to use his position on the National Executive of the LSR to press the CCF National Executive to incorporate resolutions on civil liberties and on the trade union movement at its 1937 convention. This intermediary role was not an uncommon one for Forsey, especially when it came to interaction between the LSR, the CCF, and to a lesser extent the FCSO.[51] Lewis had at first responded favourably to Forsey's initiative,[52] and he and Forsey engaged in preliminary talks to introduce resolutions through provincial councils on down to local CCF clubs. Forsey, as Chairman of the Quebec Council wasted little time in sending out an updated civil liberties "pastoral letter to [his] little flock of CCF'ers" that was to be read at club executive meetings.[53]

The CCF's subsequent actions on civil liberties did not, however, satisfy Forsey. When the time came for concrete political action Forsey's commitment to a "philosophy of action" seemed in contrast to the CCF's more tempered and calculated political inclinations. It was, therefore, becoming increasingly obvious that a separate civil liberties association was necessary. To that end Forsey joined in with Frank Scott's efforts to establish the Canadian Civil Liberties Union (CCLU).

The CCLU, Montreal Branch, was officially founded in the spring of 1937 largely in response to a perceived attempt by authorities to suppress free speech in Montreal.[54] In 1936, for example, authorities had cancelled a public speech that had been sponsored by the National Committee for Medical Aid to Spain. This League, led by the ubiquitous Frank Scott, had arranged for a public speech by a Spanish Republican-supporting Franciscan priest named Sarasola, and its cancellation raised the cry for civil liberties throughout Quebec.[55]

The Sarasola affair reminded Forsey of the type of fascist suppression of civil rights he had seen in Germany only a few short years earlier, and it fired him into action. He immediately wrote letters of protest to Premier Duplessis and to his Member of Legislative Assembly, equating the 'affair' with European fascism:

> I am writing to you, as my representative, to express my energetic protest against the suppression of free speech and assembly in Montreal on Friday, October 23. What took place then bears an uncomfortably close resemblance to events which I myself witnessed at close range in Germany, not long before Herr Hitler took power. Unless the people and their elected representatives act resolutely and promptly, law and order and constitutional liberty are in grave danger in this province.
>
> It is not a question of "French" versus "English" or Catholic versus Protestant. God forbid! It is a simple issue of freedom and justice and opinions.[56]

This event and other perceived infringements on civil liberties led Forsey into active involvement with the new Civil Liberties Union's Montreal Branch. Forsey was elected to its executive in 1937, the first year of the Union's existence, and he remained on the Executive until he moved to the United States in 1941.[57]

But as Anglophones Forsey and Scott moved carefully with their civil liberties initiatives, for they both shared a tremendous fear of an outbreak of racial fascism in Quebec. Accordingly they both appealed to Graham Spry in Toronto to initiate a CLU Branch in that city so that their work in Montreal would not appear as a move by an English minority directed against what could be perceived as French-Canadian fascism.[58] Spry had been involved in the organization of the Committee to Aid Spanish Democracy and the Canadian Branch of the League Against War and Racism, and he was a highly visible civil rights activist in Toronto. He believed it was essential that the CLU "be centralist, not leftist in character," and he asked both Forsey and Scott for names to be placed on the CLU's National Council.[59]

In 1937 Forsey became publicly associated with the cause of civil liberties when he aggressively attacked what he perceived to be two major affronts to the civil liberties movement. In late 1936 and early 1937, Mr. W. Clarke, the Secretary of the Canadian Chamber of Commerce, attacked the CCF for its "communistic," and therefore repressive, position on civil liberties and relief. Forsey interpreted Clarke's speech as an attempt to "spread mis-statements on the relations between capital and labour," and he pleaded with David Lewis to respond publicly to the charges. The CCF, however, chose not to act. Lewis explained to Forsey that he was too preoccupied with the CCF's administrative and organizational jockeying in Quebec vis-à-vis the communist trade union support and pamphlet distribution to take up the matter. Lewis added that he did not share Forsey's strong opinions on the matter.[60]

But Forsey had, for months prior to the Clarke speech, been fighting what he saw as an overall attempt by capitalists to bamboozle Canadians into accepting their condemnation of the need for socialism by picturing all Canadian working men, farmers, and industrialists as capitalists who benefited from the capitalist system.[61] Forsey responded by providing facts and figures to prove the existence of class divisions in Canadian society. To those capitalists who argued that such classes did not exist, Forsey wrote:

> I make the Chamber of Commerce a present of one answer, by John Macmurray, Professor of Philosophy in University College, London. It runs something like this: The working-class means those who will starve if they don't work; the capitalist class means those who won't starve if they don't work. This will "mean" something, I fancy, to any workingman, though it may be too subtle for the Canadian Chamber of Commerce.[62]

To Forsey, Clarke's speech was yet another attack by the "vested interests" against the civil liberties of all working men.

Once again Forsey expressed his bitter disappointment and frustration with the CCF's inaction. Lewis had explained Forsey's concern to Woodsworth, but their failure to act on his recommendation seemed, to Forsey, inexcusable:

> I am very disappointed that you people in Ottawa did nothing officially about his (Clarke's) speech. If I hadn't thought it felt safe in your hands, once I'd drawn your attention to it, I'd have sat up all night myself composing something to fire at him and had sent it up to the National Executive to issue.... It doesn't need machinery.... The press would have snapped it up.[63]

More than anything else it was the internal mechanics of the CCF that frustrated Forsey. He saw the Party's role in very simple terms. "I was brought up in a school of politics which believed that the function of an Opposition is to oppose," he wrote Lewis "and that quick, hard hitting is essential."[64] In another letter Forsey explained that he was tired of having to always push the CCF into action, adding that "glaring lies by the Secretary of the Canadian Chamber of Commerce required a response regardless of how busy you people in Ottawa are."[65]

Forsey naturally took it upon himself to provide the necessary "quick, hard hitting" response. In an open letter to Clarke and in a *Canadian Forum* article, he lashed out at Clarke's reference to the "socialists and the debating Rhodes Scholars from Oxford who gave us doles, amenities, comforts, and state benefactions – in short hand-outs without having to work for them." "Such socialists," Clarke said, would "through their covetousness, drain the vitals of the nation." Forsey chose to debate Clarke's statement that Canada's social services and liberties were improving under capitalism. He provided statistics to illustrate what he felt were unacceptable levels of public support for education, health and medical facilities, and public welfare, and the deteriorating circumstances such inadequate support produced in Canadian society.[66]

At about this same time that he was attacking Clarke's speech, Forsey became involved in what was to become for him, and for many other Canadians, a much larger battle to preserve civil liberties in Canada. Barely one year after its election, Quebec Premier Duplessis' Union Nationale government enacted legislation entitled *An Act Respecting Communist Propaganda*. This Act, soon referred to simply as the Padlock Act, gave Duplessis as Attorney General extensive powers to close, or padlock, any premises used for the purpose of "propagating Communism or Bolshevism."[67] Though the Act enraged Quebec's English-speaking minority, it appeared to have the support of a majority of French Quebeckers who favoured a frontal attack on the Communist Party, then known as the Labour Progressive Party (LPP).[68]

Even before the actual Bill was introduced, Forsey was attempting to obtain copies of it and had written to Graham Spry listing his many objections to it. Forsey complained about the Bill's widespread political powers and the fact that halls were already refusing to book organizations like the League Against War and Fascism: "The procedure," wrote Forsey, "is the most beautiful I have seen since King [Gordon] and I were in Berlin in 1932 when widespread police arrests were common."[69]

On a wider front Forsey hoped to organize a united movement of all citizens who valued civil liberties. To this end he invited several liberal-minded organizations to an upcoming CCF Provincial Council meeting to pursue the idea.[70] Within two months of the Padlock Act's passing, Forsey had published two *Canadian Forum* articles denouncing the "sweeping and arbitrary powers it granted to the Attorney General and the heavy penalties of placing the burdens of proof on the accused and the denial of the right of appeal." These, Forsey argued, were all "serious enough threats to civil liberties of all citizens," but what he found "far more sinister and menacing [was] that the Act nowhere defined Communism or Bolshevism." Forsey warned that this gave the Attorney General "practically a free hand to suppress any opinions he may happen to dislike," including private conversations in homes and the circulation of the Bible.[71] He also cited a recent midnight police attack upon the offices of the National Relief Commission Office as an example of what the new Act could permit.[72]

A month later Forsey broadened his view and fit the Padlock Act into part of a "carefully organized campaign to transform the province into a clerical-Fascist state." Forsey documented the rise of "Social Corporatism," or "the organized Church sponsored economic and social opposition to Communism, trade unionism and anti-clerical-ism," which he said had become strong enough to frighten the political hierarchy "out of its wits."[73] The spearhead of this clerical-fascist attack was the organization of Catholic trade unions, which Forsey believed was based on the proposition that workers should "love and agree with their employers and should strike only as a last resort."

This sort of policy was directly contrary to Forsey's goal of increasing class-consciousness in Canadian society, for it encouraged workers to think of themselves as part of the employers' class. That the church and government sponsored this alliance of Catholic workers and employers merely compounded the problem. Forsey believed that in this scenario the non-Catholic international unions had a key role to play not only in fighting their employers for their lives, but also in opposing the Church and the government over "the fate of democracy in this province for some years to come."[74]

The organizers of the CCLU had from their initial meetings realized that the support of French-Canadians and the Catholic clergy was extremely important to the success of their organization. In a meeting in October 1937, Forsey, Gordon, J.A. Coote, and R.B.Y. Scott passed a motion to add a member of the Roman Catholic clergy to a new CLU Committee. They also agreed that as many French-Canadians as possible should be encouraged to join the CLU.[75] But the CLU, like the Quebec CCF, was never successful in wooing French-Canadians or Roman Catholic clerical support. The English-Canadians were left largely on their own to fight the perceived threats to civil liberties.

The problem, of course, was how to go about it. Forsey believed that the federal power of disallowance was the best method, and he argued that point in CCF National Executive meetings, in the *Canadian Forum*, and in letters to David Lewis.[76] Forsey emphasized the need for federal intervention by documenting Padlock atrocities in detail, and concluded:

It seems likely that we are indeed only at the beginning of a reign of terror in which everyone who happens to incur the displeasure of Monsieur Duplessis or his august Superior, may expect to have his home or office padlocked in the approved Nazi manner.[77]

Cancellations of public lectures to be given by then CLU leader R.B.Y. Scott and CLU Counsel J.K. Mergler, and attacks on Protestant unions throughout 1938, only served to bring "the offensive against democracy and civil liberties" closer to home for Forsey.[78]

But, as had been the case in the past with the Garland and Clarke episodes, the national CCF contributed little overt action to support Forsey's case for urging disallowance of the Padlock Act. Forsey had presented his case for disallowance of the Act personally to the National Council and in written form to Lewis during the summer of 1937.[79] Lewis had forwarded Forsey's arguments on to CCF leader M.J. Coldwell, who was travelling in western Canada, and had advised Coldwell to issue a statement through the National Executive "along the lines suggested in [Forsey's] letter."[80] But Coldwell refused the advice.[81]

Forsey's case for disallowance rested on the Act's "attempt to invade the Dominion's field of criminal law." It seemed to him an obvious case for disallowance on the time-honoured grounds that it was beyond the powers of the Province and "contrary to reason, justice and natural equality."[82] Forsey relayed his comments to Lewis in the form of a speech for use by a CCF Member of Parliament, but his appeals by and large fell on deaf ears. As for the federal Liberal government, Justice Minister Lapointe had dismissed as virtually obsolete the federal power to disallow provincial legislation.[83] Forsey, who was deeply involved in the research for his doctoral thesis on the subject of federal disallowance, replied that Lapointe's arguments could only be viewed with disdain.[84]

In Forsey's eyes the CCF was making a tactical error in refusing to prepare a petition for disallowance. It should forget about its fear that its support for disallowance now might "be used to cramp the style of a CCF provincial government at some time in the future," for it was clear to Forsey that there would be no CCF provincial government for many years to come.[85] Forsey's obvious lack of tact in expressing views such as these had a great deal to do with his inability to garner support for this and numerous future proposals.

Lack of tact did not stop Forsey from continuing to present the two possible avenues that the CCF could pursue if it chose to act to protect civil liberties in Quebec. The first was the Dominion Cabinet's power under the 1927 Supreme Court Act to refer provincial legislation to the Supreme Court for a test of its validity. Secondly, there was the Dominion's power to disallow, within one year of its passing, any Act of any provincial legislature.[86]

Forsey, as usual, was certain that his recommended course of action was politically wise, as well as socially necessary to resist the power of the capitalist class:

> I am perfectly sure I am politically right on this question, and shall see my judgement vindicated by events, as I have several times before. The power is there. It will be used against us whenever it suits the capitalists to use it, or at least whenever it seems to them essential to use it. Our protestations and Lapointe's theories about provincial autonomy alike will go by the board when there is a sufficient "emergency." In plain words, our reluctance to see a power used for a good purpose for fear of setting a bad precedent will not in the least prevent its being used for a bad purpose. It's like the powers of the Crown and Underhill's Whiggism. Poor trusting soul![87]

Forsey felt strongly that the CCF convention in 1937 should recommend disallowance and repeated his warning that if and when a CCF provincial government was elected, "the power of disallowance will be used if the Big Boys see fit, regardless of what we or anyone else may have said." Meanwhile Forsey argued that Canadians were much more likely to get "a lot of perfectly hellish provincial governments doing the sort of thing Duplessis is doing now, and getting away with it partly because of our timidity and ridiculous devotion to provincial rights."[88]

Forsey also wrote to Justice Minister Lapointe and reiterated his arguments in favour of disallowance. Ironically, Lapointe did enact the federal power, but it was exactly the type of disallowance, in Forsey's view, that he had warned would occur for the benefit of the capitalists. The target of the federal action in this case was not Quebec's Padlock Act, but Alberta's Social Credit of Alberta Regulation Act. Premier Aberhart's legislation had placed the banks under the directorates appointed by his newly appointed Social Credit Board, so that their credit policies would be shaped to suit Alberta producers rather than bank shareholders. The Bank Employees Civil Rights Act made it illegal for bankers to take civil action against Alberta, and an amendment to the Judicature Act made it illegal to challenge the validity of the provincial laws in court. These acts, announced Lapointe, were an "unmistakable invasion" of federal jurisdiction.[89]

This was just the scenario that Forsey had forewarned Lewis about, and he lost no time in telling the CCF's National Secretary just that:

> The news this morning about the disallowance of the three Alberta Acts pleases me considerably. You will remember how I said to members of the National Council, to propose the Padlock Act, that I was sure we ought to press for disallowance, that I was sure their judgement was bad, and that history would prove it. I scarcely expected to be vindicated so very soon, or so strikingly.... I knew, as I said repeatedly, that as soon as the ruling class felt strongly enough that some Act should be disallowed it would insist on the power being used and would get its way. All that delightful Whiggism wasn't worth the paper it was written on or the breath it took to utter it.[90]

Forsey explained to Lewis that the CLU had also refused to act on his advice, so if he sounded bitter (as was often Forsey's reaction in situations where he was not listened to), it was because he felt trusted friends had refused his advice. "I am going to rub this thing into Frank Scott properly, and into the members of the National Council, on every possible opportunity. Good old Marx!" This vindictiveness was not an uncommon trait for Forsey to display, for he never adhered to the maxim that one should never burn one's bridges behind oneself.

Though down, Forsey was far from out. He soon took the offensive once again and urged the CCF to force Lapointe to "eat his words" and make the government "squirm." The following quote reveals very clearly the connection Forsey saw between class power in Canada and the use, or in his view abuse, of constitutional powers by a certain class:

> Think of the chance of pointing out the contrast between the treatment meted out to Alberta for these Acts and the complete passivity in regard to the Padlock Act! The civil liberties of ordinary citizens

in Quebec? Poof! But the civil liberties of bankers in Alberta? Ah! That's quite another thing! Rub it in about how the Padlock Act also closed the courts, how it vested arbitrary power in the provincial government, how it conflicted with the Dominion legislation and Dominion policy. Why the different treatment? Is there any answer except that in the one case the banks were interested (or more broadly, the capitalists were interested) and in the other they weren't? Surely it is an amazing chance to demand that the same sauce that has been served to the Alberta goose should be served to the Quebec gander?[91]

If he were in the House, Forsey wrote, he would "make the government dance on hot bricks over this business." Disallowing the Padlock, he explained, would gain the CCF support in Alberta without disapproving the use of the power of disallowance itself, which had to be avoided at all costs. At the same time such action would "do our cause in Quebec a bit of good."

He believed that the CCF need only point out to Albertans how the power had been worked against it while Quebec had been let alone, and explain why, and then insist on disallowance of at least the Padlock Act. This was the opportunity to publicly challenge the government to use its disallowance power to protect the people's civil liberties. The relentlessness with which Forsey pursued this issue despite the minimal response from the CCF National Office is a clear indication of his commitment to the issue. The reason is clear. The issue combined two important components that were necessary to achieving "real democracy." The preservation of civil liberties, and the class divisions that the disregard of those liberties revealed, were integral to Forsey's overall intellectual philosophy vis-à-vis the nature of the democratic state in Canada.

As was usual, it was Forsey's manner, rather than his insistent call to action, that may have influenced others not to act on his recommendations.[92] Witness the following excerpt from a letter to David Lewis:

I do hope the leaders will not funk this thing. If they will act, I am quite ready to forego the pleasure of saying "I told you so!" You can pass on my suggestions with that superb tact of yours and perhaps we shall get some results.[93]

Though Forsey himself soon came to admit that he and Arthur Meighen were the two poorest judges of public opinion and public reaction in Canadian history, that thought did not seem to cross his mind in the 1930s. And so he continued his arguments in CLU meetings and in the pages of the *Canadian Forum* and wherever else he felt he had an audience.[94] But the CCF organizers had long since concluded that the CCF was a weak force in Quebec. In Lewis's view the party was merely "a sympathetic bystander to a crucial social struggle."[95]

The LSR, however, still had a civil liberties role to play, and Forsey convinced its National Executive to send a letter to King urging him to accede to the CLU's recent petition for disallowance, or at least to submit the legislation to the Supreme Court for an opinion on its legality.[96] Throughout the winter of 1937 Forsey renewed his arguments in the pages of a new *CLU Bulletin*, continuing his civil liberties campaign in that journal through the autumn of 1938.[97] The CCLU was now extremely active in defending individual civil liberties cases in Montreal,[98] and Forsey was instrumental in convincing the new organization to sponsor a conference in May 1938, at which over one hundred provincial organizations and 100,000 persons formally endorsed the CLU petition for disallowance.[99] In March of that year Lapointe agreed to hear a presentation from the CLU's legal counsel, but once again he refused to act.[100]

Between June 1938 and January 1939, Forsey published three more *Forum* articles in which he cited dozens of civil liberties infringements and emphasized the overwhelming public support the CLU had garnered in Quebec. He pointed to over 124 Quebec Provincial Police raids since the Padlock Act's introduction: "And in all cases," he wrote, "not one of the persons raided has been ever charged with any offence, let alone convicted."[101]

At this same time Forsey published an article in the *Canadian Journal of Economics and Political Science* which discussed the power of disallowance in detail and established the precedents and constitutional authority for its use. This article also emphasized the importance of central political power in a federated dominion, a theme to be discussed in Chapter 9, which focuses on Forsey's constitutional theories.[102] In his CJEPS article, Forsey levelled his attacks directly at Mackenzie King. He wrote that the trampling of liberties "as old as Magna Carta" in Quebec, undoubtedly had little effect on King because they were primarily poor people's problems. Silence in the face of such abuses, he wrote, "[was] doubtless one of those imperishable Liberal principles for which the Prime Minister's grandfather risked his life."[103]

The government's inaction, Forsey told his *Forum* readers, reflected Canadian business's domination of the Canadian democratic process. Though Ottawa refused to respond to the growing public call for remedial action, it did listen and respond to the protestations raised following the introduction of the Alberta Acts. In the latter case the opposition came, in part, from the Canadian Life Insurance Association; the Dominion Mortgage and Investment Association; the Investment Dealers Association of Canada; the Edmonton and Hamilton Chambers of Commerce; the Canadian Bankers Association; the Boards of Trade of seven major cities; and "numerous other corporations and individuals in various parts of Canada, the United States and abroad.".

Forsey wrote that it was perhaps too much to expect Ottawa to disallow any legislation which "enjoyed the firm support of Montreal big business, and which had been publicly blessed by the Quebec hierarchy." In such circumstances only great statesmen would summon the necessary courage to act, and it had long been evident that Mackenzie King belonged to the "Player Toro" school of democratic leadership which leads "their regiments from behind."[104]

Forsey also shared the general uneasiness about the approaching threat of world war that many civil libertarians shared in the late 1930s. In March 1938, for example, the Montreal Branch of the CCLU[105] issued a policy statement regarding the impending war. Forsey fully supported a published warning that the CCLU issued to world leaders such as Chamberlain, King, and Roosevelt, who defined the issue of the impending conflict "as a struggle between those forces which believe in the rights of nations and individuals to liberty and those forces which would deny to nations and individuals the liberties which are their right." In response, the CCLU made clear its position on the issue:

> The Canadian Civil Liberties Union, Montreal Branch, believes that such a war can only be prosecuted with full effectiveness if the forces fighting for democracy and freedom are assured not only the maintenance but of the extension of internal democracy. The best guarantee that the war will be a war of democracy against nazism

can be provided by preserving and extending democracy in Canada during the war.

The Union realizes that in times of war there is a tendency to put into force legislation which may curtail or even abolish many of our civil liberties, and the Union is resolved to continue its opposition to any curtailment or infringement of basic civil rights unless unquestionably dictated by military necessity. The Union will combat with every means at its disposal any and every attempt to take advantage of times of war to restrict unnecessarily freedom of speech, freedom of the press, and freedom of assembly and association. All war measures will be scrutinized by the Union in this light.[106]

On the international scene Forsey advocated an all-out effort against Spain and Germany. He also clearly outlined his own view of the European situation in two lengthy letters to his mother only a few days after Britain's Prime Minister Chamberlain had flown to Munich and agreed to the partition of Czechoslovakia.[107] "The international situation is sickening," Forsey wrote, "and the fulsome praise of that creature Chamberlain makes us both [Harriet and himself] want to return our meals. If he had his deserts, he would be on trial for high treason. The whole policy of the Government for two or three years at least has been thoroughly dishonest and completely pro-Fascist."[108]

For Forsey, the problem originated with Britain's refusal to "behave properly" over the Spanish Civil War. Forsey had not only defended the Republican cause in public forums in Montreal during that war, but had left his Quaker religion over its doctrine of pacifism because he felt the Spanish conflict warranted military intervention.[109] As for Germany, Forsey believed the most realistic plan for "saving peace" was to implement non-military sanctions against Germany.[110] In a letter he wrote to the Montreal *Gazette*, Forsey condemned "the appalling policy of appeasement,"[111] and he ridiculed Chamberlain's "handiwork" in showing that Hitler's "Fuhresprinzip could be fitted into Parliamentary institutions!"[112]

Forsey did, however, fear that Canada's ruling class shared with Britain's ruling class and socialist Russia an itch for war.[113] After the outbreak of war, Forsey fully supported Canada's war effort, though he continued to speak out on the civil liberty issues surrounding the

Padlock Act, seeing it as the wartime litmus test for both the Liberal and Conservative parties as far as civil liberties were concerned.[114]

Forsey had always thought it important to defend the CLU against charges of communist association. These charges came, for example, from such establishment figures as "Ontario's paladin of anti-Communism, Colonel George A. Drew," whom Forsey would eventually face three times in elections during the 1940s. Forsey charged that in his public utterances Drew "was frightening the population into fits over a wholly mythical Communist menace," and he confronted Drew directly during a speech by the Ontario Premier at the Women's Canadian Club in Montreal:

> Forsey: Colonel Drew, the morning *Gazette* reports you as saying that the Civil Liberties Union is an organization promoted by Communists. Is that report accurate?

> Drew: Yes [and] if I have said anything wrong there is one recourse.

> Forsey: What is that?

> Drew: Libel. [Colonel Drew then repeated his remarks about knowing that the Civil Liberties Union had been promoted by Communists.]

> Forsey: Well, I was one of the chief people who promoted it, and I am not a Communist; and I know your statement is not correct. You cannot libel respectable citizens in this fashion and get away with it.

> Drew: Respectable citizens have something better to do.[115]

Drew's attack was, for Forsey, "yet another reckless and irresponsible assertion [by the] forces of reaction."[116] It was partly to counteract those forces that Forsey accepted an appointment to chair a CLU Legislative Committee in the spring of 1939. This three-member Committee was charged with "scrutinizing all legislation coming before the provincial and federal parliaments." The Committee, for example, after an examination of the Lacroix Bill, which would have amended the Post Office Act to prevent the distribution of Communist literature through the mails, made recommendations and offered the co-operation of the CLU to the CCF to combat the Bill in the House of Commons. The Bill, a private member's initiative, was "talked out" when it came before the House in March 1939.[117]

Despite these few small victories, the battle was beginning to take its toll on Forsey. He was, once again, over-committed, overworked, and over-stressed, and the forces of reaction seemed relentless. This was especially true in Quebec, where the power of the Catholic Church had virtually crushed Forsey's efforts to establish a United Popular Front of trade unions and civil liberties groups. In 1937 he had told Lewis that such a united effort was absolutely necessary in Quebec "if we are to preserve liberty at all." But now, over two years later, little had been accomplished.[118] Forsey could now only lament that "the shrieks of those poor, deluded, priest-ridden R.C.'s! La clericalisme, voila l'ennemi! I wish we were at the stage where we could say so. May I live to see it!"[119]

What Forsey saw instead was the CCF "fizzle" in the House of Commons debate on disallowance in June 1938. In that debate on the disallowance of the Padlock Act, Woodsworth spoke of the "need to protect people's liberties" and repeated the now familiar charges that the term "communism" was not defined in the Act.[120] The CCF leader also referred to the Montreal Branch of the CCLU as an example of the growing opposition to the Act, and he highlighted the fourteen months of "illegal arrests and waiting" that had occurred since the Act's passage.[121] But the CCF did not force the debate, and Woodsworth soon gave way to several strong MP's who spoke in favour of the Padlock. As the debate ended in the House it seemed only too obvious to Forsey that the CCF was not prepared to make a major political comment on Duplessis' controversial piece of legislation. What particularly offended Forsey in all this was that the CCF did not use any of his "recent material at all" during the debate. "Whether I could have persuaded them to do differently had I come up [to Ottawa]," he wondered. "I don't know, but I doubt it."[122]

As the 1930s progressed, the pressure on Forsey to participate in the SCM, FCSO, CLU, LSR, and CCF, not to mention his academic and thesis work, was becoming too much for him: "My judgement is not what it might be if I were not on the verge of a nervous breakdown," he confessed in the spring of 1938. As a result he was considering resigning from all his activities, including his written contributions to the *Canadian Forum* and the CCF's National Council, on the grounds of ill health. He had gotten to the point where "even to hear another person's voice was something I could barely endure." He hoped that a summer of quiet work on his thesis would "restore" him.[123]

He and his wife took refuge for the summer in a cottage on Inglis Island near Knowlton, Quebec, where Forsey was determined to "get clear of all his responsibilities or perish in the attempt." Both he and Harriet were exhausted and had planned to see only one other couple, the Marshes, during the entire summer. They ended up with no company, however, when the Marshes' baby died shortly before their expected arrival.[124]

The Forsey's cottage was comfortably ordered with the traditional "noble cobblestone fireplace," which they put to good use, and perhaps most important of all for the fastidious Eugene, everything was spotlessly clean. Forsey looked forward to "a grand time with bird and flower guides, and evening concerts of frogs: cello, bass viol and piccolo!"[125]

But the respite was over all too soon and he was soon back at McGill. In that autumn of 1938, Forsey was faced with an unprecedentedly large number of students, so he resigned himself to cutting out as much extra work as possible in order to get "the necessary amount of work done on his thesis."[126] But with Forsey that was usually easier said than done and within weeks he was engaged in statistical work for a Saskatchewan CCF pamphleteer; had submitted twelve hundred pages of evidence before the Senate Committee on Railways;[127] attended a special meeting of the LSR National Executive regarding the future of the *Canadian Forum*;[128] and was once again actively leading the CCF's Quebec wing.[129]

Nor could Forsey, as was suggested above, totally withdraw from his beloved CLU responsibilities. He accepted a position as one of the speakers in the Union's new Speaker Series that was launched in October 1938.[130] That winter he also published a number of economics articles in the *Forum*.[131] Nor did the spring of 1939 bring much relief, for Forsey found himself embroiled in a civil liberties issue of a different, and more personal nature. This battle was with the McGill administration, and the resulting bitterness was only resolved by Forsey departing from the University two years later.

The problem that Forsey faced at McGill was similar to that faced by a number of outspoken academics at other universities during the

1930s. And this was especially true for those members of the LSR who had contributed sections to the LSR's first published book, *Social Planning For Canada*, for its thought had become clearly socialist. And as Michiel Horn has written, five of the seven co-signers of the book held teaching posts.[132] This reportedly prompted Sir Edward Beatty, president of the Canadian Pacific Railway Company, to speak out against those academics who might "mislead students" who were susceptible to "rash remedies for visible ills."[133]

In addition to this, the recommended dismissal of Frank Underhill at the University of Toronto[134] had aroused university administrators to the potential conflict between scholarly work and public activism. In this regard Forsey had put himself in a most tenuous situation, for he was devoting a tremendous amount of time to his public interests, and this necessarily delayed the completion of his scholarly obligations, such as the submission of his doctoral dissertation and his participation in related original research.

The issue finally emerged in May 1939, when Forsey received a raise to $2,600. But in his view that was small compensation for the "gang of half-wits, boobs, ignoramuses, boors, fools and cowards" that he felt ran the place. This hardly represented a ringing endorsement of one's employers. During two interviews in May, Forsey requested, and was denied, promotion. The reason given was that he had not shown "good judgement" in his non-academic activities. In a detailed memorandum he prepared on these meetings, Forsey documented his interviewers' accusations that he was seen to have been speaking out "in an excited tone of voice" in Arts Building conversations with colleagues. Forsey's colleagues had complained about both the tone and the choice of words he had used in these conversations.

His interviewer, Dr. Hendle, also took exception to a letter which Forsey had written to the *Gazette* in which he had stated that "no one outside a lunatic asylum thinks relief a good thing." Hendle thought that some of Forsey's remarks gave the impression that Forsey was "egotistical" and had developed a reputation as a "pleader" rather than a "scholar." Forsey interpreted Hendle's comments to mean that he, Forsey, must not take sides on public questions. This Forsey considered to be a "most dangerous doctrine" from which he wholly dissented and by which he "declined to be bound."[135] Forsey presented Hendle with a list of the organizations and "things" he had resigned from and a list of the "very few in which [he] was still engaged," but he was instructed to "withdraw further from non-academic endeavours and concentrate on research." The only "intelligible meaning" that Forsey could attach to Handle's comments was that he should "resign from the CLU Executive and cease altogether contributing to the Canadian Forum." "Needless to say," Forsey added, "I ignored the hint which I consider wholly improper.[136] Though Hendle insisted that he did not wish to "muzzle" his 35-year-old lecturer, Forsey wondered how he could "keep within the bounds and still ... take my part as a citizen should in this day's generation."[137]

In summing up his thoughts on the situation, Forsey concluded that it was clear to him that promotion at McGill "did not depend on one's work, but on one's popularity and on one's observing in one's outside activities certain arbitrary and ill-defined limits."[138] Forsey was sure that he had not been given the real reasons for the decision not to promote him. His disappointment and bitterness is barely hidden in the following statement: "Oh! We have a sweet crowd in power! McGill will be lucky if it survives."[139]

That summer the Forseys once again escaped Montreal's stifling intellectual atmosphere, this time for the cool breezes of Vancouver. There they took up residence from July 3 to August 18 in the Anglican Theological College on the University of British Columbia campus.[140] Forsey found Vancouver a welcome change from Montreal and was refreshed to find how "progressive" people were there. He was accomplishing a great deal of work on his thesis and generally readying himself for the next term's work at McGill.[141]

Socially the Forsey's were kept busy visiting and entertaining, yet Forsey found time to make three public speeches. In these speeches Forsey summed up what was for him the essence of the civil liberties question in a democratic state. He warned his audience at the Greater Vancouver Youth Council to expect attacks on civil liberties to increase in the current period of rapid social change. This was especially dangerous for youth, he explained, for "the alternative to civil liberties is repression? repression breeds revolution, and in a revolution it is youth ... which will have to pay the heaviest price."[142]

With his recent experiences at McGill fresh in his mind, Forsey now added "freedom of teaching" to his list of necessary freedoms, which included freedom of religion, speech, press, assembly, and association.

Freedom of teaching, he said, had been taken for granted in the nineteenth century but was being challenged now. Those who opposed civil liberties shared a belief that it was "repugnant to reason that the true and the false should be placed on the same footing." There went with such a belief, he added, "the assumption that the person who does the suppressing is infallible." Forsey rejected this philosophy outright because he believed that man could never be sure that he was right when he was trying to suppress an opinion that he disliked. In these situations we run the risk of "depriving humanity of an idea which may be valuable."[143] Truth could only be discussed, Forsey explained, when opinions were fully discussed, for a "truth" which was never discussed "soon degenerated into a dead dogma, which commands neither assent nor loyalty because it [was] not understood." To forbid discussion of our beliefs, he concluded, "was in itself a confession of weakness, of a lack of confidence in the very ideas of whose absolute truth we profess to be so certain."[144]

These were Forsey's reasons why the public had a responsibility to do its utmost to preserve freedoms, especially in a democracy in which people had to be free to choose many differing policies in order to rule effectively. Freedom, Forsey thought, "does not mean simply freedom for the views you and I like. It means also freedom for the views you and I dislike. That is something which a good many people, even in Canada, seem to have forgotten."[145]

For Forsey the preservation of civil liberties was directly linked to economic liberty. Speaking in the strong union province of British Columbia, Forsey included the freedom of assembly and association involved in joining a union as a basic example of economic freedom:

> Absence of trade unionism, in fact means the dictatorship of the employer. It may be a benevolent dictator, or it may not; but a dictatorship it is bound to be; and it is a cardinal principle of those British institutions which we profess to revere that good government is no substitute for self government, (partly for the excellent reason that in the long run self-government will be good government.) It is as true in industry as in politics that, as Professor Laski says, "Irresponsible power is poisonous to those who exercise it."[146]

The real danger to democracy and liberty in Canada, Forsey concluded, did not come from its open enemies but from "the false friends" who in the very name of "true democracy and true liberty stand ready to betray both democracy and liberty with a kiss." It was these "unseen assassins" who love liberty but hate "license" that Forsey encouraged his audience to be on guard against. "Eternal vigilance," he dramatically concluded, "is still the price of liberty."[147]

Forsey's defence of civil liberties, then, represented them in part as a mechanism to retain order in the democratic state. Freedom ensured order, which in turn ensured freedom. In another speech he encouraged a radio audience to fight abuses such as the Padlock Act as hard as it could from the moment such measures were introduced.[148] Forsey hoped that the forthcoming Rowell Commission report would recommend the necessary constitutional changes, including a Bill of Rights, that Canada required in order to defend liberty adequately.[149]

Following his western sojourn Forsey returned in the fall of 1939 to the same problems at McGill. He was sure that his smaller class sizes were the result of the administration suggesting to students that they not take his course. Forsey did resign from the CLU,[150] but only to plunge into the planning of the CCF's provincial election campaign with Lewis, Stanley Allen, and Frank Scott.[151] Forsey canvassed and wrote speeches for the CCF's lone candidate, R.C. Calder, who ran and lost in Verdun.[152] Though he was also tied up with his "wretched thesis,"[153] Forsey did find time to lead the LSR and the CLU to publicly condemn the Defence of Canada Regulations and the CLU's decision to defend nine Montreal Communists arrested for breaking the Regulations. Forsey successfully argued for the need to defend all citizens suffering civil liberty persecutions. In this debate he was opposed by public figures such as R.B.Y. Scott. In the ensuing debate Forsey was pleased to receive "about two minutes applause," and the almost unanimous support from the CLU members in attendance.[154]

Forsey worked very hard on his thesis over the winter of 1940, since it had to be submitted by the end of April.[155] Though he agreed to draft a speech for one CCF candidate in the upcoming autumn general election, he had decided to refuse all other election work. But politics was never far from Eugene Forsey's mind: "If the election waits till May," he wrote to David Lewis, "I'm in it!!"[156] He missed his chance for his first political contest, however, as King called the election for March 26.

The results of that 1940 general election were disappointing for

Forsey and all CCF'ers. In it the CCF received almost exactly the same weak electoral support as it had in 1935.[157] In Quebec the results were especially disappointing. Despite five years of hard work by Forsey and his few CCF colleagues the CCF vote in that province increased by only 300 from its 1935 total of 7,326. Its percentage of the popular vote stayed exactly the same at 0.6 percent.[158] Disappointing as the results were, Forsey tried to be optimistic. He wrote to Lewis and suggested that once the war was over there was bound to be reaction in the CCF's favour. As for his own future, Forsey told Lewis that the moment his exams were over he meant to get back into active CCF work, and he asked Lewis how he could best make himself worthwhile. "I've been disgustingly out of touch with the active life of our movement for so long," he wrote, "that I badly need to be brought up to date." He told Lewis that his "hat was in the ring not only for the next general election but for the first bye-election that occurs."[159]

Forsey reiterated his plans for active political involvement to Frank Underhill, and he added that with his thesis complete he felt that had been just let out of jail after a long sentence.[160] Forsey's surge of interest in active politics may well have been related to the fact that he had just been informed by the McGill authorities that his contract would not be renewed for the 1941–42 academic year. Forsey almost immediately contacted Lewis regarding the possibility of full-time employment with the CCF and supported his query with the statement that he was planning to get "a packet of work done for the Quebec CCF over the balance of the summer."[161]

Forsey also set out to revise and publish his thesis. By September 1940, he had finished 155 pages, was writing an average of three thousand words a day and "enjoying, hugely, almost every minute of it."[162] He fully expected his manuscript to cause "quite a storm," but he felt it would do him no harm if he published the thesis since he had the support of Cahan and Arthur Meighen.[163] It was, in fact, Forsey's request that Meighen proofread his manuscript chapter on the Constitutional Crisis of 1926, which explained Mackenzie King's "contempt" for parliament, that reunited Meighen and Forsey and re-established a friendship that lasted until Meighen's death.[164]

Forsey had developed a professional respect for Meighen during Meighen's leadership of the Conservative Party in the 1920s.[165] That was the time when Forsey first became interested in the concept of

Tory democracy, a concept that Forsey continued to incorporate into his Depression-era work. A 1938 Forsey radio broadcast, for example, was entitled "The Two Nations," a Disraeli term referring to the two "nations" of the rich and the poor.[166] Though Meighen and Forsey would never agree on the best method of rectifying the reality of the "two nations," they did share a common respect for British Tory democratic constitutional and parliamentary principles. This common ground superseded their ideological differences, as will be illustrated in the following chapter.

To Forsey, Meighen was "the hero of my boyhood and student days in the galleries of the House of Commons," when Forsey had become captivated with Meighen's constitutional knowledge and speaking ability. "He was," said Forsey, "the unquestioned master of the House, the most brilliant Parliamentarian whom Canada has produced."[167] Forsey would often repeat the fact that he considered himself, above all else, a "John A. Macdonald Conservative," and for him Meighen's constitutional view epitomized that nineteenth-century form of conservatism. Meighen had known Forsey personally since Forsey was about fifteen years old, when Forsey and his mother often visited Meighen's Ottawa home. And Meighen always retained "the highest opinion" of them both. Despite their ideological differences, Meighen's admiration of Forsey never wavered but in fact "steadily increased" over the years.[168] Meighen followed Forsey's career closely after Forsey left Ottawa for McGill,[169] and he congratulated Forsey "on the extraordinary grasp" of British constitutional tradition and government that Forsey demonstrated in his thesis work.[170]

Forsey in turn acknowledged that he had absorbed much of his knowledge from Meighen, "the greatest master of parliamentary law and practice our country has ever produced."[171] In later years Forsey would write to Meighen: "I sometimes feel as if you and I were almost the only two people left who really care about parliamentary government and the British constitutional system."[172] Forsey encouraged Meighen to run again for the Conservative Party leadership in 1941, and he wrote on more than one occasion that if Meighen had remained leader of the Conservative Party that Forsey would not have left it in the 1920s. Instead, Forsey wrote to Meighen, he would "have had the joy of serving under you in the House. I can't think of anything I should have enjoyed more."[173]

Forsey often defended Meighen against charges that he was a virulent anti-social democratic reactionary. Forsey pointed out to many people, for example, that Meighen's stated opposition to socialism did not mean that he was opposed to a form of Tory democratic social security. Meighen had been attacked by the *New Commonwealth* journal for opposing all forms of social security, and though Forsey and his wife were then living in Cambridge, Massachusetts on a Guggenheim Scholarship, Forsey insisted on setting Meighen's record straight for the Canadian public. In letters to the *New Commonwealth* and to individuals of influence like George Grube,[174] Forsey explained that Meighen's "silly" attacks on socialism must not be mistaken as a denunciation of social security, for they were not the same thing. Not only had Meighen supported and piloted through the Senate all of Bennett's New Deal legislation, but he "welcomed as the only sensible way to deal with profiteering" the 1939 Excess Profits Tax and the later Excess Profits Tax Bill of 1940. That same year, Forsey pointed out, Meighen had even supported the principle of unemployment insurance. Some of what Meighen said in support of that measure, Forsey added, "reads like a verbatim quotation from Frank Scott."[175]

During Meighen's unsuccessful York South by-election bid following his return as leader, Forsey produced pages of evidence from Meighen's Senate speeches to show that much of the material that the political left was using to attack Meighen had been taken out of context or purposely misquoted.[176] Forsey also thought that Meighen's conscriptionist reputation was inaccurate, for surely, Forsey argued, Borden and his entire Cabinet had to share the responsibility for their policy. Meighen had moved the legislation in the House only because Borden was ill, Forsey explained. In addition to that, he had agreed to come back to the thankless job of leading the Conservative Party, – a task Forsey felt was as "attractive as a sentence to the penitentiary."[177]

Forsey also thought that Meighen's Hamilton speech, which had been interpreted as calling for a plebiscite on Canada's wartime involvement, had also been purposely misinterpreted. Meighen had not uttered one word about a plebiscite, Forsey argued, but only referred to "the will of the people." That phrase, when taken in the context of the speech and within "the British constitutional tradition which we inherit," has always meant a general election and nothing else.[178]

Forsey's impassioned defence of Meighen's Hamilton speech position rested on Forsey's belief that in that speech Meighen had proposed a novel *rapprochement* with French Canada. He explained his thoughts to Meighen:

> The Hamilton speech is something in which I feel particularly keenly, because it seems to me the only approach the Conservative party has ever made to Quebec for many years which was not only logical and straight forward but also thoroughly consistent with Conservative principles. I dare say I am doubly prejudiced on this point, but I think plenty of people who aren't would be obliged to admit, if they really thought about it, that your proposal was at least the most logical ... any Conservative leader has offered Quebec.[179]

Meighen agreed that the speech had seemed to him "a logical, frank, and wholly proper method of bridging the gulf between the Conservative Party and the Province of Quebec."[180] For the Anglophone Forsey, who spent long years of his life attempting to build a CCF bridge over that same gulf, Meighen's efforts were an example of providing the best principles of the British constitution to the bicultural realities facing Canadians in the interwar period.

Philosophically, Meighen's and Forsey's views on the nature of man differed dramatically. "Meighen," Forsey wrote in 1949, "had an eighteenth century faith in reason." Forsey thought that Meighen also attributed to most other people the same faith and "the same willingness to accept anything that can be proved by formal logic." But Forsey also believed that there was evidence in Meighen's writings and speeches to suggest that he was "not quite so remote from the real world of imperfectly rational beings."[181] Meighen's speeches reminded Forsey of "the early Laski"[182] and even Edmund Burke,[183] in that they were concerned almost exclusively with freedom, with the principles of parliamentary government, and with the British Commonwealth. "In these three central themes Meighen believes with his whole soul," wrote Forsey in his review of Meighen's speeches published under the title, *Unrevised and Unrepented*.[184] Interestingly enough, these were almost the very words chosen by Donald Creighton in his Introduction to Forsey's own book, *Freedom and Order*.

Political differences seemed not to matter a great deal in their relationship, as both men were quite open as to their views on the other's activities: "Naturally I was sorry to see you a candidate in Carleton," wrote Meighen after Forsey's nomination to oppose George Drew in a 1948 federal by-election, "but it won't affect our personal relations in any way."[185] The day after Drew had crushed Forsey at the polls, Meighen wrote to his defeated friend:

> This is the morning after!
>
> There is one thing – perhaps only one – that I liked about the contest in Carleton. The Conservative press ... spoke highly of yourself. If I must say so, the only thing I liked about the contest was the result. It is anything but happiness to me to see you defeated in whatever you try to do. My thinking is so definitely the opposite of your own in things economic and social that I could not honestly wish that your ideas would triumph.
>
> You are in the wrong company entirely and emphatically. There is no one in this Dominion I would welcome into the right company quite so ardently as yourself.[186]

Meighen doubted that Forsey had a viable strategy to combat "war against poverty, insecurity and want," and he could not accept that a society based on extensive social support for the individual citizen could regain lost morale:

> The morale of a country is measured very definitely by the willingness of its people to work. I have lived now quite a long while, and the contrast between the morale today and what it was before the hand-out era is great – very great; it is distressing.[187]

But their friendship, grounded as it was in a fervently shared commitment to the central role of civil liberties and freedom though parliamentary institutions, superseded political differences. In fact it was Forsey's constitutionally oriented Ph.D. thesis and desire to seek, on Frank Scott's suggestion, a Guggenheim Scholarship to write a book on cabinet government, that led Forsey back to Meighen in 1941 on a regular basis.[188]

That book was never written, though Forsey spent from September 1941 until the autumn of 1942 in Cambridge, Massachusetts, working on it. With academic jobs scarce in both Canada and the United States, Forsey increasingly yearned for an entrance to political life. He had always thought that a paid position with the CCF would be an excellent step in that direction and had, as mentioned above, discussed the idea with Lewis since early in 1941.[189] But now the thought of running in a federal election, Forsey told his Mother, "has very great attractions for me, for I am sure that the House is where I can do my best work."[190]

Forsey's thesis research on the dissolution of parliament had solidified his earlier commitment to parliamentary procedures and had brought him and Meighen into common agreement on Mackenzie King's total disregard for Canada's British constitutional heritage. Many of the approximately four hundred letters that Forsey and Meighen exchanged during their friendship contain examples of King's disdain for that heritage. For that reason alone Forsey wanted desperately to enter the House of Commons "before Mackenzie King gets out, so that some measure of the retribution he deserves would overtake him."[191]

Though Forsey failed in that goal, he most certainly did not fail in raising Canadian public awareness of the importance of civil liberties to the democratic state. His extensive efforts through various organizations and on his own initiative to emphasize the central importance of individual economic, social, and political freedom in the face of the "vested interests" in Canadian society laid the foundation for the planned economy that will be discussed in the following chapter. Without the acceptance of the importance of individual freedom, however, the planned economy would never arrive.

CHAPTER 8

THE **PLANNED SOCIETY**

The new decade of the 1940s brought with it many changes in Forsey's life. Academically, Forsey's career as a university instructor came to an end as nasty infighting erupted over his dismissal from McGill. A student petition and appeals for help from fellow instructors and friends such as C.H. Cahan and Arthur Meighen could not reverse the verdict. More influential were the recommendations for his dismissal by three former Deans and Stephen Leacock, who could no longer accept Forsey's politics. The decision poisoned Forsey's appetite for further university work in Canada.[1]

Forsey also found the power of big business and university administrators to control the press and academic freedom particularly disillusioning. "I wonder why it is," Forsey wrote to his mother, "that so many Canadian newspaper and public men, for that matter, seem to think that professors are a little lower on the social and intellectual and moral scale than prostitutes?" In March 1941, Forsey wrote to Meighen that he was tired of being called a communist and being misrepresented by the press. As a result, Forsey decided to refuse all future speaking engagements, a commitment that quickly fell by the wayside.[2] But Forsey's dual role of economist as citizen and scientist was clearly drawing to a close, in part because of forces clearly beyond his own control. "What a country we live in!" he exclaimed to Frank Underhill after informing Underhill of his McGill problems. Underhill could sympathize with Forsey since he was undergoing the same sort of pressure from University of Toronto administrators that Forsey had experienced at McGill.[3]

At this same time, Forsey's participation in the associations that had held so much attraction for him during the 1930s was also undergoing a metamorphosis. The LSR, Forsey explained to Underhill, was in his eyes "pretty nearly dead" and now had little effect in the community. Forsey felt it would probably be "grabbed and used by the Communist Party" within a very short time. "If only we had captured some of the young people!" Forsey lamented and he recommended to Underhill that the LSR dissolve. The Fabian dream had ended for Forsey.[4]

Similarly, the FCSO had ceased to play a role in Forsey's life. His uneasiness with that organization had begun in 1940, when he became convinced that the Fellowship had "in positions of influence people who had been and still are markedly under the influence of the Communist Party, and/or its hangers on." Forsey emphasized to the National Secretary of the FCSO that he was not a "Red-baiter" and had in fact stood up for the rights of communists many times "at some personal risk." But he feared that the Fellowship's increasing affiliation with the communists would not only undermine the CCF, but also was not in keeping with the original aims of the organization. "I do not want to see the FCSO an appendage or side-show or echo for any political party," Forsey wrote, "[and] I never have. I think it would be disastrous." He believed, rather, that the FCSO had a "special job to do" that precluded its being associated with any political party. "It looks beyond the aims of any party," he explained to its National Secretary, Fred Smith.[5]

Forsey's specific concern with the communist "infiltration" of the FCSO was that communist leadership would be unsympathetic to the war effort. This was another indicator of Forsey's strong anti-fascist feelings during the war era.[6] The previous year, the FCSO Executive had issued a statement in the *United Church Observer* that there were several legitimate expressions of Christian conscience and Christian ways of acting in relation to the war crisis. These ranged from absolute pacifism to the conviction that "aggressive nations must be resisted with any means at [the Church's] command including military force."[7] As Roger Hutchinson explained, the main emphasis of the FCSO statement was on interpreting the causes of the war, defending and extending democracy at home, and articulating clearly what Canada was fighting for as well as against. On the whole, Hutchinson concluded, the FCSO bridged the war issue successfully and avoided serious tensions over charges of its being pro-Communist until later in the 1940s.[8]

Forsey's views were especially disturbing to his Fellowship associate, and co-author of *Towards the Christian Revolution*, Gregory Vlastos. Vlastos, a Queen's philosophy professor, viewed with disdain Forsey's insinuation that it was becoming impossible for CCF people to remain in the FCSO. "Surely you have never stood for witch hunts within a left group," Vlastos asked Forsey, "nor have you ever been unwilling to enter into friendly discussion and even co-operation with other left people in any genuine socialist project." Vlastos argued that even those "definitely to the left of the CCF" had as good a right as anyone to belong to the Fellowship. He pleaded with Forsey to change his mind and attend the FCSO summer conference "to clear up this matter."[9]

But Forsey remained convinced that members of the Fellowship executive were too closely associated with Communist Party members who were pushing their candidates forward for the Fellowship's General Secretary's position.[10] Continued attempts throughout the summer to change his mind failed to dissuade him, and Forsey continued to fire what R.B.Y. Scott called "broadsides" at the fellowship Executive throughout the autumn of 1940.[11] But as Forsey explained to the FCSO Executive in October 1940, his criticisms were not intended to oppose the essence of "Christian fellowship" that the FCSO stood for. "Fellowship, surely does not mean a blind and unquestioning acceptance of anything the Executive may see fit to do," he wrote, especially "when one feels that certain acts ... may have disastrous (though unintended) consequences?"[12]

By 1941 Forsey had come to the conclusion that many of the FCSO organizers were wholly incompetent and unreliable and "devoid of the first conception of the rudiments of fair play."[13] But he was encouraged by both David Lewis and M.J. Coldwell to remain inside the Fellowship to combat any communist takeover bid: "We both feel that the organization is, at least potentially, too important to allow to fall unchallenged into the hands of the communists," Lewis wrote.[14]

Suitably encouraged, Forsey continued his efforts with the FCSO throughout the winter, writing many lengthy letters explaining his position and asking for "fair" play for himself, the CCF, and other people in the Fellowship. He also requested that more care be taken by the Fellowship in its choice of publications, in its research sources, in its confirmation of information "which is likely to arouse controversy," and in choosing the "movements to which we lend our support."[15]

As was often his unintentional practice, Forsey had by this time alienated many FCSO members on the executive and in the general membership. Vlastos, for example, scolded Forsey for his view that a communist conspiracy was afoot to capture the FCSO. "That hypothesis is so fantastic that I need not discuss it," Vlastos wrote. Vlastos also rebuked Forsey's public denunciations of the Fellowship and Forsey's predictions of its impending split from "top to bottom." Forsey dismissed Vlastos' comments, and those of his fellow Queen's philosopher Martyn Estall, as typical of Queen's academics who wrote in a "political vacuum ... a state of virgin innocence almost incredible to anyone who inhabits a less cloistered air."[16] The rebukes were many and they undoubtedly had their effect; by 1941 Forsey had withdrawn almost completely from the FCSO, though he did not formally cancel his membership until 1944, by which time he was convinced that the Fellowship had become a "front" organization for the communists.[17]

Though he remained on the executive of the Civil Liberties Union until his departure for Massachusetts in late August 1941, Forsey had very little active involvement in the organization to which he had given so much time and energy in years past. His itch for politics, however, was not so readily dropped. "I want to be in the thick of the fight," he confessed to Lewis shortly before departing for the United States.[18] Invitations from Meighen to join the Conservative Party, and from Woodsworth to join the CCF in an active capacity, did little to quell his growing appetite for political involvement.[19] Encouraged by Woodsworth's assurance that he would "crash public life" once the right opening presented itself, Forsey pressured Lewis for a decision on a CCF union job he had first mentioned while Forsey was at McGill.[20]

In the meantime the Forseys settled in at Cambridge to a life of writing and editing his thesis for publication, and teaching Sunday school.[21] Forsey was certain that the publication of his thesis's denunciation of Mackenzie King's actions in 1926 would result in King's closing virtually every door of opportunity for him in Canada, including a promising opening at the Dominion Bureau of Statistics. "What with my CCF work and this book," he wrote to Lewis, "I shall be notorious to the last degree and Mr. King and [McGill Principal Cyril] James will bolt every door they can." There was, however, one career option still open for him as he wrote Lewis. "There's still the army! That's one place they'll take even those who have made themselves obnoxious to the Grit party!"[22]

In April 1942, some promising news arrived from Ottawa when Lewis asked Forsey if he would be interested in a new Director of Research position with the Canadian Congress of Labour. The idea, explained Lewis, was to hire someone who could build up a Research Department with the CCL,[23] a new union association formed through the affiliation of former Committee for Industrial Organization (CIO) unions throughout Canada in 1940.[24]

The formation of the Canadian Congress of Labour stemmed largely from the 1939 expulsion of the CIO and its industrial unions from the Trades and Labour Congress. The TLC, a craft-oriented union, was an affiliate of the American Federation of Labour, and according to labour historian Irving Abella, both unions were "moribund in the face of the rapid advances in size, scale and technology in such related industries as electrical appliances, automobiles, chemicals and rubber." These new industries could not be accommodated within their existing craft structures, and the AFL and TLC were not willing to change their organizational policies. This set the stage for the rise of new labour organizations in the late 1920s and 1930s which challenged the TLC's control of the Canadian labour movement.[25]

Meanwhile, in the United States, a growing number of union leaders decided to create a CIO-type organization within the AFL with the goal of organizing along industrial lines. By 1937 the CIO had a membership approaching four million.[26] In response to appeals by Canadian workers, organizers then began setting up CIO unions in Nova Scotia's steel industry and in Ontario's growing automobile and mining industries, where low Depression-era wages contrasted with rising corporate profits.[27] Strikes such as the 1936 Oshawa General Motors strike gave the CIO increased publicity, though it also faced a frontal assault from both government and business which slowed its momentum considerably.[28]

Internal bickering between communist and non-communist factions also weakened the new union and membership steadily in the late 1930s. Following the AFL-inspired TLC decision to oust its CIO unions, the TLC barred the CIO from its September 1939 convention, forcing it to set out on its own.[29] Within a very short time, David Lewis had succeeded in arranging the election of active CCF supporters to the CCL's six executive offices. The CCL's constitution, passed at its September 1940 convention, re-emphasized the need for a centralized organizing fund and authority similar to the CIO's structure in the United States. The Congress adopted a policy of utilizing "persuasive powers" and educational facilities to promote the policy of having all workers in one industry and in one organization.[30] This approach necessitated an effective method of controlling information on its various unions and centralized control over official union statements in response to corporate and governmental policy.

Though Forsey seemed ideally suited to co-ordinate this centralized research task, his CCF affiliation ironically worked against his appointment, for the CCL executive had from its outset an ambivalent attitude toward political action. Though many of its leaders were partisan to the CCF, they wished, if at all possible, to avoid committing the Congress to any political activity. Many executive members feared that a positive programme of support for the CCF would further divide an already splintered Congress. Under the leadership of its Treasurer and Chief Executive Officer, Patrick Conroy, the CCL proceeded until at least 1943 to keep the CCF proponents at arm's length, "at least until the apparent anti-labour attitude of the government became too unpalatable to ignore." To this end, circulars were sent out to all Congress organizers warning them not to participate in political campaigns or to become identified with any political party.[31]

In early May 1942, Forsey travelled from Cambridge to Ottawa on the invitation of the CCL's Executive Director, Norman Dowd. The purpose of the trip was to discuss Forsey's heading up the Research Department. This would involve his setting up a library and compiling information, "particularly with regard to Labour relationships and industrial developments in Canada and in other countries." Dowd expected that a good deal of work would be necessary in connection with the coal and steel industries, for which Forsey would be called upon to prepare briefs "for the Boards of Conciliation, the National War Labour Boards ... as well as preparing material for use in wage negotiations."[32] Dowd thought the work "especially fitted" for Forsey and tentatively suggested a salary of $3,000 per year as a starting figure, with the likelihood that this would be increased within a reasonable time.[33]

Following this trip Forsey returned to Massachusetts and wrote Meighen, whose "friendship and respect" Forsey now privately "prized," about his interview and the prospective job. He explained to Meighen that his CCF affiliation had been raised by the politically concerned CCL interview panel. "My interviewers were a trifle nervous about my connection with the CCF!" Forsey wrote. Forsey also informed his friend Meighen that he had explained to his interviewers that because of the impending publication of his anti-Mackenzie King book, he was likely within a few months' time "to be roundly abused as a high Tory." Forsey was, however, pleased to discover the general support he had with the interview panel, for most had read a recent *Canadian Forum* article he had written regarding the widening gulf between wages and bond interest and dividends. This was the kind of research work that the CCL was looking for out of its own Research Department.[34]

Forsey returned to Cambridge with the knowledge that the CCL would be hiring him as its Director of Research as soon as his Fellowship ended that summer.[35] Buoyed with the prospect of returning "to the fight," Forsey exuberantly wrote Meighen that he hoped "between us to reduce King to sputtering incoherence."[36] By early August the Forseys were once again at their Inglis Island retreat, but Forsey was anything but relaxed as he eagerly awaited getting back "into the fray." He was, however, apprehensive that with the war going as it was, his work with the CCL might be abruptly cut short.[37] Later that same month he was back in his hometown of Ottawa enjoying a new home, a new baby girl, and record-high public support for the CCF party. He also was looking forward to a new career start, for the CCL offered him a new and exciting vehicle through which he could continue his role as public commentator. It was an exciting time in Forsey's life.

The Ottawa that the Forseys returned to in 1942 was bustling with new men determined to introduce new ideas for regulating and expanding Canada's position in the international arena and introducing post-war domestic planning. Of specific concern for many of these new civil servants and consultants was the need to introduce measures to meet domestic unemployment after the demobilization that everyone hoped would one day arrive. This would necessitate new jobs at the same time that Canada's war industry would be closing down. By 1942 this challenge had been taken up by "a host of agencies," boards, and commissions that had "sprung up" within, and were associated with governmental departments. Each seemed to have its own set of proposals for Canada's post-war society.[38]

One such committee was the Committee on Reconstruction, headed by Forsey's former McGill Principal Cyril James. James's Committee had been created in March 1941 to study the problems Canada was expected to face after the war. Responsible to Ian Mackenzie, the Minister of Pensions and Health, the Committee was at the time of Forsey's arrival in Ottawa gathering information for its upcoming interim report. That report was submitted in October 1942, and recommended the establishment of new structures within the federal government to handle reconstruction, including the appointment of a minister to handle all economic affairs.[39]

The Committee's report also reflected the background research and philosophy of its co-ordinator and general administrator, Leonard Marsh. Marsh was the Director of the School of Research at McGill and a well-known supporter of reform through his work with Forsey and King Gordon in Montreal in the early 1930s and his contributions to *Social Planning for Canada*. The Committee provided a vehicle by which Marsh's social reformist and pro-planning views could influence government directly.[40]

This Report, as well as the publication of other major pro-planning documents such as Britain's 1943 Beveridge Report and Marsh's personal Report published in March 1943, all suggested a view of the future that even Mackenzie King could not ignore. In 1943, the Prime Minister gave his approval for detailed reconstruction planning, and Senate and House of Commons committees were quickly established to continue a process that the new generation of social scientists and academics had subtly initiated years earlier.[41]

What is especially interesting in comparing Forsey's views of the "planned economy" with those of the "new men" is the secular nature of the bureaucratic planning. This secularism sharply contrasted with Forsey's form of Christian-moral reformism, which viewed the "planned economy" as an extension of Christian fellowship in the post-war era. The 1940s bureaucratic reconstruction process was in many ways reminiscent of the "new era" envisaged by writers in the World War I era, except that "this time the new era was defined less in moral and philosophical terms and more in material ones." The key elements of the planned state following World War II would be sound economy, controlled capitalism, and social security.[42]

Forsey's reconstructed state, on the other hand, would include most of these materialistic and economic elements, but it also maintained a strong moral Christianity related to social action. This theme Forsey had consistently supported since his adoption of Tory democratic principles and his years at Oxford. Though the CCL gave him a new secular vehicle for his pronouncements on the nature of post-war Canada, Forsey's Canada would never adhere to a purely secular society. Christ would continue to play an integral role in Eugene Forsey's "new era."

Very shortly after the assumption of his position as Director of Research, Forsey was at work preparing a memorandum that served as the basis of the Congress's July 15, 1943 submission to the House of Commons Committee on Reconstruction.[43] Later that year the CCL published Forsey's report in a pamphlet entitled *Reconstruction: The First Steps*. In it Forsey recommended a pluralistic form of "democratized" planning that differed from the centralized and bureaucratic reconstruction philosophy that was emanating from Ottawa's civil servants and their commissions and agencies. Though Forsey agreed that wartime public and co-operative enterprises could serve "the new purpose of total war on poverty, insecurity and fear" that was necessary in post-war Canada, he argued that such national planning should be pursued in a dispersed and decentralized manner. National planning for national purposes, he wrote, embodied a need not only for "provincial planning for provincial purposes [and] municipal planning for municipal purposes," but also planning by producers' and consumers' co-operatives and associations. These community groups, Forsey added, represented "organizations of the common people, by the common people, for the common people," and he argued that the remedy for any tendency toward undue centralization lay in the people's hands.[44]

Forsey also directly addressed the role that these independent social and economic units had to play in controlling the growth of a centralized bureaucracy:

> The controls we propose are controls democratized by the admission of Labour, farmer and consumer representatives. It rests with us to make them serve our purposes. The new public enterprises, like most public enterprises, will be run not by bureaucrats (which is just an abusive term for civil servants) but by competent technical and managerial staffs operating under the democratically chosen Boards of Directors. If the technical and managerial staffs get too much power, it will be our fault, and no one else's.[45]

Here Forsey drew heavily on Laski's particular form of pluralism that stressed a federal society in which it was both unwise and impossible to confine sovereignty to the state or to any of the co-ordinate groups that constituted that society. Power, Laski argued, no longer needed to be concentrated at a given point in the social structure. This thesis rejected the central role of the "monistic state to apply uniform and equal solutions to things neither uniform nor equal." Laski favoured a federal state in which sovereignty would be distributed among the people through various functional groups and associations such as trade unions, co-operatives, businessmen associations, and churches, as well as the natural geographical subdivisions of society.[46]

Forsey expanded on his thesis in November 1944, in a speech delivered to the CCF Leadership School. In that speech, which was later published as a two-part *Canadian Forum* article, Forsey stressed that the only kind of planning that should ever be accepted was what he called "planning from the bottom, democratic planning, planning by the people." He argued that planning "from the top" during wartime had worked well in wartime, but it would have worked better it had come less from the top and more from the bottom. One example of this would have been to give Labour more representation on wartime agencies of planning, control, and administration. Great national policies such as price and wage control would have worked better if they had been enacted by Parliament after full discussion by the people and their representatives.[47] But peacetime planning must, Forsey explained, be radically different from wartime planning:

> ... the only peacetime planning which can succeed in a decentralized society like ours, and with our traditions of political freedom, is planning which is democratic through and through. Planning we must have, but only planning from the bottom will be tolerable or even workable once the war is over. Peacetime planning must be based on consent, consultation and participation at every stage; consent by the people, consent with the people, participation by the people.[48]

A Parliament restored to its position of authority and supremacy, Forsey added, as well as protection of minority and individual rights, the abolition of the Senate, and democratized municipal politics, all had a role to play in guaranteeing citizen participation in a democratized political machine.[49] Forsey denied the effectiveness of a centralized state that would "run everything." Rather, all levels of government, co-operatives, and other groups in society would have a role to play:

> There will be plenty of authorities, every one of them imbued with a strong sense of its own independence, and its own importance, and every one of them prepared to fight hard for its rights. There will be plenty of employers: thousands of them, public, co-operative and private.[50]

Such diffusion of power protected the individual worker's freedom to speak out and participate in the issues affecting society. Nor would the individual stand alone: the worker would have the protection of his union; the individual farmer the protection of his farm organization; the individual consumer the protection of co-operatives and consumer organizations. "And all these organizations," Forsey explained, "will be absolutely free from government interference. The notion that they will be dominated, coerced and pushed around by the state is wholly false."[51] Politically, the CCF was Forsey's chosen political vehicle for enacting this type of state:

> The CCF is a people's movement. Workers, farmers, consumers are the people. Workers' organizations, farmers' organizations, and consumers' organizations are the people's organizations. As such they must be left absolutely free to represent the people in their capacity as workers, farmers and consumers, just as parliaments and governments represent them in their capacity as citizen.[52]

The previous chapter established Forsey's commitment to individually free citizens; now he matched those free individuals with specific organizational entities within the state. The framework that would hold this structure together was Forsey's National Plan, a Plan that envisioned free citizens and their organizations (of which their government was just one) working together. A National Plan had to be accepted by the people in order for it to work, and only a plan made by the people would be accepted by them. The mechanism for providing such input Forsey called "democratic leadership," in which Canada's twelve million citizens would speak through their representatives "in municipal councils, provincial legislatures, parliament, provincial and dominion cabinets, unions, co-operatives, farmers' and consumers' organizations."[53]

Forsey had not forgotten his earlier enthusiasm for the Russian system of planning, for he now publicly advocated that Soviet Russia's "Millions Make the Plan" slogan become the new Canadian slogan for his pluralistic state. Adult education, he argued, would be essential in order for Canada's millions to appoint wise leaders to formulate industrial policies through agencies represented by the various citizen associations. These policies would in turn be reviewed by a central planning body that would return any revised plans back to the subordinate people's agencies for final approval. Only then would the final Planning Commission draft be submitted to Cabinet. The draft as approved by the Cabinet, with or without amendments, would then go before Parliament.[54] The "people's voluntary associations" thus played a central role in Forsey's reconstructed state.

Though Forsey went to great lengths to explain the overall nature of his pluralistic national planning, he did not neglect the specific policies that he felt should compose that plan. In his *Reconstruction* pamphlet, Forsey identified six economic steps that required immediate attention. First he called for a national Transportation Plan that would facilitate the necessary readjustments from wartime to peacetime conditions. "We must not," he wrote, "go back to the chaos of unregulated road-rail-water transportation." The CPR must be brought under public ownership and "the remaining private air, road and water services should be regulated as to rates and safety."[55]

Secondly, Forsey called for a National Food Policy to ensure plenty of healthy, cheap food for low-income families and adequate markets for farmers' produce. To prove that this was necessary, he cited statistics that showed half of Canada's urban population did not have incomes sufficient to purchase a completely adequate diet "while Canadian farmers have to put up with a wretchedly inadequate standard of living because they cannot find remunerative markets." Forsey found such a situation "intolerable and inexcusable, especially in a country like Canada."[56] If the price the worker could afford to pay was not high enough to give the farmer a living income, Forsey argued, "then public funds derived from taxation based on ability to pay must bridge the gap."[57]

One cannot help but wonder what one James Committee "blue ribbon" member, J.S. McLean of Canada Packers,[58] thought as he listened to the following Forsey arguments embodied in the CCL submission:

> The provision of food must become a public service. The Big Five flour mills (with their controlled grain elevators and bakeries), the Big Three packing corporations, and the Big Two fruit and vegetable canning concerns, must be brought under social ownership, with the appropriate groups of farmers and unions represented on the Board of Directors of the public enterprises thus created. We must end the scandal of competitive waste in these industries, and subordinate not private monopoly but efficient public enterprise.[59]

Forsey called for guaranteed prices and the reconditioning and re-equipment of many farms, the rapid development of rural electrification, and the provision of rural credit at low cost. His Food Plan also called for the doubled production of milk and cheese commodities.[60]

A third step, closely associated with the rural aspects of the National Food Plan, was the need to raise Canada's rural standard of living to the equivalent urban level. "The spread between the rural and urban standards of living," wrote Forsey, "is one of the most striking features of Canadian life." As severely as Canadian industrial workers suffered during the Depression, Forsey explained, "Canadian farmers as a whole suffered even more."[61] He cited statistics that showed Canadians last out of fifteen countries in rural wages as a percentage of industrial wages. The low percentages of farm homes with flush toilets, separate bath or shower, rural lighting, refrigeration, and housing in need of external improvements all showed "the same glaring discrepancy between urban and farm conditions."[62] Forsey also urged the removal of this inequality as constituting one of the major tasks of post-war reconstruction, but he denounced the proposals of "enterprising capitalist propagandists who seem to think that it can be accomplished by bringing wages down to the prevailing level of farm incomes."[63]

Forsey continued to monitor the comparative prosperity of his "worker and farmer" throughout the 1940s, an indication of the importance he gave to this particular step. In a 1951 article in *Labour Research*, a monthly bulletin initiated by his Research Department,

Forsey compared the purchasing power of one hour's labour for the Canadian farmer and worker between 1939 and 1951. His results contradicted public pronouncements in the House of Commons by Prime Minister St. Laurent that "the average rate of pay to labour in our manufacturing industries provides a greater purchasing power today than it did before the war."[64] For almost every industrial group, an hour's labour in April 1951 would buy less than one half of one percent more in food than in October 1939. "This is progress indeed," Forsey chided, "one half of one percent in eleven-and-a-half years! Compared with the industrial worker, the farmer has on the whole gained a little more than the worker though they were still getting less than they should."[65]

Forsey's fourth reconstruction step was a National Fuel Policy that would transfer Canadian coal mines to public ownership. A Coal Import Board would arrange bulk public purchases and arrange the distribution of the resource.

The very important fifth reconstruction step was a plan that would provide good quality cheap housing. "A post-war housing programme," Forsey wrote, "must enhance both urban and rural housing [and] repair and [improve] existing housing on a scale hardly less vast." Forsey drew attention to the tremendous backlog of unbuilt houses and the "deplorable" slum conditions in rural and urban Canada. "A majority of [urban] Canadians in low and middle income groups," Forsey wrote, "lived in overcrowded conditions, and [were] by modern standards unsatisfactorily housed in sub-standard dwellings."[66]

Forsey cited statistics showing increasing housing demands from different income groups, to illustrate his point that "the construction of new housing for the low and middle income groups must be undertaken almost entirely by public authorities or with assistance from such authorities."[67] The need for a housing plan remained central to much of Forsey's writings throughout the 1940s and into the post-war era. By 1949 he was urging the Dominion government to respond to the housing emergency by using its constitutional power to pass legislation to make federal aid for low-rental housing available to the provinces. This, he argued, could be accomplished "in exactly the same fashion as with old-age pensions, unemployment relief in the thirties, [and] health grants and other things." Forsey condemned the prevailing notion that the market for housing was like the market for automobiles, "a sort of necessity-luxury commodity which [was] naturally restricted to those who can afford it. Rather, he equated the housing need to public needs such as public health or education. By providing for that need, public authorities were assisting citizens in serious distress. This service, he argued, using words that any conservative since Burke would feel comfortable with, was especially important because, by alleviating the source of the public distress, authorities were also helping to ensure social order by responding to "a source of economic and social unrest."[68] Housing was not simply an investment outlet, Forsey argued, but a "social necessity," and he condemned the Liberal government for announcing that it did not consider housing a "national emergency" and for turning to the provinces for "concrete proposals."[69]

The five reconstruction steps mentioned to this point were all central to Forsey's view of the nature of post-war Canadian society: national plans based on input from all levels of government and citizen groups were required for transportation, while rural-urban wage levels, food, fuel, and housing were all desperately needed. But perhaps the most important "step" that Forsey identified in his 1943 CCL submission and continued to write about for many subsequent years, was the necessity of solving the unemployment problem through public control of finance and investment. This step had as its ultimate goal the maximization of human and financial resources and the maintenance of consumer purchasing power.

The "great social need" of full employment, not merely the prevention of mass unemployment, could be ensured only if there was enough new investment to absorb the national savings. Since Canadian capitalists were either unwilling to assume the necessary degree of investment, or were asking too high an inducement by the public authorities to make the necessary investment, Forsey argued that "the nation will itself would have to assume full control of finance and investment." This involved the taking over of the banks and the insurance and trust companies. More importantly, perhaps, it meant ensuring that people's savings were fully used to maximize employment and directed to other "socially desirable channels." Forsey was insistent that there must be "no idle money, no idle machines, and no idle men."[70]

Forsey's financial policy was directly in accordance with the stated CCF policy, so much so, in fact, that Forsey participated in a 1944 CCF lecture series sponsored by the Ontario CCF. These sixteen lectures were given on the basic themes of the CCF political programme and then published in a book entitled *Planning For Freedom*.[71] Forsey began his January 31, 1944 lecture by mentioning that his speech was only a short overview of an issue that was covered more completely in the LSR's *Social Planning For Canada*. In his speech Forsey reiterated the need to use the financial machinery of money, banking, and investment as "an instrument of total war on poverty, insecurity and fear." Canada had the human and material resources, but it was "the business of the system to provide the money so that those resources will be used to meet the needs of the people." This approach necessitated an acceptance of the need to organize money as an instrument for promoting "the material progress of man, rather than as an end, or as itself the controller of human affairs."[72]

In addition, the financial institutions, including banks, trust, and loan companies, had to be socialized and "made an integral part of our democratic socialized economy." The socialization of finance and industry, Forsey explained, "had to go hand in hand in order to ensure private investment was directed towards projects profitable to the community, and not just profitable to the company." This ensured public access to the undistributed profits of individual corporations, which represented "a considerable amount of the supply of capital under modern conditions."[73]

Lastly, Canada's public control of the Bank of Canada had to be expanded so that the chartered banks to which it lent funds could be forced to lend that money. This ensured that all available money would be used. Also, the Central Bank should be authorized to control "the direction of the money which it makes available even if that money is actually not always lent by the chartered banks to industry." This would not always mean lending where it was the safest and most profitable to do so. "Private profit and the public interest do not necessarily coincide. A thing may be extremely profitable to the private capitalist without being correspondingly desirable from the point of view of the community."

Forsey also pointed out that the traditional argument of the mainstream reformers who favoured controlling the amount of investment, that is, the proportion of the national income which is ploughed back into production, did not go far enough.[74] "To secure a just and stable society," Forsey explained, "we must also control the kind of investment into which the available funds go, and the spending of those funds."[75] For these ends, nothing less than the socialization of all the financial machinery and the main industries would suffice. Socialization of finances was not a cure-all in Forsey's view, but it was a necessary part of the prescription.[76] Forsey used the balance of his CCF speech to explain how the financial machinery would actually administer this system.[77] He ended his presentation by emphasizing the need to reduce the public debt by simultaneously reducing taxes on the poor and decreasing interest and increasing taxes on the rich by levying a once-only graduated debt-redemption levy on capital. This policy would increase the practice of taxing those with the ability to pay, since the wealthy would be expected to pay their debt-levy in the form of their government bonds or securities in industries which were to be taken over by the public anyway. In addition to extinguishing a large part of the public debt, therefore, the levy would help in the process of social-ization of industry.[78]

But the Canadian worker also had a central role to play in this socialization process, and Forsey used his CCL position to emphasize that the success of a pluralistic society depended upon the responsi-bility of its participating social and economic units. In a 1946 speech to the Canadian Political Science Association, for example, Forsey explained that full employment could only be maintained if there was an adequate demand for consumer goods. Unions, in turn, played a key role in inducing governments to adopt social security measures that raised and stabilized consumer expenditures. But, Forsey argued, unless there was an adequate price control and an appropriate taxa-tion policy, the indirect benefits of higher wages and controlled prices "might be snatched away."

In making this argument Forsey was drawing heavily on the British economist Sir William Beveridge's influential and recently published book *Full Employment in a Free Society*, which had helped nudge even the recalcitrant Mackenzie King toward social activism.[79] Forsey rec-ommended that Canadian post-war society had to implement a method of ensuring "a new type of indirect bargaining [by labour] through government for the redistribution of real income."[80] Labour could only effectively assume its new wage co-ordination and public policy formulation powers, Forsey argued, by providing itself with a much larger and highly competent staff of expert advisers. Only then would the urgency of enacting financial and economic policies that had full employment as their top priority be accepted by Canada's private and public powers.[81] To ensure workers' participation, Forsey suggested that a fully developed workers' education programme be initiated. This would prepare unions for a responsible, reasonable, and controlled approach to the negotiation process:

> It would be rash to prophesize, but in my opinion, if the public, including the union public, is sufficiently educated; if the government shows that it really means to get and keep full employment; if it controls prices; if it takes the unions into its confidence, and gives them a real share in the formulation of its whole industrial policy; if the employers accept unions ungrudgingly and wholeheartedly, instead of dreaming of the lost delights of the non-union shop and individual bargaining, and scheming to bring them back; then the unions will act reasonably.[82]

Forsey viewed the main *raison d'être* of his new CCL Research Department as providing the intellectual and organizational leadership necessary to convince the public of the need for the policies he advocated and to resist the attacks on the "working class."[83] To this end Forsey spearheaded the organization of a CCL reference library containing books, reports, and pamphlets on Labour relations, job evaluation, union security, wages and working conditions, Labour legislation, workers' education, and reconstruction and full-employment policies.[84] This material was necessary to assist with the task of educating CCL workers to meet the post-war challenges facing them and to take a responsible place with their expert advisers as equal partners in the pluralistic policy formulation process. In his annual Director of Research Report to the CCL's 1946 convention, Forsey explained that he was personally "convinced that we must [develop] an expert union Civil Service, if the Canadian Labour Movement [is] to meet effectively the challenges which the future is certain to thrust upon it."[85]

Of all the specific post-war problems facing Canadian Labour, Forsey thought the most urgent was full employment. This was especially true in a society where Labour and the politicians knew that there was "plenty of useful work waiting and needing to be done."[86] He researched and published extensive reports in the CCL's *Labour Research* refuting industrial and governmental statements that denied

the existence of extensive unemployment. Such illusory pronouncements concealed the class nature of Canadian society that Forsey had
been fighting to reveal since his return from Oxford. Since that time
he had been socially active in raising Canadian class-consciousness of
unequal economic conditions on a major scale,[87] and his position with
the CCL provided him with an excellent vehicle for pursuing this passion for social activism. Take, for example, the following quotation,
which typically came at the end of a lengthy and statistics-laden analysis
of unemployment between 1945 and 1950, and accusations of government concealment of that information:

> More light!
>
> Unemployment has this year once more become a serious prob-
> lem; the latest figures are higher than for any corresponding period
> since the early summer of 1946. It vitally affects every citizen. It
> cannot be solved without the fullest possible information. There
> is nothing to be gained and everything to be lost by hiding, or
> neglecting to publish, any relevant figures. That just plays into the
> hands of the demagogues, irresponsible alarmists who may scare the
> public into fantastic or dangerous courses, or equally irresponsible
> optimists who may lull it into a false sense of security. Knowledge
> is our only safeguard against these perils.[88]

As solving unemployment became less of a government priority in
the early 1950s, Forsey drew attention to shortages of particular kinds
of workers an regional unemployment problems,[89] and publicly disagreed with the "official pronouncements of light unemployment."
"Slight hardly seems strong enough for unemployment which is close
to double the higher normal percentage," Forsey wrote in early 1952,
adding that "There is such a thing as carrying Anglo-Saxon understate-
ment too far."[90]

Forsey also documented the inadequacies of existing unemployment
insurance and called for the Dominion to initiate a system of public
assistance to supplement the municipalities, which did not have the
money or the means of raising it. In addition, he called for the federal
government to provide considerable assistance to prevent a winter of
"inadequacy, confusion and suffering."[91] The system, he added, need
not become a process of undue centralization, for it was the Dominion's

role merely to distribute the money through "variable payments," expert advice and uniform standards. The municipalities and provinces, in turn, would administer the programme and "set standards of administration, personnel, eligibility requirements, scale of allowance etc."[92] In this sense Forsey's pluralist and federalist beliefs prevented his becoming overly centralized in his various experiments.

But unemployment was only one of Forsey's concerns. Post-war inflation soon became a major obstacle for working people,[93] and the widening gulf between low wages and high prices consumed more and more of Forsey's attention. His carefully prepared 1948 CCL submission to the Royal Commission on Prices,[94] for example, detailed a 30 to 50 percent increase in prices between 1946 and 1948 as well as a widening gulf between wages and prices.[95]

Forsey took this opportunity to incorporate an attack on the government's failure to control prices as an indication that "[its] whole economic philosophy [was] nineteenth century laissez faire. It dislikes controls. It dislikes planning." This, Forsey wrote in his CCL brief, was unacceptable in the face of increasing working-class hardship:

> [The government] asks nothing better than to be allowed to retreat into the never-never land of "free and open competition." But it has to live in the twentieth century, and the harsh realities of the twentieth century have forced it into planning and controlling [but] it plans controls reluctantly. It plans and controls as little as it can.... it even announces measures for freeing international trade and import controls by the wildest dreams of extreme protectionism. The free trade measures are for the "normal" long run, the controls for the "abnormal" short run.

The Congress, on the other hand, believed in controls,[96] and in the need to stop inflation to preserve a free society.

This was a message that Forsey reiterated in numerous articles in *Labour Research*, the *Canadian Forum*, and letters to the editors throughout the late 1940s and 1950s.[97] A free society for Forsey meant "at least some measure of democracy in industry" through a genuine collective bargaining process that ensured working-class input into "the conduct of production." The pluralistic society ensured this through Industrial Councils and labour representation on the boards of industries and agencies of social planning and control.[98] But Canada, Forsey felt, was not receiving this sort of creative leadership in labour matters. Forsey denounced Mackenzie King as "the father of company unionism"[99] for his policies regarding collective bargaining,[100] especially his Wartime Relations Regulations.[101]

When the federal government introduced the Industrial Relations and Disputes Investigation Bill in 1948, Forsey prepared a detailed critical CCL Memorandum, which was presented to the government by CCL President A.R. Mosher and its Secretary Treasurer, Patrick Conroy.[102] Though he found the New National Labour Code an improvement over previous legislation,[103] Forsey condemned the new 1948 legislation for addressing only a few industries which were within Dominion jurisdiction. The three chief industrial provinces, Ontario, Quebec, and British Columbia, the Memorandum stated, with "about eighty percent of the country's industries," remained under three different provincial systems.[104] This Bill precluded co-ordinated nation-wide strikes, did not provide for any form of mandatory union security, and excluded any references to unfair labour practices by employers, such as refusal to bargain collectively.[105]

In a revealing analogy, Forsey wrote that the establishment of collective bargaining "democratized" industry by "constitutionalizing" it. "The establishment of the union shop," wrote Forsey, "means that industrial citizenship, like politics, becomes compulsory." This prevented non-union workers from benefiting from union agreements; in effect getting something for nothing because they did not pay for it.[106] "We do not tolerate this sort of thing in the state," Forsey wrote. "We do not allow a man to decide for himself whether he will or will not pay taxes. Exactly the same principle holds good in industry."[107]

Eugene Forsey was, however, also convinced that Labour could not depend totally upon its secular institutions, such as independent unions and its co-ordinating bodies such as the CCL, to meet these post-war challenges and responsibilities. In Forsey's pluralistic post-war society God also had a role to play in providing for the needs of Canada's workers. Despite Forsey's support for the Soviet economic system, for example, he argued that it was the very absence of any Christian element that doomed that system to failure. "Without Christianity," Forsey once wrote, "the Russians were likely to fall short of their aims."[108]

Forsey expanded on this theme in a revealing unpublished manuscript entitled "Postwar Problems of Canadian Labour, With Special Reference to the Responsibility of the Church." In it Forsey wrote that the church had "both the right and duty to pronounce on political, social and economic questions in accordance with Christian principles." "To give it up," he explained, "would be in effect to sign a treaty of partition with the devil, handing over to him vast provinces of human life."[109] The church had a responsibility like any other social unit in society; its role was to translate its fundamental Christian doctrines of freedom and equality from "mere affirmations" into social reality. As Forsey continued his campaign against unemployment, low wages, and government "misinformation,"[110] he increasingly relied on the church, for in his eyes it had always been a major active force for progressive change in his pluralistic society. The church and labour needed to work more closely, for example, to better workers' wages. "Labour wants decent minimum standards of wages, hours, and working conditions right across the country," Forsey explained, "It wants to get rid of low wage areas. This also, surely is an aim the Church must approve."[111]

Collective bargaining, social security, decent health, food, education, and recreation for all the people were all labour's aims, but they were also, in Forsey's view, the church's aim. They were, in fact, community aims. "The things Labour wants are as much in the interest of the community generally as they are of wage earners. This is the basic reason why they deserve the support of the Church."[112] In Forsey's view of the community, the church "had a special responsibility for promoting understanding among the different sections of the community." In this context, this meant promoting understanding of labour's problems by farmers and urban middle-class people.[113]

Both Christianity and labour, therefore, believed in freedom and human equality and brotherhood, and the principle that "man does not live on bread alone." This was, of course, a message that Forsey had come to wholeheartedly accept while at Oxford, and he continued to preach this message during his tenure with the CCL. Both labour and the church had to be brought closer together: "Labour has little to do with the Church and the Church has little to do with Labour," he wrote. "Each thought of the other as something outside of itself and remote from its main concerns." This, to Forsey was "true enough to be disquieting and it is certainly true enough to call for action to bring Christianity and Labour together."[114]

This unity was important for Forsey because it was essential that the church become involved with "life in this world," and shake off the lethargy of its current "pseudo-Christianity":

> It [the church] believes in freedom and equality of brotherhood; but it refers these explosive revolutionary ideas to another world, not to this. Freedom, yes; but not here and now; equality, yes, but not here and now; brotherhood, yes, but not here and now. But this is not real Christianity. Jesus taught us to pray, "Thy will be done on earth." The great religious ideas and emotions ought to be motives to action in this world. Too often we have cut the nerve between ideas and action, and of course the result has been that, although we believe all the right things, nothing happened.[115]

The reality was that too often working-class supporters in the labour movement, some of them communists with little time for religion, had "made the great Christian ideas the basis of their action, and things happened in spite of [the church], or the church stood by indifferent or even hostile." The church and labour, wrote Forsey, had sometimes been "like the two sons in Jesus' parable: the church has said, 'I go,' but has not gone; Labour has said, 'I go not,' but has gone."[116]

Forsey continued to reject the notion that the "business of Christianity [was] the development of Christian character in the individual." This notion he explained, argued that if the church could "produce enough sanctified individuals, politics, economics and social problems would solve themselves." This he found to be a false notion:

> This is a plausible argument. But it is false. Christian character does not develop in a vacuum. It is forged in the struggles of daily life and most of the daily life of most people is spent in the effort to satisfy economic wants. The struggle for bread is not the only thing in life, nor the highest thing. But it is basic, for without bread there is no life. If the economic system in which we must earn our living forces us to spend most of our waking hours in ways which thwart and deny everything for which Christianity stands, religious

leaders may preach themselves black in the face with only barely perceptible effort upon the mass of mankind. We must Christianize our society or give up preaching the Gospel of Christ.[117]

In this paper, written in 1949, Forsey concluded that "the Church must be very deeply concerned with the economic, and Labour with the spiritual. The Church must be concerned with the economic because it is concerned with the spiritual." Forsey quoted John Macmurray to illustrate his argument:

> As Professor Macmurray puts it: Our bodies are not ends in themselves. We live for the knowledge and friendship. But a serious illness puts an end to work of enormous importance.

Just as one stopped all other endeavours to right an ailing body, so too with a sick society. If the economy falls sick, Forsey explained, then nothing else is important for the time: "No real human social life is possible till the economic organization [was] restored to health." It was essential, therefore, that society recognize that the present economic system was making the personal life impossible and dehumanizing people. "That imposes on Christians," Forsey stated, "the unmistakable duty of reconstructing the economic system."[118] So too must labour be concerned with the spiritual because it was concerned with the economic. "Labour wants higher wages, shorter hours and security, not as ends in themselves, but as means to life. Take away the spiritual, and Labour's whole struggle becomes meaningless."[119]

In Forsey's view, then the church and labour were "powerful allies in a common cause." Though the emphasis was different, their basic aim was the same: abundant life. The church needed to return to its primitive, working-class origins, and recognize the revolutionary spirit of early Christianity for which it was persecuted and reviled. If the church would fight with labour for their common aim, it would have "plenty of opportunity to earn this particular blessing."[120] The church could help labour by reminding it that the end toward which it should be striving and "to which all its day to day demands and struggles" were directed, were only means. It could remind the community "that the aims of the Labour movement were essentially the aims to which the community itself was dedicated."

Perhaps the clearest articulation of Forsey's evolving philosophy of the Christian pluralist philosophy came during the summer of 1947 when he presented a series of lectures at the Alberta School of Religion, located in Calgary.[121] The lectures, which Forsey called "Economic Planning in a Free Society," were delivered over the course of one week and totalled ninety-one pages of foolscap. They represent the most comprehensive statement of Forsey's reconstructed society: a planned society built on Christian principles and moulded by the hands of its citizens acting through their respective associations, of which organized trade unions and the church were but two of many.

Forsey focused on the role of religion in these lectures, and especially its vital role in being properly concerned with economics and politics, and economic planning in particular. He also stated his clear belief that economic planning was one of the crucial issues of their time, especially for Christians who believed "in the infinite value of every human soul, and the equality of all men before God." Given this, he said, "we must believe in freedom, welcome everything that means more freedom, ... and fight everything that means less."[122]

Forsey also told his summer school audience that man was by nature a planning animal, but because man was also a social animal, planning could not proceed simply as an individual exercise, but had also to proceed on a social and national scale. But how much, what kind, and by whom? Wartime experience, he argued, had shown Canadians that the state could plan without taking over more than a small part of industry while sacrificing only a very small part of its freedom.[123] But war was not the only emergency that warranted such action: family disaster, pestilence, the lack of foreign currency to buy the food and raw materials necessary to survival, were also emergencies. "The point is," Forsey emphasized, "like war, they are emergencies, and the compulsions and restrictions they impose came from the emergency, not from the planning."[124]

Unlike wartime planning, Forsey's conception of peacetime planning did not identify with restrictions and controls. It was, rather, essentially positive in nature and aimed at abundance, not scarcity. "The greater the abundance," he explained, "the less the necessity of restrictive controls." Democratic planning, in essence, was planning by people, "frail and imperfect men and women," who will ultimately make the decisions and choose the planners. The planners, likewise, will be just as "imperfectly rational [and] just as queer a mixture of good and bad, intelligent and stupid, ignorant and well-informed, as we are now." The mechanism for this process of "planning from the bottom up" was the give and take process of pluralism in action:

> We shall act through our trade unions, our farm organizations, our co-operatives, our churches, our political parties, and other voluntary associations; through our municipal councils, our school boards, our provincial legislatures, our Dominion Parliament, our civil services, our public boards and commissions and Crown companies.

Forsey acknowledged that because of the human element, participants would not always act on the basis of "pure reason or from the highest motives or unmixed motives." Differing interests and points of view would persist and so the process of reading decisions would not be purely rational but would be partly a process of conflict and compromise. To Forsey this kind of planning was the only kind that was democratic and compatible with a free society. "Ultimately," he said, "it is the only kind that can possibly work. In economic planning as in politics, the only good government is self-government."[125]

In exploring the "philosophical jungle which surrounds this whole question of freedom," Forsey delved into the "Nature of a Free Society." In so doing he accepted the four freedoms identified by Barbara Wootton in her book *Freedom Under Planning*. The first of these were cultural freedoms, such as freedom of the press, of worship, of arts and science, and freedom of access to as much education as one could absorb. This necessitated the absolute exclusion of any attempt to impose on the people any specific doctrine, religious or anti-religious, artistic, scientific, economic or political.[126]

Secondly came civic freedoms, including freedom of speech, assembly and association, and freedom from arbitrary arrest and imprisonment. Thirdly, economic freedoms included freedom to choose one's vocation, to take, refuse or leave a particular job; to bargain collectively, to strike, and freedom of movement. Lastly, political freedoms included the right to vote and change the government without resort to force and the right to form opposition parties.[127]

Forsey agreed that this list of freedoms provided "a useful working idea of what we mean by a free society," but he emphasized that freedom encompassed the economic as well as the legal. "A society may have the absolute minimum of legal limitations on freedom," he explained, "and still be grossly unfree because most of its members are too poor to use their legal freedoms."[128] To Forsey, poverty could be a fatal barrier to the positive aspects of individual freedom such as freedom of access to education, freedom from wrongful imprisonment, freedom to choose one's vocation or to refuse or leave a particular job, or freedom of movement. He argued that, whereas nineteenth century liberalism concentrated on the legal limitations on freedom and tended to overlook the economic, socialism concentrated on the economic limitations. While Forsey acknowledged the importance of legal freedoms, he emphasized the importance of the latter type:

> Our nineteenth century, Victorian legal freedoms, though certainly incomplete, are equally certainly invaluable and provide the only solid basis for the conquest of economic freedom. But something closer to economic equality than our western societies have yet achieved is an indispensable condition of full freedom.

Forsey added that a society could not claim to be really free unless its members enjoyed both "substantial legal freedoms and also something not too far removed from equality of income." But he admitted that other elements "in the good life," such as security and the pursuit of material welfare, might justifiably "involve some sacrifice of freedom."[129]

In his analysis of the aims of planning, Forsey acknowledged that although the general aim was "the good life," different states, political parties, and effective voluntary associations all had different ideas as to what constituted that good life. This was also true with planners: some desired to use planning to effect radical change, while others were reasonably well satisfied with things as they were and wanted only enough planning to keep the status quo. These latter, conservative planners, feared that a lack of planning would mean another depression that would destroy their existing society.[130]

But all planners, Forsey argued, agreed that one aim of planning was the attainment of full employment, though differences existed as to how useful those jobs had to be to the worker and to society. Many conservative planners, for example, believed that it was not necessary to plan to make the jobs useful. "Meanwhile," Forsey said, "we must note that all planners except the most conservative think that even if the sole aim of its planning is full employment, the state will be bound to interfere to some extent with private enterprise and the mechanism of the market." This might, for example, involve special measures to stimulate consumption or investment, and this interference necessarily meant interference with private choice.

To Forsey, this distinction was crucially important. Sovereign, private choice, or "consumers' sovereignty" through the free market was for conservative planners the best basis for determining what would be produced. It worked automatically. People were entitled to get only what they themselves wanted, and the free market gave it to them more completely and cheaper than any other system could. "People buy most of what they want most," Forsey explained, "and of course the producers will therefore produce most of what people want most. So people will get what they want, as far as what is humanly possible."[131] But Forsey rejected this view of competitive capitalism because monopoly capitalism no longer produced items at the cheapest price. In addition, government price subsidies and tariffs had so distorted the system that "in the real world, as distinct from the abstract world of certain economists' studies, things [were] not always sold at the lowest possible price." Forsey also believed that "what the market place gives us is not what we want (and can pay for at the price set by our more or less monopolistic system) but what advertisers want us to want." This was not necessarily what would best satisfy our desires, "but what will give them the biggest profit. That may be a very different thing."[132]

The central point in Forsey's argument on the relationship between freedom and planning was whether the planners could have "a reasonable idea of what we want" and whether they could then give us results which most ordinary people would agree are better than what we get from lack of planning. And if they could, would they? If the answer was no to these two points, then Forsey was willing to concede that the conservatives were right, and "we should either not plan at all, or plan only with the single aim of full employment, leaving everything else to unplanned choice."

To this rhetorical question, Forsey answered that: "Despite my strong preference for conservatism, I am convinced that the conservatives are wrong." Here Forsey seemed to face the central contradictions between his Tory democratic reformist roots and his later socialist reformism. His decision to support the latter option, and to reject the controlled capitalistic reformism then in vogue in Ottawa,[133] was based on four major points: the non-comprehensive nature of "conservative planning" that excluded certain wants such as housing, health, and education; the lack of firm commitment and farsightedness of conservative planners; the commitment of "radical" planners to comprehensive consumer preferences, as opposed to the short-term market preference studies condoned by existing authorities; and lastly, "the assistance of all kinds of voluntary associations with some knowledge of what consumers want such as co-operatives, farm organizations, retail merchant organizations, trade unions, local councils of women and so forth."[134]

The economic aims of Forsey's type of planning rested on the acceptance of the above principles, and only radical planners could reasonably expect to accomplish the necessary economic aims. These aims included the maximum efficiency of society's human and mechanical resources and high levels of consumption, which required control of savings, investment, and expenditures.[135] The other aims of planning included improved health, social security, and education.

The main body of Forsey's lectures was called "The Methods of Planning," which he divided into two parts. The first dealt with economic techniques necessary to carry out the aims of the planners. Here Forsey outlined in great detail the limitations of conservative planning, which he said sought primarily to provide full employment but wanted "to leave the rest of the economic and social system as nearly as possible unchanged."[136] Forsey reiterated many of the arguments put forward ten years earlier in *Towards the Christian Revolution* and *Social Planning for Canada* in rejecting the limited planning scope inherent in the various conservative plans. These plans, in short, involved "a minimum of interference with the general structure of capitalist society." These "mere tails to the private enterprise kite" shared a tendency toward a centralized planning apparatus, an approach that Forsey's pluralism rejected as impractical in the federalized Canadian state.[137]

Forsey did, however, support the British economist William Beveridge's plan to socialize and control industrial location, investment, consumption outlay, and production. Beveridge also favoured extensive public ownership and deficit spending to meet "social priorities" and a permanent, planned total economic war "against unemployment and other social evils." This, Forsey concluded, represented "real" planning in which:

> Public choice of economic priorities takes precedence over private choice; private choice does not disappear, but it is relegated to a subordinate role. The authority of the state over economic life is vastly increased.[138]

Though Forsey labelled Beveridge's plan as being "manifestly semi-socialist," he felt that a full-scale democratic socialist plan "would probably differ from it only in assigning a considerably larger sphere to public co-operative enterprise." Forsey seemed to consider Beveridge's approach as an acceptable moderate starting point that would lead to further socialistic steps. "Beveridge's semi-socialist planning," Forsey concluded, "might well find itself pushed into socialism by the force of circumstances."[139]

Having defined his preferred socialistic planning approach, Forsey returned to the impact that socialist methods would have on freedom. He acknowledged that socialist planning posed a greater possible threat to freedom than did other forms of planning, but he emphasized that the state would not run everything in the form of the socialized state envisioned by himself and organizations such as the CCF. The whole of agriculture and a very considerable part of the other business and industry would, in fact, remain in private hands, subject only to a few social controls and legislatively approved plans. Important as this was, the central safeguard in Forsey's interpretation of Canada's democratic socialism lay in the pluralistic application of the planning process.

Eugene Forsey viewed pluralism as an integral and comprehensive component of Canadian democratic socialism. Most of the other contemporary public statements regarding CCF policy, such as the CCF's book *Planning For Freedom*, Lewis and F.R. Scott's *Make This Your Canada*, as well as the 1932 Regina Manifesto and 1956 Winnipeg Declaration of Principles, referred either to the individual role of a farm co-operative in pursuing agricultural interests, or trade unions for workers' causes. One scans the Regina Manifesto and the Winnipeg Declaration, and the more recent historical overviews of the CCF in vain to find any direct references to the importance and the centrality of pluralism in the "co-operative commonwealth."[140]

For Forsey, however, pluralism was an essential aspect in any planning system whose goal was to ensure freedom and economic democracy, and which sought to protect its citizens from becoming "mere puppets in the hands of the central government." Pluralism ensured that:

> There would be, in effect, freedom in diversity: There will be plenty of different authorities, every one of them imbued with a strong sense of its own independence, its own intelligence, and its own importance, and every one of them prepared to fight hard for its rights.

The worker, farmer, consumer, and businessman would all be individually protected by their respective organizations, which would "not only be permitted but strongly encouraged by CCF governments" but would be absolutely free from government interference. "The notion that they (associations) will be dominated, coerced or pushed around by the state," added Forsey, "is wholly false."[141]

Each of these associations would be represented on the planning bodies. These "people's" organizations provided a sense of dual representation for the people in that they would be left absolutely free to represent the people in their capacity as workers, farmers, businessmen, and consumers, just as parliaments and governments represented them in their capacity as citizens.[142]

Forsey was thus applying the duality with which he viewed himself as economist and citizen to others in Canadian society. In his view a man was part of his political entity, be that his country or province, as a "citizen." In this capacity he was necessarily a contributing member of a particular economic, religious and/or social entity. This form of planning, Forsey explained, had to be "based on consent, consultation, discussion, [and] give and take." Such was the essence of the "co-operative commonwealth." He added that any "system in which things will be done by co-operation, *by free citizens and their organizations, including their governments, working together,*" represented a harmonious planning unit. The world had witnessed compromise with democratic institutions to reach political aims; now Forsey was holding up the potential for compromise within economic and social institutions to reach economic and social aims.[143] And in so doing, Forsey added, "the political pluralism which would exist in a democratic, planned Socialist, society" would leave organizations freer than any other centralized option.

Political pluralism, therefore, ensured the freedom that was an essential precondition to the initiation of any planned society.[144] This would be true in the administration of the pluralistic plan:

> The administration of the plan, even more than its making, would fall largely to these same people's organizations. So would the reinforcement of social legislation. We hear a great deal of the army of "bureaucrats" which Socialism would let loose on the country; inspectors of this, inspectors of that; controllers of all the other things, all with enormous staffs and all accumulating mountains. of documents from a harassed citizenry. Actually there would be far less need of "bureaucrats" in a co-operative commonwealth than there would be in the controlled capitalism which is the only practical alternative.

Forsey explained that because the key industries would be under co-operative ownership, they would require less overseeing by state officials. In his pluralistic system, he explained, the public could rely on their unions, farmers' co-operatives, and other organizations involved in the planning to be "volunteer enforcement agencies."[145]

Forsey did not seem to draw his concept of political pluralism from only one source, though he did refer to Wootton's *Freedom Under Planning*.[146] His pluralist plan, however, was a very personal and unique version based on his faith that what had evolved through experience, custom, and usage in Britain's political history could repeat itself in the Canadian field. "Most of the common sense, the empiricism, the political inventiveness, the genius for compromise, which have been the glory of the British people," Forsey said, "desert us when we move from purely political to political-economic institutions."[147]

Forsey did not think that only a socialistic political party could, or would, implement the type of plan he was suggesting. Basically, he argued, specific ideology played much less of a role in the adoption of new party policies than did external factors. "The most important fact of all is that it was history itself which forced these changes in parties and their programmes." He illustrated by pointing to the fact that it was neither desire or choice that took the British Liberal Party from "a passionate belief in laissez-faire to collectivism." Nor was it desire or choice that drove the Conservative Party not only to accept but to introduce and pass "liberal collectivist measures." Rather, said Forsey, "it was the sheer pressure of events that wrought these changes in both parties and their programmes."[148]

Forsey believed that the pressure of events upon parties was both present and intensifying in post-war Canada. He predicted that just as parties in the nineteenth century accepted "the framework of a more or less unplanned, individualist economic system, and differed about the more or less and methods," so too would parties in the twentieth century be driven to accept the framework of a more or less planned and collectivist economic system, and differ over methods of implementation. His role, and the role of all Canadians, was to ensure that the need for this change was impressed upon all classes in Canadian society. Only a class-conscious Canada could effect the necessary pressure for change. The success of a pluralistic, planned society rested on his listeners becoming alert and involved in protecting their own interests:

> Ultimately the only sure shield of freedom, under any economic system [was] alert, responsible and active citizens. Proper political machinery is indispensable; but the best of it will fail if the people won't use it.

Their particular task was to ensure that citizens were educated on the issues, and secondly "to encourage voluntary associations which deal mainly with matters their members know a good deal about, and give them as large a place as possible in the scheme of things, economical and political." Thirdly, Forsey said that Canadians had to "decentralize [their] institutions, both political and economic, as much as we can. The smaller the unit, the nearer home the things it deals with, the better the citizen can cope with the problems involved, and the less lost he feels."[149]

Throughout the year following his Alberta lectures, Forsey gave serious thought to revising and publishing the speeches in book form. Those who provided him with detailed comments on his manuscript spanned the ideological spectrum. They also included some of Canada's best known public figures and thinkers, and for the most part the response was encouraging, though Forsey never did pursue the project.

One of those reviewing Forsey's work was Manitoba's Premier, Stuart Garson. Garson, who was sympathetic to the aims of reconstruction planning and held no "partisan or ideological grudges" against the Dominion's "conservative planners,"[150] had led a non-partisan coalition government in Manitoba before joining the federal Liberal Cabinet in 1948.[151] Both Garson and Forsey agreed that in his inherent nature, man was both imperfect and frail. And both men doubted whether man possessed the empirically trained, well-controlled, analytical or imaginative mind "to assess what was advantageous planning and what is [sic] not."

They could not, however, agree on the political label that best defined Forsey's social democratic planning model. Garson told Forsey that he thought it "was the liberal viewpoint that you are expounding," but neither man had much use for labels in any case. More important was the fact that Garson, like virtually all those who reviewed Forsey's work, failed to recognize the importance that Forsey gave to the concept of decentralized, pluralistic "planning from the bottom." Garson agreed with Forsey's approach but thought it "quite a different view from that of most planners" that he had met, who viewed with disdain the abilities of the people who plan. It was, Garson added, the inadequacies of the general public which convinced the centralist planners that they were fitted to do the planning and that without such planning, the rest of society would be incapable of ordering its own existence in the optimum manner."[152]

Garson concluded that Forsey's pluralistic state differed very little from the status quo, arguing that strong unions and co-operatives and business organizations were all "operating at full tilt" already. But in the end Garson could not agree with the degree of trust that Forsey gave to man. "Your scheme sounds to me something like painless dentistry: you are going to cure problems but without any of the unpleasantries of planning."[153] Garson, like so many others, failed to understand the difference between conservative planning and Forsey's full-scale pluralistic planning: "Surely to goodness," argued Garson, there was "a good deal of planning taking place in Ottawa already, with the men like Isley, Claxton, and Howe making use of experts like Dr. Clark, Sandy Skelton, Bob Bryce and Mac Mackenzie."[154]

Much the same type of response was given by former political economist A.F.W. Plumptre, who had promoted Keynesian views in Ottawa during the war.[155] Plumptre, who had subsequently become Associate Editor of *Saturday Night*, found Forsey's conclusions regarding the inability of private enterprise to plan "unnecessarily offensive," and he reiterated his belief that extensive planning already existed in Canada. He pointed out that he had done "a lot of this sort of planning" while working on the Wartime Prices and Trade Board. Plumptre also mentioned that he thought it "quite useless to expect that businessmen who have been called thieves and robbers and worse" by the CCF, "would then troop in like lambs and behave in a constructive way." He felt that the CCF approach was dividing society just as Forsey called for society to "pull together." Perhaps no other comment so revealed the distance that separated Forsey from "conservative" planners, for Forsey's social philosophy had always rested on his belief that increased class-consciousness in Canadian society was a precondition to effecting any real change in the country's basic economic structure. And increasing class-consciousness was necessarily a divisive step. In other words, the "pulling together" that Plumptre encouraged the CCF and Forsey to begin practising, could only occur after all economic classes realized that the present capitalist structure fostered the very divisiveness that Plumptre accused the CCF of fostering.[156] Only this route could ensure the economic freedom and the extension of economic democracy through decentralized pluralism that was central to Forsey's thesis.

Frank Underhill thought Forsey's manuscript was a "welcome change" from traditional CCF intellectual propaganda, though he could not accept the extensive role given to organizations in the pluralistic state. Underhill recognized the essence of Forsey's argument but he disagreed with Forsey's conclusions that the private sector could not plan.[157] Underhill did, however, encourage Forsey to revise and get his book out as soon as possible.[158]

If the "liberal-left," apart from Underhill, found Forsey's manuscript somewhat redundant and incomplete, reviewers further to the right, such as Conservative M.P. and businessman J.M Macdonnell, found Forsey's work unnecessarily and inaccurately critical of private enterprise planning. Macdonnell rejected Forsey's concept of pluralist planning as meaning that "some people give orders to other people" and was therefore unnecessarily oppressive.[159] Like Underhill, Macdonnell charged that Forsey misjudged private enterprise's ability to plan for the common good. In response to this charge, Forsey could only say that he was "sinning in good company, for Beveridge says the same thing; so do plenty of others, far more eminent than I shall ever be." "That in itself," Forsey added, "does not, of course, establish the truth of the proposition, but it suggests that I may not be so wrong-headed as you think."[160]

But the main argument put forward by Macdonnell was that Forsey's public planners who gave the orders could not be held any more responsible to the "ordered" than could private businessmen. In response, Forsey pointed to the control mechanisms inherent in the pluralistic planning process:

> Of course the state can't control itself as it controls private enterprise. But that doesn't mean that its actions can't be controlled. The controls will have to be of a different kind, applied by different people, in different ways. That is the gist of what I tried to say in the second part of Chapter IV. which I think had not reached you when you wrote.[161]

Most interesting of all the responses, perhaps, was that of Canada's "outstanding political thinker," George Grant. Labelled a "Red Tory" in his later years, Grant's "distinctive amalgam of toryism, liberalism, socialism, and nationalism" was not easily classified.[162] Grant felt that Forsey's "carefully thought out analysis," warranted publication because it addressed many "uncomfortable questions" which were often "unpleasant for socialists." At the same time, Grant pointed out, Forsey had "analyzed some of the false and misleading arguments of the free enterprisers."

Grant felt that the most important question for planning centred on the role of industrial society in realizing a decent life for individuals, "and from that more importantly, what should be the individual's attitude towards the scientific society." He foresaw little hope of increasing individual freedoms in an age of increasing mass production. "If one wants this kind of mass world," Grant wrote Forsey, "one better immediately become a member of the business elite in the U.S.A. or the Communist Party in Eurasia." So unless Forsey was willing to "put a terrific limitation on the pursuit of technical efficiency," Grant thought that he might as well abandon for the next epoch the principle of political freedom.[163]

Forsey agreed with Grant's thesis: "Your comment on the appalling authoritarianism is very much in point," wrote Forsey, as was Grant's comment that Forsey had "over-estimated human decency."[164] Forsey referred specifically to Grant's comment that in "attempting to bring up the rational in human beings, as all education must," Forsey had failed to recognize that he must first meet the "irrational."

Grant also wondered what would make the citizens want to participate as extensively as Forsey was suggesting they should? Though Forsey said he did not want to sound like "a cheery nineteenth century liberal," he did think that Grant was too pessimistic on that point. Forsey retained a belief that rational thought processes could always prevail in the pluralistic planning process.[165]

For all their differences, however, Grant's conservative view of the central role of Christianity in keeping men and women from being "content with bread and excuses," was very much in line with Forsey's view. Grant explained that it was being a Christian that kept one's motive for social action clear but that it would not happen naturally, "i.e. without a conscious effort." He added that "being a Christian, one believes that some grasp of ultimate reality in one's mind is the only thing that [would] keep one free and want to be free." This, Grant explained, was the inherent weakness of "secular pragmatists ... (like certain streams in the CCF) whose beliefs seemed useless." "In a discussion of planning and freedom," Grant concluded, "some discussion of what is going to keep the planner honest and the planned awake seem[ed] necessary."[166]

In addressing the Christian's role of equating individual freedom with Christian goals, Grant was reiterating the Christian principle that Forsey had clearly stated in the opening paragraph of his Alberta School lectures when he had written that "believing in the infinite value of every human goal and the equality of all men before God, we must believe in Freedom."[167]

Seen in this Christian light, Forsey's form of moral socialism places him very much as a transitional figure in the Canadian intellectual reform tradition. By retaining a strong Christian moralist view he differed from most of the secularly oriented economic reformers of the post-war era. Yet Forsey retained strong links with, and kept active in, many secular organizations such as the CCL and the CCF.

In 1945, for example, he was defeated in the June Ontario election that saw George Drew's Conservatives sweep to power.[168] Though he professed that he was "now the most private of private citizens, with no political hopes or aspirations,"[169] Forsey accepted a post on the Ontario

CCF Provincial Council,[170] and then ran unsuccessfully again against Drew in 1947.[171] The same scenario was then repeated in the federal election the following year. By 1949, with three political defeats in four years, a demanding job, two daughters, Margaret aged seven, and Helen aged four, and still owing four thousand dollars on his house, Forsey decided to drop politics and focus on his Christian-economic and constitutional writing.[172]

The thoughts of unfulfilled dreams remained, however, and as the 1940s drew to a close Forsey admitted his pain to his good friend Meighen. "I have been defeated in nearly everything I have undertaken for the last twenty years," he wrote, "except that book!"[173] He lamented that he had spent too much time "preaching to the converted" in his CCF work, and resigned himself to "writing and speaking to questions of constitutional practice," where he knew what he was talking about.[174]

Though Forsey's writings on the planned economy were consistent with many streams of his Christian-oriented "Tory democracy" of an earlier period, one suspects that he himself was never quite certain as to which political party he should contribute his brand of reformism. Witness this letter to Stuart Garson:

> I am almost driven to the conclusion that I am politically nonde-
> script. The late Mr. Dafoe ... described me as a Tory plotter, and
> a left wing mud slinger? Corry of Queen's says I am a disciple of
> Burke; Arthur Meighen and Jim Macdonnell are convinced I shall
> end up in the Conservative Party; you seem to think I am a spiritual
> liberal, and the CCF leaders appear to consider me an orthodox
> CCF'er! A queer beast altogether![175]

One does not, however, detect any indecision in Forsey's economic writings during this period. His commitment to socialistic planning was clear; his desire to see this planning implemented by a participatory citizenship was strong; and the Christian element in his social democracy was never far from the surface of any of his writings.

THE BRITISH CONSTITUTIONAL TRADITION

Constitutional issues always held a special place in Eugene Forsey's heart. As a boy in Ottawa, and in his later life, he idolized his grandfather Bowles for his constitutional knowledge. He had spent a great deal of his life learning history and British constitutional theory and had expanded that knowledge during his research and writing for his doctoral thesis. And since the 1930s he had written dozens of articles and letters relating to the constitutional issues that he felt were so important.

As the prospect of elected political office diminished for Forsey in the 1950s,[1] a development for which he was "devoutly thankful,"[2] Forsey dedicated more and more of his energy to defining the political idea of the British Conservative tradition for the Canadian milieu. This political philosophy stemmed from Burke, Coleridge, and the British conservatives who argued for the "British idea" of an essentially free "order of life; an historical, freely developing order; a unitary order of free inter-relationships, a truly free organic order."[3]

In this work he associated very closely with his good friend John Farthing. Forsey's work on constitutional issues from the post-war period onward places him ideologically alongside Farthing, who worked as an economist at Queen's University for many years. For Forsey, the specific issue of the era was the need to preserve Canada's British constitutional tradition as a mechanism for free and orderly growth and development. This philosophy reflected Forsey's own pragmatic approach to problem-solving, which he described as a "pragmatic, empirical, practical, traditional British and Canadian conservative philosophy."[4] This was a philosophy that also closely adhered to the evolving Burkean ideal.

One of the main political issues of the 1950s was the effort of the St. Laurent government to define Canada more within a North American framework and dramatically reduce its British and Commonwealth connection. In policy terms this meant an increasing economic association with the strong American economy and a diminished degree of interdependence with the war-shattered British economy.[5] Within a very short time the extent of American control over the Canadian economy was evident in the growth of American ownership of Canadian industry and natural resources, and also in the increasing influence of the United States on Canada's financial and commercial policies.[6] In 1957, for example, $8.4 billion of the total $10 billion foreign direct investment in Canada came from the United States.[7]

On the diplomatic scene, the St. Laurent government pursued a policy that was similarly intent on reinvigorating Canada's international relationships; yet under the leadership of Canada's Secretary of State for External Affairs, Lester Pearson, these new diplomatic initiatives were, in historian Donald Creighton's words, "[planned] instinctively in American terms."[8] In Creighton's view, Pearson's policies only confirmed and emphasized Canada's status as a military dependency of the United States in the defence of North America. He also argued that St. Laurent surrendered Canada's last chance to assert its economic self-sufficiency and independence in the construction of the St. Lawrence Seaway Project.[9]

Yet another St. Laurent policy that reflected a changed perspective of Canada's traditional orientation to Great Britain was its decision to remove many symbolic references to Canada's historical connection with Britain. This initiative was in part a response to increasing demands for national and provincial autonomy for Quebec, which experienced a virtual explosion of neo-nationalist sentiment during the late 1940s and 1950s. In Quebec, neo-nationalists had begun a campaign in schools, in organizations such as the League L'Action nationale, and in the pages of newspapers like *Le Devoir*, to decrease Canada's historical British traditions and "illustrate that a nationalism of the masses had historical roots in Quebec, [and] that in fact, it was the only authentic form of nationalism in that society."[10]

The efforts of these neo-nationalists, combined with the more traditional form of French-Canadian nationalist pressure exerted by Quebec Premier Maurice Duplessis, resulted in some tentative moves by Ottawa to define Canada's post-war image less in its traditionally British perspective. Creighton, one of Forsey's "oldest and closest friends," protested French-Canadian efforts to convince Ottawa to gradually eliminate references to "Royal" and "Dominion" from federal usage. Creighton and Forsey publicly objected to the fact that federal statutes introduced in the House of Commons, for amendment or initial passage, contained fewer references to the "Dominion of Canada" or its "Royal" heritage.[11]

To some, the removal of these colonial symbols represented an expression of Canadian nationalism. But there were a number of intellectual forces at work in the 1950s. On one hand, many intellectuals defended the preservation of traditions, social values, and a conception of Canadian culture they believed was being destroyed in the industrialized, consumer-oriented modern world of post-war American society.[12] These nationalists, who included Dalhousie academic George Grant, and westerners Hilda Neatby and Arthur Lower, sought to define Canadian nationalism in terms of Canada's own conditions, and not within a North American spectre that had as its dominant voice the United States, with its revolutionary history, its emphasis on extreme individualism, and the general absence of a sense of "social freedom," or social restraint.[13]

Lower, for example, maintained that Canada had always been in marked contrast to the United States because of Canada's inherent conservatism and by the ethic of social freedom. Lower asserted that these Canadian elements were derived from its historical experience, which had created the foundation for substantially different political and social attitudes and a moral and ordered society.[14]

But Lower could also sympathize with Canada's movement toward a more independent North American perspective. As a result, much of the impetus for the redefinition of Canada's history came from Canadian "nationalist" historians such as Lower. History for Lower, Carl Berger wrote, became a search for "a nationalist creed," which Lower found in the Canadian wilderness. For Lower, then, the New World history "had been largely the story of man's struggle with nature." The Canadian mentality, in turn, had been largely shaped through man's struggle with that wilderness.[15]

Whereas Lower's history intellectually supported some aspects of the Liberal government's general thrust for a more independent North American voice, Liberal policy in a number of areas was increasingly being shaped by men such as Jack Pickersgill. Pickersgill's rise through

201

the government's ranks from novice civil servant to "indispensable head" of the Prime Minister's Office, to Clerk of the Privy Council and finally Secretary of State, seemed to parallel the steady rise of policies challenging the relevance of the British tradition to Canada's postwar society. It seemed fitting, therefore, that many of Pickersgill's views on history and government had been shaped many years earlier by his former Wesley College friend and compatriot, Arthur Lower.[16]

In Forsey's view, Lower's and Pickersgill's initiatives represented nothing less than Canada's increasing drift away from its own British-Canadian heritage – a heritage that had little to do with the North American wilderness. It was fitting that Forsey chose the period approaching the 1952 coronation of Queen Elizabeth II to argue that the British tradition was in fact an integral and essential component of that Canadian heritage. The essence of that Canadian heritage, Forsey wrote in an unpublished article entitled "Crown, Parliament and Canadian Freedom," was first and foremost a tradition firmly rooted in the past. Whereas the Americans had chosen to break with their past, Canadians "had deliberately and repeatedly chosen to preserve theirs, both our French past and our British past." Forsey explained that Canadians had chosen not to join with the United States, but as John A. Macdonald had said, chose to retain our relations with Britain and "to give a distinct declaration on that point." Thus, said Forsey, the first sentence in the Canadian constitution states that:

> The Executive Authority of the Government shall be vested in the Sovereign of the United Kingdom, and be administered according to the well understood principles of the British Constitution by the Sovereign personally or by the Representative of the Sovereign duly authorized.[17]

For Forsey the facts clearly established that the Fathers of Confederation had deliberately chosen a constitution "similar in principle to that of the United Kingdom." This discussion ensured that the Canadian tradition would be one not only of continuity with its past, but with a corresponding element of "continuity in change." As it had for Burke and many other British conservative thinkers, this sort of tradition provided a conservative humanitarian like Forsey with the ideal mechanism for preserving basic economic, social, and political individual rights within an ordered and stable structure. On this point Forsey argued:

> The men who made this country were not men who preferred oppression to liberty, or stagnation to progress. But they sought liberty and progress not by revolution but by ordered and orderly development. They never let the past master them, but they never forgot it; they built upon it.[18]

A second basic element of the Canadian tradition that followed from our choosing Britain's system of gradual and orderly change was the non-partisanship of the state as represented in the monarchy.[19] And the third basic element in this tradition, which made the first two elements possible, was parliamentary responsible government. "This, above all," Forsey wrote, was "what makes the boundary [between Canadians and Americans] real, not imaginary. This is the heritage of all Canadians, whatever their race, creed, class or party. And of this the Crown is the centre and symbol."[20]

Forsey believed that this "wonderfully sensitive, flexible and effective instrument" of parliamentary responsible government "was responsible not only to Parliament or to the electorate, still less to party, but to the interests of the nation as a whole." And the Crown was the indispensable centre of the whole democratic order, the guardian of the Constitution. Ultimately, wrote Forsey, the Crown represented the sole protection of the people.[21]

Forsey believed, therefore, that Canada's "British tradition" of constitutional government was based on three basic elements: our deliberate choice of a constitution similar in principle to Britain's; this constitution's foundation in a strong non-partisan monarchy; and lastly, the monarch's power in ensuring the continuance of parliamentary responsible government. This tradition, Forsey argued, though British in design, was in fact Canada's own "tradition." It did not rest either on a sentimental attachment to England, nor did it evolve out of any "cult of racial superiority." Rather, the British tradition represented the best mechanism for ensuring the free and ordered growth for Canadians of all social origins.

In response to the claims of Lower and the Liberal nationalists of the post-war era, Forsey argued that Canada's true British heritage had been freely chosen by her own English- and French-speaking forefathers and had achieved the credibility associated with experience:

> To uphold the British tradition simply because it is British would be as irrational as the cult of "pure" Canadian Nationalism. The only rational ground preserving the British tradition in Canada is that it has proved itself; that experience shows it is, with the companion French tradition, the best guarantee for the preservation of our national prosperity, the best hope for its free and ordered growth.[22]

Forsey, therefore, like Edmund Burke, exhibited a conservative's clear preference for experience and practical, established traditions and structures, especially if those structures fostered calm and reasoned discussion.[23]

Thus the "British Tradition," as Forsey labelled Canada's British constitutional heritage, represented a reasoned response to the rise of both English-speaking and French-speaking "nationalists." Not one of these latter groups, Forsey argued, had presented any reasoned arguments. Rather, they argued based on the way they felt, believing that mere feeling was a valid substitute for reasoned discussion through established institutions. He argued, for example, that it was unreasonable to remove from use references to Canada's British tradition, such as the words "Dominion" and "Royal," simply because the Nationalists and some politicians in Ottawa thought the words "incompatible with equality of status for Canada." This impulsive initiative had convinced a majority of Canadians to dislike the words and agree that "they had to go."[24] "This sort of thing," Forsey wrote, "is much more than an attack on the British tradition in Canada. It is a revolt against reason. It is a blow at the very foundations of democracy."[25]

Like Burke, who exalted the allegedly "British" middle road of compromise and reason over the "French" propensity for extreme doctrinaire theories based on eighteenth century rationalism,[26] Forsey viewed the democratic process as not "simply a matter of counting heads instead of breaking them, [but] a matter of using them." And, he argued: "We can't use them if somebody's mere 'feeling' settles everything. Freedom of discussion is essential to democracy, but it must be both free and discussion. Compromise is also essential to democracy." Forsey believed that if one side's mere feelings were to settle discussions, then compromise was impossible and "one side would get everything and the other side would receive nothing."[27]

It was this almost fervent belief in the importance of free, reasoned, and democratic discussion that directed Forsey's adherence to the keystone of the British tradition, parliamentary responsible government. This form of government was for Forsey the "essential British tradition" in Canada that separated Canadians from Americans. Both countries shared many democratic principles, including a respect for the constitution, the rule of law, and personal freedom, and both countries shared the English common law principle that an accused was innocent until he or she was proven guilty. It was Canada's parliamentary responsible form of government, however, that made the boundary line between the two North American nations real and not imaginary. "That is our essential, our priceless British heritage," Forsey wrote, "And it's ours, and it's British."[28]

But what were the essential features of this parliamentary system, this "government of men, not of laws; this organic living thing which has taken root and grown in our soil and climate"?[29] In this regard Forsey's view of Canada's constitutional government was similar to Burke's view of an orderly, progressive universe governed by "the great law of change, the most powerful law of nature."[30] For Burke, political progress meant adjustment of each part of the social order to all the others. This adjustment of social institutions to changing circumstances, in turn, ensured the gradual realization of right and justice.[31] For Forsey, this system of constitutional government gave Canadians "the most delicate, the most flexible, the most efficient system of government yet devised, and the one most responsive to the public will."[32]

Forsey's first central feature in this political process was the monarchy and its "Anglo-Saxon alliance." The deliberate and resolute acceptance of the monarchical principle, Forsey argued, was unanimously agreed upon by both the Anglophone and the Francophone Fathers of Confederation. And one particular reason for the overwhelming preference for retaining the monarchy and the British connection was the ubiquitous "horror of abstract principles" that had led to revolution in France and the United States.[33]

To Forsey, the Crown is the "symbolic embodiment of the people; not a particular group or interest or party, but the people, the whole people." In this sense the Crown preserves "the common interest in the commonwealth against the particular interests of governments or party majorities, by ensuring that the appeal routes of the people are never blocked and that the people retain ultimate control over their representatives and their servants."[34] It is "our business to govern ourselves," Forsey wrote, "[and] the Crown's business to see that our power to govern ourselves is preserved and that her servants, our servants, not become our masters."[35] The Constitutional Monarch exercised this power through the preservation and use of its "reserve powers." These powers were intended to be used in those "rare and exceptional circumstances, without or against the advice of the Ministers in office, to preserve the rights of Parliament ... and the people against the Cabinet or Prime Ministerial despotism."[36]

Monarchical power was not a new area of expertise for Forsey. Largely because of his wife's encouragement,[37] he had written his Ph.D. thesis on the subject of the royal power of dissolution. In this work, which was later published as a book, Forsey meticulously documented the principle that the monarch or his or her representative "may, in law, grant, refuse or force the dissolution of the Lower House of the Legislature." And in recognition of his original exposure to British constitutional practice, Forsey dedicated the 1943 published version of his thesis to the memory of his grandfather, William Cochrane Bowles, to whom, Forsey wrote, "I owe my first understanding of the principle of constitutional government."[38]

Forsey's book, entitled *The Royal Power of Dissolution of Parliament in the British Commonwealth*, reflected the point that Forsey's whole upbringing had been steeped in the parliamentary tradition. The book, therefore, articulated a lifetime of thought and belief.[39]

Forsey had first stated his main themes as early as 1930 in a speech to the Canadian Political Science Association, in which he referred to the Crown's absolute discretionary power being regulated by "convention." This term, he explained, went beyond the traditionally interpreted view of convention as "precedent" to include "unprecedented" situations. Although Forsey was in 1930 actively engaged in activities that were perceived by many of his contemporaries as somewhat radical, his speech to the CPSA illustrated his profound adherence to adaptive and reasoned evolutionary change.[40] Precedent, he argued, was an important element in the conventions of the Constitution, but it was not, and could not be, the only element. "History seldom repeats

itself," Forsey explained to his CPSA audience, because "unprecedented situations arise and precedents ... have to be applied or adapted
to new conditions. This adaptation involves the use of reason, in the
eighteenth century sense of the term." Because every precedent began
by being unprecedented, Forsey said, it was essential to consider not
merely the letter of precedent, but the spirit and intention of the constitution as well.[41]

One such precedent for the power of dissolution, he explained,
was that for two centuries the prerogative of dissolution had never
been exercised except on the advice of Ministers. Secondly, on at least
three occasions the prerogative had been used to enable a government
defeated in the House of Commons to appeal to the electorate.[42] But
Forsey qualified the approach of looking strictly to precedents in cases
such as these. Rather, he argued, the precedents merely established
that "in ordinary circumstances the prerogative is used according to
the advice of Ministers provided that no motion of censure is pending
in the House of Commons"; and provided that the government was
not appealing to the monarch, or his or her representative, "to escape
adverse verdict of a House of Commons elected as the result of a dissolution already granted to that same Ministry."[43]

The use of precedent was limited, however, in Forsey's view. It was
necessary, therefore, to look past its "strict letter [and] to turn not to
history, but to reason and the spirit of the Constitution."[44] He also
came to believe that conventions and the constitution were not "rigid
and immutable codes but living organic entities that are born, grow and
decay." Their value, therefore, lay in their flexibility and ability to con-
form more closely to the will of the nation.[45]

In practical terms this meant that the Crown had not only the
reserve power to refuse the advice of a Prime Minister or a Cabinet
in certain circumstances, but also the power "to see that the people
themselves [were] directly consulted in a general election."[46] Forsey
adhered, therefore, to the principle that an essential right in British
political history was the power and the rights of the people against
the partial, particular interest of the governments or party majorities.
This tradition established that Parliament "was not the Government's
Parliament but the Queen's, the people's." But precedent was a crucial
ingredient in the defence of that tradition. Forsey cited numerous
scenarios, for example, in which a government could seek to avoid

responsibility to the people through the House of Commons, while not committing "one single illegality; not one thing the Courts could even consider let alone pronounce judgement on, provide redress for, or give protection against." In each scenario, he added, "the only protection would lie in the reserve power of the Crown."[47]

In one of his dozens of articles and speeches on the subject of the monarchy, Forsey summed up his interpretation of the monarchical role in the British constitutional tradition:

> In short, the Queen or her representative is the guardian of our democratic Constitution against subversion by a Prime Minister or Cabinet who might be tempted to violate that Constitution and deprive us of our right to self-government; but it makes sure that we, the people, are not prevented from governing ourself.[48]

Given the central role that Forsey gave to the monarchy, it is not surprising that he reacted so strongly to efforts to abolish various symbols of Canada's British tradition. Forsey, who often has described himself as a "Sir John A. Macdonald Conservative,"[49] condemned the efforts of the St. Laurent government to abolish the term "Dominion." He brought to the attention of the Canadian public the fact that Macdonald had wanted to call the country the Kingdom of Canada, but that the "British Government jibbed because it was afraid the Americans would be offended." The word Dominion, Forsey argued, was good enough for every major Canadian statesman down to Mackenzie King in 1947. But now Forsey feared that Canadians were going to wake up some morning to "find themselves citizens of the Republic of Canada."[50] Symbols of Canada's British tradition were especially important to Forsey because they were "intended to assert Canada's adherence to the Monarchy." The Crown, Forsey maintained, was something the Fathers of Confederation considered no less important than national unity itself. In a phrase that Burke might well have written, Forsey explained to the Canadian public that their Fathers of Confederation wanted to maintain "the sense of freedom slowly broadening down from precedent to precedent, [as] symbolized by our ancient Anglo-Norman monarchy."[51]

In the years following the publication of his book through to the end of his career, Forsey published a number of articles that reinforced his constitutional belief that a government's ultimate authority in the British constitutional system derived "solely from the Crown" and that a government was responsible to the House and the electorate. To Forsey the Crown was not "just a rubber stamp for the Cabinet." Rather, it had the power to refuse a Cabinet's request to prolong a government's life if that request might abuse the people's fundamental rights. The Canadian constitution, he argued, regulates such matters by convention, custom, and usage. The reserve power of the Crown was then, in fact as well as symbolically, the guardian of the Constitution and the mechanism for avoiding chaos and confusion.[52]

This power, Forsey argued, has been retained in Canada by the Governor General, who has exercised it periodically, most notably in Canada's constitutional crisis of 1926.[53] Forsey did not draw a distinction between the issues involved in the King-Byng episode and more symbolic issues such as the removal of the word "Royal" from a mailbox or the Union Jack from the Canadian flag. For him these instances all represented challenges "to our priceless heritage of British responsible government."[54]

The "King-Byng affair" had been a particularly interesting issue for Forsey since he began researching it for his thesis. That the 1925–26 affair played such a huge role in his work[55] should not be surprising given Forsey's belief that the duty of the Governor General is "to make sure that responsible government is maintained, that the rights of parliament are respected, that the still higher rights of the people are held sacred."[56]

Forsey's work on the 1926 crisis is also important because it was his research and writing on the subject that led to his friendship with Arthur Meighen; this despite that fact that at the same time Forsey was using his knowledge of constitutional issues to convince Canadians that the CCF was in the mainstream of the British constitutional tradition.[57] Much more important, however, was Forsey's growing realization that the 1926 debate fundamentally challenged the Canadian heritage of British parliamentary responsible government.

But what did that phrase exactly mean to Forsey? Simply put, Forsey viewed parliamentary responsible government as a system that was parliamentary, that is, involving a "talking-place, a parlement with full and free reasoned discussion." Secondly, parliamentary responsible government was "responsible," in that the government was answerable to Parliament (which includes both Houses and in Canada's case, the monarch's representative) and responsible or accountable to the people.[58] On both these counts, Forsey's preliminary thesis research had by 1932 strongly indicated that Mackenzie King's actions in 1925 and 1926 were "a violation of responsible government."

Throughout his research and writing, Forsey was aided tremendously by Arthur Meighen. Forsey had privately acknowledged his "socialist views" to Meighen as early as 1932. Forsey confessed that although he did not personally enjoy differing from his family and friends on political issues, they were nevertheless very tolerant of his "eccentricities" and he hoped Meighen would be similarly patient. Forsey added that he and Frank Scott were contemplating writing a book on the Canadian Constitution which would focus on the King-Byng episode, and he hoped that his own change of political "opinions" would not jeopardize Meighen's "friendship and co-operation," which he had always prized.[59] Quite obviously the two men's differing political views did not affect their co-operating in the preparation of Forsey's thesis.[60] And Meighen obviously enjoyed Forsey's arguments regarding King's "sabotage of parliamentary institutions."[61] "I can say without reservation at all," Meighen wrote in 1940 after reviewing one of Forsey's chapters on the 1926 crisis, "that this chapter brought me a great deal of pleasure. It is excellently written, clear and thorough."[62]

When put into an overall perspective, the Meighen-Forsey friendship could be seen as a natural relationship between two men who shared more than a mutual disdain for Mackenzie King. More important was their shared belief in the central role of the "British tradition" in the Canadian state. Meighen's views regarding the Monarchy, for example, were similar to Forsey's in that he, like Forsey, believed that the Governor General was "the guardian of the rights of Parliament."[63] In the *Royal Dissolution of Parliament*, Forsey lay the detailed groundwork from which both he and Meighen argued for decades that Lord Byng's 1926 actions in guarding those parliamentary rights were absolutely proper and necessary. Forsey's two thesis chapters given over to the King-Byng affair chronicle in intricate detail the flow of events during 1925 and 1926: motions, amendments, speeches, and discussions in Parliament and at the Governor General's residence were reviewed and placed in context. Forsey also documented King's "unprecedented" actions in refusing to hold office until his Conservative successors were appointed following King's resignation after Byng's refusal to grant King dissolution.[64]

Though the details of the issue need not be dealt with here, it is important to note that in his book and in a multitude of letters, articles, and speeches in subsequent years, Forsey condemned Prime Minister King's "abuse" of Parliament through his "unprecedented request for dissolution while a motion of censure was under debate." That, plus a number of additional acts on King's part, in Forsey's view formed a "constitutional annus mirabilis in Canadian history."[65]

In a 1951 speech to the Canadian Political Science Association, Forsey emphasized that his research proved that King's political theory was not parliamentary responsible government, but "the negative of that system." He argued that in King's view, Parliament was the "mere creature of the Cabinet, meeting, doing, acting and concluding only when, for so long, and under such conditions as the favour of the Cabinet may be ordained."[66] Such an approach ran contrary to Forsey's own view of Parliament as "parlement": a forum for reasoned discussion leading, if necessary, to gradual change. It was fitting, therefore, that in his speech, in countering King's methods, Forsey quoted that great British advocate of reason and conservative, gradual change, Edmund Burke. "It is not in the choice of Ministers," Forsey quoted Burke as writing, "to resort to Parliament or the electorate as may best suit the purpose of their sinister ambition." "But," Forsey added, "in Mr. King's theory it is."[67]

Though Forsey argued that he set about preparing his speech "in a spirit of stern academic objectivity," he only found more and more evidence that King believed himself to be above both Parliament and the people in 1926. Forsey reviewed the evidence he had presented in his book eight years earlier, but he added that his subsequent research had produced "important new facts" to support his conclusions. The most important fact in this regard was Mr. King's statement in the 1925 election campaign that if the election failed to produce a clear majority, he would "ask for another dissolution of Parliament to get this matter straightened out, until we got a majority sufficient for the country's needs." Forsey considered this statement "the most extraordinary of Mr. King's career, for if Parliament had any rights at all, surely it had the right 'to come into existence.'" Yet, Forsey argued, "Mr. King asserted that the Prime Minister has the right to kill it before it is born.... For those who really believe in parliamentary government, that fact will go down against him to the last syllable of recorded time."[68] Forsey added that if Canadians accepted the fact that the 1926 election gave the country "Mr. King's Constitution, then our freedom [was] gone." King's principle was nothing more than an assertion that a people could "vote away its liberties." This, Forsey believed, was nothing short of "nonsense, hideous appalling nonsense."[69] Forsey felt that his book had been one of the few redeeming features of his career, but he now expressed his hope that this June speech would be another such accomplishment. If the speech went well, Forsey confided to his friend, he hoped to collect and publish his constitutional writings, thereby putting "my Cat among the Grit political scientists."[70]

Forsey prepared for his speech with typical thoroughness. For two months he "por[ed] over" King's speeches and Meighen's responses. "What a soul destroying business it must have been replying to him!" Forsey wrote to Meighen. "There was really nothing to reply to.... You had to keep grasping at vapour, which swirled away from you as you touched it."[71] As the date of the speech approached, Forsey seemed to be warming to the prospect of making a definitive statement as an important clarification of the public's mistaken perspective of King's constitutional beliefs. He explained this personal 'mission' to Meighen shortly before his speech:

> King erected a gigantic fabric of lies on this subject of the Constitution; it has got to be destroyed.... The worst of his productions, I think, are the sanctimonious professions of his undying devotion to parliamentary government. It is like listening to Satan on the doctrines of the Church. It would be easy to write a pretty complete account of what parliamentary government is by just taking King's statements on the subject and putting down the opposite. If I am provoked in the discussion, I shall probably say something very much like this.[72]

Between mid-May and the June 16 date of the speech Forsey and Meighen exchanged a flurry of correspondence. Meighen reviewed Forsey's drafts and the two men collectively decided on which material to include in the speech.[73] Forsey's speech was eventually published in the *Canadian Journal of Economics and Political Science* in November 1951, soon after King's death.[74] In the published article Forsey re-emphasized his firm belief that "parliamentary democracy was the essence of our Constitution," and cited examples from 1925–26 and statements made by King in the 1930s and 1940s that "proved" King's ignorance in this subject area. Forsey again quoted Burke at length, citing references from Burke's writings that denounced any action that would "shrink [the House of Commons] into a mere appendage of administration and destroy the dearest rights and liberties of the nation."[75]

Forsey stated in his 1942 review of King's constitutional views and actions on labour policy that "in the whole of history of Canada no public man has been as vociferous about the rights and supremacy of Parliament" as King had been. It was ironic, wrote Forsey, that it was King's fervent professions of devotion to this principle which had helped to put him "in the lofty political heights that he came to inhabit."[76] Forsey's goal was to destroy this myth which was fostered by King and the "riff raff of Liberals and professional Nationalists" who were associated with him.[77]

To this end much of Forsey's energies in the 1950s focused on warning the Canadian public against "innocently swallowing the Liberal-Nationalist fairy-tales"[78] expounded by men such as John Dafoe of the *Winnipeg Free Press*, with whom Forsey engaged in a heated exchange of correspondence following the publication of Forsey's book.[79] Much of their debate focused on Forsey's extensive reliance on Burke's writings in Forsey's book, *The Royal Power of Dissolution*.[80] The debate raged on for three months, and ended, so Forsey believed, with his leaving "Dafoe dead upon the field."[81]

Forsey also found fault with yet another "liberal historian," Bruce Hutchinson. Hutchinson's "political crooning" throughout his biography of Mackenzie King, Forsey wrote, was nothing short of "historical and political romance." Such work, though "good entertainment," in Forsey's view bore little resemblance to actual people or events and was little more than "a wonderfully adroit piece of Liberal propaganda." Hutchinson, wrote Forsey, was "utterly blind to the fact that parliamentary responsible government means that the Government is responsible, answerable to Parliament." Mr. King's request for a dissolution while awaiting a vote of censure was "a brazen attempt to establish the principle that Parliament henceforth would vote on a motion of censure only if the Government saw fit; that no Government would be condemned save by its own consent." Forsey added:

213

[This] was an unparalleled contempt of Parliament. It was the most deadly blow conceivable against responsible government. Mr. Meighen made this crystal clear during the election.... If a Government which can't be removed except by its own consent is "responsible," what on earth is it responsible to? If the Crown has no power to prevent a Government from defying Parliament and the people alike, what protection have we against the tyranny of any jack in office? The fact is Mr. King in 1926 tried to kill parliamentary responsible government. He tried to make Lord Byng his accomplice. Lord Byng refused.

Hutchinson had stood "the whole story on its head" by making Lord Byng out to be wrong by "invading the rights of parliament" and placing himself above Parliament and the people.[82]

Eugene Forsey's active opposition to perceived abuses of "our heritage of parliamentary government" continued well into the 1950s. In 1957, for example, he attacked the Liberal Government's "murder" of Parliament during the Pipeline debate. During his work on this debate, Forsey, as was by then his habit, acknowledged "the Right Honourable Arthur Meighen as the greatest master of parliamentary law and practice our country has ever produced." It was from Meighen, Forsey explained in a November 1956 speech at University of Toronto's Osgoode Hall, that he had personally "absorbed much of the little I know of these great [constitutional] matters." In particular Forsey cited the "principle of our British parliamentary government: first, that our government is parliamentary; second, that it is responsible; third, that it rests on the rule of law; fourth, that it rests also on an unwritten code of self-restraint, moderation, decency and fair play."[83]

Forsey thought that the Liberals' decision to implement closure to restrict debate did not allow Parliament to function in its proper manner. "What the pipe line debate revealed, above all," wrote Forsey in a 1957 article, "was that the Government and the presiding officers alike had simply no understanding of the basic principles of parliamentary government. They had no understanding that it rests on discussion."[84] And in a letter to the Ottawa *Journal* Forsey added that, "all the pipelines that were ever built or ever will be, are as dust in the balance beside our heritage of parliamentary government."[85]

In a second 1957 article, entitled "What's Wrong With the Liberals?" Forsey concluded that "twenty-two years of unbroken and unchallenged power" had convinced the Liberals that they had arrived at "final truth." In fact they had flouted Parliament and avoided reasoned, informed discussion in dozens of instances.[86] "Canadian freedom is very sick," Forsey concluded, and "the sickness will not be cured 'till [sic] the Canadian people win back parliamentary government. The first step is to turn the Liberals out."[87]

But as far as his becoming actively becoming involved in politics to help accomplish that goal, Forsey remained an interested bystander. Despite his 1948 and 1949 electoral losses to George Drew, Forsey remained fascinated and tempted at the prospect of re-entering the political arena. Two weeks after his 1949 defeat, Forsey explained to Meighen that he had refused offers to run as a "parachute" candidate for the CCF in at least six constituencies in Ontario for that same 1949 election. He had agreed with his employer, CCL Secretary Treasurer Pat Conroy, that such a move would make Forsey appear to be "a seat-seeker, scampering around looking for an easy thing." For that reason, and because of family and work commitments, Forsey had chosen to stay and face certain defeat in Carleton.[88]

In the 1950s Forsey continued to resist the urge to run again for elected office. By 1950 he was very busy with his family, teaching an advanced seminar in Canadian Government at Carleton College,[89] and co-ordinating an increasingly heavy workload in his expanding Research Department at the Congress.[90] Despite more staff support and an increased budget at the CCL, Forsey remained "frantic with work" in the Union office throughout the 1950s. In a January 1950 letter to Meighen, Forsey described a typical monthly schedule. It began with his preparing a "factum" for the Congress for the Supreme Court of Canada and another memorandum which "ultimately ran to over 10,000 words and involved my working at the office until 11:30 two nights, 1:10 a.m. another, 3:30 a.m. another, and 4:30 another." Following that task, Forsey had "to pop off to Quebec City to appear before the Massey Commission" and from there he went to Montreal to appear before a Railway Conciliation hearing. From Montreal it was on to Brantford, Ontario, for a conference of local union officers of the United Automobile Workers and then back to Montreal to sit on

a Steelworkers' Arbitration Board, all of which involved preparing follow-up rebuttals back in Ottawa. January also involved a debate at the
University of Toronto's Hart House "and a variety of other things,"
including a number of reviews and letters to various newspaper editors concerning Meighen's recently published collection of speeches
entitled *Unrevised and Unrepented*.[91]

Politics, however, was never far from Forsey's mind. His job itself
was political. In October 1950, for example, the CCL formally encouraged its members to vote CCF and make "real progress" for labour by
developing a political party strong in both the provincial and national
fields.[92] But Forsey confessed to Meighen in March of the following
year that he was "devoutly thankful to be out of politics," largely
because he felt that too many voters who were to "decide the destinies
of civilization, perhaps of life itself on this planet, [were] just ignorant
numbskulls." Forsey had come to the conclusion that there was little
room in any of Canada's political parties for men with a "reasonable
view, or even a view with a modicum of reason to it."[93]

For many reasons, including the nature of his own personality,
Forsey had come to the realization that he had little future in politics:

> Actually, though I remain convinced that I'd be a good Member,
> I remain equally convinced that I'm a poor candidate. I lack the
> common touch. I am too stiff. I haven't enough friends. I don't
> belong to enough things. I don't get about enough. I don't remem
> ber people well enough. I can't spin my speeches with homely anec
> dotes. I am too much the "professor." Worst of all, perhaps, I have
> very little confidence in myself, except on a very few subjects....
> Lacking confidence in myself, I can hardly expect the electors to
> have much in me.[94]

And so Forsey declined the opportunity in the fall of 1951 to run in
Ottawa, seeing "no reason that I should be taken out of mothballs."[95]

During the 1950s Forsey continued to concentrate on constitutional
issues, preparing a book of constitutional essays and a book on King
and the Constitution.[96] But his hectic work schedule and a dearth
of financial resources resulting from the cancellation of his Carleton
course and mounting family medical bills prevented his running for
office.[97] It must have been very difficult for him when he politely

refused Meighen's offer of financial assistance,[98] for he still privately yearned to enter the House of Commons.[99] With his self-styled "Great Campaign" over the retention of British traditions in Canada bringing forth a full uproar of opposition from Quebec nationalists, and from many federal politicians of all parties who wished to pacify Quebec voters, Forsey was anxious for "battle."[100]

But he remained on the political sidelines, receiving moral support and encouragement in dozens of letters from Meighen, who simply could not understand those English-Canadian politicians who spurned Forsey's position for fear they would violate some sacred French-Canadian right to eliminate symbols of Canada's British heritage.[101] Meighen's support became especially meaningful because Forsey had so very little self-confidence. Witness the following extract from a Meighen to Forsey letter regarding newspaper praise over Forsey's efforts to retain British traditions:

> Well you deserve it! What the Conservative Party means by even
> delaying a powerful attack on this sinister, subterranean programme
> that St. Laurent has going is more than I can ever understand.[102]

This was just the sort of rhetoric that bolstered Forsey's confidence and set his indignation ablaze. "The more I contemplate this dismal affair the more disgusted I get," replied Forsey. "I am becoming sorry I ever left the Conservative Party. I might have been some use in it."[103] Forsey reviewed recent speeches by Members of Parliament in the House of Commons who disagreed with him about "dropping the Queen and other obsolete words." "This sounds ominous," he wrote to Meighen, "and just strengthens my suspicions that the people behind this won't stop till [sic] they have wiped out the Monarchy. The whole thing is just sickening."[104]

Forsey believed that the 1926 election was, in retrospect, a "fatal event" because it released in the country a "flood of nonsense" that deliberately falsified history. He found it particularly lamentable "the way some people [were] ready to give up everything to please the French Canadians, whatever piece of nonsense they may happen to have got into their noodle."[105] Forsey's approach to dealing with Canada's bicultural society was the same as his approach to any political, social or economic issue. The answers to the problems lay in reasoned discussion that would lead to "change if necessary, but not change for change's sake."[106] And he was certain that the Conservative Party had the central role to play in ensuring that this process in fact occurred. But such appeared not to be the case in the 1950s.

It has been suggested that during the 1950s the Conservative Party under George Drew's leadership was more interested in salvaging whatever was left of the alleged "Drew-Duplessis" axis that had given the Conservatives some degree of hope for a political breakthrough in 1949.[107] Forsey believed that such an attitude prevented the type of balanced discussion that was necessary between Ottawa and Quebec City, and he denounced any English-Canadian who refused to discuss these issues at all or opposed his own view, "in order not to disturb national unity." He had no patience with French-Canadians who professed as "sacred dogma [any] piece of nonsense which entered his head" and he rejected outright the claims of the French-Canadian nationalists who were causing their more reasoned Quebeckers to question any reference to Canadian autonomy and its British heritage. Forsey also denounced those who feared to challenge those same nationalists. "It was time to speak out and treat French Canadians like men instead of spoiled children. As long as we go around hush-hushing for fear we'll wake the baby, of course they'll behave like babies."[108]

Forsey rejected the view that "those of us who don't swallow the liberal policy line, hook and sinker, are against Canada" and agreed with Meighen that the answer to that particular "line" lay with the now dormant Conservative Party. Forsey wrote:

> The preservation of our history and our traditions is pre-eminently the task of the Conservative party. If it shirks that task, it has no reason for existence. At the same time this ought not to be a party question.... Our history, our traditions, our British institutions are not the property of any party; they ought to be the object of a common veneration by all parties. The Conservative Party ought to take the lead in the face of Liberal efforts since Mackenzie King to make Canada's heritage the property of that party.[109]

But the present Conservative leaders, Forsey concluded in a letter to Meighen, suffered from having "no nerve, no backbone," for backing down from carrying the fight on in Quebec against nationalistic politicians and journalists:

> I groan inwardly to think of the Conservative Party [falling] to this. I can imagine Sir Robert or yourself, deferring to any journalist on such a matter, or Sir John! ... I think the only way to deal with this thing, in Quebec or elsewhere, is to tell the truth and rely on the good sense of the people to grasp it. I don't think any other policy will win votes, even in Quebec. But perhaps you, ... and I, in this respect, all belong to a vanishing generation.

Forsey felt strongly that the entire issue went far beyond a fight over "a couple of words." Rather, he felt it went "to the very heart of things – honesty, honour, justice, to the men who made us what we are, and to our children's children, to whom we owe it to pass on the great heritage we received."[110] He added:

> Nothing is more revolting than the continuous application that the Fathers of Confederation ... were a crew of lickspittles, with no pride, no self-respect, no real patriotism; the further implication that a nation can grow great, can only grow great, by wiping the slate clean of its past. This is as false as hell, and to hell it will certainly lead us.[111]

Though Forsey felt that something a good deal bigger than merely writing articles was required, he was at a loss as to which way to turn. He believed that he had "no right or title" in stating his arguments directly to the Conservatives; nor was there any use, he wrote Meighen, "in saying anything to the leaders of my own party, who have so far, been content to be feeble echoes of the Government." He felt sure that any formal protest would be met by the CCF leaders as an "eccentricity" by one who took "too little part in the donkey-work of the party, in any work, to have any influence."[112] But Forsey could still dream:

> How I wish I were in the House for occasions like this! I'm convinced I could do better than anyone there now.... We need that kind of leadership ... and I could make clear that all hope of social or economic or any other kind of reform disappears if we surrender

that most incomparable instrument the British Constitution, to
which, incidentally, the French Canadians owe at least as much as
the English Canadians do.... The French Canadians are proud of
their traditions and properly so. Why shouldn't we be proud of
ours? "Notre langue, nos institutions, nos lois," is just as appropriate for us as for them. I am sick of the way some of our people
of British stock almost apologize for it. I was brought up to be
proud of the great deeds of the early French soldiers, explorers
and missionaries in Canada, and of the French-speaking Fathers of
Confederation etc.; but also of our own ancestors.[113]

Eugene Forsey's views on the place that the French-Canadians held in
Canada's "British Traditions" was clear. He argued that one of the main
features of John A. Macdonald's Constitution was "a limited official
bilingualism, for the Dominion Parliament, the Courts, and the Quebec
Legislature and the courts." It was, Forsey wrote, "the degree of bilingualism called for by the needs of the time," but the beautifully flexible
constitution left "room for administrative or legislative adaptations or
extensions beyond that minimum at Ottawa and at Quebec, and elsewhere total freedom in the matter."[114] By so doing, the Fathers of
Confederation guaranteed to Quebec "the specific rights which French
Canadians then felt to be indispensable to [their] survival and development." To Forsey those included language rights, its own Civil Law, and
lastly, complete control of its educational system, subject to certain guar-
antees for the Protestant minority in Quebec.[115] By taking this limited
bicultural approach, Forsey later wrote, Canada rejected the American
melting pot theory "by deliberately writing into our Constitution a limited, but considerable bilingualism and biculturalism."[116]

The fluently bilingual Forsey, who lived a great many years in
Montreal as part of the English-speaking minority, had always been
aware of the need to protect French-Canadian linguistic and cultural
rights. "Let us give a resounding Yes!" wrote Forsey, "to demands that
would strengthen the same principles as the Fathers applied to the
smaller French Canada of their day, and so make French Canadians of
today feel, as their Fathers did, that the whole country is their show as
well as ours."[117]

Forsey had, therefore, consistently rejected any suggestion that the
arrangements agreed to by the Fathers of Confederation represented a

"compact" between French and English-speaking delegates at Quebec City and Charlottetown. This was the very principle that drove him from the newly formed New Democratic Party in 1961,[118] and for which he denounced the Conservative Party in 1967.[119] This "fairy-tale" just did not stand up to the facts as far as Forsey was concerned. Its proponents were misreading an arrangement that was agreed upon, not by "two founding peoples" through bilateral negotiations, but by representatives from the Maritimes and the two Canadas who "declared emphatically, and in both languages, that they were creating 'a new nation, a new and great nation, une nouvelle nation, une seule et grande nation....' Or in Sir George Cartier's phrase, 'a new political nationality.'"[120]

To Forsey, the French-Canadians had "received the framework of the single new political nation," and Forsey steadfastly maintained that no one participating in the Confederation debates had seriously questioned that approach.[121] And as a former member of a minority in Quebec, Forsey was sensitive to the difficulties faced by the French-Canadian minority in North America. This is illustrated in the following statement:

> First and foremost, we must try to understand the position of French Canada as a tiny island of people who speak French; in a vast North American sea of people who speak English; and an island upon which that sea beats incessantly and thunderously. We should try to imagine what it would be like if we were the island and they were the sea ... a satisfied majority, just because it is a satisfied majority, has a special obligation to try to understand the situation of a dissatisfied minority ... so that we can see whether there are changes in the terms which will satisfy him without reducing the partnership to a cobweb or destroy it altogether.[122]

But Forsey expected this process of listening and understanding to be mutual, in that the French-Canadians had an obligation to understand the English-Canadian situation through "dialogue." Forsey was proud of his British heritage, but he felt that the French-Canadians often misunderstood the fact that English-Canadians had their own history, "not the history of their forebears in England, Scotland, Iceland, or any other of the old countries." Forsey felt strongly that English-Canadians, as Canadians of British ancestry, should be proud of the "Imperial fountain" of their freedom, and to their worldwide, interracial Commonwealth to whose development French-Canadians like Laurier and St. Laurent had made vital contributions. Though Forsey also believed that all Canadians should feel a "pride in, and attachment to the historic provincial communities we belong to," we had also to remember that "first and foremost we are Canadians; that is where our primary loyalty lies."[123]

It was that Commonwealth link with the heritage of parliamentary responsible government, however, that had served as the guardian of French-Canadian minority rights since 1867, and which offered the French-Canadian minority in Canada its best chance to grow and prosper within that English-Canadian sea. "If the British element in our heritage goes," Forsey wrote, "the French element, equally essential, will not survive it, because annexation [with the United States] will follow inevitably, and Canada will be just a memory."[124] To Forsey, French-Canadians who urged on radical cultural and political rights for Quebec were attempting to establish in that Province a "hemi-demi-semi separatism: a loose confederation, in which an almost independent Quebec would have jurisdiction over most every service and activity." That prospect, concluded Forsey on more that one occasion, "is a recipe for total paralysis [and] the end of any attempt at biculturalism."[125]

Forsey felt strongly enough on this point that he resigned from the New Democratic Party following its 1961 founding convention, which endorsed the Two Nations principle. This endorsement precipitated Forsey's resignation from a movement that he had served for almost thirty years. Forsey specifically objected to the Convention's deletion of the word "national" throughout the NDP's official documents without its replacing the word with any suitable substitute. This deletion, wrote Forsey, "was avowedly part of a general scheme to make the New Party deny the existence of the Canadian nation, and affirm instead that there is not one nation but two; a French-Canadian nation and English Canadian nation in a bi-national State."[126] To Forsey, such a philosophy represented "a denial of the existence of the Canadian nation founded by the Fathers of Confederation ninety-four years ago."[127]

Forsey warned the convention leaders and delegates that accepting the French-Canadian notion of "nation" in a sociological and cultural sense would lead to demands for political national rights. He spoke out at the Convention a number of times, imploring the delegates to realize "that they were letting loose a devil, and that they had not the faintest idea of the consequences of their actions." "The result of the whole performance," Forsey added, "was, of course, to make it utterly impossible for me to remain in the NDP. I had been made ineligible since I could not for a moment accept the mutilated, expurgated party Constitution."[128]

Forsey believed that to try to understand the French-Canadians should really amount to nothing more than an exercise in calm, reasoned, rational discussion. But he believed it was also a particular challenge for "those of us who profess Christian convictions." Christians, Forsey maintained, were challenged "to try and think ourselves into the skins of the French Canadians.... But we've got to try to understand with our hearts and our heads."[129] Forsey never rejected any French-Canadian claim for special consideration. He had no doubt but that the Province of Quebec had every reason to request "careful considered extensions of special provisions because of its special character. It is not simply a province like all the others."[130] But those same French-Canadian claims had to be carefully considered on an individual basis and within the Christian mentality of love and understanding; not to pacify Quebec nationalists but to strengthen the Canadian nation:

> We should be inspired by Christian love, not a sickly desire to *be* loved [by French-Canadians].
>
> Christian love is not witless amiability, or absolute unselfishness. "Thou shalt love the Lord thy God with all thy mind," or, as our French Protestant Bible says, "*tu aimeras l'Eternal ton Dieu ... avec toute ta pensée*," all thy thought. And the second commandment is like unto it: thou shalt love thy neighbour as thyself, "*comme toi-même.*"[131]

Forsey believed that if a person's love of neighbour was to be "like unto" one's love of God, it must then be a love in which "we use our minds, in which we think." This also demanded that we love and respect ourselves, since a Christian's love for others was to be like his or love of self. "We must will the good of our neighbour, which involves using our heads to discover what that good is."[132] For the Christian Forsey, ensuring the continuation of a single national entity within a bicultural state required the active application of Christian principles in much the same way as the Christian worked to preserve a humanitarian society.

The foundation of Forsey's response to French-Canadian nationalism is similar to his response to English-Canadian nationalists: Canadians had their own history to respect, a Christian's responsibility to understand their neighbours, and a political responsibility to pursue change through reasoned debate. But this did not mean giving any group, including the French-Canadians, "instantaneously, invariably anything they happened to get into their heads they wanted." That kind of knee-jerk response would not exemplify Christianity in action, but merely appeasement, "the result of which could only be the flight of reason from human affairs; the triumph of the brutal; and in the life of the community, the dictatorship of whoever can shout the loudest or shake the biggest fist or make the biggest nuisance of himself."[133]

Forsey understood the French word "nation" to mean more than recognizing French-Canadians as a distinct "cultural and sociological group." Rather, it had two meanings: first, as a cultural or sociological nation like Scotland, Wales, or England; and secondly as a political "nation" like the United Kingdom, France and Canada. "As long as we allow ourselves to be fooled by this kind or verbal juggling," concluded Forsey, "we shall be sitting ducks for every separatist, or hemi-semi-demi-separatist in the country."

During the tense constitutional discussions surrounding Ontario Premier John Robarts' Confederation of Tomorrow conference in 1967,[134] Forsey stated his belief that Quebec already had a "special status" within the British North America Act through its unique official bilingualism and its jurisdiction over property and civil rights. Forsey had no opposition to giving any province a particular power, or powers, merely on the ground that this would make it different from the others: "But," he added, "I want to know first what power or powers, and why, and what the effect would be on the country as a whole."[135]

Forsey's commitment to the country as a whole was the same commitment that had led him to speak against French-Canadian attempts to incorporate the word "nation" into constitutional discussions since the mid-1960s. Forsey was certain that anyone who read the documents that had been submitted to various conferences by the Quebec government since 1966 would have no difficulty in showing how its representatives "slide from the cultural to the political meaning with a quickness of the hand which deceives the unpracticed eye." Analyzing the meaning of words had always been a Forsey specialty, and in the case of Quebec nationalistic literature, Forsey had frequently retreated to one of his constitutional and political mentors, John A. Macdonald, for clarification: "Subtlety! As Sir John A. Macdonald said, Marsh means marsh, bog means bog, yes means yes, and no means no."[136] Forsey often found that Quebec's submissions concerning special status have often purposely lacked such clarity.

Forsey's allegiance to Macdonald's vision of the nature of the political nation created by the Fathers of Confederation long predated the constitutional turbulence of the 1960s and 1970s. "Personally I have never been able to take much stock in the pact theory," Forsey wrote in 1946. "I remain on this subject an obstinate and unrepented follower of John A. Macdonald; indeed, in this respect I think I am a better Conservative than a good many members of the party."[137]

Forsey's constitutional sympathies for the Conservative Party increased after his resignation from the NDP in 1961. He provided Conservative leader John Diefenbaker with quotations from his Tory democratic mentor, Lord Randolph Churchill, who at one point in his career had denounced his own party for its "crowning desertion of Tory principles." That phrase was now resurrected by Forsey and Diefenbaker in the mid-1960s and applied to the followers of Dalton Camp and the "two nations monstrosity." Diefenbaker shared Forsey's view that what many French-Canadians in Quebec during the 1960s had in mind was "a politically sovereign entity equal in status with the federal parliament."[138] The ironic aspect here was that Forsey felt sure that by the early 1960s French-Canadians had much more in the way of bilingualism and biculturalism in the central government and its affairs than they were ever promised, "explicitly or implicitly at Confederation, or than they [ever] got in Sir John's time."[139]

Forsey's views regarding the dangerous rhetoric that often surrounded "nationalistic" appeals placed him in agreement with a new breed of French-Canadians who were emerging from Quebec in the mid-1960s. In a letter to Jim Macdonnell in late 1963, Forsey discussed his "100 per cent" backing of a political newcomer named Marc Lalonde. "You may possibly know him," Forsey wrote to Macdonnell, his old friend and a former Conservative M.P. "He was for a while Davie Fulton's Special Assistant."[140] Forsey viewed favourably Lalonde's comments that "he was neither a French-Canadian Nationalist nor a Canadian Nationalist." Rather, Lalonde believed that nationalism was for the most part a backward concept.[141] And Forsey especially liked Lalonde's call to end the informal method of handling serious problems through ultimatums, press conferences, and television appearances. What was needed, both Lalonde and Forsey agreed, was "to have people on both sides sit down, look carefully at particular problems, see what was required to work out the costs, and negotiate sensible conditions which would really produce the results that were needed." Forsey also agreed with Lalonde's claim that "our Dominion politicians were not strong, [while] our provincial politicians were so strong that there were few or no people here in Ottawa capable of standing up to them." This was particularly true, Lalonde thought, in the Dominion Cabinet, where for the most part there were poor French-Canadian ministers.[142]

Forsey's agreement with the philosophy expounded by Marc Lalonde placed him ideologically close to Lalonde's close friend, and rising political star, Pierre Trudeau. Trudeau's preoccupation with the individual and freedom, the equation of freedom through reasoned, rational discussion, and his "functional" abhorrence of ideologies such as irrational nationalism, paralleled Forsey's personal philosophy very closely.

Forsey and Trudeau met in the late 1940s,[143] and the two men slowly developed a mutual respect for one another following Trudeau's response to Forsey's public warnings during the early 1950s about the dangers of French-Canadian nationalism and English-Canadian "nationalistic fairy-tales." "Though perhaps my subconscious sympathies tend at times to fall with *messieurs les autonomistes*," Trudeau wrote to Forsey, "I must recognize that my reason was swayed by your argument."[144]

Forsey and Trudeau also exchanged information concerning trade union activities since both men were engaged in union-related work,[145] and discussed the power of dissolution to safeguard civil liberties in the Canadian state: "On the power of the Dominion Parliament in such matters," Forsey wrote Trudeau that "[I take my] stand with the Fathers of Confederation for whom I retain an obstinate respect." "Perhaps," added Forsey, "it is merely that I was brought up a Tory.... I believe in Dominion status for the provinces." Forsey then summed up his own non-ideological political ideology for Trudeau:

Perhaps you can convert me to "high Grittism" but I warn you will have your hands full with an old "bleu" like me. I think I really should not describe my political opinions as CCF, but rather as "Independent Continuing Unprogressive Conservative CCF!"[146]

Forsey continued to assist Trudeau in the 1950s by editing a brief that Trudeau was submitting to the Quebec Federation of Independent Unions. Later, in the early 1960s, Forsey read over Trudeau's "Concepts of Federalism" paper, in which Trudeau quoted Forsey's "thorough and convincing" work in Forsey's 1962 CJEPS article "Canada: Two Nations or One." In his reference to this article, Trudeau also thanked his "friend Eugene Forsey" for not only reading Trudeau's manuscript, but also for helping Trudeau to clarify several other ideas.[147] Later, Trudeau wrote Forsey that he was "most impressed with [Forsey's] thesis concerning the concept of special status for Quebec."[148] In response, Forsey lamented the fact that his position on the Conservative Party's Two-Nations policy "had put him in the doghouse with my Conservative friends."[149] In 1968 Trudeau wrote to Forsey and told him that:

I need not insist that I am in complete agreement with your views in the relations between French-speaking and English-speaking Canadians, and between Quebec and the rest of Canada. Your statements stand upon the most conclusive ones ever made on the subject.[150]

And shortly before Trudeau's June 1968 election, Trudeau wrote a similarly complimentary note to Forsey in which he stated:

I feel so indebted to you for your invaluable help and encouragement on so many occasions. I have to tell you how much I have appreciated everything you have done for me. I hope I shall always be worthy of the privilege of counting on your support and friendship.[151]

Forsey, himself never one to hold back on praise for those he admired, personally praised Trudeau for giving an "excellent, first-rate speech" during a Toronto campaign stop. "Trudeau just sort of stepped back as if he'd been hit," recalled an aide after Forsey's statement, "and I swear that for a moment he looked like he was going to burst into tears."[152]

Forsey's support for Trudeau's political career was based on a number of factors which Forsey outlined in a 1967 pre-Liberal convention newsletter supporting Trudeau. In his article, Forsey praised Trudeau's intelligence, knowledge, and his intellectual "toughness" which was "mixed with understanding, sympathy and tolerance." Forsey particularly stressed Trudeau's rational approach to discussion and his views on federalism that were totally in accord with his own views:

> On the biggest question that faces Canada today, the question of keeping it Canada and making it the Canada of all Canadians, he is, I think, completely and profoundly right. If the country breaks up, or if the central Government is reduced to impotence or chaos, then the best plans of the other parties will be just waste paper. Keeping Canada together, making it the Canada of all Canadians, is going to take intelligence, knowledge, hard work, judgement, candour, courage: all of them qualities in which Pierre Trudeau, in my long experience of him, is pre-eminent.[153]

In Trudeau, Forsey, like so many Canadians of the era, saw a man able to deal with a Quebec society that seemed in the mid-1960s to be in crisis: "a society adrift without a rudder," in the words of Trudeau biographer George Radwanski.[154] But despite the social turmoil of the 1960s, Forsey shared Trudeau's view that the Fathers of Confederation had "arrived at as wise a compromise and drew up as sensible a constitution as any group of men anywhere could have done." Trudeau, like Forsey, shared a conservative suspicion that radical change in the constitution was not necessary to make Canada work.[155] And most importantly, the two men had long shared the goal of steering Canada away from its drift toward some sort of special status for Quebec. They both perceived that special status would not prevent the breakup of Confederation, but would make it nearly inevitable in the long run.[156]

From the pre-war political battles, to the constitutional debate surrounding the 1987 Meech Lake Accord, Eugene Forsey had steadfastly opposed any massive transfer of powers to any provincial legislature. "Such a policy," argued Forsey, "would be just a transitory chilly, half-way house on the road to complete separation."[157] For example, Forsey had argued as far back as 1936 that no Dominion government could carry through a socialist plan for the Dominion without complete control of the monetary and financial system.[158] Since the early 1940s Forsey had repeatedly stated his strong belief in the need to maintain the strong central government that was intended by John A. Macdonald and the Fathers of Confederation. "The Fathers," he wrote, "clearly intended the powers of the Dominion to cover such matters as labour and social legislation, marketing and price control, insurance, liquor traffic, and social security." But this original constitutional principle, Forsey argued, had over the years been "stood on its head by those old rascals" in the Judicial Committee of the Privy Council. In this regard Forsey could support the CCF in its desire to see the Dominion given back its power to regulate the various legislative areas originally intended to be under its authority.[159]

Forsey continued to preach his "strong central government" message into the 1950s and throughout the 1960s following his resignation from the NDP.[160] In July 1969, Forsey retired from the CLC after having reached the age of sixty-five,[161] and after completing a Special Research Project which led to the publication of his labour history book *Trade Unions in Canada, 1812–1902*. In this work Forsey argued that Canada's tradition of labour organization and collective work was in fact a long and well-established historical fact in Canada dating back well into the early nineteenth century. Forsey's thesis in *Trade Unions* was consistent with his constitutional arguments in the sense that the Canadian working class, like its political leadership, drew upon long-established British traditions.[162]

The completion of this research project left Forsey free to consider new opportunities, one of which was Trudeau's offer to become Canada's Commissioner of Indian Affairs. Forsey declined that position as well as Trudeau's offer of the Ambassadorship to the Vatican. He did however, readily accept the Senate seat that Trudeau offered to him the following year.

In his Senate position Forsey was influential in publicly advocating his continuing support for "setting [Canada] back to an up-date version of the kind of thing that the Fathers of Confederation were trying to do" more than one hundred years earlier. Forsey was particularly active on the Joint Senate and House Committee on the Constitution of Canada, whose report was tabled in March 1972.[163] Though he had some specific concerns with the wording of the final document, Forsey basically agreed with the Committee's recommendations to draw a distinction between great economic questions which affected the whole country, which would be left to the Parliament of Canada, and socio-cultural matters, which would be left predominantly to the provinces, "sometimes with some overriding provision for paramountcy for the legislation of the Parliament of Canada, or the actions of the Government of Canada, sometimes not."[164]

Forsey supported Trudeau's opposition to "special status" in any form for Quebec as well as Trudeau's efforts to prevent a massive decentralization of power to the provinces. Forsey believed that Canada was already the most decentralized federation in the world. "How much further can we go," wrote Forsey, "without making Canada a political Cheshire Cat, of which you remember, nothing remained but the smile?"[165]

Forsey, who often stated that he sat as a Pierre Trudeau Liberal Senator because he was a John A. Macdonald Conservative,[166] also referred to himself as a "continuing Conservative" as opposed to a "Progressive Conservative." Forsey added that he thought that Donald Creighton and himself were perhaps "the only two survivors of this almost extinct species of John A. Macdonald Conservative."[167] Forsey also added that he could not see how Canada could accomplish the economic and humanitarian goals that he as a "Tory democrat" believed necessary, if the country was "being run by a set of provincial potentates with enormous power; Electors of a resurrected Holy Roman Empire." "And you remember what Voltaire said," Forsey reminded his listeners: "It was neither holy, nor Roman, nor an empire." Likewise, Forsey did not think that Canada could do much in the way of national economic planning "if the country was led by a series of fragments of Canada ... by the Electors of an un-holy, un-Canadian, un-Empire."[168]

Forsey often argued that the British North America Act was an effective vehicle for dealing with "totally new situations of nation-wide interest and importance" because it was flexible. He saw the BNA Act as providing the flexibility to manoeuvre through "twentieth century" traffic because much of the wording was not written down. As a result, both it and the Constitution Act (1982) could be changed by a simple Act of Parliament or by a provincial legislature.[169] Much of the BNA Act, Forsey wrote, fostered reasoned discussion and common sense debate between national parties and between Ottawa and the provinces. The Act, he added, was "pure convention," that is, habits, practices, usages, and customs which have grown out of repeatedly successful ways of dealing with particular problems.

Because Forsey shares Burke's suspicion of intense idealism,[170] he favours a system in which problems "can be changed or abandoned when they cease to work satisfactorily, without any change at all in the law."[171] One example of this adaptation was found in "the essence of responsible government; that a cabinet defeated in the House of Commons on a motion of want of confidence must either resign or ask for a fresh election." This accountability to the electorate, Forsey once wrote, was an "unwritten" aspect of our Constitution that ensured ample room of change and innovation as well as "what Robert Borden called the common-place quality of common sense. The much criticized silences or gaps in the BNA Act are among its greatest glories."[172]

Another very important example of the power that the BNA Act gave Canadians to make special arrangements to meet special needs lay in its claim that Quebec was not a province like the others. It was clear to Forsey that Quebec had two examples of special constitutional status: alone of all the provinces it could not abolish the use of English in its legislature and courts; and alone of the provinces it could not surrender any of its jurisdiction over property and civil rights. Special needs in the Canadian Constitution could be met only with these examples of special constitutional status, explained Forsey, but could also be met by "administrative delegation" and through reasoned discussion between the Dominion and one or more provinces. During these discussions each government and legislature would undertake to use its powers through concurrent legislation, such as the case in family allowances.[173]

One of the criteria, therefore, that Forsey consistently used in evaluating any suggested amendment to the Constitution is the degree to which the amendment would diminish not only the Dominion powers, but diminish the Constitution's overall flexibility. For example, he supported the Conservative government's Fulton amendments in 1960 not because he favoured their institutionalization of certain unwritten conventions, such as the unanimous consent of the provinces for some major federal initiatives, but because these changes were already established conventions. "In fact," Forsey explained, "the Fulton proposal give the provinces, including Quebec, nothing beyond what they have already."[174]

For Forsey the real strength of the Fulton proposal was its principle that if Quebec, or any other province, did not wish to delegate specific proposals to the Dominion, it did not have to do so. But those provinces could not stop the rest of the provinces from doing so if they wanted to. In this regard Forsey felt that the Fulton proposal ensured the continuation of a strong Dominion government while maintaining a flexible constitution.[175] Likewise Forsey supported the Liberal government's 1964 Fulton-Favreau amendments because under those provisions any four provinces could delegate to the Dominion their power to legislate on any matter whatsoever.[176] These matters could include, for example, items of "local works, property and civil rights" which would otherwise be beyond the power of Parliament. Thus the flexibility of the Constitution worked to enhance Dominion powers that Forsey believed would "open up new avenues to social progress which [were] now completely blocked. It would build barriers against national disruption." The resulting uniformity of social legislation was a goal that Forsey had long sought within the Labour/CCF ranks, a position that Forsey thought "was historically sound and valid until King, St. Laurent, Diefenbaker and the NDP sold the pass."[177] The Fulton-Favreau formula requiring unanimous provincial consent over any future amendments did not, Forsey believed, make the Act any more rigid, since it "put into a law what is already there in constitutional convention (usage) as unbreakable as any law."[178]

Forsey's strong support for the retention of "conventions" and "silences" in the BNA Act and the Constitution Act of 1982 was based on his belief that those conventions permitted common sense discussion and adaptation to take place. It was precisely for this reason that Forsey opposed the 1978 Bill C60 amendment, which included a clause stating that the "institution of the Canadian federation shall be governed by the Constitution of Canada and by the conventions, customs and usages hallowed by it." This clause, Forsey argued, would place the conventions at the mercy of the Supreme Court of Canada and represent a subversion of parliamentary government.[179]

And so Forsey defended as "crucially important" the flexibility of "John A. Macdonald's Constitution ... which provided the nation with room to grow and left people to use their heads." Like the other important elements that have been identified in this chapter, including the monarchy, parliamentary responsible government, and limited bilingualism, the element of flexibility was essential if Canada was to maintain a strong, powerfully active Dominion government capable of initiating the social and economic legislation that the nation required. For Forsey, Canada's British tradition was the keystone of its constitutional system. That tradition provided an effective, workable system that protected individual and minority rights and ensured that the will of the people as a whole would be carried out. And just as importantly, it encouraged reasoned discussion and responded to the changing needs of the twentieth century.

Forsey's published and unpublished material on the Constitution is extensive; yet he was, and continued to be, very consistent in what he argued for and against. If an idea or a recommended change was in keeping with British constitutional tradition and would work, chances were good that Forsey would support it. But if it went "against the grain" of British constitutional traditions and it appeared less than well thought-out and reasonable, chances were very good that Forsey would oppose it. There were few grey areas in the sphere of constitutional debate.

CONCLUSION

In his conclusion to his book entitled *Edmund Burke,* historian Frank O'Gorman writes that "Underpinning Edmund Burke's political philosophy was a mentality which rendered coherent the diverse and seemingly unconnected experiences of his career."[1] In a similar vein, one can conclude that Eugene Forsey's underpinning mentality was forged by the "diverse and seemingly unconnected experiences" of his life. To understand Forsey one must always keep in mind the secure and comfortable middle-class experiences of Forsey's very political and religious Ottawa boyhood home. These experiences are central to understanding the missionary zeal with which Forsey approached political and constitutional issues throughout his life.

Forsey's maternal and paternal families were rooted in "old country" British and Loyalist ways, and this fact was always very important to Forsey. This heritage was especially important to Forsey because of his unique ability to perceive and retain certain personal idiosyncrasies in others, and then to relate them to that person's ethnicity and family roots. In this sense Forsey shared Burke's belief that "real individuals [are] not abstract men," but "Englishmen, Frenchmen, Irish Catholics, Indians and Americans." And these "real men," Burke added, "lived in and through specific social institutions."[2] Forsey was always very aware of his English, Welsh, and Irish bloodline, and his Loyalist, Maritime, and Quebec family roots, and his awareness of this heritage was a major factor in shaping his attachment to British constitutional principles.

Of the "social institutions" that Burke also referred to above, Forsey, like Burke, always considered the family and the Christian Church the two most important institutions in society. To Forsey, one's behaviour was largely determined by the "genes" he or she carries, as well as the environmental experiences of his or her family during past generations. Forsey revealed his commitment to these influencing factors of family and environment in a lengthy letter he wrote to his wife during the early 1960s. Forsey, who was undergoing a difficult personal depression at this time, wrote that it was "absolutely essential to find out all we can about the conditions – physical, chemical, social, family, religious, or any other which produce aberrant behaviour or state of mind."[3] His attachment to "the value of tradition" can be applied to his family history as well as to the political milieu. Forsey's attachment to family tradition was so strong, in fact, that he became depressed when he discovered that some of his own perceived failings as a father resulted from his failure to pass on to his wife and two daughters his own family and personal traditions and traits. "I totally failed to make available to you and the girls any of the heritage I had, religious or other," Forsey wrote. "I had political and social convictions [but] I said almost nothing about them. I could easily have given the girls a good deal more equipment for facing and enjoying life than I have done."[4]

Forsey's mother and grandfather Bowles provided him with much of the experience and "equipment" that largely shaped Forsey's allegiance to Jesus Christ and the British constitution. Within this context, Forsey's allegiance to family as a strong, independent unit responsible for controlling social actions represented one of the cornerstones of his political pluralism. This philosophy was clearly articulated by Edmund Burke:

> We began our public affections in our families [and] we pass on to
> our neighborhoods, and our habitual provincial connections. These
> are inns and resting-places, ... divisions of our country as have been
> formed by habit, and not by a sudden jerk of authority.... The
> love to the whole is not extinguished by this subordinate partiality.
> Perhaps it is a sort of elemental training to those higher and more
> large regards.[5]

A second aspect of Forsey's "elemental training" was his strong Methodist upbringing, which was reinforced during his first years at McGill through his exposure to the personality and messages of Reverend Allsworth Eardley. The church, like family, was always a very important "resting-place" where Forsey formulated his passion for

236

moral reform of self and society through individual Christian social activism. This passion is also partly an outgrowth of Forsey's attachment during the early 1920s to British conservatism and in particular to its Tory-democratic morality.

Though Forsey personally doubted his own Christian convictions at various points in his life,[6] he retained a personal commitment to a nineteenth century form of the "moral imperative" as the necessary basis of a well-ordered society. This is a philosophy that for the most part had disappeared in Canada by the end of World War I.[7] But for Forsey, there were just too many continuing influences that kept his moral reformism central to his thought processes: his Methodist upbringing; the impact of Reverend Eardley; his readings in Tory democracy; and the powerful influences of academics like J.C. Hemmeon and, more importantly, John Macmurray, all contained elements of the moral imperative's balance "between individual autonomy and the social good, between the myth of freedom and the myth of concern."[8] And like so many of Canada's pre-World War I moral idealists, Forsey's philosophy was shaped by the conditions of the his times. In Forsey's lifetime these conditions included the economic uncertainty of the 1920s and more importantly the devastating social impact of the Depression. All of these influences, therefore, contributed to Forsey's lifelong belief in the individual's Christian responsibility to actively work to better one's society.

This was a philosophy that had its intellectual roots in the Burkean ideal of morality as the cement of society. For Burke, as for Forsey, religion represented one of the key foundations of society. Forsey always believed that just as Jesus "lived a perfect human life," so too did every Christian have a responsibility to seek perfection through his or her actions toward others.[10] In this effort Forsey believed that every person was guided by the presence of God in the form of the Christian Holy Spirit. It was because this goal of moral reform was so central to Forsey's psyche that he eventually embraced Quakerism, and its focus on the "Inner Light" as a powerful force aiding one's struggle for perfection in thought and action.[11]

The social reform that would result from this individual effort was, in Forsey's view as it had been for Burke, necessarily a slow and gradual process not in any way meant to be a revolutionary event. For this reason Forsey shared Burke's suspicion and slight disdain for the "intellectuals" of society. Both men believed that the "intelligentsia" of society often initiated momentum for radical social change when steadfastness or moderate gradual social reform and guidance was called for.[12]

But Forsey had times in his life when he questioned his personal commitment to "live what [he] was supposed to believe." "You know," he wrote to his wife, "that Jesus' test was 'By their fruits ye shall know them'; and my fruits [have been] microscopic." Forsey's barometer of social action, based as it was on the moral goal of individual and social regeneration, ideologically bridged the cautious social reformism of conservative Methodism with the "full program of social regeneration of liberal Presbyterians."[13]

Perhaps Forsey's clearest expression of this philosophy is found in an unpublished, handwritten manuscript located in Forsey's personal papers. This extensive, undated work is almost certainly the outline of one of Forsey's church sermons that he occasionally gave. A main theme in this sermon is the failure of Christianity to become a major transforming force in Canadian society:

> Instead of the Church Militant, we have the Church Quiescent. In no sphere is this more true than in that of politics and economics.
>> Some still believe that these are outside Church's realm.
>> Some still believe we should sign a Treaty of Partition with the Devil, leaving politics and economics as his Kingdom.
>> Some pray that the King may have wise and upright counsellors, but with a truly remarkable "faith" leave the Devil to provide them.[14]

Forsey cited the failure of prohibition to eradicate alcohol, militarism's exploitation of fellow human beings, and the failure of the missionary ideal, as examples of Christianity's failure to foster meaningful social change. The result, Forsey concluded, was predictable:

> Does anyone seriously believe that we can establish the Kingdom of God on earth if all our political and economic machinery is in the hands of the enemies?
>> I acknowledge no boundary to Christ's Kingdom. What becomes of Christianity if you do? Christ is the complete fulfillment of the world's needs and some of those needs are political and economic, and can be met only with political and economic means. [15]

Though Forsey at times personally doubted his commitment to living out this challenge, his life experiences suggest that he at least made a concerted effort to contribute to the goal of Christianity as stated above. His philosophy, shaped over the years by academic and religious figures and the moral and social devastation of the Depression years, was expressed through his association with Christian activist organizations such as the United Church's Committee of Social and Economic Research, the Student Christian Movement, the Quaker Church, and the Fellowship for Christian Social Order. Ideologically, Forsey viewed each of these entities as mechanisms for individual and social regeneration. And, like Burke's, Forsey's philosophy was presented within a pluralist framework that provided the socialism, or social interaction, of these interdependent collective units, each striving to protect its own interests while co-operatively contributing toward the betterment of all classes in society.

Forsey believed that it was Jesus Christ who provided the necessary context for this process. It was He who provided the moral standard which guided individuals through their small, local associations such as the church, unions, businessman associations, and co-operatives. The achievement of those Christian goals, in turn, provided both personal liberty and social harmony between the naturally different classes in society. "Personal liberty" to Forsey, therefore, was based on the maintenance of a social condition that provided an individual with the opportunity "to rise to higher things, to live a broad, rich, abundant life."[16] In his notes Forsey cites T.H. Green as the intellectual source for this philosophy, and for good reason, since freedom, for Green and Forsey, was "the greatest of blessings, but did not mean freedom from restraint or compulsion or to do as we like irrespective of what it is that we like."[17] Nor was freedom something that could be enjoyed by one person, or set of persons, at the cost of a loss of freedom to others. For Forsey this meant that mankind "needs a positive power or capacity of doing or enjoying something in common with others."[18]

Forsey shared Green's belief that freedom, the goal of all social effort, was a positive "liberation of the powers of all men equally for contributions to a common good."[19] This is most clearly shown through Forsey's work for the League for Social Reconstruction, the Co-Operative Commonwealth Federation, and the Canadian Congress of Labour, all of which involved his efforts to introduce "real democracy" for the working classes, a democracy that provided opportunities for constructive, meaningful work. To Forsey this meant preserving both individual civil rights and utilizing society's human and material resources to the fullest possible degree. "The establishment of Social Justice and industrial peace" according to Christ's teachings was for Forsey the only philosophy that made sense.[20] "The Church's duty – not methods, but goals," Forsey wrote, was to fearlessly proclaim the:

1. Consecrated ministry of political and economic research and action.
2. Respect and love of those whose methods may differ from our own – Socialists vs. our brothers all.

But most important of all, Forsey wrote, was the third duty – the Proclamation of general principles. First of all, these principles included the task of preserving personality, that is, the principle that mankind must take precedence over money in order to provide the "chance to develop personality." A second principle was ensuring that industry provided "a living wage," and that its production was directed toward "channels of necessities for the many rather than the luxuries of the few."[21]

As earlier illustrated, this duty for Forsey required a degree of collective long-range planning which would ensure specific idealistic social goals. "Idealism," wrote Forsey, "[is] the only realism – the other policy is short-sighted and has been tried long enough [with] disastrous results."[22] Forsey admitted that his "revolutionary" ideas were not likely to be popular, but he was convinced that "Our Lord's ways of life [was] the only solution to world problems." His call was a call to action to the Church, and to the individual, and neither entity could ignore the call.

There is no doubt that Forsey's belief in religious social radicalism contrasts with his political conservatism and belief in a stable, gradually reformist society. He was well aware that a person's individual "hypothesis, theories, and doctrines" would change during one's lifetime "with advances in knowledge (coming mostly from thought, partly from experiences and experiment.)"[23] In this regard Forsey's own theories and doctrines changed over the course of his lifetime and in so doing appear to contain inherent contradictions. But the consistent thread was his belief in the need for individual moral regeneration and responsibility for Christian action within the context of a social whole. This principle permeated his life's work after his return from Oxford in 1929.

Closely tied to this principle was Forsey's belief in the right of individuals to live and work in a free and stable society. The preservation of that freedom and stability was, in turn, the task performed by the political institutions associated with Canada's British constitutional heritage. This heritage ensured that the necessary changes were pursued within an ordered framework that allowed individuals of differing abilities to contribute to the social good in accordance with those abilities. All persons were not equal in Eugene Forsey's eyes; but he always believed that no person should suffer because of that reality. In this sense the health of corporate society was, for Forsey, analogous to the health of a living human body:

> In a body, there [are] different jobs to do, all good and knowledgeable and necessary to the health, the wholeness, of the whole body, and the eye and the ear [do not] fight for recognition of superiority but just do their job as parts of the body.[24]

As the above quotation suggests, Forsey was never hesitant to clothe his message in emotionalism. Whether in detailed, personal letters to his loved ones, short acerbic letters to newspapers editors, or lengthy articles, Forsey's emotions were usually quite observable. "There is nothing wrong with emotions," Forsey once wrote, "provided they are rational, that is in accord with and springing from the facts."[25]

Forsey always shared Burke's disdain for "abstract principles and emotional doctrine," largely because the two men shared a belief in the limitations of human abilities.[26] Thus the need to solve problems using reason and rational discussion through the mechanism of pluralism. For Eugene Forsey, life was a constant struggle to maintain his sense of Christian brotherhood in the face of emotional persons of "less ability." It was a challenge that Forsey, the twentieth century conservative, Christian humanitarian, continued to face until the end of his life.

NOTES

CHAPTER

1

THE **EARLY YEARS**

1 Eugene Forsey, "Multiculturalism: An Anglo-Celtic View," n.d.,
Eugene Forsey Papers (hereafter cited as EFP), Public Archives of
Canada (hereafter cited as PAC), Ottawa.
2 Eugene Forsey, "The British Fact in Canada," Speech, n.d., EFP.
3 Eugene Forsey, *Freedom and Order: Collected Essays* (Toronto, 1974),
vii.
4 Forsey Family Records, EFP.
5 Ibid. Eugene Forsey senior was discharged as "Seaman, A.B." in
Halifax in July 1899.
6 Ibid., vol. 46, File 20, Letters from Eugene Forsey senior to George
Forsey, 1889–99.
7 Ibid., Family Tree Scrapbook, vol. 46, File 25.
8 Ibid.
9 Ibid., Biographical Note on Eugene Alfred Forsey, and Family
Records, vol. 46, File 15.
10 Eugene Forsey to Arthur Meighen, June 17, 1943, Arthur Meighen
Papers (hereafter cited as AMP), PAC, Ottawa. Cahan's friendship
with the Forsey family continued through the subsequent decades.
See Eugene Forsey to C.H. Cahan, May 30, 1943, AMP.
11 Forsey to C.H. Cahan, May 30, 1943, AMP.
12 Baptismal Register and Birth Certificate of Eugene Alfred Forsey,
Methodist Church, Grand Bank, Newfoundland, Family Records,
vol. 46, File 21, EFP.
13 Forsey, *Freedom and Order,* vii.
14 Forsey Family Records, vol. 46, File 5, EFP.
15 Forsey, *Freedom and Order,* vii.
16 Forsey Family Records, vol. 46, File 5, EFP.
17 Forsey, *Freedom and Order,* vii.
18 John George Bourinot, *Parliamentary Procedure and Practice in the
Dominion of Canada,* Reprint ed. (Shannon, 1971), Introduction.
19 Ibid.
20 Carl Berger, "Race and Liberty: The Historical Ideas of Sir John
Bourinot," *Canadian Historical Association Annual Report,* 1965, 92.

21 Ibid., 104.
22 Interview with Eugene Forsey, Ottawa, March 18, 1986.
23 Ibid.
24 Ibid.
25 Quoted in Forsey, *Freedom and Order,* vii.
26 W.C. Bowles to Hazel Bowles, April 5, 1911, vol. 46, W.C. Bowles Correspondence File, EFP.
27 Eugene Forsey, "A Delightful Incident on my Holidays," School Essay, vol. 46, File 17, EFP; and W.C. Bowles to Mrs. Florence Forsey, August 17, 1915, EFP; Forsey Interview, Ottawa, May 30, 1987.
28 See, for example, a school essay written by Forsey when he was fourteen years old entitled "Armistice in Ontario," vol. 46, File 17, EFP.
29 See vol. 46, Files 8–19, EFP.
30 Ibid., Forsey Family Records, Family Tree Scrapbook.
31 Alberta and Theresa Moritz, *Leacock: A Biography* (Toronto, 1985), 98, 154.
32 Doug Owram, *The Government Generation: Canadian Intellectuals and the State, 1900–1945* (Toronto, 1986), 12.
33 Owram, *The Government Generation,* 32, 90–91, 103–4, 122, and Chapter 5, passim.
34 Eugene Forsey to his mother, October 1, 1922, EFP.
35 Forsey Interview, March 1984.
36 Stephen Leacock to Eugene Forsey, Personal Correspondence Files, 1920s and 1930s, EFP.
37 See Alberta and Theresa Moritz, *Leacock,* Chapter 6, passim. Forsey's thoughts on the importance of the British connection in Canada will be fully discussed in Chapter 9.
38 Leacock to Forsey, 'June the Something,' 1925.
39 Eugene Forsey to his mother, October 1, 1922, EFP.
40 J.C. Hemmeon to Eugene Forsey, July 27, 1924, EFP.
41 J.C. Hemmeon to Frank Scott, February 16, 1934; Harry Cassidy to Frank Scott (n.d.); Frank Scott to Hemmeon, April 16, 1935, Frank Scott Papers, PAC, Ottawa.
42 D.G. Goodwin, Secretary C.C.L.U. to Neil Morrison, Secretary, Student Christian Movement in McGill University, February 8, 1943, Student Christian Movement Papers, Canadian Civil Liberties Union File, United Church Archives, Toronto.
43 Hemmeon to Forsey, April 7, 1943 and March 17, 1954, EFP.
44 Forsey to his mother, October 29, 1922; July 27, 1924; November 24, 1924, EFP.
45 Forsey to his mother, November 19, 1922, EFP.
46 J.W. Jenks and Walter Clark, *The Trust Problem: Economic Power in a Free Society* (New York, 1929). See 'A Note About This Book.'
47 Richard Hofstadter, *The Age of Reform: From Bryan to F.D.R.* (New York, 1955), Introduction and 134.
48 Jenks and Clark, *The Trust Problem,* 147–49.
49 Ibid., 149–50.
50 Ibid., 306, 309, 312.
51 McGill Transcripts, vol. 46, File 14, EFP.
52 Ibid. Forsey received first class standings in all his third and fourth year classes. These courses, listed below, indicate the mixed nature of Forsey's work, for though he had decided to major in Political Economy he continued to study a great deal of Literature.

THIRD YEAR – Economics 3 (Political and Social Theories of
Modern Times)
Economics 4 (Labour Problems)
Economics 5 (Money and Banking)
Economics 6 (The Government of Canada)
Economics 7 (Canada: Industrial and Economic Problems)
English 7 (Poetry and Drama)
English 9 (Poets of the Nineteenth Century)

FOURTH YEAR – Economics 8 (Political Economy Till 1776)
Economics 9 (Political Economy From 1776)
Economics 10 (International Trade)
Economics 11 (Public Finance)
Economics 14 (Economic Factors in the Evolution of Society)
Economics 15 (Economic Factors in the Evolution of Society
   After 1800)
English 10 (The English Novel)
English 12 (Anglo-Saxon)
English 14 (Chaucer)

53 *Montreal Gazette* clipping, n.d., EFP.
54 *Montreal Daily Star* clipping, May 28, 1925, EFP.
55 *McGill Daily Supplement* clipping, n.d., EFP. This was a position
Forsey would hold for many subsequent years.
56 Owram, *The Government Generation*, 122.
57 Ibid., 122.
58 See Barry Ferguson, "The New Political Economy and Canadian
Liberal Democratic Thought: Queen's University, 1890–1925," Ph.D.
dissertation, York University, 1982. See especially Chapter 9, "The
Political Economists and Post-War Canada: An Agenda for Reform,"
370–84, 405.
59 See Stanley Frost, *History of McGill*, vol. 1.
60 Eugene Forsey, "Economic and Social theories of Adam Smith," EFP.
Though undated, this paper was probably written over the course of
two years. In November 1922, Forsey wrote to his mother that he was
studying *The Wealth of Nations* in political economy and was "taking
a swat at Adam Smith" in his outside reading course work. The paper
itself has a 1925 notation on it that has been added in recent years. See
vol. 8, File "Arts and Speeches, 1925–1971."
61 Forsey did not, however, reflect McKillop's additional "liberal" and
"secular" dominant notes of Canadian intellectual life. See A.B.
McKillop, *A Disciplined Intelligence: Critical Inquiry and Canadian
Thought in the Victorian Era* (Montreal, 1979), 230.
62 Forsey, "Economic and Social Theories," 3.
63 Ibid., 1–2.
64 Ibid.
65 Ibid.
66 Ibid., 3.
67 Smith's " division of labour" discussion focuses on the division
of tasks in the production process that led to "a proportionable
increase in the productive powers of labour." This, in turn, led to
the separation of different trades and employment from one another.
The degree of separation, Smith wrote, increased with the degree of

industrialization of a particular country. Forsey basically agreed with this explanation, calling Smith's treatment of the issue "one of the classics of Economic Science." See Adam Smith, *An Inquiry Into the Nature and Causes of The Wealth of Nations* (New York, 1937), 4–5; and Forsey, "Economic and Social Theories," 4.

68 Forsey, "Economic and Social Theories," 8.
69 Ibid., 25–26.
70 Ibid., 29.
71 Forsey to his mother, June 12, 1931, EFP.
72 Forsey, "Economic and Social Theories," 8.
73 Smith, *The Wealth of Nations*, p. 61.
74 Jenks, *The Trust Problem*, 308–09.
75 See, for example, David P. Noble, *The Progressive Mind, 1890–1917* (Chicago, 1970); John Chambers II, *The Tyranny of Change; America in the Progressive Era, 1900- 1911* (New York, 1980); Robert M. Crunden, *Ministers of Reform: The Progressive Achievement in American Civilization, 1889–1920* (New York, 1982).
76 Forsey, "Economic and Social Theories," 18.
77 Ibid., 2.
78 Smith, *The Wealth of Nations*, Book IV, Chapter 7, passim, and 625–26.
79 Forsey, "Economic and Social Theories," 24.
80 Ibid., 26–27.
81 Ibid., 21.
82 Ibid., 3–4.

CHAPTER

EUGENE FORSEY AND TORY DEMOCRACY

1 John Herd Thompson with Allen Seager, *Canada 1922-1939: Decades of Discord* (Toronto, 1985), 76.
2 Thompson, *Decades of Discord*, 76.
3 James Struthers, *No Fault of Their Own: Unemployment and the Canadian Welfare State, 1914–1941* (Toronto, 1983), 25, 37.
4 See Christopher Armstrong, *The Politics of Federalism: Ontario's Relations With the Federal Government, 1867–1942* (Toronto, 1981), 33–48.
5 Paul-André Linteau, René Durocher and Jean-Claude Robert, *Quebec: A History, 1867–1929* (Toronto, 1983), Chapters 26–28.
6 Ibid., 434–35.
7 Terry Copp, *The Anatomy of Poverty: The Condition of the Working Classes in Montreal, 1897–1929* (Toronto, 1974), Chapter 2, passim.
8 Ernest R. Forbes, *Aspects of Maritime Regionalism* (C.H.A. Booklet), 18; and Ernest Forbes, *The Maritimes Rights Movement, 1919–1927: A Study in Canadian Regionalism* (Montreal, 1979).
9 W.L. Morton, *The Progressive Party in Canada* (Toronto, 1950), 268.
10 J.L. Granatstein, Irving M. Abella, David J. Bercuson, R. Craig Brown, and H. Blair Neatby, *Twentieth Century Canada* (Toronto, 1983), 188.
11 See Tom Traves, *The State and Enterprise: Canadian Manufacturers and the Federal Government, 1917–1931* (Toronto, 1979).
12 Ibid., 80–82.

13 See Hofstadter, *Age of Reform*, 142; and Morton Keller, *Affairs of State:
  Public Life in Late Nineteenth Century America* (Cambridge, 1977),
  Chapter 10; George Mowry, *The Era of Theodore Roosevelt, 1900–1912*
  (New York, 1959); Gabriel Kolko, *The Triumph of Conservatism:
  A Reinterpretation of American History, 1900–1916* (Chicago, 1963),
  98–103.
14 See, for example, Traves, *The State and Enterprise*.
15 Ibid.
16 Ibid.
17 Robert Bothwell, Ian Drummond, and John English, *Canada,
  1900–1945: Power, Politics, and Provincialism* (Toronto, 1989), 225.
18 Owram, *The Government Generation*, 121.
19 See Thompson, *Decades of Discord*, Chapter 6; R. MacGregor Dawson,
  William Lyon Mackenzie King: A Political Biography (Toronto, 1958),
  Chapter 15; H. Blair Neatby, *William Lyon Mackenzie King: The Lonely
  Heights, 1924–1932*, Chapter 2; Roger Graham, *Arthur Meighen, vol.
  2: And Fortune Fled* (Toronto, 1963), Chapters 5 and 10; Traves, *The
  State and Enterprise*, 90–126.
20 Forsey Interview, March 11, 1984.
21 Graham, *And Fortune Fled*, 259–60.
22 Ibid., 131.
23 Roger Graham, *Arthur Meighen, vol. 1: The Door of Opportunity*
  (Toronto, 1960), 285–92.
24 Dawson, *William Lyon Mackenzie King*, 380–92, 441–45.
25 Neatby, *The Lonely Heights*, 18.
26 Ibid., 20.
27 J. Murray Beck, *Pendulum of Power: Canada's Federal Elections*
  (Toronto, 1968), 174–75.
28 Graham, *And Fortune Fled*, 259–69.
29 Ibid., 263–67.
30 Claude Bissell, *The Young Vincent Massey* (Toronto, 1981), 148–49.
31 Forsey to his mother, September 2, 1924, EFP.
32 Ibid., September 2, 4, 9, 11, 14, and 21, 1924.
33 Bissell, *The Young Vincent Massey*, 150–53.
34 Forsey Interview, Ottawa, May 29, 1987.
35 Bissell, *The Young Vincent Massey*, 149.
36 Ibid., 149.
37 Ibid., 85 and 249, n. 17.
38 Forsey to his mother, September 4 and 14, 1924, EFP.
39 Bissell, *The Young Vincent Massey*, 78 and 103–4.
40 Ibid., 104.
41 Neatby, *The Lonely Heights*, 18.
42 Ibid., 67.
43 Bissell, *The Young Vincent Massey*, 107–8.
44 Neatby, *The Lonely Heights*, 67; Bissell, *The Young Vincent Massey*,
  107–11.
45 John Buchan (Lord Tweedsmuir) was a Scottish novelist who was
  appointed Canadian Governor General in 1935. He was a personal
  friend of the Massey family and met Massey while the two were at
  Oxford. Thompson, *Decades of Discord*, 237.
46 Forsey to his mother, September 2, 1924, EFP.
47 Charles Stewart, a former Premier of Alberta, was King's Minister of
  Mines and Interior in 1924. He aggressively sought to demonstrate

how close the government was to the Progressives by stressing the severity of the 1924 tariff reductions and announcing the budget as "the death knell to protection." Neatby, *The Lonely Heights*, 19

48   Arthur Cardin, a Quebec M.P., was appointed Minister of Finance and Fisheries in January 1924 to increase Quebec's representation in Cabinet. Neatby, *The Lonely Heights*, 16, 67.

49   Forsey to his mother, September 11, 1924, EFP.

50   Ibid.

51   Ibid., Forsey to his mother, September 4, 1924.

52   Ibid., September 11, 1924.

53   Ibid., September 4, 1924.

54   Ibid.

55   Ibid., September 11, 1924.

56   Ibid., September 14, 1924.

57   Paul Smith, *Disraelian Conservatism and Social Reform* (Toronto, 1967), 4.

58   Ibid., 4.

59   Geoffrey G. Butler, *The Tory Tradition: Bolingbroke–Burke–Disraeli–Salisbury* (London, 1914), 90–91.

60   See Stephen Graubard, *Burke, Disraeli and Churchill: The Politics of Perseverance* (Cambridge, Mass., 1961), 125–36 and Chapter 2, passim; Butler, *The Tory Tradition*, 80–85; Norman Gash, Donald Southgate, David Dilks and John Ramsden, *The Conservatives: A History from Their Origins to 1865* (London, 1977), Chapter 3, passim.

61   See Smith, *Disraelian Conservatism*, 17, 161.

62   For a more detailed discussion of Disraeli's political platform, see Robert Scheuttinger, ed., *The Conservative Tradition in European Thought* (New York, 1970), 225–45.

63   Philip W. Buck, ed., *How Conservatives Think* (Baltimore, 1975), 17.

64   Ibid., 18.

65   See William J. Wilkinson, *Tory Democracy* (New York, 1925), Chapter 4; Robert Blake, *The Conservative Party From Peel to Churchill* (London, 1970), 148–53.

66   Wilkinson, *Tory Democracy*, 227–29.

67   Gash, Southgate, Dilks and Ramsden, *The Conservatives*, 199–208.

68   See Wilkinson, *Tory Democracy*, 14. See also Blake, *The Conservative Party*, 154; and Smith, *Disraelian Conservatism*, 323.

69   Smith, *Disraelian Conservatism*, 325.

70   Peter Viereck, *Conservatism: From John Adams to Churchill* (New York, 1956), 40–42.

71   Ibid., 45–46.

72   Lord Hugh Cecil, *Conservatism* (London, 1912), 195–96.

73   Forsey to his mother, September 4, 9, 11, 1924, EFP.

74   Ibid., September 9, 1924.

75   Ibid., September 11, 1924. No record of this article appears in the Forsey Papers.

76   Ibid., September 4, 1924.

77   Ibid.

78   Ibid., September 11, 1924.

79   Neatby, *The Lonely Heights*, 18.

80   Ibid.

81   Forsey to his mother, September 11, 1924, EFP.

82   Ibid.

83   Ibid.
84   See Wilkinson, *Tory Democracy*, 213.
85   Forsey to his mother, September 11, 1924, EFP.
86   Ibid., October 21, 1924.
87   Ibid., November 23, 1924.
88   Ibid., November 28 and November 30, 1924.
89   Eugene Forsey, "My Discovery of Montreal," *McGill Daily Literary Supplement*, December 3, 1924, vol. 1, no. 9, 1–2, 4.
90   Ibid., Part II, December 10, 1924, vol. 1, no. 10, 1.
91   Ibid. Part III, December 19, 1924, vol. 1, no. 3, 1.
92   Ibid., 4.
93   Ibid., 4.
94   See David Dilks, *Neville Chamberlain, vol. 1* (Cambridge, 1984), 397.
95   Ibid.
96   Ibid.
97   Ibid.
98   Forsey to his mother, November 30, 1924, EFP.
99   For a description of Meighen and this Imperialist issue, see Graham, *The Door of Opporunity*, 335–55.
100 Forsey Interview, November 13, 1984.
101 Ibid.
102 Forsey Interview, Ottawa, June 1985.

CHAPTER *3*

THE ROOTS OF CHRISTIAN ACTIVISM

1   Viereck, *Conservatism*, 13–14.
2   Russell Kirk, *The Conservative Mind: From Burke to Santayana* (Chicago, 1953), 7.
3   Ibid., 26.
4   For further discussions of the centrality of religion in Burke's conservative thought, see Kirk, *The Conservative Mind*, 27–33; Michael Freeman, *Edmund Burke and the Critique of Political Radicalism* (Oxford, 1980), Chapter 3, passim; Frederick A. Dreyer, *Burke's Politics: A Study in Whig Orthodoxy* (Waterloo, 1979), 45–53; R.J. White, ed., *The Conservative Tradition*, 2nd ed. (London, 1964), Chapter 1, passim; Scheuttinger, *The Conservative Tradition in European Thought*, 55–58; Russell Kirk, ed., *The Portable Conservative Reader* (New York, 1982), 25–35; James McGoldrick, "Edmund Burke as a Christian Activist," *Modern Age* 17 (1973): 275–86.
5   Cecil, *Conservatism*, 86.
6   Ibid., 115–16.
7   Ibid., 115–16.
8   Richard Allen, *The Social Passion: Religion and Social Reform in Canada, 1914–1928* (Toronto, 1971), 3.
9   Richard Allen, "The Social Gospel in Canada," *Canadian Historical Review* 49 (1968): 382.
10 Ibid., 382–93; Allen, *The Social Passion*, Chapter 5, passim.
11 See Owram, *The Government Generation*, 112–14; Allen, *The Social Passion*, Chapters 13, 16, and 17.
12 Allen, *The Social Passion*, 261.

13 Ibid., 261; Roger Hutchinson, "The Fellowship for a Christian Social Order: A Social Ethical Analysis of a Christian Socialist Movement," Ph.D. dissertation, University of Toronto, 1970, 23.

14 Forsey to his mother, October 1, 1924, EFP.

15 Biographical File, "Reverend Allsworth Eardley," United Church Archives; see also *The New Outlook*, November 17, 1926, 26, and July 11, 1928, 17.

16 Benjamin G. Smillie, "The Social Gospel in Canada: A Theological Critique," in *Papers of the Inter-Disciplinary Conference on the Social Gospel*, National Museum of Man Mercury Series (Ottawa, 1975), 229–30.

17 Forsey to his mother, October 16, 1922, EFP.

18 Ibid.

19 Ibid.

20 Ibid., October 20, 1922.

21 Ibid., October 16, 1922.

22 Ibid., October 20, 1922.

23 Ibid., October 26, 1926.

24 A.M.S. Hutchinson, *This Freedom* (Toronto, 1922), 1–29.

25 Ibid., 256.

26 Ibid., 369.

27 See Veronica Strong-Boag, "Intruders in the Nursery: Childcare Professionals Reshape the Years One To Five, 1920–1940," in Joy Parr, ed., *Childhood and Family in Canadian History* (Toronto, 1982), passim.

28 Forsey to Mrs. Forsey, October 16, 1922, EFP.

29 Ibid., October 29, 1922.

30 Ibid.

31 Quoted in McKillop, *A Disciplined Intelligence*, 198–99.

32 Ibid., 198–202; see also 269 n. 89.

33 Leslie Armour and Elizabeth Trott, *The Faces of Reason: An Essay on Philosophy and Culture in English Canada ,1850–1950* (Waterloo, 1981), 234–35 and 308–10.

34 McKillop, *A Disciplined Intelligence*, 198; Armour and Trott, *Faces of Reason*, 103.

35 Thompson, *Decades of Discord*, 58.

36 S.E.D. Shortt, *The Search for an Ideal: Six Canadian Intellectuals and Their Convictions in an Age of Transition, 1890–1930* (Toronto, 1976), 147.

37 Ibid., 145–46.

38 Eugene Forsey, 1925 McGill Arts Valedictory Address, 2, EFP.

39 Ibid., 4.

40 Ibid., 5.

41 Ibid., 5.

42 Ibid., 5–6.

43 The literature concerning conservatives' view of the nature of man is extensive. See, for example, W.L. Morton, "Canadian Conservatism Now," in H.D. Forbes, ed., *Canadian Political Thought* (Toronto, 1985), 302–9; Schuettinger, *The Conservative Tradition in European Thought*, 10–14; Cecil, *Conservatism*, 86–91; Kirk, *The Conservative Mind*, 29–32; Russell Kirk, "Edmund Burke: The Tension of Order and Freedom," in Kirk, ed., *The Portable Conservative Reader*, 44–45; Dreyer, *Burke's Politics*, 26–27; Freeman, *Edmund Burke and the Critique of Political Radicalism*, 37–53; Smith, *Disraelian Conservatism*, 32–33.

44 Forsey, Valedictory Address, 6.
45 For more on this secularism see Owram, *The Government Generation*, 120.
46 Forsey Interview, Ottawa, May 28, 1987.
47 Eugene Forsey, "The Economic and Social Aspects of the Nova Scotia Coal Industry," M.A. thesis, McGill University, 1926, 229–30, copy in EFP. This thesis was published by Macmillan as a book with the same title in 1926.
48 Ibid.
49 See Forsey, "Economic and Social Aspects," Chapter 7, "Finance, Management and Markets (1914–1926)," 112–48.
50 Ibid., Chapter 8, "Industrial Relations and Social Conditions," 155–229; Thompson, *Decades of Discord*, 142–44.
51 Thompson, *Decades of Discord*, 144.
52 Forsey Interview, Ottawa, May 28, 1987.
53 Ernest Forbes, *Aspects of Maritime Regionalism, 1867–1927*, C.H.A. Booklet no. 36 (Ottawa, 1983), 19–20.
54 Forsey Interview, Ottawa, May 28, 1987.
55 Ibid.
56 See Research Committee for the League for Social Reconstruction, *Social Planning For Canada* (Toronto, 1935), 446.
57 Herbert A. Deane, *The Political Ideas of Harold J. Laski* (New York, 1955), 33.
58 Forsey Interview, Ottawa, May 28, 1987.
59 Forsey, "The Economic and Social Aspects," 70–76 and 247–55. In fact Forsey concluded that the central question in the labour issue in the coal industry was the poor living conditions, especially poor housing conditions and high rents.
60 Ibid., 75–189; Eugene Forsey, *Trade Unions in Canada, 1812–1902* (Toronto, 1982), 65–67.
61 Ibid., 192–96.
62 Forsey Interview, Ottawa, May 28, 1987.
63 Ibid.
64 Ibid.
65 Ibid.
66 Ibid. Forsey recalled, for example, that Hemmeon urged him to read works by the American "muckraker" Upton Sinclair, whose book *The Jungle* was a lurid exposé of the disgusting practices in the meat-packing industry of the age. (See also Arthur M. Schlesinger Jr., ed., *The Almanac of American History* (New York, 1983), 413.) Hemmeon also encouraged Forsey to read Gustavus Myer's slashing attack on Canadian wealth in his *History of Canadian Wealth* (Chicago, 1914).
67 Hubert Kemp to Forsey, May 10, 1926, EFP. Kemp, a University of Toronto economist, was Forsey's outside examiner for his Masters' thesis. Kemp later wrote to Forsey's supervisor, J.C. Hemmeon, that Forsey's thesis was the most careful and thorough piece of writing that he had seen "for a considerable time." Kemp also encouraged Forsey to go further if his inclinations lay in that direction.
68 Ibid., Leacock to Forsey, n.d., 1925.
69 C. Bailey, Tutor for Admissions, Balliol College, Oxford to Forsey, February 6, 1926, EFP.

CHAPTER 4

THE OXFORD TRADITION

1   See Kenneth McNaught, *A Prophet in Politics: A Biography of J.S. Woodsworth* (Toronto, 1959), 10; and David Lewis, *The Good Fight: Political Memoirs, 1909–1958* (Toronto, 1981), 50.

2   See Christopher Hobhouse, *Oxford As It Was and It Is Today* (London, 1939), 292–93; Ann Thwaite, ed., *My Oxford* (London, 1977). See recollections in that book by Raymond Massey, 37–58, and John Betjeman, 69.

3   Hugh Gaitskell, "Oxford In The Twenties," in Asa Briggs and John Saville, eds., *Essays in Labour History: In Memory of G.D.H. Cole, 1889–1959*, revised ed. (London, 1967).

4   H.W.C. Davis, *A History of Balliol College* (Oxford, 1963), 256.

5   Ibid., 250–53.

6   I.M. Greengarten, *Thomas Hill Green and the Development of Liberal-Democratic Thought* (Toronto, 1981), 128. Greengarten also places Edward Caird in this same intellectual stream, as do Armour and Trott, *The Faces of Reason*, 222.

7   Greengarten, *Thomas Hill Green*, 1–11; John Passmore, *A Hundred Years of Philosophy* (London, 1957), 56–58; and C.B. Macpherson, *The Political Theory of Possessive Individualism: Hobbes to Locke* (Oxford, 1962), 2–3.

8   Davis, *A History of Balliol College*, 257.

9   See David Sidorsky, ed., *The Liberal Tradition in European Thought* (New York, 1970), 347; Greengarten, *Thomas Hill Green*, 90.

10 Forsey to his mother, October 25, 1926, EFP.

11 Forsey Interview, May 29, 1987.

12 Ibid.

13 Davis, *A History of Balliol College*, 251–53.

14 Ibid., 221–24.

15 Armour and Trott, *The Faces of Reason*, 217–22.

16 See Passmore, *A Hundred Years of Philosophy*, 53–54; McKillop, *A Disciplined Intelligence*, 183–86.

17 Davis, *A History of Balliol College*, 249.

18 EFP, Forsey to his mother, October 17, 1926.

19 Ibid.

20 The concept of pluralism is important in understanding both the roots of Forsey's intellectual development and his subsequent thought and activities after returning to Canada. Pluralism is frequently used to denote any situation in which no particular ideological, cultural, or ethnic group is dominant in society. See A. Bullock, ed., *The Fontana Dictionary of Modern Thought*, 478. Pluralism can also be defined "as a line of thought that dissolves and divides the sovereignty of the state among a number, or plurality, of different groups or communities." Ernest Barker, *Age and Youth* (London, 1953), 76.

This devotion to diversity has been cited as a conservative principle though it has remained rather inconspicuous. Edmund Burke, who has been called a pluralist, argued that tyranny could be prevented in society if its people could remain "attached to the subdivision, to love the little platoon we belong to in society" as the people's first principle of attention. Burke's pluralism provided the philosophical basis for many a conservative's defence of local autonomy and support of natural institutions in an organic society, such as churches, trade unions, universities, newspapers, farmers' unions, and businessmen's clubs. All have a special role in standing between the citizen and his government. By strengthening the power of one the stability of the other is ensured.

The conservatives' attachment to pluralism, or social diversity, is rooted in their love of diversity of groups in society which nurture individuality and individual freedom, while providing barriers against the pressures for uniformity emanating from the central authority. Conservative ideologists, therefore, have seen this individual freedom as an inextricable aspect of a kind of social pluralism, one rich in autonomous, or semi-autonomous, communities and institutions.

It should also be noted that the benefits of pluralism to the modern state have been championed by non-conservatives as well. Harold Laski, for example, whom Forsey once referred to as the greatest living political thinker of the twentieth century, was a leading pluralist during the early part of his academic career.

See Quinton Hogg, *The Case for Conservatism* (London, 1974), 90–93; Russell Kirk, *The Portable Conservative Reader,* 15–19; Michael Clark, *Coherent Variety: The Idea of Diversity in British and American Thought* (Westport, Conn., 1983), passim; Robert Nisbet, *The Twilight of Authority* (New York, 1975), 48; R.J. White, *The Conservative Tradition,* 86–88; Herbert A. Deane, *The Political Ideas of Harold Laski* (New York, 1955), 22–23.

21 See W.D. Ross, *Aristotle* (New York, 1924), Chapter 7.
22 Ibid., 188–95.
23 Davis, *A History of Balliol College,* 252.
24 Ibid., 252, and Appendix IV, 314.
25 See Hobhouse, *Oxford,* 93; Davis, *A History of Balliol College,* 140–42.
26 Forsey to his mother, October 26, 1926, EFP.
27 Passmore, *A Hundred Years of Philosophy,* 322.
28 See ibid., Chapter 11, "The New Realists," and Chapter 12, "Critical Realism and American Naturalism."
29 M.M. Waddington, *The Development of British Thought From 1820–1890* (Toronto, 1919), 12–19.
30 Passmore, *A Hundred Years of Philosophy,* 280–83.
31 John Macmurray, *Search for Reality in Religion* (London, 1965), 10–11.
32 Ibid., "Biographical Note," 10–14.
33 Ibid., 11.
34 See Passmore, *A Hundred Years of Philosophy,* 322–44.
35 See Armour and Trott, *The Faces of Reason,* 13.
36 Forsey to his mother, October 25, 1926, EFP.
37 Forsey Interview, November 16, 1984.
38 University *News* Modern Greats Class List For Oxford, July 19, 1928, EFP.
39 Master A.D. Lindsay to Forsey, July 22, 1928, EFP.
40 Thwaite, *My Oxford,* 42–43.
41 Macmurray, *Search for Reality in Religion,* 13.
42 Forsey to his mother, March 9, 1927, EFP. Forsey's involvement in the Student Christian Movement will be discussed in detail in Chapter 5.
43 Macmurray, *Search for Reality in Religion,* 1.
44 Forsey to his wife, Harriet Forsey, n.d., 1962, EFP.

45 Eugene Forsey, "Christianity and Communism," Unpublished manuscript, n.d., EFP.
46 John Macmurray, "Religion in the Modern World," Lectures transcribed by Harriet and Eugene Forsey (Montreal, 1936), 25 pages, EFP and SCM Papers, UCA.
47 Eugene Forsey, "Bedtime Stories For Workingmen," *Canadian Forum* 16 (December 1936): 24–26.
48 See R.B.Y. Scott and Gregory Vlastos, eds., *Towards the Christian Revolution* (Chicago, 1936).
49 Forsey to his mother, February 20, 1940, EFP.
50 See, for example, Eugene Forsey, "The Church and Labour," *Presbyterian Record* (September 1958), 6–9.
51 See Rev. Leland J. White, "John Macmurray's Theology as Philosophy," *Scottish Journal of Theology* 26 (November 1973): 449–65, for a general overview of Macmurray's theory of theological philosophy.
52 Macmurray, *Search for Reality in Religion*, 22–23.
53 See Thomas A. Langford, "The Natural Theology of John Macmurray," *Canadian Journal of Theology* 12 (1966): 10–12.
    Langford concludes that although Macmurray differed from Kant on some aspects of critical philosophical study, the two shared a central interest in discovering knowledge through faith. Macmurray's acceptance of the primary practical reason, Langford argues, also places him very close to the philosophy of Richard Niebuhr. See also J. Blaikie, "Being, Process and Action in Modern Philosophy and Theology," *Scottish Journal of Theology* 25 (1972): 146–50, for a more critical view of Macmurray and Kant's similarities.
54 Macmurray, *Search for Reality in Religion*, 16.
55 Ibid., 16
56 Ibid., 19.
57 John Macmurray, *The Philosophy of Communism* (London, 1933), 22–26.
58 Ibid., 25.
59 John Macmurray, "The New Materialism," in J. Middleton Murry, J. Macmurray, N.A. Holdaway and G.D.H. Cole, *Marxism* (London, 1935), 51.
60 Ibid., 43.
61 Ibid., 44.
62 B.H. Streeter, *Reality; A New Correlation of Science and Religion* (London, 1926), 292–93. In this book Streeter acknowledged that he had rediscovered religion "through the gateway of T.H. Green's philosophy" (p. vii). Like Macmurray, Green had discovered a religion that correlated the reality of scientific knowledge with the concept of a living Christ.
63 John Macmurray, "Beyond Knowledge," in B.H. Streeter, ed., *Adventure: The Faith of Science and the Science of Faith* (London, 1926), 41.
64 See, for example, Arthur O. Lovejoy, *The Revolt Against Dualism* (New York, 1930), passim.
65 Forsey Interview, Ottawa, May 29, 1987.
66 Macmurray, "Religion in the Modern World," 23.
67 Ibid., 14.
68 John Macmurray, *The Clue to History* (London, 1938), 6–9.
69 Ibid., 113–14.
70 Macmurray, "The New Materialism," 47.

71 John Macmurray, "The Nature and Functions of Ideologies," in Murry et al., *Marxism*, 73.

72 Ibid., 70–71.

73 Ibid., 70–71.

74 Forsey, "The Economic Problem," in Scott and Vlastos, eds., *Towards the Christian Revolution*, 118. The purpose here is merely to establish Forsey's acceptance of Macmurray's philosophy of activism and his rejection of dualism. The specific reformist means advocated by Forsey during the 1930s will be addressed in Chapters 5 and 6.

75 Macmurray, *The Clue to History*, 21–28.

76 Forsey, "The Economic Problem," 117.

77 Macmurray, *Search for Reality in Religion*, 221–23.

78 Macmurray, *The Clue to History*, 21–28.

79 Forsey, "Church and Labour," 6. It was this separation between ideas and action that Forsey condemned in the Canadian Social Gospel movement of the early twentieth century. Forsey was never much attracted to the writings of Salem Bland or other Social Gospel writers. The Social Gospel, he believed, had a destructive influence on people's faith through its emphasis on the need for "works" at the expense of an "individual, personal faith relationship with God." Christianity, Forsey later said, should not advocate the "choosing of one or the other"; the two have to be held in balance. This balanced approach has been the approach taken by the "orthodox churches" such as the Roman Catholic, Anglican, and Greek Orthodox. Forsey Interview, Ottawa, May 29, 1987.

80 Eugene Forsey, "Postwar Problems of Canadian Labour, With Specific Reference to the Responsibility of the Church," Unpublished article, EFP.

81 Eugene Forsey, "The Canadian Trade Union Movement," Unpublished article (1949), EFP.

82 Eugene Forsey, "The Marxist Challenge," in Scott and Vlastos, eds., *Towards the Christian Revolution*, 256.

83 Macmurray "Religion in the Modern World," 17.

84 Ibid., 4.

85 Forsey, "Church and Labour," 3.

86 Forsey, "Postwar Problems," 4.

87 John Macmurray, ed., *Some Makers of the Modern Spirit* (London, 1933), 17.

88 Macmurray, ed., *Some Makers of the Modern Spirit*, 17.

89 Ibid., 20–23.

90 See, for example, Eugene Forsey, "Christianity and Communism."

91 See Frank H. Underhill, "Bentham and Benthamism," *Queen's Quarterly* 39 (1932): 658–68 for an overview of Benthamism; and Macmurray, *Some Makers of the Modern Spirit*, 34.

92 Macmurray, *The Philosophy of Communism*, 96.

93 See Macmurray, *Search for Reality in Religion*, 79.

94 Eugene Forsey, "The Preservation of Democracy," Radio Address, EFP. Though there is no date given on this transcript, the contents suggest that it was delivered in either 1935 or 1936.

95 Forsey, "The Canadian Trade Union Movement," 6.

96 Forsey, "Postwar Problems of Canadian Labour," passim.

97 Macmurray, "Religion in The Modern World," 14–19.

98 Forsey, "Christianity and Communism," 8–9.

99 Gaitskell, "Oxford in the Twenties," 7.

100　See ibid., 8-9; ibid., Stephen Bailey, "What Cole Really Meant," 20-24; and G.D.H. Cole, *Guild Socialism,* Fabian Tract no. 192 (1915).

101　Forsey to his mother, October 25, 1926, EFP.

102　Forsey Interview, March 24, 1986.

103　Forsey Interview, June 9, 1984.

104　Forsey to his mother, March 9, 1927, EFP; Forsey Interview, November 1984.

105　G.D.H. Cole, *The Simple Case For Socialism* (London, 1935), 161–68.

106　Ibid., 174; Cole, *Guild Socialism,* passim.

107　G.D.H. Cole, *Capitalism in the Modern World,* Fabian Tract no. 315, n.d., 32.

108　Anne Fremantle, *This Little Band of Prophets: The Story of the Gentle Fabians* (London, 1959), 71.

109　Forsey to his mother, April 12 and November 22, 1927, EFP.

110　Ibid., September 6, 1928.

111　Ibid.

112　Ibid.

113　Ibid., July 31, August 6, August 29, and September 6, 1928.

114　Ibid., September 6, 1928.

115　C.P. Stacey, *Canada and the Age of Conflict, vol. 2: 1921–1928* (Toronto, 1981), 100–103. The Kellogg Pact was an American-sponsored document that called for a renunciation of war as an instrument of policy to be subscribed to by all the nations of the world. See p. 96.

116　Forsey to his mother, September 6, 1928, EFP. The quote is Forsey's.

117　J.C. Hemmeon to Forsey, January 29, 1929, EFP.

118　Forsey to his mother, May 9, 1929, EFP.

CHAPTER 5

DEPRESSION-ERA CHRISTIANITY

1　Forsey Interview, March 24, 1986, Ottawa.

2　Forsey to his mother, April 12, 1927, EFP.

3　J.M. Winter, ed., *History and Society: Essays by R.H. Tawney* (London, 1978), 2–14.

4　See ibid., 1–40; R.H. Tawney, *Religion and the Rise of Capitalism: A Historical Study* (London, 1926), Chapter 3.

5　Forsey Interview, March 24, 1986.

6　Ibid.; Forsey to his mother, March 23, 1934, EFP.

7　Forsey Interview, March 24, 1986. For a short overview of the Friends' position on pacifism, see Balwant Nevaskar, *Capitalists Without Capitalism: The Jains of India and the Quakers of the West* (Westport, Conn., 1971), 77–80.

8　Nevaskar, *Capitalists Without Capitalism,* 79–98.

9　Ibid., 98.

10　See ibid., 96–99; and John Greenwood, *Quaker Encounters, vol. 1: Friends and Relief* (York, 1978). This latter book lists and describes the many relief projects that the Quakers were sponsoring during the period that Forsey was at Oxford.

11　Biographical Note, Eugene Alfred Forsey, n.d., EFP.

12　"Graduates and the SCM," SCM Pamphlet, SCM Papers, UCA, Toronto; Margaret Beattie, "Pressure Group Politics: The Case of the Student Christian Movement in Canada, 1920–1941," Ph.D. dissertation, University of Alberta, 1972, 1–16.

13 Ernest A. Dales, *Twenty-One Years A-Building: A Short Account of the Student Christian Movement in Canada, 1920–1941* (SCM, n.d.), 9–12.

14 Ibid., 8.

15 Ramsay Cook, *The Regenerators: Social Criticism in Late Victorian English Canada* (Toronto, 1985), 9–12.

16 "History of the Student Christian Movement," n.d., SCM Papers, UCA.

17 Ibid.

18 Ibid.

19 Forsey to his mother, October 21, 1924, EFP.

20 Ibid., March 9, 1927.

21 Macmurray, *Search for Reality in Religion*, 1.

22 Beattie, " Pressure Group Politics," 42.

23 Dales, *Twenty-One Years A-Building*, 36.

24 Forsey to his mother, February 20, 1940, EFP.

25 Dales, *Twenty-One Years A-Building*, 15.

26 "The SCM At McGill: Graduates and The SCM,"n.d., SCM Pamphlet, SCM Papers, UCA.

27 Ibid., "Draft Constitution As Amended by the Provisional Organizational Meeting," September 28, 1937.

28 Ibid., "SCM in McGill University," Brochures, June 1934 and Autumn 1935; McGill University Students Conference Brochure, 1937.

29 Interview with J. King Gordon, Ottawa, March 1986.

30 Ibid.

31 Ibid. Various SCM brochures during the 1930s contain references to Forsey's involvement in study groups, lectures, and the summer conferences.

32 J. King Gordon Interview, Ottawa, March 1986.

33 Forsey was also an avid reader of Shaw's work.

34 J. King Gordon, "The Politics of Poetry," in Sandra Djwa and R. St. J. Macdonald, eds., *On F.R.Scott: Essays on His Contributions to Law, Literature and Politics* (Montreal and Kingston, 1983), 17–18; J. King Gordon Interview, Ottawa, March 1986.

35 Ibid., 18–19.

36 Ibid., 19.

37 Ibid., 19; Michiel Horn, *The League For Social Reconstruction: Intellectual Origins of the Democratic Left in Canada* (Toronto, 1980), 4, 23.

38 See, for example, the 1936–37 SCM Brochure list of Study Group Topics, SCM Papers, UCA. The SCM Papers also contain a number of published and unpublished speeches and papers by Macmurray.

39 "The Monitor," December 14, 1933, J. King Gordon Papers (hereafter cited as KGP), Private Collection, Ottawa. Gordon arranged for Niebuhr to give two lectures in Montreal in 1933. They were entitled "The Urgency of the Present Situation," and "The World Outlook: Reconstruction or Reaction." *McGill Daily News*, December 14, 1933.

40 Beattie, "Pressure Group Politics," 52.

41 Ibid., 53.

42 Ibid.

43 H. Blair Neatby, *The Politics of Chaos: Canada in the Thirties* (Toronto, 1972), 21.

44 Ibid., 22 and Chapter 2, "The Personal Impact of the Depression," 20–49; Bothwell, Drummond, and English, *Canada, 1900–1945*, Chapter 15, "The Social and Economic Impact of the Depression,"

244–58; Thompson, *Decades of Discord*, Chapter 9, "The Crisis of Capitalism," 193–221.

45 *Information Bulletin* , vol. 1, no. 1, November 1932, KGP.
46 Ibid., vol. 1, no. 2, December 1932.
47 Ibid.
48 Ibid.
49 Gordon to Gerard Tremblay, Deputy Minister of Labour, January 19, 1933, KGP.
50 Gordon to Gustav Franz, December 21, 1932, KGP.
51 "Report of the Presbytery's Committee on Economic and Social Research," December 6, 1932, KGP.
52 Leonard Marsh to Harry Cassidy, December 11, 1931, Harry Cassidy Papers, University of Toronto Archives; Allan Irving, "Leonard Marsh and the McGill Social Science Research Project," *Journal of Canadian Studies* 21 (September 1986): 6–25; Gordon, "The Politics of Poetry," 23.
53 "Report of the Presbytery's Committee," KGP.
54 *Information Bulletin*, vol. 1, no. 5, June 1933, KGP.
55 Ibid., vol. 1, no. 2, December 1932.
56 Ibid., Forsey Research Notes.
57 Ibid.
58 See Thompson, *Decades of Discord*, Table Xa, 347.
59 Ibid., Table XIV, 351.
60 Neatby, *Politics of Chaos*, 46.
61 *Information Bulletin*, vol. 2, no. 4, November 1933, KGP.
62 Ibid.
63 Ibid.
64 Ibid., vol. 1 (no month), 1932.
65 Thompson, *Decades of Discord*, 222–26.
66 Ibid., 227.
67 Section 98 made it illegal for any individual or association to advocate "governmental, industrial or economic change within Canada by the use of force, violence or physical injury to person or property, or by threats of such injury." Membership in, or financial contributions to, such an association was also made unlawful. The maximum penalty under Section 98 was twenty years in prison. See ibid., 227; and Walter Tarnopolsky, "Frank R. Scott: Civil Libertarian," in Djwa and Macdonald, eds., *On F.R. Scott*, 134–35.
68 Tarnopolsky, "Frank R. Scott: Civil Libertarian," passim.
69 *Information Bulletin*, vol. 1, no. 4, February 1933, KGP.
70 *Montreal Gazette*, March 9, 22, 23, 24, 1933.
71 *Information Bulletin*, vol. 2, no. 4, February 1933, KGP.
72 Ibid.
73 Ibid.
74 Ibid.
75 Ibid.
76 Ibid., vol. 1, no. 2, December 1932.
77 Ibid., vol. 1, no. 5, June 1933.
78 Hutchinson, "The Fellowship For a Christian Social Order," 74–75.
79 J.S. Woodsworth to King Gordon, February 12, 1932, KGP.
80 J.A. Ewing to King Gordon, June 29, 1933, KGP.
81 Gordon, "The Politics of Poetry," 23–24.
82 Anonymous to Eugene Forsey, June 29, 1933, KGP.
83 Ernest Thomas to King Gordon, January 18, 1933, KGP.

84 "Report of the Presbytery's Committee," KGP.
85 Gordon Interview, October 3, 1986; *Information Bulletin*, vol. 1, no. 5, June 1933, KGP.
86 *Record of the Proceedings of the Montreal Presbytery of the United Church of Canada, vol. 2*, February 28, 1933, KGP.
87 Ibid.; Hutchinson, "The Fellowship for a Christian Social Order," 33.
88 Gordon, "Politics of Poetry," 23; Gordon Interview, March 1986; Hutchinson, "The Fellowship for a Christian Social Order," 33.
89 Gordon, "Politics of Poetry," 23.
90 Beattie, "Pressure Group Politics," 19.
91 Ibid., 91.
92 Ibid., quoted from an SCM document entitled "Some Canadian Questions: Society and Industrial Discord," 61.
93 James Struthers, *No Fault of Their Own: Unemployment and the Canadian Welfare State, 1914–1941* (Toronto, 1983), 22, 29, 234 n. 58.
94 Eugene Forsey, *Unemployment in the Machine Age: Its Causes* (Ottawa, 1935), 1.
95 Ibid., 2–58.
96 Ibid., 12.
97 Ibid., 16.
98 See Beattie, "Pressure Group Politics," 246.
99 Gordon Interview, October 1986.
100 Ibid.
101 John Macmurray, "The Philosophy of Jesus," n.d., 9, SCM Papers, UCA.
102 Eugene Forsey, "The Role of the Christian in Today's World (Especially Canada)," Unpublished article, n.d., EFP.
103 Ibid.
104 Ibid.
105 See ibid., n. 74.
106 Hutchinson, "The Fellowship for a Christian Social Order," 75–79.
107 Laurel Sefton MacDowell, "The Impact of the Great Depression and the Second World War on the Social Policy of the United Church of Canada," Unpublished paper, Erindale College, University of Toronto, July 1986, 4–5.
108 See "The Board of Evangelism and Social Service," Unpublished church document, United Church Council Papers File, UCA; see also the "Constitution of the Board of Evangelism and Social Service," in the Minutes of the Eighth Meeting of the Board, March 29 and 30, 1933, BESS Annual Reports File, 1933, United Church Council Papers, UCA.
109 D.N. McLachlin to the Ministers of the United Church Council, August 23, 1933, BESS Annual Reports File 1933, United Church Council Papers, UCA.
110 Minutes of the Executive Committee of the Christian Social Order Commission (Falconer Commission), United Church Council Papers, UCA.
111 Ibid., 2–3.
112 Ibid.
113 MacDowell, "The Impact of the Great Depression," 55.
114 Irene Biss, "The Essential Conditions for Good Society," Submission to the Commission on Christianizing the Social Order, United Church Council Papers, UCA.
115 MacDowell, "The Impact of the Great Depression," 10–11.

116 John Line, "Introduction," to Scott and Vlastos, eds., *Towards the Christian Revolution* (Toronto, 1935), passim. This book will be referred to hereafter as *TCR*.

117 Ibid., 73.

118 Hutchinson,"The Fellowship for a Christian Social Order," 25 and Chapter 3, passim.

119 Ibid., Chapter 3, passim.

120 References to Macmurray's works occur regularly throughout the pages of *TCR*. See, for example, 54 n. 23, 59, 63, 91, 111, 115–17, 134–35, 237, 259.

121 See Thomas Langford, "The Natural Theology of John Macmurray," *Canadian Journal of Theology* 12 (1966): 14–15.

122 Harriet and Eugene Forsey, "Notes on John Macmurray's Religion in the Modern World" (Montreal, 1936), 25 pages. This publication can be found in the Forsey Papers and the SCM Papers.

123 King Gordon to Frank H. Underhill, August 30, 1935, Frank Underhill Papers, LSR Correspondence File, PAC.

124 Forsey Interview, Ottawa, May 29, 1987.

125 Eugene Forsey to G. D. Ferguson, November 17, 1954, EFP.

126 Forsey Interview, Ottawa, May 29, 1987.

127 See Paul F. Boiler Jr., *American Thought in Transition: The Impact of Evolutionary Naturalism, 1865–1900* (Chicago, 1969), Chapter 6, "William James and the Open Universe," 123–47.

128 Ibid.

129 Forsey Interview, Ottawa, May 29, 1987.

130 Harriet and Eugene Forsey, "Notes on John Macmurray."

131 Ibid., 2.

132 Eugene Forsey, "The Economic Problem," in *TCR*, 2.

133 Ibid., 118.

134 Forsey, "Notes on John Macmurray," 13.

135 Ibid., 14.

136 Ibid., 25.

137 Forsey, "The Economic Problem," 118–19.

138 Ibid., 119.

139 Ibid., 120.

140 Ibid., 120.

141 Ibid., 121.

142 Ibid., 121–22.

143 Ibid., 122.

144 See Thompson, *Decades of Discord*, 258–61, for a brief outline of the Price Spreads Commission and its mandate.

145 Forsey, "The Economic Problem," in *TCR*, 122–38.

146 Forsey drew this quote from Harold Laski, the British economist and political scientist whom Forsey would later refer to as "The greatest living political thinker in the English speaking world." (Eugene Forsey, "Democracy," Radio Broadcast (1939), EFP.) In 1939 Forsey listened to Laski speak in New York and found it personally "refreshing to hear good orthodox socialist analysis again." Forsey was familiar with Laski's writing during the successive stages of Laski's career, which took him from being a proponent of pluralism to Fabianism, and finally Marxist socialism. See Herbert A. Deane, *The Political Ideas of Harold Laski* (New York, 1955), 2–6.

147 Forsey, "The Economic Problem," in *TCR*, 130.

148 Ibid., 132–33.
149 Ibid., 135.
150 Ibid., 137–40.
151 Ibid., 140–41.
152 Ibid., 142. Beatty was also a Chancellor of McGill University and
     in 1935 had publicly attacked the socialist theorists involved in the
     League for Social Reconstruction and the CCF. See Albert and
     Theresa Moritz, *Leacock: a Biography* (Toronto, 1985), 244–46.
153 Ibid., 144–45.
154 J. King Gordon Interview, October 1985.
155 Forsey, "The Economic Problem," 153–54.
156 Ibid., 154.
157 Ibid., 157.
158 Ibid., 159.
159 Ibid., 159.

CHAPTER

"REAL DEMOCRACY": 1930–1935

1   See R.D. Francis and H. Ganzevoort, eds., *The Dirty Thirties in
    Prairie Canada* (Vancouver, 1980), 5; Gerald Friesen, *The Canadian
    Prairies: A History* (Toronto, 1984), 382.
2   John Kendle, *John Bracken: A Political Biography* (Toronto, 1979), 107.
3   Armstrong, *The Politics of Federalism*, 151.
4   Herbert F. Quinn, *The Union Nationale: A Study in Quebec Nationalism*
    (Toronto, 1963), 43.
5   J.R. Noel, *Politics in Newfoundland* (Toronto, 1971), 97.
6   Struthers. *No Fault of Their Own*, 42.
7   Brooke Claxton to Professor Burton Hurd, February 21 and August
    12, 1930; Claxton to Graham Spry, July 17, 1930, Brooke Claxton
    Papers, PAC, Ottawa.
8   Neatby, *The Politics of Chaos*, 48.
9   Ibid.
10 Beck, *Pendulum of Power*, 201.
11 Brooke Claxton to W.B. Hurd, February 21 and August 12, 1930,
    Brooke Claxton Papers.
12 Unpublished book manuscript, n.d., CCF Papers, LSR File, vol.
    16; Claxton to Professor C.R. June 21, 1930; Claxton to Percy E.
    Corbett, August 4, 1930, Brooke Claxton Papers.
13 Book manuscript, Introduction, CCF Papers.
14 Ibid., passim in chapter outlines.
15 Eugene Forsey, "The Function of the Economist," Radio Broadcast,
    January 19, 1934, 1, EFP.
16 Ibid., 2.
17 Ibid., 4.
18 Ibid., 5–6. The book Forsey referred to in this speech was *Social
    Planning for Canada*, which was sponsored by the LSR and published
    in September 1934.
19 Eugene Forsey, "Planned Economy," Proceedings of the Canadian
    Political Science Association, Fourth Annual Meeting, vol. 4 (May
    1932), 175–76.
20 Ibid., 176–77.

21 Ibid., 177.
22 Ibid.
23 Ibid.
24 Ibid., 178.
25 Ibid.
26 Ibid.
27 Ibid., 179.
28 Ibid., 178–79.
29 Ibid.
30 Ibid., 179.
31 A.D. Lindsay, *The Essentials of Democracy* (Philadelphia, 1929), 80–82.
32 Ibid., 81.
33 See Chapter 4.
34 J. King Gordon, "The Politics of Poetry," in Djwa and Macdonald, eds., *On F.R. Scott*, 18–19.
    The Fabian Society was founded in 1884 as an assorted group of middle class ethical and social reformers. It developed a distinctive non-Marxist doctrine of gradual collectivism during the late nineteenth century. The Society took as its leading principle the need for "the reconstruction of a Society in accordance with the highest moral possibilities." This principle was based on the Society's recognition that the competitive system was not working. The Fabians formed study groups and promoted the need for local society committees to educate and convert the middle classes to socialism. During the 1920s the Fabians were "in a fine frenzy of writing and publishing" led by Sidney and Beatrice Webb, R.H. Tawney, Harold Laski and, during the early part of the decade, G.D.H. Cole. See Patricia Pugh, *Educate, Agitate and Organize: One Hundred Years of Fabian Socialism* (London, 1984); Anne Fremantle, *This Little Band of Prophets: The Story of the Gentle Fabians* (London, 1960).
35 R. Douglas Francis, *Frank H. Underhill: Intellectual Provocateur* (Toronto, 1986), 84; Horn, *The League for Social Reconstruction*, 20–22.
36 Frank Scott to Frank Underhill, November 6, 1931, Frank Scott Papers.
37 Gordon, "Politics of Poetry," 19; Horn, *The League for Social Reconstruction*, 21–22.
38 Scott to Underhill, November 6, 1931, Frank Scott Papers.
39 Unpublished manuscript, "The League for Economic Democracy," as amended by Eugene Forsey, LSR File, vol. 17, n.d., Frank Scott Papers.
40 Ibid., Frank Scott to Underhill, January 18, 1932.
41 Michiel Horn, "Frank Scott, The Great Depression and the League for Social Reconstruction," in Djwa and Macdonald, eds., *On F.R. Scott*, 74.
42 Eugene Forsey, "Canada's Foreign Trade," Supplement to the *McGill News*, September 1930, 1–9, copy in AMP. In this article Forsey also condemned protectionism and the power of Canada's manufacturing interests. He called for investment controls and stronger trade unions and "a more sensitive professional conscience" by Canadian economists.
    See also the "Handbook of the League for Social Reconstruction," February 1933 (hereafter cited as LSR Handbook); Manifesto, 3–4, vol. 18, Frank Scott Papers.

43   Report of the Activities of the Montreal Branch of the League for
     Social Reconstruction, vol. 18, Frank Scott Papers.
44   Ibid., 2.
45   Ibid.
46   Ibid.
47   Minutes of April 23, 1932 Meeting of the Montreal Branch of the
     LSR, Frank Scott Papers.
48   League for Social Reconstruction Membership List, LSR Papers,
     University of Toronto Library, Toronto.
49   Minutes of April 23, 1932 Montreal Branch debate.
50   Eugene Forsey to C.H. Cahan, November 3, 1936, copy in AMP;
     J. King Gordon Interview, Ottawa, June 1984 and March 1986.
51   R.R. Palmer, *A History of the Modern World* (New York, 1951), 736–39.
52   Ibid., 738.
53   Eugene Forsey, Diary of Russian Trip (1932), 4, EFP.
54   See Chapters 5 and 7.
55   Forsey, Diary of Russian Trip, 5.
56   Ibid.
57   J. King Gordon Interview, Ottawa, October 1986.
58   Forsey, Diary of Russian Trip, 13.
59   Ibid., July 5, 6, 13.
60   Ibid., 15.
61   Ibid., 17.
62   Ibid., 18.
63   Ibid., July 28.
64   Ibid.
65   Gustav Cassel was an Economy Professor at the University of
     Stockholm. Cassel viewed his field of study as "economic science,
     whose ways and views are different from those of the business man
     and the politician." Cassel advocated the field of "social economy"
     because it allowed human will to determine the direction and the
     extent of economic activity in the state. In this way individual citizens
     could contribute to the whole economic process. This was a message
     that blended with Forsey's pluralism.
         Cassel's "exchange economy" stipulated only that it would allow
     for "the individual freedom to choose employment freedom of
     consumption within his means." He also favoured socialism because
     it permitted the community some control over production and
     reserved to itself the ownership of the material means of production.
     Technically this resulted in "a self-contained exchange economy in
     which the entire production is conducted by and for the community
     itself through officials appointed for the purpose and in which
     there is still freedom of work and consumption." Forsey was also
     undoubtedly impressed with Cassel's exacting methodology and with
     his condemnation of the vagueness of many early twentieth century
     economists, "who express themselves in vague phrases which commit
     them to nothing, but which also make nothing clear."
         See Gustav Cassel, *Fundamental Thoughts in Economics* (New York,
     1925), 18–19, 34–35; *The Theory of Social Economy* (New York, 1924),
     128–33; *Post War Monetary Stabilization* (New York, 1928); *Money and
     Foreign Exchange After 1919* (London, 1922).
66   Forsey, Diary of Russian Trip, July 29.
67   Ibid., July 28.

68 Ibid.
69 Minutes of the Second Annual Meeting of the Montreal Branch of the LSR, March 13, 1933, Frank Scott Papers.
70 See Michiel Horn " Frank Underhill's Early Draft of the Regina Manifesto, 1933," *Canadian Historical Review* 59 (December 1973): 394; Horn, *The League for Social Reconstruction*, 37.
71 Minutes of the September 23, 1932 Executive of the Montreal Branch of the LSR, Frank Scott Papers.
72 Horn, *The League for Social Reconstruction*, 37.
73 Minutes of September 26, 1932 Executive of the Montreal Branch of the LSR, Frank Scott Papers.
74 Annual Convention Summation, LSR Handbook, 6–7, Frank Scott Papers.
75 J. King Gordon Interview, Ottawa, October 1984.
76 Forsey Interview, June 1985.
77 Joseph Parkinson Interview, Ottawa, October 1, 1986.
78 Ibid.
79 See A.G. Mills, "The Canadian Forum, 1920–1934: A Study in the Development of English Canadian Socialist Thought," Ph.D. dissertation, University of Waterloo, 1976, Abstract and p. 23.
80 Eugene Forsey, "Concentration in Canadian Industry," *Canadian Forum* 14 (October 1939): 9.
81 Ibid., 9–13.
82 Eugene Forsey, "Equality of Sacrifice: Dividends, Salaries and Wages in Canada in the Great Depression," *Canadian Forum* 14 (November 1933): 47.
83 Ibid., 49.
84 Eugene Forsey, *Dividends in the Depression* (Toronto, 1934); Forsey, "Wages and Dividends in the Depression," Speech, n.d. EFP.
85 Forsey, "Equality of Sacrifice," 51.
86 Ibid., 51.
87 Forsey, "Wages and Dividends in the Depression," 4.
88 Harry Cassidy to Frank Pedley, February 29, 1933, Harry Cassidy Papers.
89 See Michael Bliss's Introduction to the reprint edition of *Social Planning for Canada* (Toronto, 1975 [1935]), xvi.
90 Stuart Legge to E.J. Cummings, February 1, 1934, LSR Papers, J.S. Woodsworth Collection, Fischer Rare Book Room, University of Toronto Archives, Toronto.
91 Horn, *The League for Social Reconstruction*, 67.
92 Forsey to Underhill, n.d., Frank Underhill Papers, University of Toronto Archives.
93 Forsey to his mother, March 4 and March 5, 1935, EFP.
94 Frank Scott to Harry Cassidy, February 22, 1935, Harry Cassidy Papers.
95 Anonymous to Frank Scott, June 28, 1935, Frank Scott Papers.
96 Forsey to Underhill, September 28, 1935, Frank Underhill Papers.
97 Transcript of a Paul Fox interview with Frank Underhill, LSR File, Frank Underhill Papers.
98 Research Committee of the League for Social Reconstruction, *Social Planning for Canada* (Toronto, 1975 [1935]), 218–19.
99 Ibid., 215, 220–21, 223 n. 9.
100 Ibid., 222.

101 Ibid.
102 Ibid., 225.
103 This constitutional theme is discussed in detail in Chapter 9.
104 Ibid., 225.
105 Ibid., 225.
106 Ibid., 225–26.
107 Ibid., 226.
108 Ibid., 228, 239–40.
109 Ibid., 235.
110 Ibid., 246.
111 Ibid., 247.
112 Ibid., 246–47.
113 Ibid., 285.
114 Research Committee of the League for Social Reconstruction, *Democracy Needs Socialism* (Toronto, 1938).

CHAPTER

CIVIL LIBERTARIAN AND THE FORCES OF REACTION

1   LSR Handbook, 14, LSR Papers, J.S. Woodsworth Collection, University of Toronto Archives. See also ibid., "LSR Reading List."
2   See, for example, Walter Tarnopolsky, "F.R.Scott: Civil Libertarian," in Djwa and Macdonald, eds., *On F.R. Scott*, 133–50.
3   Stiernotte to Frank Scott, October 25, 1932; February 10, 1933; Frank Underhill to A. Stiernotte, November 23, 1932 (copy), Frank Scott Papers.
4   Frank Scott to Harry F. Ward, April 10, 1934; Roger Baldur, Director, American Civil Liberties Union, to Frank Scott, April 18, 1934; Frank Scott to Ella Timbres, June 14, 1934, Frank Scott Papers.
5   Frank Scott to Graham Spry, April 13, 1935, Frank Scott Papers.
6   Ibid.
7   Ibid., "Report of the Activities at LSR Week-End Conference, June 15–16, 1935," 4–5.
8   Struthers, *No Fault of Their Own*, 168; Thompson, *Decades of Discord*, 285.
9   Eugene Forsey, "Recovery – For Whom?" *Canadian Forum* 17 (August 1937): 156.
10 Ibid., 158.
11 Irving M. Abella, *Nationalism, Communism and Canadian Labour: The CIO, the Communist Party and the Canadian Congress of Labour, 1935-1956* (Toronto, 1973), 22–23.
12 Ibid., 27.
13 Thompson, *Decades of Discord*, 285.
14 See Chapter 5.
15 Thompson, *Decades of Discord*, 285.
16 Forsey, "Recovery – For Whom?", 158.
17 Struthers, *No Fault of Their Own*, 155.
18 Forsey, "Recovery – For Whom?", 158.
19 Struthers, *No Fault of Their Own*, 168–69.
20 Eugene Forsey, "From the Seats of the Mighty, Part II: Dives and Lazarus," *Canadian Forum* 17 (April 1937): 10.

21 Eugene Forsey, "From the Seats of the Mighty, Part I: The Simple Faith of the Chamber of Commerce," *Canadian Forum* 16 (March 1937): 22.

22 Forsey, "From the Seats of the Mighty, Part I," 11; see also Eugene Forsey, "Facts, Figures and Finance," *Canadian Forum* 16 (March 1937): 17.

23 Struthers, *No Fault of Their Own*, 18.

24 Ibid., 197.

25 Eugene Forsey, "More Unemployment – Less Relief," *Canadian Forum* 18 (February 1939): 331; Eugene Forsey, "Unemployment and Relief," *Canadian Forum* 19 (May 1939): 42.

26 Ibid.

27 Forsey, "More Unemployment – Less Relief," 332.

28 See Struthers, *No Fault of Their Own*, 190–200. In July 1940, the British Parliament amended the BNA Act, giving the federal government control over unemployment insurance. The Unemployment Insurance Act was passed a month later. See Struthers, *No Fault of Their Own*, Chapters 5 and 6.

29 Eugene Forsey, " The Taxpayers' Money," *Canadian Forum* 19 (July 1939): 106.

30 Ibid., 106–7; "The Budget," *Canadian Forum* 19 (May 1939): 76–77; "The Budget," *Canadian Forum* 20 (August 1940): 136–37.

31 Eugene Forsey, "Immigration Ballyhoo," *Canadian Forum* 16 (February 1937): 8–10.

32 Eugene Forsey, "The Immigration Question," *Social Welfare* 17 (March 1937): 7–10, 17.

33 Ibid., 17; "Immigration Ballyhoo," 10.

34 M. Sedgewick to Eugene Forsey, September 17, 1937, LSR Papers; Eugene Forsey, *Does Canada Need Immigrants?* (Montreal, 1937), 1–8.

35 Forsey to Frank Underhill, December 5, 1935, Frank Underhill Papers.

36 See Donald MacGregar, Department of Political Science, University of Toronto, to Stuart Legge, March 19, 1934, LSR Papers; Forsey to Bea and Harry Cassidy, January 19, 1936, Harry Cassidy Papers.

37 Horn, *The League for Social Reconstruction*, 55.

38 Mark Farrell to Leonard Marsh, October 29, 1937, LSR Papers.

39 Proceedings of the LSR's Sixth Annual Convention, March 20–21, 1937; LSR's Seventh Convention Pamphlet, LSR Papers.

40 Helen Marsh, Secretary's Report of the Proceedings of the LSR's Sixth Annual Convention, LSR Papers.

41 Beck, *Pendulum of Power*, 220.

42 Forsey to Underhill, October 15, 1935, Frank Underhill Papers.

43 Forsey to Cassidy, January 19, 1936, Harry Cassidy Papers.

44 CCF Records, LSR File, vol. 168, PAC, Ottawa.

45 Quebec Council Notes, August 1, 1937, LSR Papers.

46 Lewis, *The Good Fight*, 116–17.

47 Ibid., 127.

48 J.T. Morley, *Secular Socialists: The CCF/NDP in Ontario, A Biography* (Kingston and Montreal, 1984), 41.

49 E.J. Garland to Forsey, n.d., David Lewis Papers, CCF Records, PAC, Ottawa.

50 Lewis to Forsey, March 8, 1937, David Lewis Papers.

51 See, for example, Forsey to Lewis, April 24, 1937, David Lewis Papers.

52 Lewis to Forsey, April 26, 1937, David Lewis Papers.

53 Forsey to Lewis, May 9, 1937, David Lewis Papers.
54 Canadian Civil Liberties Union, Montreal Branch *Bulletin*, no.1, February 2, 1938, SCM Papers, UCA.
55 F.M. Ackroyd to Members of the Montreal Branch of the LSR, n.d. (1936), Frank Scott Papers.
56 Eugene Forsey to Hon, Thomas Coonan, MLA, November 2, 1936, EFP.
57 D.G. Goodwin to Neil Morrison, February 8, 1938, Canadian Civil Liberties Union Papers, SCM Papers, UCA. The Montreal Branch also happened to be the only CLU Branch at this time.
58 Forsey to Graham Spry, March 17, 1937; Graham Spry Memoirs (Rough Notes), Graham Spry Papers, vol. 85, File 33, PAC, Ottawa.
59 Interview with Irene Spry, Ottawa, June, 1985; Graham Spry to Frank Scott, January 13, 1937, Graham Spry Papers.
60 Forsey to Lewis, February 2, 1937; Lewis to Forsey, February 3; Forsey to Lewis, February 4; Lewis to Forsey, February 5; Forsey to Lewis, February 7, 1937, David Lewis Papers.
61 See Eugene Forsey, "Bedtime Stories for Workingmen," *Canadian Forum* 16 (December 1936): 24–26; Eugene Forsey, "Every Man a Capitalist," *Canadian Forum* 16 (January 1937): 18–20.
62 Forsey, "Bedtime Stories for Workingmen," 24.
63 Forsey to Lewis, February 7, 1937, David Lewis Papers.
64 Forsey to Lewis, February 11, 1937, David Lewis Papers.
65 Ibid., February, 7, 1937.
66 Forsey to W. Clarke, February 13, 1937, copy in David Lewis Papers; Forsey, "From the Seats of the Mighty, Part I," 22–23.
67 Herbert F. Quinn, *The Union Nationale: A Study in Quebec Nationalism* (Toronto, 1963), 126.
68 Ibid., 127.
69 Forsey to Spry, March 17, 1937, Graham Spry Papers.
70 Ibid.
71 Eugene Forsey, "Civil Liberties in Quebec," *Canadian Forum* 17 (May 1937): 42.
72 Ibid., 43.
73 Eugene Forsey, "Clerical Fascism in Quebec," *Canadian Forum* 17 (June 1937): 91.
74 Ibid., 92.
75 Minutes of Meeting held in Strathcona Hall Regarding "Freedom of Speech," October 27, 1937, Frank Scott Papers.
76 See Forsey, "Civil Liberties in Quebec," 43.
77 Eugene Forsey, "Quebec on the Road to Fascism," *Canadian Forum* 17 (December 1937): 300; Forsey, "The Padlock Act Again," *Canadian Forum* 17 (February 1938): 382.
78 See Eugene Forsey, "Under The Padlock," *Canadian Forum* 18 (May 1938): 41.
79 Forsey to Lewis, August 18, 1938, David Lewis Papers.
80 Lewis to Forsey, August 19, 1937, David Lewis Papers.
81 Forsey's frustration resulting from the reluctance of the CCF's leaders to aggressively pursue the civil liberties issue suggests that traditional interpretations of the CCF as a party deeply involved in the preservation of civil liberties may not be accurate. See, for example, Kenneth McNaught, *A Prophet in Politics: A Biography of J.S. Woodsworth* (Toronto, 1959), 290–93.
82 Forsey to Graham Spry, March 22, 1937, copy in David Lewis Papers.

83 Thompson, *Decades of Discord*, 295.
84 Forsey Interview, October 1986.
85 Forsey to Lewis, July 22, 1937, David Lewis Papers.
86 Forsey, "Civil Liberties in Quebec," 43.
87 Forsey to Lewis, July 22, 1937, David Lewis Papers.
88 Ibid.
89 Thompson, *Decades of Discord*, 295.
90 Forsey to Lewis, August 18, 1937, David Lewis Papers.
91 Ibid.
92 Interviews with King Gordon, Irene Spry and Joseph Parkinson suggest that Forsey was at the time regarded as particularly vociferous and strident in making his arguments. He was often regarded as humourless and overly dramatic.
93 Ibid.
94 Forsey, "Quebec on the Road to Fascism," *Canadian Forum* 17 (December 1937): 300; Forsey to Lewis, January 6, 1937, David Lewis Papers.
95 Lewis, *The Good Fight*, 332.
96 Minutes of January 28, 1938 LSR National Executive Meeting, LSR Papers, University of Toronto Archives.
97 Forsey to his mother, May 2, 1938, EFP.
98 See CLU Information Bulletin no. 1 (February 1938), SCM Papers, UCA; and nos. 2–11 (March 1938 to April 1940), Frank Scott Papers.
99 Eugene Forsey, "Mr. Lapointe and the Padlock," *Canadian Forum* 18 (August 1938): 149.
100 CLU Information Bulletin no. 2 (March 1938); no. 4 (July 1938), Frank Scott Papers.
101 Eugene Forsey, "Disallowance: A Contrast," *Canadian Forum* 18 (June 1938): 74.
102 Eugene Forsey, "Disallowance of Provincial Acts, Reservation of Provincial Bills, and Refusal of Assent by Lieutenants General Since 1867," *Canadian Journal of Economics and Political Science* 4 (February 1938): 47-59.
103 Forsey, "Disallowance: A Contrast," 75; Forsey, "Mr. Lapointe and the Padlock," 150.
104 Ibid.
105 It was at this time the only CCLU branch.
106 "Statement of Policy," CCLU, Montreal Branch, n.d., copy in Frank Scott Papers.
107 Bothwell, Drummond and English, *Canada, 1900–1945*, 314.
108 Forsey to his mother, October 15, 1938, EFP.
109 Forsey Interview, March 1986.
110 Forsey to his mother, October 5 and 6, 1938, EFP.
111 Ibid.
112 Ibid., November 20, 1938.
113 Ibid., September 14, 1939.
114 Forsey Interview, Ottawa, June 1985.
115 Eugene Forsey, "Colonel Drew Attacks the Civil Liberties Union," March 12, 1938, EFP (copy of Montreal *Gazette* article).
116 "Eugene Forsey Replies to Drew's Attack on the Civil Liberties Union," Unpublished Notice, Dr. E.A. Forsey File, CCF Records, PAC.
117 CLU Information Bulletin no. 8 (April 1939), Frank Scott Papers.

118   See Forsey to Lewis, October 1, 1937; Lewis to Forsey, August (n.d.), September 30, and November 7, 1937, David Lewis Papers.
119   Forsey to Lewis, March 23, 1937, David Lewis Papers.
120   Canada, Debates of the House of Commons, June 2, 1938, 3374–75.
121   Ibid., 3378.
122   Forsey to his mother, June 3, 1939, EFP.
123   Forsey to Lewis, April 23, 1938, David Lewis Papers.
124   Forsey to his mother, June 3, 1938, EFP.
125   Ibid.
126   Ibid., October 5, 16, 1938.
127   Ibid., November 5, 1938.
128   Minutes of November 17, CCF Committee, CCF Records.
129   John Risk to M.J. Coldwell, December 21, 1938, CCF Records.
130   CLU Information Bulletin no. 6 (October 1938), 5, Frank Scott Papers.
131   See Chapter 6.
132   The five were Forsey, Leonard Marsh, Joseph Parkinson, Frank Scott and Frank Underhill. See Michiel Horn, "Academics and Canadian Social and Economic Policy in the Depression and War Years," *Journal of Canadian Studies* 13 (Winter 1978–79): 4.
133   Ibid., 5.
134   See Michiel Horn, "Free Speech Within the Law: the Letter of the Sixty-Eight Toronto Professors, 1931," *Ontario History* 72 (March 1980: 27–48.
135   Eugene Forsey, "Memorandum on Promotion," June 19, 1939, EFP.
136   Ibid., 2.
137   Ibid.
138   Ibid.
139   Ibid.
140   Forsey to his mother, May 28, 1939, EFP.
141   Harriet Forsey to Mrs. Forsey, August 15, 1939, EFP.
142   Eugene Forsey, "Youth and Civil Liberties," Unpublished Speech, n.d., EFP.
143   Ibid., 13.
144   Ibid.
145   Ibid., 4.
146   Ibid., 5.
147   Ibid., 6.
148   Eugene Forsey, "Civil Liberties in Canada," Radio Broadcast, August 15, 1939, EFP.
149   Ibid., 7.
150   Forsey to his mother, September 26, 1939, EFP.
151   Allen was Professor of Natural Science at Sir George Williams University. He was a member of the Provincial and National Executive of the CCF and at one time had been a Montreal City Councillor. Forsey to Ernest Lapointe, Minister of Justice, May 10, 1941, EFP.
152   Forsey to his mother, October 8 and 22, 1939, EFP.
153   Forsey to Albert Macleod, January 28, 1940, EFP.
154   Forsey to his mother, November 19 and 28, 1939, EFP.
155   Ibid., February 20 and March 17, 1940, EFP.
156   Forsey to Lewis, n.d., 1938, David Lewis Papers.
157   Beck, *Pendulum of Power,* 220–21, 238–39.

158 Ibid.
159 Forsey to Lewis, March 31, 1940, David Lewis Papers.
160 Forsey to Frank Underhill, March 31, 1940, Frank Underhill Papers.
161 See Forsey to Lewis, July 17, 21, 1940; Lewis to Forsey, July 12, 1940. David Lewis Papers.
162 Forsey to his mother, September 23, 1940, EFP.
163 Forsey to Frank Underhill, October 10, 1040, Frank Underhill Papers.
164 Forsey to Arthur Meighen, October 10, 1940; Meighen to Forsey, October 16, 1940, AMP.
165 See Chapter 2.
166 Eugene Forsey, "The Two Nations," Radio Broadcast, 1938, EFP.
167 Eugene Forsey, *Freedom and Order,* x, 86.
168 Arthur Meighen to Gratton O'Leary, July 26, 1949, AMP.
169 Meighen to Guggenheim Foundation, November 28, 1941, AMP.
170 Meighen to Forsey, November 27, 1940, AMP.
171 Eugene Forsey, "The British Tradition in Canada, Part II," n.d., Unpublished manuscript, EFP.
172 Forsey to Meighen, March 13, 1944, EFP.
173 Forsey to Meighen, December 6, 1947, EFP.
174 Grube was a Classics Professor and Department Head at Trinity College, University of Toronto. He was a former LSR Toronto Branch President and a close associate of the editors at the *New Commonwealth.*
175 Forsey to George Grube, January 6, 1942, copy in David Lewis Papers; Forsey to the Editor of the *New Commonwealth*, February 6, 1942, EFP.
176 Ibid.
177 Forsey to Miss Godfrey, December 2, 1941, copy in Frank Underhill Papers.
178 Forsey to Grant Dexter, Editor, *Winnipeg Free Press*, June 24, 1949, EFP.
179 Forsey to Meighen, July 21, 1949, AMP.
180 Meighen to Forsey, July 26, 1949, AMP.
181 Forsey to Professor R. MacGregor Dawson, December 28, 1949, copy in AMP.
182 Eugene Forsey, Review of Arthur Meighen's *Unrevised and Unrepented: Speeches of Arthur Meighen* in the *Ottawa Citizen*, December 24 and 27, 1949, copy in AMP.
183 Forsey to Meighen, December 29, 1949, AMP.
184 Forsey Review of *Unrevised and Unrepented*, 1.
185 Meighen to Forsey, December 8, 1948, AMP.
186 Meighen to Forsey, December 21, 1948, AMP.
187 Ibid.
188 Henry Allen Moe, Secretary, Guggenheim Memorial Foundation, to Forsey, March 12, 1941; Forsey to his mother, March 13, 1941, EFP.
189 Forsey to Lewis, January 24, 1941, David Lewis Papers.
190 Forsey to his mother, February 4, 1941, EFP.
191 Ibid.

CHAPTER

THE **PLANNED SOCIETY**

1 See Forsey to David Lewis, March 21, 1941, David Lewis Papers;
   Forsey to his mother, March 21, 26, 1941, EFP; Forsey to Underhill,
   May 2, 1941, Frank Underhill Papers; Forsey to Meighen, July 12,
   1941, AMP.
2 Forsey to Meighen, March 5, 1941, AMP.
3 See R. Douglas Francis, *Frank H. Underhill: Intellectual Provocateur,*
   108–26; Forsey to Underhill, October 10, 1940, Frank Underhill
   Papers.
4 Forsey to Underhill, May 4, 1941, Frank Underhill Papers.
5 Forsey to Fred Smith, National Secretary of the FCSO, July 25, 1940,
   EFP.
6 Ibid.
7 Hutchinson, "The Fellowship For a Christian Social Order," 155–57.
8 Ibid., 156, 192.
9 Gregory Vlastos to Forsey, August 1, 1940, EFP.
10 Forsey to Vlastos, August 2, 1940, EFP.
11 See Gregory Vlastos to Forsey, August 7, 1940; Fred Smith to Forsey,
   September 11, 16, 17, 30, 1940; R.B.Y. Scott to Forsey, September
   17, 1940, EFP.
12 Forsey to National Executive Members, October 14, 1940, EFP.
13 Forsey to Morton Freeman, General Secretary, FCSO, January 3, 7,
   1941; Freeman to Forsey, January 6, 1941, EFP.
14 Lewis to Forsey, January 17, 1941, David Lewis Papers.
15 Forsey to Martyn Eastall, January 20, 1941. See also Estall to Forsey,
   January 11; Forsey to Jarvis McCurdy, January 19; Forsey to John
   Davidson, January, 27, 1941, EFP.
16 Forsey to his mother, January 24, 1941, EFP.
17 Forsey to Alex Cameron, National Secretary, FCSO, November 15,
   1944; Cameron to Forsey, November 22, 1941, EFP.
18 Forsey to Lewis, August 2, 1941, David Lewis Papers.
19 Meighen to Forsey, October 29, 1941, AMP; J.S. Woodsworth to
   Forsey, December 13, 1941, EFP.
20 Forsey to Lewis, December 7, 1941, EFP.
21 Forsey to Lewis, May 12, 1942, EFP; Forsey to Meighen, February
   2, 1942, AMP.
22 Forsey to Lewis, April 21, 1942, David Lewis Papers.
23 Lewis to Forsey, April 29, 1942, David Lewis Papers.
24 Irving Abella, *Nationalism, Communism and Canadian Labour: The
   CIO, the Communist Party and the Canadian Congress of Labour,
   1935–1950* (Toronto, 1973), 49–53.
25 Ibid., 2
26 Ibid., 4.
27 Ibid., 6–10.
28 Ibid., 27.
29 Ibid., 40.
30 Ibid., 50–53.
31 Ibid., 74.
32 Norman Dowd to Forsey, April 29, 1942, CCF Records.
33 Ibid.

34   Eugene Forsey, "Distribution of Income in Ontario," *Canadian Forum* 22 (March 1942): 374–76; Forsey to Meighen, May 18, 1942, AMP. See also Forsey, "Distribution of the National Income in Canada," *Canadian Forum* 22 (October 1942): 214–15; Forsey, "Distribution of Income in British Columbia," *Canadian Forum* 22 (August 1942): 148–49.
35   Forsey to Frank Underhill, May 1942, Frank Underhill Papers; Forsey to Meighen, May 14, 1942, AMP.
36   Forsey to Meighen, May 2, 1942, AMP.
37   Forsey to Meighen, August 7, 1942, AMP.
38   See J.L. Granatstein, *The Ottawa Men: The Civil Service Mandarins, 1935–1957* (Toronto, 1982), 140, 161–63.
39   Ibid., 161.
40   Owram, *The Government Generation*, 281.
41   Ibid., Chapters 10 and 11.
42   Ibid., 303–4.
43   Forsey to Meighen, June 17, 1943, AMP.
44   Eugene Forsey, *Reconstruction: The First Steps* (Ottawa, 1943), 3, 19.
45   Ibid., 19.
46   Deane, *The Political Ideas of Harold Laski*, 23–24.
47   Eugene Forsey, "Planning From the Bottom – Can It Be Done?" *Canadian Forum* 24 (March 1945): 277.
48   Ibid.
49   Ibid., 277–78.
50   Ibid.
51   Ibid., 278.
52   Ibid., 278.
53   Eugene Forsey, "Planning From the Bottom – Can It Be Done? Part II," *Canadian Forum* 25 (April 1945): 20.
54   Forsey, *Reconstruction: The First Steps*, 6.
55   Ibid., 7.
56   Ibid., 7.
57   Ibid., 7.
58   Granatstein, *The Ottawa Men*, 161.
59   Forsey, *Reconstruction: The First Steps*, 8.
60   Ibid.
61   Ibid., ,14.
62   Ibid., 14–15.
63   Ibid., 16.
64   Eugene Forsey, "Worker and Farmer: What An Hour's Labour Would Bring, 1939–1951," *Labour Research* 4 (November–December 1951): 1–8.
65   Ibid., 8.
66   Ibid., 9.
67   Ibid., 12.
68   Eugene Forsey, "Housing – Unfinished Business," *Labour Research* 2 (May 1949): 3.
69   Eugene Forsey, "What's Ahead for 1949?" *Labour Research* 2 (March–April 1949): 3.
70   Forsey, *Reconstruction: The First Steps*, 6.
71   See Lewis, *The Good Fight*, 199.
72   Eugene Forsey, "The CCF Policy on Money," in CCF, ed., *Planning For Freedom* (Toronto, 1944), 86.
73   Ibid., 87.
74   For a detailed discussion of the specific arguments advanced by

these mainstream "macroeconomic" managers, see Owram, *The Government Generation*, Chapter 2, passim.

75 Forsey, "The CCF Policy on Money," 88.
76 Ibid., 88.
77 Ibid., 89–91.
78 Ibid., 91.
79 Owram, *The Government Generation*, 289–91.
80 Eugene Forsey, "Trade Union Policy Under Full Employment," *Canadian Journal of Economics and Political Science* 12 (August 1946): 345.
81 Ibid., 349.
82 Ibid., 351.
83 Eugene Forsey, Report of the Director of Research to the CCL's Fifth Annual Convention, Proceedings of the Fifth Annual Conference, Quebec, 1944, Canadian Labour Congress Records (hereafter cited as CLC Records), PAC.
84 Eugene Forsey, Report of the Director of Research to the CCL's Sixth Annual Convention, Convention Proceedings, Toronto, 1946, 31, CLC Records. Forsey's mother assisted her son in building up the research library and keeping it in "a state of efficiency." She was well qualified for the task, having been employed for many years as the Librarian at the Geological Society of Canada in Ottawa.
85 Ibid., 33.
86 Ibid., 2.
87 See Eugene Forsey, "Religion and Society: The Canadian Trade Union Movement," Unpublished manuscript, May 30, 1949, EFP.
88 Eugene Forsey, "The Labour Force, Labour Market and Unemployment, 1945–1950," *Labour Research* 3 (July-September 1950): 11.
89 Eugene Forsey, "Labour, Supply Defence and Welfare," *Labour Research* 4 (April 1951): 1–4.
90 Eugene Forsey, "Unemployment Again," *Labour Research* 5 (February–March 1952): 2.
91 Eugene Forsey, "Full Employment?", *Labour Research* 5 (July–September 1952): 2.
92 Ibid., 6.
93 See Jack Pickersgill and D.F. Forster, *The Mackenzie King Record, vol. 4, 1947–1948* (Toronto, 1970), 313.
94 See Report of Research Director to the Ninth Annual Convention of the CCL (1941), CLC Records.
95 CCL Submission to the Royal Commission on Prices, December 9, 1948, CLC Records.
96 Ibid., 16.
97 See, for example, "Labour and Inflation," *Labour Research* 1 (August 1948): 1–4; "Higher Prices Pick Your Pocket!" *Labour Research* 3 (October–November 1950): 1–5; "Corks and Bottles: Prices and Price Controls," *Labour Research* 4 (December 1950–January 1951): 1–8; "The Case For Price Controls," *Canadian Forum* 31 (June 1951): 54–55; Eugene Forsey to the Editor, *The Letter Review*, April 4, 1951, EFP.
98 Eugene Forsey, "Post-War Problems of Canadian Labour, With Special Reference to the Responsibility of the Church," Unpublished manuscript, CCF Records, 2.
99 Eugene Forsey, "Meet Mackenzie King," *Saskatchewan Commonwealth* 9 (June 1945): 4.

100 Ibid., 17.
101 See "Memorandum on a Permanent Peacetime, National Collective Bargaining Act" (1947), CCF Records. Forsey is the probable author of this extensive twenty-page review document which was attached to the CCL's Review of the Industrial Relations and Disputes Investigation Act of 1947.
102 Eugene Forsey, CCL Memorandum Submitted to the Dominion Government, April 5, 1946, vol. 171, File 43, CCF Records.
103 See Department of Research, "Memorandum on Bill 338: An Act to Provide for the Investigation, Conciliation and Settlement of Industrial Disputes," Submitted to the House of Commons Committee on Industrial Relations, June 30, 1947, CCF Records.
104 Eugene Forsey, "The New National Labour Code," *Canadian Forum* 28 (July 1948): 73.
105 Ibid., 73–77.
106 Forsey, "Post-War Problems," 3.
107 Ibid.
108 Forsey to his mother, December 18, 1939, EFP.
109 Eugene Forsey, "Post-War Problems."
110 See, for example, Forsey, "The Economic Situation: Mid-Year Review," *Labour Research* 7 (August–September 1954): 1–8; and "There is Some Unemployment in Canada," *Labour Research* 8 (March 1955): 1–4.
111 Forsey, "Post-War Problems," 2.
112 Ibid.
113 Ibid., 4.
114 Eugene Forsey, "Religion and Society: The Canadian Trade Union Movement," 4.
115 Ibid.
116 Ibid.
117 Ibid.
118 Ibid.
119 Ibid.
120 Ibid., 6.
121 This school was apparently located in Calgary, for in his Director's Report to the 1947 CCL Convention, Forsey explained that he could not attend a Union Summer School because "a longstanding previous engagement in Calgary" prevented him from doing so. Eugene Forsey, Report of the Executive Director to the Seventh Annual CCL Convention, 35, CLC Records.
122 Eugene Forsey, "Economic Planning in a Free Society," Introduction, 1. Unpublished Manuscript, EFP.
123 Ibid., 4–6.
124 Ibid., 7.
125 Ibid., 8.
126 Ibid., Chapter 2, "The Nature of a Free Society," 2.
127 Ibid., 2–3.
128 Forsey's conception of freedom as a positive communal force in society has similarities to the idea of "positive liberty," a tradition dating back to Oxford and to people like Thomas Hill Green. See I.M. Greengarten, *Thomas Hill Green and the Development of Liberal Democratic Thought* (Toronto, 1981).
129 Forsey, "Economic Planning in a Free Society," 4–5.
130 Ibid., Chapter 3, "The Aims of Planning," 1.
131 Ibid., 3–4.

132 Ibid., 5.
133 See Owram, *The Government Generation*, Chapter 11, "The Triumph of Macro-Economic Management"; and Granatstein, *The Ottawa Men*, Chapter 6, "New Men, New Ideas"; Robert Bothwell, Ian Drummond, and John English, *Canada Since 1945: Power, Politics and Provincialism* (Toronto, 1981), 70–101.
134 Forsey, "Economic Planning in a Free Society," Chapter 3, 7.
135 Ibid., Chapter 4, "The Methods of Planning," 11.
136 This section alone runs to over twenty typed pages.
137 Ibid., 13.
138 Ibid., 20.
139 Ibid., 30–31.
140 See CCF, *Planning For Freedom*, 11, 19; David Lewis and Frank Scott, *Make This Your Canada: A Review of CCF History and Policy* (Toronto, 1943); Walter Young, *The Anatomy of a Party: The National CCF, 1932–1961* (Toronto, 1969); David Lewis, *The Good Fight*.
141 Forsey, "Economic Planning in a Free Society," 3.
142 Ibid., 4.
143 Ibid., 5–6.
144 Ibid., 5.
145 Ibid., "Methods of Planning – Part II," 10.
146 Ibid., "Planning and Parliamentary Democracy," 10.
147 Ibid., 22.
148 Ibid., "Planning and Parliamentary Democracy," 4.
149 Ibid., 9.
150 Owram, *The Government Generation*, 324.
151 Gerald Friesen, *The Canadian Prairies: A History* (Toronto, 1984), 403, 420.
152 Stuart Garson to Eugene Forsey, July 8, 1948, EFP.
153 Ibid.
154 Ibid.
155 Owram, *The Government Generation*, 186, 294–301.
156 A.F.W. Plumptre to Forsey, June 16, 1948, EFP.
157 Frank Underhill to Forsey, October 28, 1947, EFP.
158 Ibid.
159 Forsey to J.M. Macdonnell, September 18, 1947, EFP.
160 Ibid.
161 Ibid.
162 H.D. Forbes, ed., *Canadian Political Thought* (Toronto, 1985), 284.
163 George Grant to Forsey, n.d. (received in Ottawa, July 3, 1948), EFP.
164 Forsey to George Grant, August 3, 1948, EFP.
165 Ibid.
166 George Grant to Forsey, October 3, 1948, EFP.
167 Forsey, "Economic Planning in a Free Society," Introduction.
168 Beck, *Pendulum of Power*, 250.
169 Forsey to J.M. Macdonnell, September 18, 1947, EFP.
170 Forsey to Lewis, April 23; Lewis to Forsey, May 25, 1946, David Lewis Papers.
171 Forsey to Meighen, December 20, 1947, AMP.
172 Forsey to Meighen, June 17, 1949, AMP.
173 Forsey to Meighen, December 20, 1948, AMP. Forsey was referring to his published thesis, *Royal Dissolution of Power*.
174 Forsey to A.F.W. Plumptre, June 28, 1948, EFP.
175 Forsey to Garson, July 13, 1948, EFP.

CHAPTER *9*

THE BRITISH CONSTITUTIONAL TRADITION

1   Forsey to [Unknown], September 11, 1957, EFP.
2   Forsey to Meighen, March 25, 1951 and November 28, 1951, AMP.
    This did not mean the end of temptations, however, for Diefenbaker
    attempted on more than one occasion to convince Forsey to run as
    a Conservative.
3   John Farthing to Arthur Meighen, December 12, 1953, copy in EFP.
        Forsey's notations on this letter illustrate the strong regard he
    had for Farthing's work, which Farthing clearly expressed in what
    Forsey referred to as Farthing's "precious little book," *Freedom Wears
    a Crown* (Toronto, 1957). That book was finished and edited by
    their mutual friend, Judith Robinson, following Farthing's premature
    death in 1954.
        Farthing, Robinson and Forsey had been working on a joint book
    which they were to call *The British Tradition in Canada*. When
    the project faltered, Farthing went on to work on his book and
    Forsey began a book of his own which was to include nineteen of
    his constitutional articles, running to three hundred pages. This
    indicated the intensity with which Forsey approached the subject of
    the constitution in the 1950s. Forsey's proposed book went through
    many alterations in content and was eventually published as *Freedom
    and Order* in 1974, over twenty years after he first planned the work.
    Forsey's original idea for his book was to define the meaning of the
    British tradition in Canada and the essentially British character of the
    Canadian people. The British tradition, he concluded in the 1950s,
    had two characteristics – the monarchy and an organic order.
        See Forsey's original outline for his book called *The British
    Tradition in Canada*, EFP; Forsey's "In Memoriam" for Farthing
    (1954), EFP; and Forsey to Farthing, March 31, 1953, EFP.
4   Forsey to the Editor of the *Ottawa Journal*, March 21, 1961.
5   See Granatstein et al., *Twentieth Century Canada*, 140, 150–51.
6   Donald Creighton, *The Forked Road: Canada 1939–1957* (Toronto,
    1976), 23.
7   Ibid., 259.
8   Ibid., 240–41.
9   Ibid., 241.
10 Michael D. Behiels, *Prelude to Quebec's Quiet Revolution; Liberalism
    Versus Neo-Nationalism, 1945–1960* (Kingston and Montreal, 1985), 49.
11 Creighton, *The Forked Road*, 226–27.
12 See Erma Buffie, "The Massey Report and the Intellectuals:
    Tory Cultural Nationalism in Ontario in the 1950's," M.A. thesis,
    University of Manitoba, 1982, 4.
13 Ibid., 131.
14 Ibid., 131–39.
15 Carl Berger, *The Writing of Canadian History: Aspects of English
    Canadian Historical Writing, 1900–1970* (Toronto, 1976), 112–13,
    117. See also A.R.M. Lower, *Colony to Nation: A History of Canada*
    (Toronto, 1946 [1977]); and Lower, *My First Seventy-Five Years*
    (Toronto, 1967).

16 See Granatstein, *The Ottawa Men*, 208–25.
17 Eugene Forsey, "Crown, Parliament and Canadian Freedom,"
     Unpublished article (1952), copy in AMP.
18 Ibid., 2.
19 Ibid.
20 Ibid.
21 Ibid., 3.
22 Eugene Forsey, "The British Tradition in Canada, Part II,"
     Unpublished Article (circa 1943), EFP.
23 See Frank O'Gorman, *Edmund Burke: His Political Philosophy* (London,
     1973), 47; Viereck, *Conservatism*, 22–30; Freeman, *Edmund Burke and
     the Critique of Political Radicalism*, 18–23, 27–31.
24 Forsey, "The British Tradition in Canada, Part I," Rough Notes
     taken from the drafting of this unpublished manuscript, n.d., EFP;
     Forsey, "Depriving Canada of Its History," Unpublished manuscript,
     copy in AMP.
25 Ibid., 2.
26 Viereck, *Conservatism*, 30.
27 Forsey, "The British Tradition, Part I," 2.
28 Ibid.
29 Ibid., 3.
30 Freeman, *Edmund Burke and the Critique of Political Radicalism*, 77–79.
31 Ibid., 78–79.
32 Eugene Forsey, "In Defense of Macdonald's Constitution,"
     Unpublished speech, n.d., 4, EFP.
33 Ibid., 6; Forsey, "The Monarch and the Canadian Constitution,"
     Unpublished manuscript, n.d., EFP.
34 Eugene Forsey, "Crown and Commonwealth," Unpublished article,
     August 1973, 3, EFP; Forsey, "Democracy in Action," 8; Forsey,
     "Why the Monarchy? Why Not?" Speech (n.d.), 9, EFP; Forsey,
     "The British Tradition, Part II," 5.
35 Forsey, "Crown and Commonwealth," 9–12.
36 Forsey, "The British Fact in Canada," Unpublished manuscript, n.d.,
     2, EFP.
37 Forsey Interview, Ottawa, May 1987.
38 Eugene Forsey, *The Royal Power of Dissolution of Parliament in the
     British Commonwealth* (Toronto, 1943).
39 See ibid., Chapter 4, 106–29.
40 Ibid., Chapters 5 and 6. In a 1984 article, Forsey explained in more
     detail his view that "conventions" were very much a part of the
     "working Constitution of Canada." Conventions helped to make
     up the rules by which we were governed by acknowledging the
     extralegal "customs, usages, practices, and understandings by which
     our system of government operated." They were, Forsey wrote, the
     "sinews and nerves of our body politic." The basic convention of the
     Canadian Constitution, he added, was the convention of responsible
     government itself. Eugene Forsey, "The Courts, the Conventions and
     the Constitution," *U.N.B. Law Journal* 33 (April 1984): 11–41.
41 Eugene Forsey, "The Royal Prerogative of Dissolution of
     Parliament," Proceedings of the Canadian Political Science
     Association, II (1930), 81–82, copy in AMP.
42 Ibid., 82.
43 Ibid., 83.

44　Ibid., 83.

45　Ibid., 81, 86.

46　Forsey, "Crown and Commonwealth," 8.

47　Ibid., 10.

48　Forsey, "The Monarchy and the Canadian Constitution," 5.

49　Forsey used this term in at least five different taped interview sessions.

50　Eugene Forsey, "Republic of Canada?" *Public Affairs* (1952): 11–17.

51　Eugene Forsey, "The Meaning of Dominion Day," Address to the Men's and Women's Clubs of Edmonton, June 19, 1956, EFP. See also Forsey's comments on this subject in the following letters to editors: "Depriving Canada of Its History," *Globe and Mail*, November 26, 1951; December 4 and 12, 1951; and February 16 and August 5, 1952; United Church *Observer,* July 2, 1952 and July 21, 1964.

52　See, for example, the following Forsey articles: "The Crown and the Cabinet: A Note on Mr. Isley's Statement," *Canadian Bar Review* 25 (February 1947): 185–87; "The Crown and the Constitution," *Dalhousie Review* 33 (1953–54): 41–45; "Constitutional Issues in Ontario," *Canadian Forum* 25 (May 1945): 37; "The Role of the Crown in Canada Since Confederation," *The Parliamentarian* 60 (January 1979): 14–20; "The Role and Position of the Monarch in Canada," Unpublished manuscript, n.d., 1–11, EFP; "The Constitutional Amendment Bill, 1978," *The New Brunswickian* (1978).

　　See also the following series of *Ottawa Journal* articles in the Forsey Papers: "The Election and the Constitution, I: The Reserve Power of the Crown," April 3, 1963; "The Election and the Constitution, II: Resignation or Dissolution," April 4, 1963; "The Election and the Constitution, III: Before Parliament Opens," April 5, 1963. The basic thesis of this series of articles is that a number of basic principles are in place to ensure that "the reserve power is in fact held in reserve for use only in the rarest and most extraordinary emergencies, when it offers the sole protection against the divine right of Prime Ministers."

53　See Forsey, "The Role of the Crown in Canada Since Confederation," 16; "The Role and Position of the Monarch in Canada," 1–11.

54　Forsey, "The Meaning of Dominion Day," 12.

55　Two full chapters entitled "The Canadian Crisis of 1926," Parts I and II, are included in Forsey's *The Royal Power of Dissolution*. Together the chapters are 120 pages in length.

56　See Forsey's introductory comments to the article "The Crown and the Constitution," in his *Freedom and Order: Collected Essays*, xi.

57　See Eugene Forsey, "The Crown, the Constitution and the C.C.F." *Canadian Forum* 23 (June 1943): 54–56; Forsey, "Memorandum on the Relations of the Crown to Its Advisers," Unpublished article, n.d., 1–6, EFP.

58　Forsey, "The Meaning of Dominion Day," 13.

59　Forsey to Meighen, January 25, 1932, AMP.

60　See Meighen to Forsey, January 29, 1932; and Meighen's detailed "Report" on the first draft of Forsey's thesis, n.d. (circa 1939), Letter no. 09725 in AMP.

61　Eugene Forsey, "Shaping a New Government," Unpublished manuscript, n.d., 10, EFP.

62　Meighen to Forsey, November 19, 1940, AMP.

63　Meighen to Forsey, October 16, 1940, AMP.

64　Forsey, *The Royal Power of Dissolution*, 133–35.

65 Eugene Forsey, "Constitutional Annus Mirabilis," *Public Affairs* 14 (Autumn 1951): 43–45.

66 Press Release, June 6, 1951, copy in AMP.

67 Ibid., 1.

68 Ibid., 2.

69 Ibid., 3.

70 Forsey to Meighen, April 28, 1951, AMP.

71 Forsey to Meighen, May 11, 1951, AMP.

72 Forsey to Meighen, May 16, 1951, AMP.

73 Forsey to Meighen, May 11, 16, 23, 25 and 28, 1951; and Meighen to Forsey, May 14 and 22, 1951, AMP.

74 See Forsey's introductory comments in *Freedom and Order,* xiii.

75 Eugene Forsey, "Mr. King and Parliamentary Government," *Canadian Journal of Economics and Political Science* 17 (November 1951): 452–55, 458–59, 464.

76 Eugene Forsey, "Mr. King, Parliament, the Constitution and Labour Policy," *Canadian Forum* 21 (January 1942): 296.

77 Forsey to Meighen, November 30, 1940, AMP.

78 Forsey to Dr. John Stewart, June 21, 1954, EFP.

79 See "Mr. Forsey Offers Replies to Free Press Criticisms," *Winnipeg Free Press,* June 12, 1943, 22–23; and Forsey's *Free Press* letters, "The Record Remains Clear," August 31, 1942; "Excitable Letter-Writer," June 12, 1943; "Mr. Forsey Writes Final Letter in Controversy," June 26, 1943; see also unpublished letters to Dafoe, copies of which can be found in the AMP, dated June 4, 1943, July 1, 1943, July 18, 1943, and January 4, 1944.

80 See Forsey, *The Royal Power of Dissolution,* 8–10, 75, 185, 257–58, and Dafoe's "Mr. Forsey Offers Replies," *Winnipeg Free Press,* June 12, 1943.

81 Forsey to George Drew, February 6, 1969, EFP.

82 Eugene Forsey, "A Gamble and the Constitution: A New Telling of the King–Byng Affair," *Saturday Night,* January 3, 1953, 9–11, 34.

83 Eugene Forsey, "Constitutional Aspects of the Pipe Line Debate," Speech, November 6, 1956, 1, EFP.

84 Eugene Forsey, "Constitutional Aspects of the Canadian Pipe Line Debate," *Public Law* (Spring 1957): 24–25.

85 Forsey to the editor of the *Ottawa Journal,* May 21, 1957, EFP.

86 Eugene Forsey, "What's Wrong With the Liberals?" Unpublished article (1957), 1–2, EFP.

87 Ibid., 5.

88 Forsey to Meighen, July 5, 1949, AMP.

89 Forsey to Meighen, September 6, 1949, and November 29, 1950, AMP.

90 Research Director's Report to the 1951 CCL Congress, CLC Records, PAC.

91 Ibid., January 20, 1950; Eugene Forsey, "Treachery, The CCF and Mr. Meighen," *Ottawa Citizen,* n.d., EFP.

92 CCL News Release, September 27, 1950, CLC Records.

93 Forsey to Meighen, March 28, 1951, AMP.

94 Ibid., October 23, 1951.

95 Ibid., October 1, 1951.

96 Ibid., October 23, 1951.

97 Ibid.

98 Meighen to Forsey, December 20, 1951; Forsey to Meighen, December 26, 1951, AMP.

99   Forsey Interview, Ottawa, June 1984.
100 Ibid.
101 See, for example, Meighen to Forsey, December 12, 1951, AMP.
102 Ibid.
103 Forsey to Meighen, December 26, 1951, AMP.
104 Forsey to Meighen, December 17, 1951, AMP.
105 Forsey to Meighen, December 17, 1951, AMP.
106 Forsey Interview, Ottawa, November 1984.
107 See Beck, *Pendulum of Power,* 267–68.
108 Forsey to Meighen, December 26, 1951, AMP.
109 Ibid.
110 Ibid.
111 Ibid.
112 Ibid.
113 Ibid.
114 Forsey, "In Defence of Macdonald's Constitution," 10.
115 Forsey, "Concepts of Federalism: Some Canadian Aspects," Speech to
     the Thirty-Fourth Annual Couchiching Conference, August 21, 1965, 2.
116 Forsey, Letter to the Editor, *Vancouver Province,* June 25, 1965, EFP.
117 Ibid.
118 See Eugene Forsey, Speech to the Board of Men of the United
     Church of Canada, n.d., Audio Tape, UCA.
119 See Forsey's article "Deux Nations," *Ottawa Citizen,* March 15,
     1969, EFP; Forsey to John Diefenbaker, February 5, 1967, EFP; John
     Diefenbaker to Eugene Forsey, March 24, 1967, EFP.
120 Ibid.
121 Eugene Forsey, *Our Present Discontents: The George P. Nowlan Lectures*
     (Acadia University, 1968), 21–26.
122 Ibid., 27–29.
123 Ibid., 31.
124 Eugene Forsey, "And When They Were Half-Way Up, They Were
     Neither Up Nor Down," Unpublished manuscript, copy in AMP, 13.
125 Eugene Forsey, "The United Church and Biculturalism," n.d., 2,
     EFP. See also Forsey, Letter to the Editor, *Globe and Mail,* July 22,
     1964, EFP; Forsey to Bruce Hodgins, June 20, 1965, EFP; Forsey,
     "Deux Nations," *Ottawa Citizen,* March 15, 1969, EFP; Forsey, "The
     Language Bill: Are The Prairie Provinces Off Base?" *Globe and Mail,*
     February 8, 1969, 7–10; Forsey, "Quebec's Language Bill 22 Said
     Fueling Flames," *Vancouver Province,* October 16, 1976, EFP; Forsey,
     The Official Languages Act (Bill 22), Unpublished manuscript, EFP.
126 Eugene Forsey, Letter to the Editor, *Canadian Forum,* September 7,
     1961, EFP.
127 Eugene Forsey, Letter to the Editor, *Montreal Star,* September 13,
     1961, EFP. See also Forsey, Letter to the Editor, *Regina Leader-Post,*
     November 9, 1961, EFP.
128 Forsey to Herbert W. Herridge, M.P., January 31, 1966, EFP.
129 Forsey, "Speech to the Board of Men of the United Church of
     Canada."
130 Ibid.
131 Forsey, *Our Present Discontents,* 33.
132 Ibid., 38–39.
133 Ibid.
134 See Bothwell, Drummond and English, *Canada Since 1945,* 379–80.

135 Forsey, *Our Present Discontents*, 39.
136 See Forsey's, "Deux Nations," *Ottawa Citizen*, March 15, 1969; Letter to the Editor, *Ottawa Journal*, December 5, 1967; "Quebec and the Constitution," *Financial Post*, December 4, 1976, EFP; "English and French," *Toronto Star*, August 25, 1967; and Forsey to Mr. Arthur Stimson, January 11, 1968, EFP.
137 Forsey to Meighen, June 6, 1946, EFP.
138 John Diefenbaker to Forsey, September 10, 1967 and September 19, 1968, EFP.
139 Forsey to Jim Macdonnell, July 19, 1963; Forsey to Macdonnell, September 12, 1963, EFP.
140 The fact that Lalonde was an advisor to Davie Fulton, Diefenbaker's Minister of Justice, from 1960 to 1961, would have been seen in a favourable light by Forsey, who fully supported Fulton's constitutional amendment formula. Fulton, however, failed to acquire the necessary unanimous provincial support when the Saskatchewan CCF–NDP government objected to the rigid entrenchment of provincial jurisdiction over property and civil rights clauses. Meanwhile, Quebec objected to leaving intact Section 91, Head 1, of the BNA Act, which gave the Dominion Parliament power to change the Constitution by ordinary legislation, if supported by two-thirds of the provinces containing 50 per cent of the population. In the end Quebec rejected the "Fulton Formula" because it did not give the provinces control over unemployment insurance even though the draft bill entrenched all provincial powers and rights, languages, and education. See Bothwell, Drummond, and English, *Canada Since 1945*, 239.
141 Forsey to Jim Macdonnell, November 8, 1963, EFP. For Forsey's views on the Fulton Formula, see Forsey, "The New Constitutional Amendment Formula," *IODE Echoes* (Spring 1965): 24–25.
142 See George Radwanski, *Trudeau* (Toronto, 1978), Chapter 7, 119–45.
143 Forsey to John Harbon, November 6, 1968, EFP.
144 Trudeau to Forsey, June 10, 1950, EFP.
145 Forsey Interview, Edmonton, June 10, 1985.
146 Forsey to Trudeau, July 4, 1950, EFP.
147 Trudeau to Forsey, June 9, 1964, EFP.
148 Trudeau to Forsey, March 2, 1967, EFP.
149 Forsey to Trudeau, September 29, 1967, EFP.
150 Trudeau to Forsey, March 2, 1967, EFP.
151 Trudeau to Forsey, May 13, 1968, EFP.
152 Radwanski, *Trudeau*, 41–42.
153 Eugene Forsey, "Why a Rank Outsider Chooses Pierre Trudeau," *Trudeau Today*, n.d., copy in EFP.
154 Radwanski, *Trudeau*, 311–12.
155 Ibid., 313.
156 Ibid., 314; Forsey Interview, Ottawa, November 1984.
157 Eugene Forsey, "The Consequences of Special Status," *Ottawa Journal*, November 18, 1977.
158 Forsey, "The Question of a Provincial Bank," *Canadian Forum* 16 (September 1936): 15–16.
159 Forsey, "Shaping a New Government," *Glace Bay Gazette*, April 25, 1944.
160 See Forsey, "Concepts of Federalism: Some Canadian Aspects."
161 Forsey to Frank Howard, November 9, 1970, EFP.

162 Eugene Forsey, *Trade Unions in Canada: 1812–1902* (Toronto, 1982). See Trudeau to Forsey, July 23,1969, EFP; Forsey Interview, Ottawa, May 29, 1987; see *Globe and Mail* editorial, October 8, 1970; R.B.Y. Scott to Forsey, October 20, 1970, EFP.

163 Canada, Senate Debates, March 23, 1972, 222–25.

164 Ibid., 224.

165 See Sunday Magazine Television Transcript, September 25, 1977, copy in EFP; CTV Question Period Transcript, July 22, 1978, copy in EFP; Forsey, Transcript of a Broadcast on the Manifesto of the Committee For a New Constitution, April 23, 1977; Forsey, "Speech to Men's Canadian Club of Calgary," June 7, 1978, EFP.

166 Forsey interview, Ottawa, March 1984; November 1984.

167 Forsey, "Speech to the Ontario Conference on Economic and Cultural Nationalism," June 24, 1971, EFP.

168 Ibid.

169 Eugene Forsey, "The British Share in the Canadian Identity," Unpublished manuscript, 4, EFP.

170 See O'Gorman, *Edmund Burke: His Political Philosophy*, 146.

171 Ibid.

172 Forsey, "The British Share in the Canadian Identity"; Forsey's Course Outline for Political Science 47.300 at Waterloo University, EFP.

173 Forsey, "Submission to the Task Force on National Unity," copy in EFP.

174 Eugene Forsey, "Note on the Fulton Proposals for Amending the BNA Act," Unpublished manuscript, EFP.

175 Ibid., 4.

176 For Forsey's description of the terms and significance of the Fulton-Favreau Formula, see Forsey's "The New Constitutional Amendment Formula," *IODE Echoes* (Spring 1965): 25.

177 See Forsey, "Note on the Fulton Proposals," 24.

178 Eugene Forsey, "The Price of Keeping One Canada," *Information*, 3.

179 Eugene Forsey, "The Courts, the Conventions and the Constitution," *U.N.B. Law Journal* 33 (April 1984): 41.

CHAPTER

CONCLUSION

1 O'Gorman, *Edmund Burke: His Political Philosophy*, 144.

2 Freeman, *Edmund Burke and the Critique of Political Radicalism*, 61.

3 Forsey to his wife, Fall–Winter 1962, EFP.

4 Ibid., 15.

5 Freeman, *Edmund Burke Burke and the Critique of Political Radicalism*, 61–62.

6 Forsey to his wife, Fall–Winter 1962, 16–19.

7 See Chapter 3.

8 McKillop, *A Disciplined Intelligence*, 231.

9 Freeman, *Edmund Burke and the Critique of Political Radicalism*, 59, 64.

10 Forsey to his wife, Fall–Winter 1962, 12.

11 Ibid., 22.

12 See Freeman, *Edmund Burke and the Critique of Political Radicalism*, 64. Forsey had frequently written and spoken with suspicion on the worth of the "intelligentsia," of whom Forsey stated, "Lord knows why they are called so."

13 See Ramsay Cook, *The Regenerators*, 179; McKillop, *A Disciplined Intelligence*, 229–32.

14 Eugene Forsey, Untitled manuscript, vol. 47, File 26, EFP.

15 Ibid., 2.

16 Ibid., 3.

17 Quoted in Greengarten, *Thomas Hill Green and the Development of Liberal Democratic Thought*, 97.

18 Ibid.

19 Ibid., 98.

20 Forsey, Handwritten manuscript, EFP.

21 Ibid.

22 Ibid.

23 Ibid.

24 Ibid.

25 Forsey to F.W. MacLean, January 24, 1957, EFP.

26 See Forsey to his wife, Fall–Winter 1962, 23–25; Forsey to Bruce [No last name], September 12, 1963, EFP.

BIBLIOGRAPHY

A. PRIMARY AND MANUSCRIPT SOURCES

PRIVATE COLLECTIONS

J. King Gordon Papers (Ottawa)
Public Archives of Canada
E. A. Forsey Papers
Arthur Meighen Papers
Canadian Labour Congress Records
CCF Records
Brooke Claxton Papers
David Lewis Papers
Frank Scott Papers
Graham Spry Papers
Frank Underhill Papers
University of Toronto Archives
Harry Cassidy Papers
LSR Papers (contained in the J. S. Woodsworth Collection)
Provincial Archives of Manitoba
W. L. Morton Papers
United Church Archives
Student Christian Movement Papers
United Church Records and Papers

INTERVIEWS

Biss, Irene. Ottawa, Ontario, June 1985.
Gordon, King. Ottawa, Ontario, June 1984; October 1985; March 1986;
    October 1986.
Parkinson, Joseph. Ottawa, Ontario, October 1986.

GOVERNMENT DOCUMENTS

Canada, House of Commons Debates
Canada, Senate Debates

B. FORSEY SOURCES

UNPUBLISHED ARTICLES
(FORSEY PAPERS UNLESS OTHERWISE CITED)

"A Bi-National Second Chamber?" n.d., 8 pp.
"And When They Were Only Half-Way Up They Were Neither Up Nor Down." n.d. 16 pp. Copy in Meighen Papers, 146065–146091.
"Can Mankind Really Achieve Human Rights?" n.d. (1950's), 5 pp.
"Christianity and Communism." n.d.
"Church and Labour." 3 pp.
"Combines and the Constitution." (November 1949), 5 pp. Copy in Meighen Papers., 145251–145255.
"Constitutional Issues in Canada." n.d., 4 pp.
"Crown and Cabinet." (August 1973), 12 pp.
"Crown, Parliament and Canadian Freedom." (1953), 5 pp. Copy in Meighen Papers, 146270–75.
"Depriving Canada of its History." n.d. 12 pp. Copy in Meighen Papers, 14567–145773.
"Looking Backward and Looking Forward." (1967), 13 pp.
"Memorandum on Monopoly in Canada." n.d., 2 pp. United Church Archives, University of Toronto.
"Memorandum on the Relations of the Crown to its Advisers." n.d., 6 pp.
"Mr. Hutchinson and the Constitution." n.d., 10 pp.
"Multiculturalism: An Anglo-Celtic View." n.d.
"No Constitution Can Stand a Diet of Dissolutions." (June 1952), 4 pp. Copy in Meighen Papers.
"Notes on the Ryan Proposals: A New Canadian Federation, Part I." n.d., 7 pp.
"Notes on the Fulton Proposals for Amending the British North America Act." n.d., 4 pp.
"Notes on the Ryan Proposals, Part II." n.d., 13 pp.
"Our Canadian Party System and Political Structure." n.d., 6 pp.
"Post-War Problems of Canadian Labour, With Special Reference to the Responsibility of the Church." n.d., 4 pp. CCF Records.
"Professor Angus on the British Columbia Elections: A Comment." (January 1953), 6 pp. Copy in Meighen Papers, 146165–146170.
"Professor Scott and the 'No' Vote." (1942), 11 pp.
"Submission to the Task Force on National Unity."
"The British Share in the Canadian Identity." n.d.
"The British Tradition in Canada, Part I." n.d., 8 pp.
"The British Tradition in Canada. Part II." n.d. (circa 1943), 9 pp.
"The Cabinet." n.d., 7 pp.
"The Canadian Constitution: Report of the Joint Parliamentary Committee." n.d., 19 pp.
"The Canadian Trade Union Movement." (May 1949), 7 pp. Forsey also called this article "Religion and Society."

"The Constitution: Whence and Whither?" (1967), 6 pp.

"The Constitutional Amendment Formula." n.d., 2 pp.

"The Incredible Mr. Hutchinson." n.d., 1 p.

"The Official Quebec Languages Act ("Bill 22")." (December 1974), 25 pp.

"The Progressive Conservative Party and *Social Planning for Canada*." n.d., 16 pp.

"The Role and Position of the Monarch in Canada." n.d., 11 pp.

"The Senate." (July 1961), 6 pp.

The United Church and Biculturalism. n.d.

"Wages and Dividends in the Depression." (1933–34), 4 pp.

"What's Wrong With the Liberals?" (1957), 5 pp.

"Why a Rank Outsider Chooses Pierre Trudeau." *Trudeau Today*, n.d.

PUBLISHED ARTICLES

"A Gamble and the Constitution." *Saturday Night*, January 3, 1953.

"A Note on the Dominion Factory Bills of the 1880's." *Canadian Journal of Economics and Political Science* 12 (November 1947): 580–83.

" A Rose by Any Other Name." *Canadian Forum* 17 (September 1937): 201.

"After the Ball Was Over." *McGill Fortnightly Review*, November 21, 1925, pp. 5–6.

"Alexander Mackenzie's Memorandum on the Appointment of Extra Senators, 1873–78." *Canadian Historical Review* 27 (June 1946): 189–94.

"Appointment of Extra Senators Under Section 26 of the British North America Act." *Canadian Journal of Economics and Political Science* 12 (May 1946): 159–67.

"Are the Provinces to Have Dominion Status?" *Saturday Night*, February 28, March 20, April 24, May 15, June 26, 1948.

"At the Outbreak of War." *Canadian Forum* 19 (December 1939): 272.

"Automation: Part I." *Labour Research* 8 (October–December 1955): 1–12.

"Automation: Part II." *Labour Research* 9 (March 1956):1–12.

"Bedtime Stories for Workingmen." *Canadian Forum* 16 (December 1936): 24–26.

"Boom – and Unemployment." *Labour Research* 9 (April 1956): 1–4.

"British Columbia, Coal and Petroleum Products Commission." *Canadian Journal of Economics and Political Science* 5 (1939): 225–28.

"British Labour and the Cost of Living." *Labour Research* 4 (February–March 1951): 1–3.

"Canada and Alberta: The Revival of Dominion Control Over the Provinces." *Politica* 4 (June 1939): 95–123.

"Canada's Foreign Trade." *McGill News Supplement*, September 1930, pp. 1–9.

"Canadian Labor and Political Action." *Nation* 165 (July 12, 1947): 42–44.

"Canadian Labour and Postwar Reconstruction." *International Post-War Problems* 1 (September 1944): 549–59.

"Church and Labour." *Presbyterian Record* (September 1958): 6–9.

"Civil Liberties in Quebec." *Canadian Forum* 17 (May 1937): 42–43.

"Clerical Fascism in Quebec." *Canadian Forum* 17 (June 1937): 90–92.

"Concentration in Canadian Industry." *Canadian Forum* 14 (October 1933): 9–12.

"Constitutional Annus Mirabilis." *Public Affairs* 14 (Autumn 1951): 43–45.

"Constitutional Aspects of the Canadian Pipe Line Debate." *Public Law* (Spring 1957): 9–27.

"Constitutional Issues in Ontario." *Canadian Forum* 25 (May 1945): 35–37.

"Corks and Bottles: Prices and Price Controls." *Labour Research* 4 (December 1950–January 1951): 1–8.

"Cost of Living Bonuses." *Labour Research* 4 (April 1951): 4.

"Disallowance: A Contrast." *Canadian Forum* 18 (June 1938): 73–74.

"Disallowance of Provincial Acts, Reservation of Provincial Bills, and Refusals of Assent by Lieutenant-Governors Since 1867." *Canadian Journal of Economics and Political Science* 4 (February 1938): 47–59.

"Disallowance of Provincial Acts, Reservation of Provincial Bills, and Refusals of Assent by Lieutenant-Governors, 1937–1947." *Canadian Journal of Economics and Political Science* 14 (February 1948): 94–97.

"Disarmament Legend." *Canadian Forum* 18 (December 1938): 262–63.

"Distribution of Income in British Columbia." *Canadian Forum* 22 (March 1942): 148–49.

"Distribution of Income in Ontario." *Canadian Forum* 22 (March 1942): 375–76.

"Distribution of the National Income in Canada." *Canadian Forum* 22 (October 1942): 214–15.

"Duplessis Marches On." *Canadian Forum* 18 (January 1939): 298–99.

"Election and the Constitution." Three parts, *Ottawa Journal*, April 3–5, 1963.

"Equality of Sacrifice: Dividends, Salaries and Wages in Canada in the Great Depression." *Canadian Forum* 14 (November 1933): 47–51.

"Every Man a Capitalist." *Canadian Forum* 16 (January 1937): 18–20.

"Facts, Figures and Finance." *Canadian Forum* 16 (March 1937): 17.

"From the Seats of the Mighty." *Canadian Forum* 17 (May 1937): 54.

"From the Seats of the Mighty, Part I: The Simple Faith of the Chamber of Commerce." *Canadian Forum* 16 (March 1937): 22–23.

"From the Seats of the Mighty, Part II: Dives and Lazarus." *Canadian Forum* 17 (April 1937): 10–11.

"Full Employment?" *Labour Research* 5 (July–September 1952): 1–6.

"Higher Prices Pick Your Pocket!" *Labour Research* 3 (October–November 1950): 1–4.

"Housing – A National Emergency." *Labour Research* 3 (January–February 1950): 1–8.

"Housing – Unfinished Business." *Labour Research* 2 (May 1949): 1–4.

"How Much Food for an Hour's Work Again." *Labour Research* 5 (February–March 1952): 7–8.

"Immigration." *Labour Research* 6 (May–July 1953): 1–12.

"Immigration Ballyhoo." *Canadian Forum* 16 (February 1937): 8–10.

"Inflation in Canada." *Canadian Forum* 13 (December 1932): 88.

"Is Labour Pricing Itself out of the Market?" *Labour Research* 8 (April–June 1955): 1–12.

"Is the Union Ship Democratic?" *Maclean's Magazine*, November 1, 1945, pp. 46–48.

"Labour and Inflation." *Labour Research* 1 (August 1948): 1–4.

"Labour and Rearmament." *Public Affairs* 13 (Spring 1951): 55–63.

"Labour and Research." *Canadian Forum* 16 (June 1942): 8–9.

"Labour and the Constitution in Atlantic Canada," in *Centre for Canadian Studies. Perspectives on the Atlantic Canadian Labour Movement and the Working-Class Experience*; Winthrop Pickard Bell Lectures 1984–1985, Winter Series. Sackville, NB: Centre for Canadian Studies, 1985.

"Labour in the Post-War Period." *Canadian Welfare* 20 (April 15, 1944): 2–6.

"Labour Supply, Defence and Welfare." *Labour Research* 4 (April 1951): 4.

"Land of the Padlock's Pride." *Canadian Forum* 19 (July 1939): 109–11.

"Meet Mackenzie King." *Saskatchewan Commonwealth* 9 (June 1945): 4–5.

"Montreal is a Quiet City." *Canadian Forum* 11 (June 1931): 131–32.

"More Socialists on the Monarchy?" *Canadian Forum* (February 1937): 17.

"More Unemployment – Less Relief." *Canadian Forum* 18 (February 1939): 331–32.

"Mr. King and Parliamentary Government." *Canadian Journal of Economics and Political Science* 17 (November 1951): 451–67.

"Mr. King and the Government's Labour Policy." *Canadian Forum* 21 (November 1941): 231–32.

"Mr. King, Parliament, the Constitution and Labour Policy." *Canadian Forum* 21 (January 1942): 296–98.

"Mr. Lapointe and the Padlock." *Canadian Forum* 18 (August 1938): 148–50.

"New Ontario Labour Relations Act." *Labour Research* 3 (April–May 1950): 6–8.

"Oaths of Ministers Without Portfolio." *Canadian Journal of Economics and Political Science* 14 (May 1948): 246–47.

"Organized Industry: A Reply to Miss Dennis." *Dalhousie Reivew* 25 (January 1946): 475–84.

"Parliament is Endangered by Mr. King's Principle." *Saturday Night*, October 9, 1948, pp. 10–11.

"Pecuniary Degrees." *Canadian Forum* 16 (December 1936): 24–26.

"Planned Economy." (May 1932). Proceedings of the Canadian Political Science Asociation, Fourth Annual Meeting, May 1932: 175–86.

"Planning From The Bottom: Can It Be Done?" *Canadian Forum* 24 (March 1945): 277–79.

"Planning from the Bottom: Can It Be Done?" *Canadian Forum* 25(April 1945): 18–22.

"Politics in Quebec." *Canadian Forum* 13 (June 1933): 326–27.

"Productivity in Canada, 1946–1950." *Labour Research* 4 (September–October 1951): 1–7.

"Proposed Installment Buying." *The Canadian Unionist*, August 1945, p. 198.

"Provincial Collective Bargaining Legislation." *Public Affairs* 11 (December 1947): 35–50.

"Quebec on the Road to Fascism." *Canadian Forum* 17 (December 1937): 298–300.

"Recovery – for Whom?" *Canadian Forum* 17 (August 1937): 156-59.

"Regional Distribution of Investment." *Labour Research* 2 (March–April 1949): 3–5.

"Republic of Canada?" *Public Affairs* (1952): 11-17.

"Sectional Representation in Maritime Provincial Cabinets Since Confederation." *Public Affairs* 4 (Autumn 1942): 23–24.

"Sheep's Clothing." *Canadian Forum* 13 (August 1933): 409–11.

"Should the Senate Be Abolished?" *Information* (Autumn 1961): 12–13, 32.

"Social Planning in Canada." *Plan Age* 3 (January 1937): 15–19.

"Some Facts About Railway Wages." *Labour Research* 1 (July 1948): 1–2.

"Some Questions for Mr. Macdonnell." *Canadian Forum* 23 (September 1943): 133–34.

"The Budget." *Canadian Forum* 19 (June 1939): 76–77.

"The Budget." *Canadian Forum* 20 (August 1940): 136–37.

"The Budget." *Labour Research* 1 (June 1948): 1–4.

"The Budget." *Labour Research* 2 (March–April 1949): 5–6.

"The Budget Speech." *Labour Research* 7 (April–May 1954): 4–8.

"The Budget White Paper." *Labour Research* 2 (March–April 1949): 6–8.

"The Case for Price Controls." *Canadian Forum* 31 (June 1951): 54–55.

"The CCF Policy on Money," in CCF, *Planning for Freedom.* Ottawa: CCF, 1944.

"The Constitutional Amendment Bill, 1978." *The New Brunswickian* (1978).

"The Crown and the Cabinet: A Note on Mr. Ilsley's Statement." *Canadian Bar Review* 25 (February 1947): 185–87.

"The Crown and the Constitution." *Dalhousie Review* 33 (1953–54): 31–49.

"The Crown, the Constitution and the C.C.F." *Canadian Forum* 23 (June 1943): 54–56.

"The Consumer Price Index." *Labour Research* 5 (October–November 1952): 1–8.

"The Courts, the Conventions and the Constitution." *U.N.B. Law Journal* 33 (April 1984): 11–41.

"The Economic Outlook for 1954." *Labour Research* 7 (January–March 1954): 1–12.

"The Economic Situation: Mid-Year Review." *Labour Research* 7 (August–September 1954): 1–8.

"The Future of Canadian Politics." *Canadian Mercury,* June 1929, pp. 123–25.

"The Immigration Question." *Social Welfare* 17 (March 1937): 7–10, 17.

"The Labour Force, Labour Market and Unemployment, 1945–1950." *Labour Research* 3 (July–September 1950): 1–11.

"The Literary Consequences of Section 98." *Canadian Forum* 12 (January 1932): 131–32.

"The National Income, 1926–1951." *Labour Research* 5 (April–June 1952): 1–10.

"The New Constitutional Amendment Formula." *IODE Echoes* (Spring 1965), pp. 24–25.

"The New National Labour Code." *Canadian Forum* 28 (July 1948): 73–74, 77.

"The Padlock Again." *Canadian Forum* 17 (February 1938): 382.

"The Padlock Act Again." *Canadian Forum* 17 (February 1938): 382.

"The Padlock... New Style." *Canadian Forum* 18 (March 1939): 362–63.

"The Price of Keeping One Canada." *Information.*

"The Prince Edward Island Trade Union Act, 1948." *Canadian Bar Review* 26 (October 1948): 1159–81.

"The Pulp and Paper Industry." *Canadian Journal of Economics and Political Science* 1 (August 1935): 501–9.

"The Quebec Labour Code." *Labour Research* 2 (January 1949): 1–4.

"The Question of a Provincial Bank." *Canadian Forum* 16 (September 1936): 15–16.

"The Role of the Crown in Canada Since Confederation." *The Parliamentarian* 60 (January 1979): 14–20.

"The Royal Prerogative of Dissolution of Parliament." *Proceedings of the Canadian Political Science Association* 2 (1930): 81–94.

"The Taxpayers' Money." *Canadian Forum* 19 (May 1939): 42–43.

"The Taxpayers' Money." *Canadian Forum* 19 (July 1939): 106–7.

"There is Some Unemployment in Canada." *Labour Research* 8 (March 1955): 1–4.

"Trade Union Policy Under Full Employment." *Canadian Journal of Economics and Political Science* 12 (August 1946): 343–55.

"Under the Padlock." *Canadian Forum* 18 (May 1938): 41–44.

"Unemployment Again." *Labour Research* 4 (November–December 1951): 1–6.

"Unemployment Again." *Labour Research* 5 (February–March, 1952), p. 2.

"Unemployment and Relief." *Canadian Forum* 19 (May 1939): 42.

"Wanted: Complete Relief Statistics." *Canadian Forum* 17 (September 1937): 211.

"What's Ahead for 1949?" *Labour Research* 2 (January 1949): 1–3.
"What's in a Name?" *Canadian Forum* 18 (September 1938): 180.
"Worker and Farmer: What An Hour's Labour Would Bring, 1939–1951."
    Labour Research 4 (November–December 1951): 1–8.

BOOKS AND PAMPHLETS

Canada in a New World. Toronto: Ryerson Press, 1948.
The Canadian Labour Movement, 1812–1902. Ottawa: Canadian Historical
    Association, 1974.
Dividends in the Depression. Toronto, 1934.
Does Canada Need Immigrants? Montreal: League for Social Reconstruction,
    1937.
Economic and Social Aspects of the Nova Scotia Coal Industry. Toronto,
    Macmillan Co. of Canada for the Dept. of Economics and Political
    Science, McGill University, Montreal, 1926.
Freedom and Order: Collected Essays. Toronto: McClelland and Stewart, 1974.
How Canadians Govern Themselves. (4th ed.). Ottawa: Public Information
    Office, Library of Parliament, 1997.
Les Canadiens et leur Système de Gouvernement. (4e éd.). Ottawa: Service
    d'information publique, Bibliothèque du Parlement, 1997.
Le Mouvement Ouvrier au Canada, 1812–1902. Trans Guy Courtel. Ottawa:
    Société Historique du Canada, 1975.
A Life on the Fringe: The Memoirs of Eugene Forsey. Toronto: Oxford
    University Press, 1990.
*Our Present Discontents: The George P. Nowlan Lectures at Acadia University,
    1967.* Wolfville, NS: Acadia University, 1968.
*Perspectives on the Atlantic Canadian Labour Movement and the Working Class
    Experience.* (Eugene A. Forsey, J. Albert Richardson and Gregory S.
    Kealey). Sackville, N.B.: Centre for Canadian Studies, Mount Allison
    University, 1985.
Reconstruction: The First Steps. Ottawa: The Canadian Congress of Labour,
    1943.
The Royal Power of Dissolution of Parliament in the British Commonwealth.
    Toronto: Oxford University Press, 1943 (new edition 1968).
*Second report of the Standing Joint Committee of the Senate and of the House of
    Commons on Regulations and other Statutory Instruments.* Standing Joint
    Committee on Regulations and other Statutory Instruments. Ottawa:
    Queen's Printer for Canada, 1977.
Trade Unions in Canada, 1812–1902. Toronto: University of Toronto Press,
    1982.
Unemployment in the Machine Age; Its Causes. 2nd ed. Toronto: Social Service
    Council of Canada, 1936.

THESES

"The Economic and Social Aspects of the Nova Scotia Coal Industry." M.A.
    thesis, McGill University, 1926.

SPEECHES, LECTURES AND CONVOCATION ADDRESSES
(FORSEY PAPERS UNLESS OTHERWISE CITED)

"Acadia University Convocation Address." n.d.

"Brandon University Convocation Address, 1974." 8 pp.

Canada in a New World: Addresses Given at the Canadian Institute on
Public Affairs, 1947. Edited by Eugene Forsey. Toronto: Canadian
Institute on Public Affairs, Ryerson Press, 1948.

"Carleton University Convocation Address. 1976." 9 pp.

"Concepts of Federalism: Some Canadian Aspects," Speech to the Thirty-
Fourth Annual Couchiching Conference, August 21, 1965.

"Constitutional Aspects of the Pipe Line Debate." Speech at Osgoode Hall
Law School, Toronto. November 6, 1956, 14 pp.

"Contributions Made By Early British Immigrants." n.d., 7 pp.

"Dalhousie University Convocation Address, 1971." 8 pp.

"Defence Regulations." Montreal Civil Liberties Union Speech. Autumn
1939, 6 pp.

"Democracy." Radio Address. February 1939, 5 pp.

"Democracy in Action." n.d., 10 pp.

"Ecaenial Address." University of New Brunswick. May 17, 1962, 16 pp.

"Economic Growth." Sixth Morrison Memorial Lecture, Ontario
Agricultural College, Guelph, Ontario. October 31, 1961, 9 pp.

"Economic Planning in a Free Society." Alberta School of Religion, Calgary.
1948, 86 pp.

"In Defence of Macdonald's Constitution." 1973, 13 pp.

"McGill University Convocation Address, 1978." 5 pp.

"McGill University Valedictory Address, 1925." 6 pp.

"McMaster University Convocation Address, 1984." 5 pp.

"Mount Allison Convocation Address, 1973." 6 pp.

"Multiculturalism: An Anglo-Celtic View." n.d., 9 pp.

Papers, National Conference on Canadian Goals. Progressive Conservative
Association of Canada. Fredericton, Ottawa, 1964.

"Negotiations and Arbitration for Professional Civil Servants." n.d., 4 pp.

"On the Manifesto of the Committee for a New Constitution." Radio
Broadcast. April 23, 1977, 4 pp.

"Our Canadian Party System and Political Structure of Canada." Speech to
a Steelworkers Conference, n.d., 4 pp.

"Queen's University Convocation Address, 1979." 4 pp.

"Question Period: A CTV Television Interview With Senator Eugene
Forsey." June 11, 1971, 12 pp.

"Question Period: A CTV Television Interview With Senator Eugene
Forsey." July 21, 1978, 12 pp.

"Remarks by the Honourable Eugene Forsey, Senator, to the Ontario
Conference on Economic and Cultural Nationalism." June 24, 1971, 10
pp.

"Speak for Canada!" 1980 Queen's University Alumni Address. Copy in
Harry Cassidy Papers. 3 pp.

"Speech to the Board of Men of the United Church of Canada."

"Speech to the Ontario Conference on Economic and Cultural
Nationalism." June 24, 1971.

"Task Force on Canadian Unity: Answers to Canadian Unity." n.d., 5 pp.

"The British Fact in Canada." n.d., 6 pp.

"The British Share in the Canadian Identity." n.d., 7 pp.

"The Constitution Amendment Bill, 1978." 1979, 6 pp.
"The Constitutional Amendment Formula." CBC Radio Commentary. November 1964, 2 pp.
"The Function of the Economist." McGill University Graduates' Society Radiologue. January 19, 1934, 6 pp.
"The Meaning of Dominion Day." Speech to the Men's and Women's Canadian Clubs, Edmonton, Alberta. June 19, 1956.
"The Monarchy and the Canadian Constitution." n.d., 6 pp.
"The Preservation of Democracy." Circa 1938, 7 pp.
"The Two Nations." Circa 1939, 9 pp.
"The United Church and Multiculturalism." n.d., CCF Papers.
"Transcript of the Hamilton Labour Council Radio Series." September 1953, 4 pp. CCL Papers.
"Transcript of Interview with Senator Eugene Forsey on Sunday Magazine." September 25, 1977, 11 pp.
"Transcript of Interview with Eugene Forsey." Vancouver Radio Station C.J.O.R. August 1939, 9 pp.
"University of Saskatchewan Convocation Address, 1967." 9 pp.
"University of Toronto Convocation Address, 1968." 8 pp.
"Untitled Speech to the Men's Canadian Club of Calgary, Alberta." June 7, 1978, 4 pp.
"Why the Monarchy? Why Not?" n.d., 3 pp.
"World University Services Seminar, India, 1953." 1953, 5 pp.
"York University Convocation Address, 1972." 7 pp.
"Youth and Civil Liberties." 1939, 6 pp.

BOOK REVIEWS

Review of *Mr. Prime Minister,* by Bruce Hutchinson. Copy in Forsey Papers.
Review of *The Crown and Parliament*, by Sir Cecil Carr. London *Sunday Times*, 20 August 1944. Copy in Forsey Papers.
Review of *The Progressive Party*, by W. L. Morton. *Canadian Journal of Economics and Political Science.* Copy in Meighen Papers, 145404–408.
Review of *Unrevised and Unrepented*, by Arthur Meighen. *Ottawa Citizen*, 24 and 27 December 1949.

NEWSPAPERS

Forsey wrote hundreds of short articles and letters to newspapers editors around the world. The following papers were his 'favourite targets,' though no attempt has been made to list the individual letters amid articles.

Glace Bay *Gazette*
The Financial Post
McGill Daily News and Literary Supplement
Montreal *Daily Star*
Montreal *Gazette*
Montreal *Star*
Ottawa *Citizen*
Ottawa *Journal*
Toronto *Globe and Mail*

Toronto *Star*
Vancouver *Province*
Winnipeg *Free Press*

INTERVIEWS

Ottawa, March 11, 14; June,
November 13, 16, 1984.
June 9, 10, 1985.
March 18, 23, 24 1986.
Edmonton, May 27, 28, 29, 30, 1987.

C. SECONDARY AND PUBLISHED SOURCES

BOOKS

Abella, Irving M. *Nationalism, Communism and Canadian Labour: The CIO, the Communist Party and the Canadian Congress of Labour, 1935-1956.* Toronto: University of Toronto, 1973.

Allen, Richard. *The Social Passion: Religion and Social Reform in Canada, 1914–28.* Toronto: University of Toronto Press, 1971.

Armour, Leslie, and Elizabeth Trott. *The Faces of Reason: An Essay on Philosophy and Culture in English Canada, 1850–1950.* Waterloo, Ontario: Wilfrid Laurier Press, 1981.

Armstrong, Christopher. *The Politics of Federalism: Ontario's Relations with the Federal Government, 1867–1942.* Toronto: University of Toronto Press, 1981.

Barker, Ernest. *Age and Youth.* Oxford: Oxford University Press, 1953.

Beck, J. Murray. *Pendulum of Power: Canada's Federal Elections.* Scarborough, ON: Prentice-Hall, 1968.

Behiels, Michael D., ed. *The Meech Lake Primer: Conflicting Views of the 1987 Constitutional Accord (with a foreword by Eugene Forsey).* Ottawa : University of Ottawa Press, 1989.

———. *Prelude to Quebec's Quiet Revolution: Liberalism versus Neo-Nationalism, 1945–1960.* Kingston and Montreal: McGill-Queen's University Press, 1985.

Berger, Carl. *The Writing of Canadian History: Aspects of English-Canadian Historical Writing, 1900–1970.* Toronto: Oxford University Press, 1976.

Bissell, Claude. *The Young Vincent Massey.* Toronto: University of Toronto Press, 1981.

Blair, R.S., and J.T. McLeod (eds.). *The Canadian Political Tradition: Basic Readings.* Scarborough, Ont.: Nelson Canada, 1989.

Blake, Robert. *The Conservative Party from Peel to Churchill.* London: Methuen, 1970.

Boiler, Paul Jr. *American Thought in Transition: The Impact of Evolutionary Naturalism, 1865–1900.* Chicago: Rand McNally, 1969.

Bothwell, Robert; Ian Drummond, and John English. *Canada, 1900–1945.* Toronto: University of Toronto Press, 1987.

Bothwell, Robert; Ian Drummond; and John English. *Canada Since 1945: Power, Politics and Provincialism.* Toronto: University of Toronto Press, 1981.

Bourinot, John George. *Parliamentary Procedure and Practice in the Dominion of Canada*. Reprint ed., Shannon, Ireland, 1971.

Buck, Philip, ed. *How Conservatives Think*. Baltimore: Penguin, 1975.

Butler, Geoffrey G. *The Tory Tradition: Bolingbroke–Burke–Disraeli–Salisbury*. London: J. Murray, 1914.

Cassel, Gustav. *Fundamental Thoughts in Economics*. New York: Harcourt, Brace, 1925.

———. *Money and Foreign Exchange After 1914*. London: Constable, 1922.

———. *Post-War Monetary Stabilization*. New York: Columbia University Press, 1928.

———. *The Theory of Social Economy*. New York: Harcourt, Brace, 1924.

Cecil, Lord Hugh. *Conservatism*. London: Williams & Norgate, 1912.

Chambers, John. *The Tyranny of Change: America in the Progressive Era, 1900–1911*. New York: A. Knopf, 1980.

Clark, Michael. *Coherent Variety: The Idea of Diversity in British and American Thought*. Westport, CT: Greenwood, 1983.

Cole, G.D.H. *Capitalism in the Modern World: Fabian Tract No. 315*. London: Fabian Society, n.d.

———. *Guild Socialism: Fabian Tract No. 192*. London: Fabian Society, 1915.

———. *The Simple Case for Socialism*. London: Harcourt, 1923.

Cook, Ramsay. *The Regenerators: Social Criticism in Late Victorian English Canada*. Toronto: University of Toronto Press, 1985.

Copp, Terry. *The Anatomy of Poverty: The Condition of the Working Classes in Montreal, 1897–1929*. Toronto: McClelland and Stewart, 1974.

Creighton, Donald. *The Forked Road: Canada, 1939–1957*. Toronto: McClelland and Stewart, 1976.

Crunden, Robert M. *Ministers of Reform: The Progressive Achievement in American Civilization, 1889–1920*. New York: Basic Books, 1982.

Dales, Ernest A. *Twenty-One Years A-building: A Short Account of the Student Christian Movement in Canada, 1920–1941*. Student Christian Movement, n.d.

Davis, H.W.C. *A History of Balliol College*. Oxford: Clarendon Press, 1963.

Dawson, R. MacGregor. *William Lyon Mackenzie King: A Political Biography*. Toronto: University of Toronto Press, 1958.

Deane, Herbert A. *The Political Ideas of Harold J. Laski*. New York: Columbia University Press, 1955.

Dilks, David. *Neville Chamberlain, Vol. 1*. Cambridge: Cambridge University Press, 1984.

Dreyer, Frederick A. *Burke's Politics: A Study in Whig Orthodoxy*. Waterloo, ON: Wilfrid Laurier University Press, 1979.

Farthing, John. *Freedom Wears a Crown*. Toronto: Kingswood House, 1957.

Forbes, Ernest. *Aspects of Maritime Regionalism*. C.H.A. Booklet No. 36. Ottawa, 1983.

———. *The Maritimes Rights Movement, 1919–1927: A Study in Canadian Regionalism*. Montreal: McGill-Queen's University Press, 1979.

Francis, R. Douglas. *Frank H. Underhill: Intellectual Provocateur*. Toronto: University of Toronto Press, 1986.

Francis, R.D., and Ganzevoort, H., eds. *The Dirty Thirties in Prairie Canada*. Vancouver: Tantalus Research, 1980.

Freeman, Michael. *Edmund Burke and the Critique of Political Radicalism*. Oxford: Basil Blackwell, 1980.

Fremantle, Ann. *This Little Band of Prophets: The Story of the Gentle Fabians*. London: Allen and Unwin, 1960.

Friesen, Gerald. *The Canadian Prairies: A History.* Toronto: University of Toronto Press, 1984.

Gash, Norman, Donald Southgate, David Dilks, and John Ramsden.*The Conservatives: A History.* London: Allen & Unwin, 1977.

Graham, Roger. *Arthur Meighen, Vol. 2: And Fortune Fled.* Toronto: Clarke-Irwin, 1963.

——. *Arthur Meighen, Vol. 1: The Door of Opportunity.* Toronto: Clarke-Irwin, 1960.

Granatstein, J.L. *The Ottawa Men: The Civil Service Mandarins, 1935–1957.* Toronto: Oxford University Press, 1982.

Granatstein, J.L., Irving M. Abella, David J. Bercuson, R. Craig Brown, and H. Blair Neatby. *Twentieth Century Canada.* Toronto: McGraw-Hill Ryerson, 1983.

Graubard, Stephen. *Burke, Disraeli and Churchill: The Politics of Perseverance.* Cambridge, MA: Harvard University Press, 1961.

Greengarten, I.M. *Thomas Hill Green and the Development of Liberal-Democratic Thought.* Toronto: University of Toronto Press, 1981.

Greenwood, John. *Quaker Encounters, Vol. 1: Friends and Relief.* York: William Sessions, 1978.

Hobhouse, Christopher. *Oxford As It Was and It Is Today.* London: B.T. Batsford, 1939.

Hodgetts, J. E. *The Sound of One Voice: Eugene Forsey and his Letters to the Press.* Toronto: University of Toronto Press, 2000.

Hofstadter, Richard. *The Age of Reform: From Bryan to F.D.R.* New York: Vintage, 1955.

Hogg, Quinton. *The Case for Conservatism.* London: Oxford University Press, 1974.

Horn, Michiel. *The League for Social Reconstruction: Intellectual Origins of the Democratic Left in Canada.* Toronto: University of Toronto Press, 1980.

Hutchinson, A.M.S. *This Freedom.* Toronto: McClelland and Stewart, 1922.

Jenks, J.W., and Walter Clark. *The Trust Problem: Economic Power in a Free Society.* New York: Doubleday, Doran and Co., 1929.

Keller, Morton. *Affairs of State: Public Life in Late Nineteenth Century America.* Cambridge: Harvard University Press, 1977.

Kendle, John. *John Bracken: A Political Biography.* Toronto: University of Toronto Press, 1979.

Kirk, Russell. *The Conservative Mind: From Burke to Santayana.* New York: Chicago: Henry Regnery, 1953

——, ed. *The Portable Conservative Reader.* New York: Viking, 1982.

Kolko, Gabriel. *The Triumph of Conservatism: A Reinterpretation of American History, 1900–1916.* Chicago: Quadrangle, 1963.

League for Social Reconstruction Research Committee. *A criticism of the Book written by Eugene Forsey [and others],* published by the League for Social Reconstruction under the title "Social Planning for Canada." n.p., n.d.

Lewis, David. *The Good Fight: Political Memoirs, 1909–1958.* Toronto: Macmillan of Canada, 1981.

—— and Scott, Frank. *Make This Your Canada: A Review of CCF History and Policy.* Toronto: CCF, 1943.

Lindsay, A.D. *The Essentials of Democracy.* Philadelphia: Twilight Press, 1929.

Linteau, Paul-André, René Durocher; and Jean-Claude Robert. *Quebec: A History, 1867–1929.* Toronto: James Lorimer, 1983.

Lovejoy, Arthur. *The Revolt against Dualism.* New York: W.W. Norton, 1930.

Lower, Arthur R.M. *Colony to Nation: A History of Canada.* Toronto: Longman's Green, 1946. Reprint ed., Toronto: McClelland and Stewart, 1977.

————. *My First Seventy-Five Years.* Toronto: Macmillan of Canada, 1967.

Ludovici, Anthony M. *A Defence of Conservatism: A Further Text-Book for Tories.* London: Faber and Gwyer, 1927.

Macmurray, John. *Search for Reality in Religion.* London: G. Allen and Unwin, 1965.

————, ed. *Some Makers of the Modern Spirit.* London: Methuen, 1933.

————. *The Clue to History.* London: SCM Press, 1938.

————. *The Philosophy of Communism.* London: Faber and Faber, 1933.

Macpherson, C.B. *The Political Theory of Possessive Individualism: Hobbes to Locke.* Oxford: Clarendon Press, 1962.

McKillop, A.B. *A Disciplined Intelligence: Critical Inquiry and Canadian Thought in the Victorian Era.* Montreal and Kingston: McGill-Queen's University Press, 1979.

McNaught, Kenneth. *A Prophet in Politics: A Biography of J.S. Woodsworth.* Toronto: University of Toronto Press, 1959.

Moritz, Alberta and Theresa. *Leacock: A Biography.* Toronto: Stoddart, 1985.

Morley, J.T. *Secular Socialists: The CCF/NDP in Ontario, A Biography.* Kingston and Montreal: McGill-Queen's University Press, 1984.

Morton, W.L. *The Progressive Party in Canada.* Toronto: University of Toronto Press, 1950.

Mowry, George. *The Era of Theodore Roosevelt, 1900–1912.* New York: Harper, 1958.

Myers, Gustavus. *History of Canadian Wealth.* Chicago: C.H. Kerr & Co., 1914.

Neatby, H. Blair. *William Lyon Mackenzie King: The Lonely Heights, 1924–1932.* Toronto: University of Toronto Press, 1958.

————. *The Politics of Chaos: Canada in the Thirties.* Toronto: Gage Publishing Ltd., 1972.

Nevaskar, Balwant. *Capitalists without Capitalism: The Jains of India and the Quakers of the West.* Westport, CT: Greenwood, 1971.

Nisbet, Robert. *The Twilight of Authority.* New York: Oxford University Press, 1975.

Noble, David P. *The Progressive Mind, 1890–1917.* Chicago: Rand McNally, 1970.

Noel, J.R. *Politics in Newfoundland.* Toronto: University of Toronto Press, 1971.

O'Gorman, Frank. *Edmund Burke: His Political Philosophy.* London: George Allen and Unwin, 1973.

Owram, Doug. *The Government Generation: Canadian Intellectuals and the State, 1900–1945.* Toronto: University of Toronto Press, 1986.

Palmer, R.R. *A History of the Modern World.* New York: Alfred A. Knopf, 1951.

Passmore, John. *One Hundred Years of Philosophy.* London: Duckworth, 1957.

Pickersgill, J.W., and Forster, D.F. *The Mackenzie King Record: Vol. 4, 1947–48.* Toronto: University of Toronto Press, 1970.

Pugh, Patricia. *Educate, Agitate and Organize: One Hundred Years of Fabian Socialism.* London, Methuen, 1984.

Quinn, Herbert F. *The Union Nationale: A Study in Quebec Nationalism.* Toronto: University of Toronto Press, 1963.

Radwanski, George. *Trudeau.* Toronto: Macmillan of Canada, 1978.

Research Committee of the League for Social Reconstruction. *Social Planning For Canada.* Toronto: Thomas Nelson and Sons, 1935.

Research Committee of the League for Social Reconstruction. *Social Planning For Canada.* Reprint ed. With new introduction by Michael Bliss. Toronto : University of Toronto Press, 1975.

Research Committee of the League for Social Reconstruction. *Democracy Needs Socialism.* Toronto: Thomas Nelson and Sons, 1938.

Ross, W.D. *Aristotle.* New York: Scribner, 1924.

Schlesinger, Arthur M., ed. *The Almanac of American History.* New York: G.P. Putnam's Sons, 1983.

Schuettinger, Robert, ed. *The Conservative Tradition in European Thought.* New York: G. P. Putnam's Sons, 1970.

Scott, R.B.Y., and Gregory Vlastos, eds. *Towards the Christian Revolution.* Chicago: Willett, Clark & Co., 1936.

Shaw, William F. and Lionel Albert, foreword by Eugene Forsey. *Partition: the Price of Québec's Independence: A Realistic Look at the Possibility of Quebec Separating from Canada and Becoming an Independent State.* Montreal: Thornhill, 1980.

Shortt, S.E.D. *The Search for an Ideal: Six Canadian Intellectuals and Their Convictions in an Age of Transition, 1890–1930.* Toronto: University of Toronto Press, 1976.

Sidorsky, David, ed. *The Liberal Tradition in European Thought.* New York: G.P. Putnam's Sons, 1970.

Smith, Adam. *The Wealth of Nations.* Reprint ed. New York: Random House, 1937.

Smith, Paul. *Disraelian Conservatism and Social Reform.* London: Routledge and Kegan Paul, 1967.

Stacey, C.P. *Canada and the Age of Conflict, Vol. 2: 1921–1948.* Toronto: University of Toronto Press, 1981.

Streeter, B.H. *Reality: A New Correlation of Science and Religion.* London: Macmillan, 1926.

Struthers, James. *No Fault of their Own: Unemployment and the Canadian Welfare State, 1914–1941.* Toronto: University of Toronto Press, 1983.

Tawney, R.H. *Religion and the Rise of Capitalism: A Historical Study.* London: J. Murray, 1926.

Research Committee of the League for Social Reconstruction. *Social Planning for Canada.* Michael Bliss, gen. ed., *The Social History of Canada.* Toronto: University of Toronto Press, 1975.

Thompson, John Herd, and Allen Seager. *Canada: 1922–1939, Decades of Discord.* Toronto: McClelland and Stewart, 1985.

Thwaite, Ann. *My Oxford.* London: Robson, 1977.

Traves, Tom. *The State and Enterprise: Canadian Manufacturers and the Federal Government, 1917–1931.* Toronto: University of Toronto Press, 1979.

Viereck, Peter. *Conservatism: From John Adams to Churchill.* New York: Van Nostrand Reinhold, 1956.

Waddington, M.M. *The Development of British Thought from 1820–1890.* Toronto: J.M. Dent and Sons, 1919.

White, R. J. *The Conservative Tradition.* 2nd ed. London: Adam and Charles Black, 1964.

Wilkinson, William J. *Tory Democracy.* New York: Columbia University, 1925.

Winter, J.M., ed. History and Society: Essays by R.H. Tawney. London: Routledge & Kegan Paul, 1978.

Young, Walter D. *The Anatomy of a Party: The National CCF , 1932–1961.* Toronto: University of Toronto Press, 1969.

ARTICLES

Allen, Richard. "The Social Gospel in Canada." *Canadian Historical Review* 49 (1968): 382.

Bailey, Stephen."What Cole Really Meant," in Asa Briggs and John Saville, eds., *Essays in Labour History: In Memory of G.D.H. Cole, 1889–1959,* revised ed. London: Macmillan & Co., 1967: 20-25.

Berger, Carl. "Race and Liberty: The Historical Ideas of Sir John Bourinot." *Canadian Historical Association Annual Report,* 1965.

Blaikie, Rev. R.J. "Being, Process, and Action in Modern Philosophy and Theology." *Scottish Journal of Theology* 25 (May 1972): 129–54.

Gaitskell, Hugh. "Oxford in The Twenties," in Asa Briggs and John Saville, eds., *Essays in Labour History: In Memory of G.D.H. Cole, 1889–1959,* revised ed. London: Macmillan & Co., 1967: 6-19.

Gordon, J. King. " The Politics of Poetry," in Sandra Djwa and R. St. J. Macdonald, eds. *On F.R. Scott: Essays on His Contributions to Law, Literature and Politics.* Kingston and Montreal: McGill-Queen's University Press, 1983: 17–28.

Hoffman, John C. "Religion and Religious Experience in the Thought of John Macmurray: A Critique." *Sciences Religieuses/Studies in Religion* 4 (1974): 2–7.

Horn, Michiel. "Academics and Canadian Social and Economic Policy in the Depression and War Years," *Journal of Canadian Studies* 13 (Winter 1978–79): 4.

Horn, Michiel. "Free Speech Within the Law: the Letter of the Sixty-Eight Toronto Professors, 1931," *Ontario History* 72 (March 1980): 27–48.

Horn, Michiel. "Lost Causes: The League for Social Reconstruction and the Co-Operative Commonwealth Federation in Quebec in the 1930s and 1940s." *Journal of Canadian Studies* 19 (Summer 1984): 133–57.

Horn, Michiel. "Frank Scott, The Great Depression and the League for Social Reconstruction," in Djwa, Sandra and R. St. Macdonald, eds. *On F.R. Scott: Essays on His Contributions to Law, Literature and Politics.* Kingston and Montreal: McGill-Queen's University Press, 1983: 71–77.

Horn, Michiel. " Frank Underhill's Early Draft of the Regina Manifesto, 1933." *Canadian Historical Review* 59 (December 1973): 394.

Irving, Allan. "Leonard Marsh and the McGill Social Science Research Project." *Journal of Canadian Studies* 21 (September 1986): 6–25.

Langford, Thomas A. "The Natural Theology of John Macmurray." *Canadian Journal of Theology* 12 (1966): 10–12.

MacDowell, Laurel Sefton. "The Impact of the Great Depression and the Second World War on the Social Policy of the United Church of Canada." Unpublished Paper, Erindale College, University of Toronto. July 1986, 36 pp.

Macmurray, John. "Beyond Knowledge," in B.H. Streeter, ed. *Adventure: The Faith of Science and The Science of Faith.* London: Oxford University Press, 1926.

———. "Religion in the Modern World," as transcribed by Harriet and Eugene Forsey. Montreal: Associational Literary Services, 1936.

———. "The Nature and Functions of Ideologies," in J. Middleton Murry, J. Macmurray, N.A. Holdaway and G.D.H. Cole, *Marxism.* London: Trinity Press, 1935.

———. "The New Materialism," in J. Middleton Murry et al., *Marxism.* London: Trinity Press, 1935.

———. "The Philosophy of Jesus." Student Christian Movement Papers, United Church Archives, n.d.

McGoldrick, James. "Edmund Burke as a Christian Activist." *Modern Age* 17 (1973): 275–86.

Morton, W.L. "Canadian Conservatism Now," in H.D. Forbes, ed., *Canadian Political Thought*. Toronto: Oxford University Press, 1985: 301–9.

Smillie, Benjamin G. "The Social Gospel in Canada: A Theological Critique." *Papers of the Inter-Disciplinary Conference on the Social Gospel*. National Museum of Man Mercury Series. Ottawa: National Museum Commission, 1975: 317–42.

Strong-Boag, Veronica. "Intruders in the Nursery: Childcare Professionals Reshape the Years One to Five, 1920–1940," in Joy Parr, ed., *Childhood and Family in Canadian History*. Toronto: McClelland and Stewart, 1982: 160–78.

Tarnopolsky, Walter. "F.R. Scott: Civil Libertarian," in Sandra Djwa and R. St. Macdonald, eds., *On F.R. Scott: Essays on His Contributions to Law, Literature, and Politics*. Kingston and Montreal: McGill-Queen's University Press, 1983: 133–50.

Underhill, Frank. "Bentham and Benthamism." *Queen's Quarterly* 39 (1932): 658–68.

White, Leland J. "John Macmurray: Theology as Philosophy." *Scottish Journal of Theology* 26 (November 1973): 449–65.

THESES

Beattie, Margaret. "Pressure Group Politics: The Case of the Student Christian Movement in Canada, 1920–1941." Ph.D. dissertation, University of Alberta, 1972.

Buffie, Erma. "The Massey Report and the Intellectuals: Tory Cultural Nationalism in Ontario in the 1950's." M.A. thesis, University of Manitoba, 1982.

Ferguson, Barry G. "The New Political Economy and Canadian Liberal Democratic Thought: Queen's University, 1890–1925." Ph.D. dissertation, York University, 1982.

Hutchinson, Roger. "The Fellowship for a Christian Social Order: A Social Ethical Analysis of a Christian Socialist Movement." Ph. D. dissertation, University of Toronto, 1970.

Mills, A.G. "The *Canadian Forum*, 1920–1934: A Study in the Development of English Canadian Socialist Thought." Ph.D. dissertation, University of Waterloo, 1976.

SOUND RECORDINGS

Forsey, Eugene A. *How Canadians Govern Themselves* (3rd ed.). Toronto : Canadian National Institute for the Blind, 1991.

———. *The Senate. / Speaker of the House of Commons/ James Jerome*. Toronto: OISE, c1977.

Canadian Government Policy and Process: a Series of Interviews with Prominent Canadians, in conversation with F. Conrad Raabe. Toronto: OISE, in cooperation with the Department of External Affairs, Ottawa, 1978.

INDEX

C

I

idealism, 55–56, 64, 94, 231, 240
immigration
    controls in Planned Society, 105
    Forsey's condemnation of government policy, 79–80, 132
individualism, 40, 44, 56, 60–62, 87, 101, 103
industrial democracy, 65, 180
Industrial Democracy (Webb), 45
Industrial Relations and Disputes Investigation Bill, 181
inflation in post-war Canada, 180
investment controls in Planned Society, 104–5

J

James, Cyril, 164, 167–68
James, William, 89
Jenks, J.W., 6–7
Jung, Carl, 89

K

Kellogg Pact, 66, 255 n. 115
Kemp, Hubert, 251 n. 67
Kerr, F.W., 82
King, Mackenzie
    economic relief strategy, 130
    Forsey's views on, 22, 160, 164, 167, 181, 210–14
    inaction on civil liberty infringements, 145–46
    at League of Nations, Geneva, 66
    and post-WWII reconstruction plans, 168
    response to social crisis in 1920s and 1930s, 16–17, 100
    on tariff issue, 21, 22
King-Byng affair, 209, 210–14
Kirk, Russell, 33–34

L

labour movement. *See also* Canadian Congress of Labour (CCL); trade
  unions
    Forsey's interest in, 44, 45–46, 48
    Labour and Christianity, 182–84
Labour Progressive Party (LPP), 139
labour relations in Nova Scotia coal industry, 44–46
Labour Research, 173, 178, 180
labour supply. *See also* immigration
    controls in Planned Society, 105
Lacroix Bill, 148–49
Lake Wonish, 100
Lalonde, Marc, 225–26

U

V

W

Y

Z